PROFESSIONAL WORKFLOW IN SHAREPOINT® 2010

PROFESSIONAL

Workflow in SharePoint® 2010

PROFESSIONAL

Workflow in SharePoint® 2010

REAL WORLD BUSINESS WORKFLOW SOLUTIONS

Paul J. Galvin
Udayakumar Ethirajulu

John Wiley & Sons, Inc.

Professional Workflow in SharePoint® 2010: Real World Business Workflow Solutions

Published by
John Wiley & Sons, Inc.
10475 Crosspoint Boulevard
Indianapolis, IN 46256
www.wiley.com

Published simultaneously in Canada

ISBN: 978-0-470-61788-5
ISBN: 978-1-118-21972-0 (ebk)
ISBN: 978-1-118-21971-3 (ebk)
ISBN: 978-1-118-21973-7 (ebk)

Manufactured in the United States of America

10 9 8 7 6 5 4 3 2 1

Library of Congress Control Number: 2011939654

This book is dedicated to the SharePoint community.

ABOUT THE AUTHORS

PAUL J. GALVIN is a four-time Microsoft SharePoint MVP. Paul is a prolific blogger and writes for a wide array of online periodicals and has contributed to two other SharePoint books. He regularly speaks at SharePoint conferences throughout the United States on a monthly basis. He is the Principle SharePoint Architect at BrightStarr, US.

UDAYAKUMAR ETHIRAJULU is a Microsoft SharePoint MVP, frequent blogger and public speaker at SharePoint events. Uday works at RSC Solutions as Vice President & Chief Architect in New York.

CREDITS

ACQUISITIONS EDITOR
Paul Reese

PROJECT EDITOR
Kelly Talbot

TECHNICAL EDITOR
Fabio Claudio Ferracchiati

PRODUCTION EDITOR
Kathleen Wisor

COPY EDITOR
San Dee Phillips

EDITORIAL MANAGER
Mary Beth Wakefield

FREELANCER EDITORIAL MANAGER
Rosemarie Graham

ASSOCIATE DIRECTOR OF MARKETING
David Mayhew

MARKETING MANAGER
Ashley Zurcher

BUSINESS MANAGER
Amy Knies

PRODUCTION MANAGER
Tim Tate

VICE PRESIDENT AND EXECUTIVE GROUP PUBLISHER
Richard Swadley

VICE PRESIDENT AND EXECUTIVE PUBLISHER
Neil Edde

ASSOCIATE PUBLISHER
Jim Minatel

PROJECT COORDINATOR, COVER
Katie Crocker

PROOFREADER
Sheilah Ledwidge, Word One

INDEXER
Robert Swanson

COVER DESIGNER
Mike Trent

COVER IMAGE
© Remus Eserblom / iStockPhoto

ACKNOWLEDGMENTS

I COULD NEVER HAVE FINISHED this project without the sustained support of my loving wife, Samantha, and my son, Aidan. This project has been looming over the Galvin family household for a mighty long time. "The Book" has been used as a legitimate (and occasionally illegitimate) reason to cancel or defer various social and household obligations. These obligations inevitably fell upon Samantha and Aidan's shoulders. Samantha and Aidan: Thank you.

Many others have contributed to this effort, and although I don't think I can remember all of them, let me try. Thank you Bob for inspiring me to really join in the SharePoint community. Thanks Mark for opening my eyes to the world of SharePoint end users (and for writing the Foreword to this book). Thank you my co-authors and contributing writers, starting with Uday (who was always there to help me talk things through), Peter Ward for his contributions, and Chris Beckett for a brilliant effort. I need to acknowledge the various potential writers who never quite found time to contribute. The universal support and enthusiasm you displayed helped me to keep working at it.

Lastly, I wish to acknowledge the members of the Heart Circle Sangha. Despite my prolonged absence, you always made me feel welcome when I did (occasionally) show up for service. I truly value that support.

CONTENTS

FOREWORD

SharePoint workflow comes in many shapes and flavors, yet to the average SharePoint user it is a master magician's art learned through a formidable journey. Why is it that one of the most important aspects of SharePoint is also one of the hardest to comprehend and learn? SharePoint default workflows, SharePoint Designer workflows, custom-made workflows using Visual Studio, Visio exporting to SharePoint Designer, third-party tools including BPM suites . . . the choices for creating workflows are confusing and complex. How is one to choose a solution for solving real business problems?

Research confirms it takes 10,000 hours of concentrated practice to internalize, truly understand, and become a master of your chosen topic. With the speed of change in the technology field and the complexity of the solutions, there is no longer time to become conversant in every aspect of the field. There is no longer an apprentice program where you can learn your craft under the watchful eye of a master craftsman while building your 10,000 hours of expertise.

Adult learning is a difficult process. We are constantly comparing ideas with our past experiences, while trying to comprehend new concepts. Too often, there is a lot of "how" to do something and not enough "why" to do it in technical books. That is why this book is different.

Paul Galvin and the team he has assembled are trying to shorten the learning cycle by supplying you with the tools you need to get started or continue your education in SharePoint workflow. This team, with combined experience of well over 10,000 hours building enterprise-level workflow solutions, can help shortcut your learning cycle by showing the essentials of workflow applications.

Professional Workflow in SharePoint 2010: Real World Business Workflow Solutions begins by laying the foundation for your first workflow project through analyzing your existing systems, walking through the discovery process to generate requirements, and then using this knowledge to understand basic design considerations. For intermediate workflow developers, you will find outlines to real-world solutions that can be used for solving universal business problems. Advanced developers will find concepts that far exceed many people's expectations of SharePoint workflow through the use of advanced customization scenarios.

Save yourself a couple thousand hours of frustration and head banging. Use this book as your guide. Whether you are a novice workflow builder or expert craftsman, you are sure to find a solution that will help trigger a new way to look at and manage workflow in SharePoint. Consider yourself a true master when you can pass that knowledge down to the next generation.

I wish you the best of luck on your new adventure.

MARK MILLER
Founder and Editor, EndUserSharePoint.com
Chief Community Officer and SharePoint Evangelist, Global 360
Founding Member, NothingButSharePoint.com

INTRODUCTION

SHAREPOINT 2010 IS THE TALK OF THE TOWN. You can barely take a subway ride in NYC these days without bumping into someone doing something with SharePoint. These are exciting times for the SharePoint community. The entire world seems to be implementing SharePoint.

And that's great. However, when you survey the SharePoint landscape, you find that many organizations just barely scratch the surface of SharePoint 2010's capabilities. They install and configure SharePoint and quickly turn it into an overpriced "S Drive" (shared network drive). Too many companies put up an out-of-the box team site, create a few document libraries with some views, start uploading documents left and right, and call it a day. That's a real shame and one of the key motivations for the authors of this book.

Why is it a shame? It's a shame because SharePoint can do a lot more than the simple stuff such as document management, lists and views, search, and so on. That's not to say that the simple stuff isn't valuable or unworthy in any way. However, the platform offers a lot more capability. The authors aim to expose and dive deep into one of those capabilities: business process automation using workflow.

Why does this happen? Why do so many companies underutilize this gem of a platform? It happens for a number of reasons. First, SharePoint is to a great extent a victim of its own success. It's a very successful platform in part because it's so very easy to install and set up. IT departments don't need to spend anything close to the kind of time and energy for an ERP system, a CRM system, or even a moderately complicated custom/bespoke application. Consider what happens when you combine easy installation with near immediate realization of value. End users adopt that functionality quickly and painlessly (at least in the short term). IT can move on to other complex projects. This happens quite often. That's only one part of the picture, and it's an incomplete picture at that. Another, less obvious barrier to increased adoption can be summed up by the phrase "The spirit is willing, but the body is weak."

In SharePoint terms, it's more appropriate to say "The spirit knows how and desperately wants to extend SharePoint's reach, but other IT projects stand in the way." Historically, IT is asked to do an absurdly large amount of work in a very short amount of time. It's just a fact of life for an IT person. We are constantly forced to allocate ever diminishing slices of our time to "mission critical" projects day in and day out. If you're in an IT role, you know this feeling very well and have no doubt spent a lot of time working with your co-workers and management to devise ways to become more efficient. Everyone wants to get more work done in less time. It's a losing battle, however. No matter how efficient you and your team become, you are still forced to choose between projects and deliver less functionality and capability than you want.

To be clear — the authors do not assert that IT is lazy or focusing on the wrong things. If you're in IT, you love technology and it's a binding passion that that we all share. You want to make the best use of the tools you have and just about every IT pro quickly learns that SharePoint is far more than a document management and search platform.

IT departments use various techniques to tackle this problem. They devise and implement efficiency programs such as good governance, automation, source code control, and intellectual property (IP) databases. They also increase bandwidth by hiring more staff. This book takes the latter head on by helping you to find new staff, but not how you might expect. Instead of hiring new people (a difficult proposition in these challenging economic times), you can look inside your organization for some part-time IT talent that is often hidden in plain view.

SharePoint offers a new way of building business applications. It enables a business-centric approach to creating business solutions that require very little IT support. SharePoint 2010 offers tools that enable the IT department to take on an advisory role rather than the traditional hands-on approach that is the root cause of so many IT project bottlenecks. Properly trained and motivated end users can step up and help IT with its mission. Of course, the key is finding and creating those "properly trained" end users. This book can't help you with the former, but it aims to solve the latter.

These motivated end users (or activist users as we'll be calling them in the Chapter 1) can't take up all the slack. After all, they aren't training IT pros. They are, however, business experts. The aim of this book is to provide those experts with the baseline knowledge they need to create business process automation solutions that leverage SharePoint workflow and SharePoint Designer.

IT still plays a critical role. End users will hit walls as they develop their solutions. IT is there to help and assist and in some cases, take over. This book addresses these scenarios with an eye toward empowerment. One example is creating a custom workflow activity. Your end users won't be creating custom activities. It requires Visual Studio and lot of detailed technical knowledge. However, they are the business experts. Once they are skilled with SharePoint Designer and its capabilities, they will know how to communicate their custom activity requirements to you and know how to use it once you develop it for them.

In summary, this book's goal is to empower your organization's activist end users to partner with IT to create business process automation solutions in SharePoint.

WHO THIS BOOK IS FOR

The authors have two audiences in mind: SharePoint end users and IT developers. End users will learn how to define business problems, identify real business requirements and create effective business solutions. IT developers will learn how to create advanced business solutions using SharePoint 2010.

The ultimate goal, however, is to show how IT and activist end users can partner together to create real value for their organization using SharePoint 2010's business process automation capabilities. This book is for those organizations that want to forge such a partnership.

WHAT THIS BOOK COVERS

As stated earlier, this book's goal is to empower your organization's activist end users to partner with IT to create business process automation solutions in SharePoint. In support of this goal, the core of this book is about business scenarios — problems that companies face every day and want to solve using technology. You dive into each of these scenarios and explore them in great detail.

The book follows the typical progression: Teach the basics, introduce increasingly complex business and technical patterns using SharePoint Designer, and then when we you outgrow it, move into the world of Visual Studio. You'll learn how to use Visual Studio to create custom activities that enable you to extend SharePoint Designer's capabilities and then step outside of SharePoint Designer altogether and to create a workflow solution using pure visual studio.

This book is heavily tilted toward specific real-world scenarios (for example, Human Resources on-boarding processes) that serve as examples for a class of similar business problems. After you solve one HR on-boarding process problem, you can solve a whole class of similar problems, whether oriented around Human Resources or not. You explore each problem in depth, starting with a simplistic overview and forging ahead and into the business ramifications and their impact on SharePoint. You then are provided with a step-by-step guide that describes how to solve those business problems with SharePoint 2010. We really mean "step by step." These chapters are full of detailed instructions and screenshots that walk you through the solution from start to finish. Finally, recognizing that some problems are simply too hard to solve without going the extra mile technically, things are rounded off by discussing advanced topics related to the business problem.

HOW THIS BOOK IS STRUCTURED

The book is organized into the following chapters:

- Chapter 1, "Introduction": This chapter provides a general introduction to the book. It discusses business and technical patterns. You'll also see what's new in SharePoint 2010 workflow.
- Chapter 2, "Workflow Basics": This chapter lays down the foundational concepts for everything that follows. You'll create a classic "Hello, World" workflow. Subsequently, you'll learn about a requirements gathering process that helps you to identify "great" requirements. Figuring out what your user community wants SharePoint to do is easier said than done. SharePoint has, over time, become increasingly accessible to more and more activist users. With new-found power comes new responsibility. This chapter discusses why it's important to learn the lingo of your IT department (hint: they won't take you seriously if you don't talk their language) and teach the lingo itself. The chapter is a primer on business requirements gathering and solution design. It describes an approachable and highly effective method to engage with end users (and to probe your own business requirements), guaranteeing high-fidelity results that will naturally lead to a spot-on solution to your organization's real business problems.
- Chapter 3, "HR On-Boarding": Even in these days of high unemployment and low turnover, companies still need to hire new staff. For this reason, it's more important than ever that companies bring their few new employees into the fold efficiently, quickly, and correctly so that they and their new employees don't waste unnecessary time and effort during their first day on the job. This business chapter explains how to use SharePoint Designer workflow to create a top-notch on-boarding solution. This chapter provides a simple real-world introduction to SharePoint workflow by building upon Chapter 2.
- Chapter 4, "Helpdesk Ticketing": Things go wrong all the time in a busy work environment. People forget passwords. Printers break. You name it, something will

go wrong with it and IT must fix it. The helpdesk ticketing chapter introduces a ticket management solution. It provides the first real treatment of delegation and plants the seeds for building a dashboard in later chapters.

- Chapter 5, "Time Off Management": This chapter introduces the time bank concept. Companies provide time-off benefits to employees based on seniority, years of service, and sometimes, whimsy. You can think about this allocated time off as money in the bank. When you spend it, it's out of the bank and won't be replenished until the company deposits more time into it later (typically, one year later in the United States). It's actually more complicated than that, as the time bank isn't fungible. That's to say that some of those allocated hours can be used only for sick days, personal days, bereavement, and the like. This chapter explains all of that in great detail and then builds the most complex solution so far in the book. It explains how to use math in SharePoint, and when you follow it closely, you can build your first audit trail. (This is important because everyone's a lawyer when their vacation time is at stake, and you want a clear, unambiguous history of a given employee's time bank.)
- Chapter 6, "Interview Scheduling": Remember Chapter 3's difficult economic times? This chapter addresses the result of that problem: fewer managers on hand to interview more people than ever, even if for fewer open positions. The ratio of open positions to job applicants may be in the company's favor, but that doesn't make the interview scheduling problem any easier. Overworked managers have to work harder, and nothing is more important than finding the best talent available. This solution introduces SharePoint 2010 document sets. It explains the business uses for document sets (in this case, bundling up all of a job applicants' documents) and how to use document sets in SharePoint Designer workflow. It also introduces the checklist pattern, which HR can use to manage the overall process and ensure the best outcome for the company.
- Chapter 7, "Facilities Management": Cousins to the IT Helpdesk Ticketing solution in Chapter 4, the Facilities Management solution focuses on physical maintenance. It ranges from the simple (change a broken light bulb) to the complex (move my office). Your company's maintenance department is busy and has a long backlog of requests. This solution provides a request and multilevel approval mechanism that enables employees to request maintenance services and enables the facilities managers to estimate costs and seek approval (or automatically approve if possible) for these requests. Lastly, the chapter explains SharePoint 2010's new mobile interface capabilities and illustrates how the maintenance team can update its work queue directly from its mobile phones.
- Chapter 8, "Enterprise: Authorization for Expenditure Capital": This concept-heavy chapter describes how you can use SharePoint to manage capital expenditure requests and approvals.
- Chapter 9, "Marketing Contact Management": Everyone has it: the "contact us" form on their public web site. Some companies integrate that form into a well-designed CRM system and never lose a potential lead because of it. If that is your approach, this chapter is not for you. Instead, it's for those companies that want to track these kinds of customer contacts.
- Chapter 10, "R&D Gateway Process": Good companies are always thinking of new and interesting ways to bring products to the market. There's no shortage of good ideas, but how to choose between them? This chapter describes a gateway process. Tracking ideas

from concept through to production, each new product idea has to pass through several gates if it's ever to see the light of day.

- Chapter 11, "Enhancing the User Interface": At first, people are pleasantly surprised that SharePoint provides so many useful default user interfaces. Define some columns and glue them together via a content type and SharePoint provides a full-blown create/update/delete (CRUD) UI that is consistent with everything else. Upon further inspection, however, people quickly wish that they could make minor changes to functionality, such as cascading drop-downs, better end-user feedback options, and colorful dashboards. This chapter, written with the most advanced end users in mind, describes how to achieve useful effects without programming.
- Chapter 12, "Custom Activities": Up to this point, you've been working within the confines of SharePoint Designer, and the book has activist users first and foremost in mind. By now, you have learned that as powerful as SharePoint Designer workflows are, they are limited at times and crippled in others. Fortunately, Microsoft is in the habit of providing extensibility into its products, and SharePoint Designer is no exception. You can build custom action and conditions using Visual Studio and integrate them directly into SharePoint Designer. This provides a great teaming opportunity between activist users and IT. IT creates the activity, and the end users create more complex and on-target solutions using SharePoint Designer, the tool best suited for them. This chapter solves the "future business day" problem. Business days are not calendar days. SharePoint Designer workflow, by itself, cannot easily calculate business days. This custom activity solves that problem.
- Chapter 13, "Site Governance": Governance plans save SharePoint from turning into a confusing mess of disorganized sites and end user frustration. However, most governance plans live on paper and in people's heads. People make mistakes or ignore the paper rules out of laziness or a desire to just "get it done." The "human problem" can never be solved, but you can help people by automating some elements of your governance plan. This chapter automates that part of the plan that governs ad-hoc sites: short- or long-term project or other sites that don't have a place in your company's permanent information architecture (which is typically most visible as the global navigation). To this end, you create a custom activity that creates the actual site, and by means of this, cement your understanding of custom activities. The chapter introduces a SharePoint timer job. The timer job inspects these ad-hoc sites and determines whether they are approaching or have exceeded their expiration date and also attempts to identify whether they have been abandoned.

As you can see, the book presents two types of chapters: business scenario chapters using SharePoint Designer workflow to implement the solution and highly technical chapters that use Visual Studio. Chapter 13 breaks the mold a bit by using Visual Studio to implement a business solution by very technical means.

The business solutions, pattern-heavy as they are, themselves follow a pretty standard pattern, organized as follows:

- **"What is" section:** Describes the business problem, its place in the world as a representative of a business pattern, and which business and technical patterns the chapter addresses

- **Business requirements:** Includes a detailed discussion of the business problem broken down into specific requirements. These sections build upon, extend, and generally illustrate the requirements-gathering process first introduced in Chapter 2.
- **High-level solution:** Describes how the various SharePoint tools and workflow will operate together to meet the requirements
- **Detailed technical implementation:** Offers step-by-step instructions on how to implement the solution. This is a screenshot-heavy detailed walk-through.
- **Summary:** In addition to summarizing the chapter, it points out advanced topics and scenarios that flow naturally from the chapter's topic but that are too advanced or complex for the discussion or that will be explored in future chapters.

By following this pattern, the book enforces the concept of "patterns" and puts some predictability of flow in place that we hope you'll find helpful.

WHAT YOU NEED TO USE THIS BOOK

To successfully execute the many walk-throughs in the book, you'll need the following tools:

- A SharePoint 2010 environment. In most cases, SharePoint Foundation will suffice. In some cases, you'll need SharePoint 2010 Enterprise Edition. The individual chapters will explain when this is the case.
- SharePoint Designer. This tool is used in every chapter.

There are three advanced technical chapters. For these chapters, you will need the following additional tools:

- Visual Studio 2010
- InfoPath 2010

Chapter one explains this in greater detail and offers some ideas on how to obtain a SharePoint environment if you don't already have one.

CONVENTIONS

To help you get the most from the text and keep track of what's happening, we've used a number of conventions throughout the book.

Boxes with a warning icon like this one hold important, not-to-be-forgotten information that is directly relevant to the surrounding text.

The pencil icon indicates notes, tips, hints, tricks, and/or asides to the current discussion.

As for styles in the text:

- We *highlight* new terms and important words when we introduce them.
- We show keyboard strokes like this: Ctrl+A.
- We show file names, URLs, and code within the text like so: `persistence.properties`.
- We present code in two different ways:

```
We use a monofont type with no highlighting for most code examples.
```

```
We use bold to emphasize code that is particularly important in the present context
or to show changes from a previous code snippet.
```

ERRATA

We make every effort to ensure that there are no errors in the text or in the code. However, no one is perfect, and mistakes do occur. If you find an error in one of our books, like a spelling mistake or faulty piece of code, we would be very grateful for your feedback. By sending in errata, you may save another reader hours of frustration, and at the same time, you will be helping us provide even higher quality information.

To find the errata page for this book, go to `www.wrox.com` and locate the title using the Search box or one of the title lists. Then, on the book details page, click the Book Errata link. On this page, you can view all errata that has been submitted for this book and posted by Wrox editors. A complete book list, including links to each book's errata, is also available at `www.wrox.com/misc-pages/booklist.shtml`.

If you don't spot "your" error on the Book Errata page, go to `www.wrox.com/contact/techsupport.shtml` and complete the form there to send us the error you have found. We'll check the information and, if appropriate, post a message to the book's errata page and fix the problem in subsequent editions of the book.

P2P.WROX.COM

For author and peer discussion, join the P2P forums at `p2p.wrox.com`. The forums are a Web-based system for you to post messages relating to Wrox books and related technologies and interact with other readers and technology users. The forums offer a subscription feature to e-mail you topics of interest of your choosing when new posts are made to the forums. Wrox authors, editors, other industry experts, and your fellow readers are present on these forums.

At `p2p.wrox.com`, you will find a number of different forums that will help you, not only as you read this book, but also as you develop your own applications. To join the forums, just follow these steps:

1. Go to `p2p.wrox.com` and click the Register link.
2. Read the terms of use and click Agree.

3. Complete the required information to join, as well as any optional information you wish to provide, and click Submit.
4. You will receive an e-mail with information describing how to verify your account and complete the joining process.

You can read messages in the forums without joining P2P, but in order to post your own messages, you must join.

Once you join, you can post new messages and respond to messages other users post. You can read messages at any time on the Web. If you would like to have new messages from a particular forum e-mailed to you, click the Subscribe to this Forum icon by the forum name in the forum listing.

For more information about how to use the Wrox P2P, be sure to read the P2P FAQs for answers to questions about how the forum software works, as well as many common questions specific to P2P and Wrox books. To read the FAQs, click the FAQ link on any P2P page.

1

Introduction to SharePoint 2010 Workflow

SharePoint 2010 is an exciting technology platform that continues to deliver the promise that Microsoft made with its earliest commercial version, SharePoint Team Services (STS) in 2001. A lot of people in the industry are excited by the product's new technical features (including the authors!) but the real power of the product shouldn't be reduced down to a spreadsheet showing new or upgraded features. Instead, SharePoint 2010, like its predecessors, provides a powerful platform on which skilled technologists can deliver business value and solutions to your customers, your fellow employees, your trading partners, and indeed, almost anyone you can imagine. This book can help you become one of those skilled technologists.

SharePoint has always been like this. STS made this promise in 2001 by focusing on providing basic document sharing and collaboration features primarily for departments. WSS 2.0 and SharePoint Portal Server 2003 expanded this to be enterprise-capable; although, it still had a long way to go. WSS 3.0 and Microsoft Office SharePoint Server (MOSS) extended this even further and represented a leap forward in scalability, functionality, technical extensibility, and overall suitability for solving business problems.

And now you have SharePoint 2010, which delivers even more on the promise, and in many respects, for the first time, the product is truly accessible to the large number of nontechnical users — power users, hands-on business analysts, and site administrators — that form the backbone and embody every company's core competency. A successful car franchise once ran a summertime advertisement with the tag line, "If you can sign your name, you can buy a car!" If Microsoft asks, the authors would suggest a similar tagline, "If you can use a web browser, you can create your own business solution!"

Thousands of organizations learned the truth of this as they rolled out Windows SharePoint Services 3.0. WSS frequently started as a department-level proof of concept (POC). Installed by the IT department, it was quickly handed off to a departmental-level power user to "play around with." Suddenly, IT learned that the little POC had turned into a mission-critical application while they had eyeballs on another, more elaborate project. SharePoint generated a large and varied following, and other departments clamored for the functionality. As you read this book, you can understand that if WSS 3.0 were that successful, you haven't seen anything until you've seen SP 2010.

EXPANDING THE CIRCLE OF TRUST

And so the world finds itself with this interesting and relatively new thing under the sun: a highly advanced technical system that does not require an army of well-trained IT workers to properly use. This isn't to say that your army of well-trained IT resources will find themselves with nothing to do. Far from it! This is discussed in greater detail in the book's final chapters, and indeed, each chapter describes opportunities for advanced technical work. But that doesn't change that suddenly, almost anyone can sit down at a computer, fire up a web browser, point it at an SP 2010 environment, and create nontrivial applications with no coding whatsoever.

Different people will take this in their own personal way. Power users will rejoice for a variety of reasons. These users, typically highly dedicated and on the fast track to increasing levels of responsibility and influence in the company (or leaving for bigger and better opportunities elsewhere), can take matters into their own hands. They know the problems they face. Now they have a tool and platform that empowers them to solve those problems.

IT people may take a different position. Classically trained computer scientists are frankly going to quail at the prospect of untrained, albeit smart, users creating business applications. The authors concur, and that concern gets right to the heart of the problem and one that this book aims to solve.

It is literally true that some CIOs regret bringing SharePoint into their environment. They regret it for the simple reason that they can't effectively control what is happening with the platform. They see the formula for this as something like the following:

Easily configurable environment (SharePoint) + Untrained Power User = Confusing Mess

Actually, their math is 100% accurate. And it's even worse than that. SharePoint projects and implementations managed by highly trained IT people, following tried-and-true development processes, still create confusing messes with SharePoint. The SharePoint technical community (including the authors of this book) has responded with an explosion of articles, blogs, books, and conferences to define "best practices" for SharePoint. These range from best practices around governance, best practices around development, best practices around implementation for scalability, best practices for Internet facing sites with content management, and even best practices for documenting best practices. (That last is only half in jest.)

SP 2010 is the new kid in town, and it's bending, stretching, and in many cases throwing out the old rules altogether. SP 2010 platform features and enhancements over MOSS extend SharePoint's sphere of influence in many ways. Power users and other nontraditional application builders are entering the field of battle, so to speak, and they have a lot to learn if they want to avoid getting bogged down in a SharePoint quagmire. In this book, we strive to fill the gap between accepted best practices for MOSS and the new territory in which organizations shall soon find themselves with SP 2010. This book provides reliable information that these new application builders can use to create comprehensive, stable, and most important, effective solutions that solve business problems. How is this done? By break things down into three parts:

- Business patterns
- Technical patterns
- Real-world examples that illustrate business and technical patterns.

Now consider each in turn.

ON THE FRUSTRATING LACK OF A GOOD WORD

The Spanish language has a word, *simpatico*, that translates literally to the word "nice" in English. However, it actually embodies more than just a description such as "That's a nice haircut!" It describes a state of being at the same time, more along the lines of having performed a good deed. There is no single word in English equivalent to *simpatico*.

We have a similar problem describing a kind of user, probably you, dear reader. This user is often called a "power user" or even more loosely, an "end user." Microsoft tends to use the word "information worker." Sadly, none of these words capture the meaning of an important role that always exists in successful companies. What do we mean? We're talking about user who are "plugged in" and dedicated to their job. They may get in early or stay late. They put in some serious hours and focus on doing a good job for the company at all times. These are the kind of people who work in department [X] but for whatever reason, know what's going on in other departments even though they aren't connected to those other departments. When they go to conferences, they agonize over that they can't attend every session they want rather than sneak off to the golf course for a few rounds.

The current lexicon fails because of the following:

- "Power users" traditionally mean individuals who are experts at a software application, such as Microsoft Excel. All of you know an "Excel guy" who can navigate around Excel, fix your pivot table problems, and help you write a macro.
- End users are normally the last users in the solution food chain. IT creates a solution and deploys the solution, and end users use the solution. End users figure prominently in usability tests and scenarios, but end user is too broad a term and frankly, a little derogatory at times.
- The term "information worker" is more or less a fancy term for "end user." This is someone that uses tools to manage information. You're all information workers. Whoop-dee-doo.

None of these words catch the meaning of the extraordinary professionals at every company who spend their days "in the trenches," pushing and prodding their co-workers and their company to greater success on a daily basis. The authors tried to come up with a good word, such as "educated user" or "motivated user." But these are problematic because everyone in a company is in some sense educated and motivated (or so we hope). The term "activist user" seems to be as close as we can come to coining a term that matches well with the envisioned kind of person.

In any event, a label doesn't matter too much in daily terms. You know who you are, and your peers know what you do. This book is for you.

PATTERNS

What does the word, pattern, mean in the context of a book on SharePoint workflow? It boils down to the old cliché: If you've seen it once, you've seen it a thousand times. This book includes almost a dozen real-world business scenarios. However, it doesn't dive deeply into more than a tiny fraction of the business and technical problems you'll face on a regular basis in your job (although those scenarios are common and valuable in their own right). But, if this is all that is offered, it would hardly be worth your time. This problem can be solved by focusing on patterns as much or more than focusing on the individual business problem.

This book outlines and explains specific business solutions, which serve as a single example of an entire class of similar business problems. Chapter 6, "Interview Scheduling," as its name implies, explains how to implement an interview scheduling system in SP 2010. However, after you've seen this problem solved once, you can use this technique to solve a wide array of resource scheduling business problems, such as conference room scheduling.

There's nothing new in computer science about patterns. Microsoft, Oracle, HP, and university scientists across the globe have defined various patterns. They are defined by and for their fellow technologists and as a result are inaccessible to the rising new crop of activist users in the SP 2010 world. In response, the authors define a set of business-oriented patterns with you in mind.

Business Patterns

The book's chapters walk you through the process to create a solution for about a dozen business problems. These problems show you how to identify a problem and apply the correct business pattern to solve it. In these chapters, you learn about the following business patterns:

- **Time Bank:** The time bank pattern describes how to manage limited resources, such as allocated time off for an employee. A typical employee in the United States is offered 2 weeks (80 hours) vacation per year. The time bank pattern helps you use SharePoint workflow to control access to that time and ensure that it's properly managed as it's consumed. More broadly, it addresses the category of business problems that have this nature.
- **Simple and multilevel approval:** Many business solutions require an approval mechanism. This pattern explains how to think about approvals from a management and maintenance perspective.
- **Routing:** Frequently working with approval patterns, the routing pattern explains how to move the ball from one person to the next. That may mean identifying the sequence of approvers for a given request, or it may be as simple as assigning work to a series of individuals to complete a project.
- **Reminders:** In the real world, stuff has to get done, and it has to get done *fast*. The reminders pattern helps keep everyone on task by reminding busy people of pending obligations.
- **Checklist:** Many business processes are checklist-driven. For example, people fill out online forms to join an organization. The organization needs to vet these people before

enrolling them as full members. The vetting process includes a reference check, validating professional credentials, and other tasks. The checklist pattern ensure that the process tracks the vetting process and provides a single authoritative source of status information.

- **KPI Feeder:** Key performance indicators (KPIs) provide a great visual to a business process — what's going well, what's going poorly, and what's heading toward disaster? To work well, KPIs need data upon which to report. The KPI feeder pattern ensures that your business solutions provide the raw data upon which KPIs are built.
- **Anonymous users:** SharePoint provides a lot of functionality that works well for employees and trusted partners. You can also create business solutions targeted at anonymous users. To provide solutions for anonymous users, you need to address security and overall processing issues that SharePoint solves automatically for named users. This pattern helps you address them early and rigorously.
- **Security:** There isn't only one business pattern for security. You infuse security throughout your solutions. The business solution chapters explain the need for security and how to think about security in the context of the specific solution.
- **Mobile Interface:** This pattern identifies both when it's appropriate to provide a mobile interface and second, when it's technically feasible to do so. SharePoint 2010 is better than any other SharePoint platform as far as mobile options go, but it's still relatively limited.
- **Delegation:** The delegation pattern recognizes the reality of real-life schedules. Many business processes assign tasks to people or request approval dispositions. If that person is on vacation, the task may miss its due date, causing difficulties for all concerned. The delegation pattern identifies and provides a solution for this problem.

Technical Patterns

Technical patterns describe the work you do "under the covers," so to speak. There isn't a clear business purpose for it, but it lives in service to the business solution it supports. The book's technical patterns provide answers to questions such as "How do I embed a hyperlink into the body of an email I send from my workflow?"

- **Simple approval:** How do you find the current user's manager? How do you assign a task to that manager and receive the response?
- **Multilevel and variable approvals:** Picking up from simple approval, how do you create multiple approvals serially or in parallel?
- **Time Bank:** How do you find time bank records? How do you increment, decrement, and execute other operations against them? How do you use the time bank to approve, deny, or otherwise affect the workflow process?
- **Dashboards:** What kinds of dashboards can you create with SharePoint 2010? How do you feed a dashboard with content, both in terms of design (making sure you generate the raw data needed to create an effective dashboard) and implementation (what content types, lists, and key values make up the dashboard)?

- **Rich content in emails:** How do you create an email message that contains rich formatting and lots of great contextual information that helps your fellow employees and managers make quick and correct decisions?
- **Dates and times:** How do you manipulate dates and work with them in SharePoint Designer workflow?
- **Document sets:** How can you use document sets and manipulate them and their metadata?
- **Auditing:** Similar to dashboards, how do you ensure you produce long-lived audit trails that link back to original data sets, provide good context and serve as reliable data sources for audit reports?
- **Delegation:** How do you implement delegation using SharePoint Designer workflow?

What's New in SharePoint 2010 Workflow

At this point, the authors want to make a point about what this book is not: It's not a survey of SharePoint workflow features. It covers a lot of SharePoint workflow, both from a SharePoint Designer perspective and Visual Studio perspective. However, every specific feature that a chapter covers is done purely in service to the business problem that the chapter solves. You won't find a chapter devoted to state machines or a chapter devoted specifically to site workflows. You learn about these things in the book, but always in the context of a business problem. That said, you probably want to hear about "What's new in SharePoint 2010?" Like the newly minted Don Corleone, you can ask the question once — just this one time — and we will answer it.

SharePoint 2010 enhanced SharePoint Designer workflow in the following key ways:

- **Transportability:** If you've lived in the SharePoint 2007 world for a while (MOSS or WSS, or even earlier) you know about SharePoint Designer's many frustrating limitations. Well, there's good news in SharePoint 2010: Many of those limitations have been removed or at least their impact muted. For starters, SharePoint Designer workflows can now be moved around from list to list. In WSS/MOSS, your workflows were tied to a specific SharePoint list, and if you wanted to reuse the same workflow in another list, you had to rekey the whole thing from scratch. Thankfully, Microsoft addressed this problem. This is the single-most important enhancement from a workflow perspective because it enables activist users to follow change control procedures that were impossible before.
- **Scope:** SharePoint Designer workflows used to be confined to specific lists. Now you can create a workflow by connecting it to a content type. If you understand content types, you understand the implications of this feature. It means that you can reuse the workflow anywhere you can use that content type. Beyond content types, you can create workflows at the site level. You don't even need a SharePoint list or content type to do it.
- **Security:** In the past, using SharePoint Designer was an all-or-nothing affair. And because SharePoint Designer in the wrong hands is rightfully called "SharePoint Destroyer," many

IT departments disabled it altogether. As a result, activist users who could be trusted to use the tool were punished for the sins of their less careful co-workers. Microsoft added some granularity to SharePoint Designer , which should go a long way toward allaying its concerns and allowing activist users to jump in and use it.

CONCLUSION

This book is about building solutions using SharePoint's tools and primarily using SharePoint workflow. It's not a reference manual, but by working within the context of real-world business problems, it can be more valuable and provide a better learning experience than a cut-and-dry reference book.

Enough said. It's time to start with the basics in anticipation of your first real-world business problem.

2

Workflow Basics

WHAT'S IN THIS CHAPTER?

- Creating content types
- Making custom lists
- Creating custom workflows
- Working with SharePoint Designer

Welcome to Chapter 2, "Workflow Basics." This chapter introduces you to SharePoint Designer, workflows, and content types. It then shows you how to design business solutions using swim lane diagrams and reusable patterns.

The walk-through sections of the book's remaining chapters focus on solving business problems with a practical approach based on SharePoint 2010 functions and tools (primarily workflow). They do not explain how to create a content type but instead provide instructions, such as "create a site content type with the following site columns...." Refer back to this chapter for detailed instructions for those kinds of tasks if you need to.

GETTING STARTED

In the next few pages, you learn what you need to create your first workflow solution. Attempts were made to ignore the "Hello, World" siren song, but we failed. First, you learn what you need to create the workflow (hardware and software), then you create the simple "Hello, World" workflow solution.

The origin of "Hello, World" is somewhat obscure, but it dates back at least as far as the introduction of the C programming language. Many books and tutorials use "Hello, World" as a way to introduce a new programming concept.

What You Need

To create business solutions in a SharePoint 2010 world, you need the following:

- **Hardware:** A laptop or desktop to run the client tools.
- **Software:** SharePoint Designer 2010 is the most essential tool for creating the kinds of business solutions this book describes.
- **Access to a SharePoint server:** You need a SharePoint 2010 environment and you need appropriate privileges.

The next sections discuss each of these in detail.

Hardware

Hardware needs depend on whether you want (or must) run SharePoint 2010 on your laptop/ workstation. This gives rise to two scenarios:

- **Remote SharePoint environment:** You have access to a SharePoint environment within your business or hosted someplace other than your workstation. In this case, you need only the client tools.
- **Local SharePoint environment:** You do not need access to a remote environment, or you want to have a local environment for personal reasons.

Local SharePoint environments require much more horsepower than remote environments because you are, after all, running an entire server application (SharePoint) on your workstation. The following table displays minimum recommended configurations for remote and local SharePoint hardware requirements:

Remote SharePoint environment:

- 64-bit hardware recommend, 32-bit supported
- 50 gigabytes free disk space
- 4 gigabytes RAM
- Single core 1.66GHZ CPU, equivalent or higher

Local SharePoint environment:

- 64 -bit hardware required
- 8 gigabytes RAM (more can make a huge improvement)
- 150 gigabytes free disk space
- Dual core 1.66GHZ CPU, equivalent or higher

You can survive with less. You can squeeze the entire development and server environment onto a single laptop. But, you won't be happy about it.

Software

As with hardware, required software depends on whether your SharePoint environment is local or remote.

Both local and remote:

- SharePoint Designer 2010
- InfoPath 2010
- Internet Explorer 7.x or higher

Local environment:

- Windows Vista or Windows 7 (64 bit)

Access to SharePoint 2010

You can't create a SharePoint 2010 business solution if you don't have access to a SharePoint 2010 environment. Your path to solving this problem can vary based on your current situation. Your company may already be up and running with SharePoint 2010. You may be in a 2007 (or earlier!) SharePoint environment. You may be new to SharePoint altogether.

If you already live with SharePoint 2010, work with your IT administrator to create a separate site collection for you to use while you learn how to create business solutions in SharePoint 2010. Describing site collections beyond the most cursory level of detail is beyond the scope of this book. A site collection is a section of a SharePoint environment carved out by SharePoint administrators that provides a reasonable level of isolation from other areas in the environment. In other words, if you make some kind of killer mistake in your site collection, the damage will (probably) be limited to your site collection.

Site collections have profound implications on your SharePoint environment, and you need to understand a few things about them to be successful with the platform. Site collections are actually a big bucket of content. You put stuff, such as sites, documents, lists, and workflows into the bucket. That sounds straightforward, right? In general it is, and it's not stretching the analogy too far to talk about SQL databases. Site collections always live in one, and only one, SQL database. In many cases, one SQL database holds multiple site collections. You can, however, force a site collection to reside in its own SQL database, which can be handy indeed. (Ask your SQL admin why.)

It's not all beds of roses, however, with site collections. Site collections also serve as a strong barrier between other site collections. This can be good, but most often, it's frustrating, especially when the person who designed your site's information architecture had a tenuous hold on the concept.

The technical definition and scourge of the "site collection" concept hinges upon the word scope. Many SharePoint objects are scoped to the site collection in which they reside. They live within that collection and can't get out of it. Objects are site content types, site columns, lists and libraries, (most) security configurations, and so on. Most out-of-the-box SharePoint tools function within the scope of a single site collection, including SharePoint Designer workflow solutions. (The kind of workflow solutions this book describes.) As a result, if you want your workflow to access content in another site collection, or create tasks in more than one site collection, well . . . you can't.*

Finally, site collections are not mile-high walls of steel. Some SharePoint functions operate across site collections. Search is the most obvious and most useful such feature. SharePoint Search locates content anywhere it can find it and as long as the user executing the search has the necessary permission to view the results.

** I say "most" because there are some coarse-grained security features available at the web application level that do span site collections. You can think of a web application as an even bigger bucket that holds site collections (a bucket of buckets).*

If you don't have access to a SharePoint 2010 environment (either because your company isn't running SharePoint 2010 or your IT department learned at the Soup Nazi school of IT administration), you can create your own. This too is beyond the scope of this book, but excellent online resources are available from Microsoft, Microsoft MVPs and other helpful people, and organizations on the Web.

Create the "Hello, World" Solution

Now dive right in and create a workflow solution by following these steps:

1. Create a sandbox site.
2. Create a list in that site.

3. Create the "Hello, World" workflow on that list.
4. Test your creation.

If you have created a workflow solution in SharePoint Designer 2010 in the past, you can skip this section and move on to "Business Solution Lingo."

Create a Sandbox Site

You do a lot of experimenting with SharePoint as you learn the platform. Developers use the term *sandbox* to denote a location in a SharePoint environment whose purpose is to "play around" with different SharePoint features and functions without worrying that they might break something important. Because this is exactly what you do, you create the sandbox site. First, open up Internet Explorer and connect to your SharePoint environment. SharePoint responds with a screen similar to Figure 2-1.

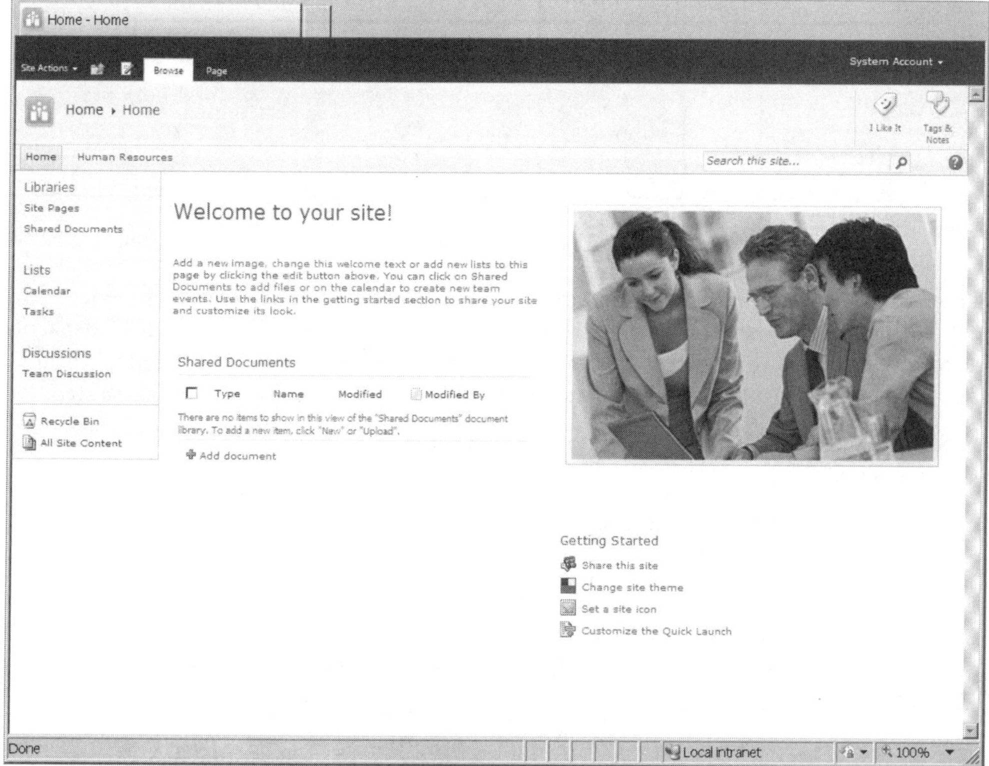

FIGURE 2-1

Focus your eyes on the upper-left corner. This is the famous ribbon you hear so much about. For some people, it takes some getting used to and draws the (slightly more than) occasional complaint.

Click Site Actions, and SharePoint responds with the drop-down, as shown in Figure 2-2.

Hover your mouse over New Site, and click the mouse. SharePoint now prompts you for new site information, as shown in Figure 2-3.

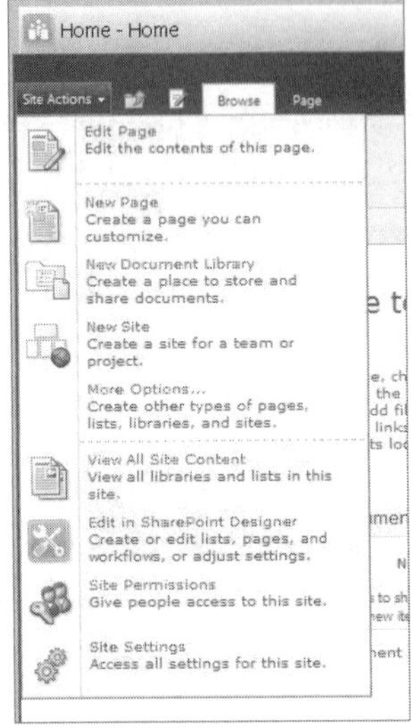

FIGURE 2-2

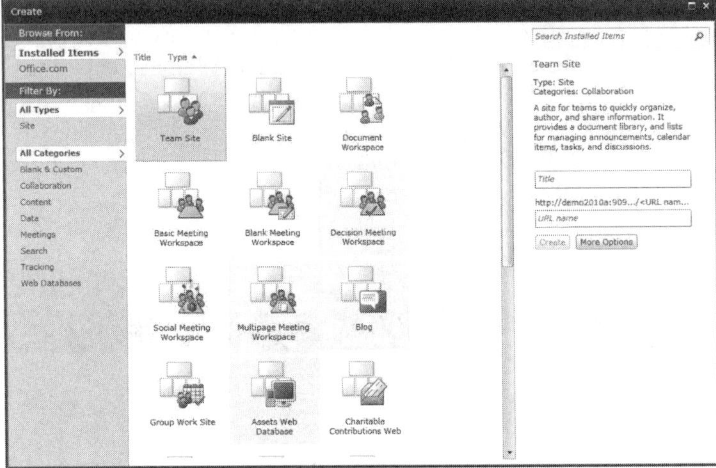

FIGURE 2-3

SharePoint presents you with a variety of templates. The templates you see may vary from Figure 2-3 depending on the version of SharePoint you run and whether you (or your IT department) has created and installed third-party custom site templates. For purposes of the "Hello, World" workflow, you can use just about any of these site templates. For simplicity, follow these steps:

1. Select Blank Site (normally listed immediately after Team Site).
2. On the right side of the screen, in the Title field, enter `Hello World Sandbox`.
3. In the URL field, enter `helloworldsandbox`.

A URL by any other name . . .

Why pick `helloworldsandbox` *instead of* `Hello, World Sandbox`*? The latter is a valid URL. The reason is that a name like that needs the comma and spaces "escaped" so that they can work properly. So, instead of* `Hello, World Sandbox`*, users see the escaped version,* `Hello%2C+World+Sandbox`*, or worse,* `Hello%2C%20World%20Sandbox`*. Everyone can agree that* `helloworldsandbox` *is not especially attractive in a URL, but it's better than the alternatives.*

If you followed these steps correctly, SharePoint enables the Create button, and your screen should look similar to Figure 2-4.

Click the Create button. Congratulations! You created a sandbox site (the first of many), which should look similar to Figure 2-5.

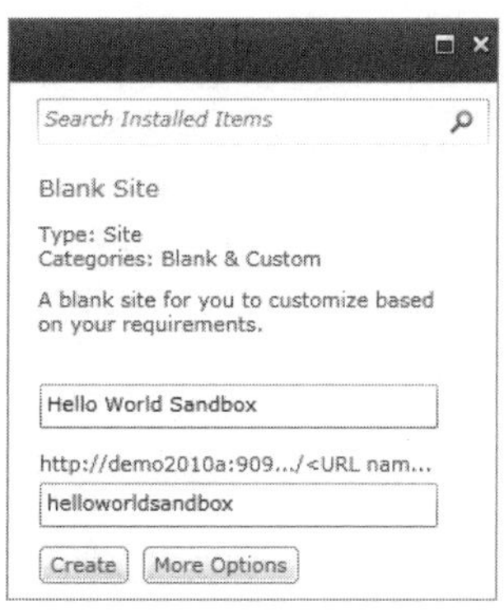

FIGURE 2-4

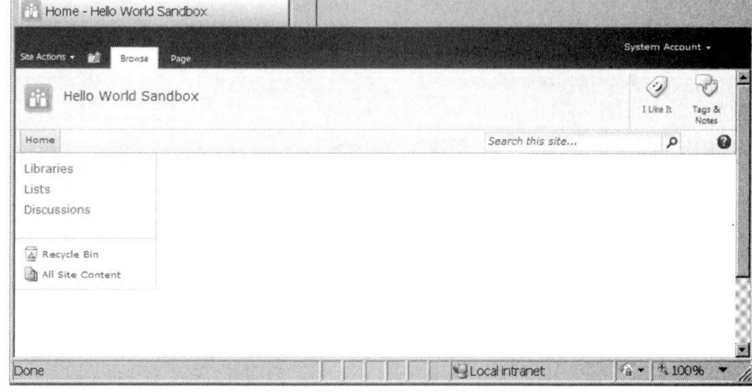

FIGURE 2-5

This provides a clean starting point for your next step.

Create a Custom List

SharePoint workflows must ultimately run in response to actions on a list of one kind or another. The "list" is a fundamental concept in SharePoint, and you need to understand this core idea. In SharePoint, a *custom list* is just a list with columns and rows of data. That's obvious enough. However, a document library is also a *list* — it just happens to be a list that must always have one, and only one, attached document. Image libraries are lists. KPIs are lists. Tasks are lists. You get the picture. To create the sample "Hello, World" workflow, you need a list. Now create a custom list for this purpose by following these steps:

1. Go to your site.
2. Click Site Actions from the upper-left corner.
3. Click More Options.
4. Fill out the SharePoint form, as indicated in Figure 2-6.

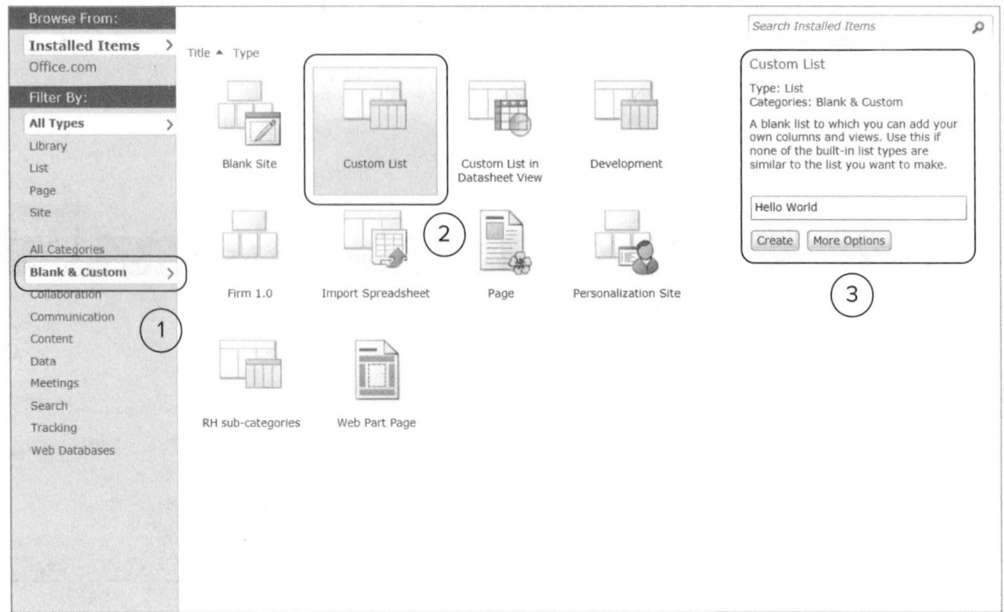

FIGURE 2-6

5. Select Blank & Custom from All Categories.
6. Select Custom List.
7. Name the list Hello World.
8. Click Create.

Congratulations! You created a custom list. Many more will follow over the course of this book. Now you can finally create the "Hello, World" workflow.

Create the "Hello, World" Workflow

You use SharePoint Designer 2010 to create the "Hello, World" workflow. SharePoint Designer 2010 is the successor to SharePoint Designer 2007 and is now the premier site editing tool for SharePoint. If you worked with SharePoint 2007 in the past and SharePoint Designer 2007 in particular, you will be presently surprised (even overjoyed). SharePoint Designer 2010 is leaps and bounds ahead of its predecessor.

There's a good chance that you've used (fought with, cried over) SharePoint Designer 2007 in the past. You'll be glad to know that SharePoint Designer 2010 is far, far superior to SharePoint Designer 2007. It is now a first-class tool for interfacing with and configuring SharePoint, including previously inaccessible elements such as content types and security. Workflow received much of Microsoft's love, however. As you'll see later in this chapter, SharePoint Designer now supports a proper software development life cycle (SDLC) and enables you to do the following:

- ***Reuse a workflow:*** *Create the perfect workflow on list A and reuse it again on list B.*
- ***Export a workflow:*** *Export from your development environment and import it directly into another site.*

SharePoint Designer 2007 does not enable you to reuse a workflow within a site or export it to another site. This may be the most welcome addition to the product line for business solution designers.

There are two ways to fire up Designer: through the web browser UI or directly via the Start menu. The easiest way is through the web browser ribbon. First, access the sandbox site (see Figure 2-7).

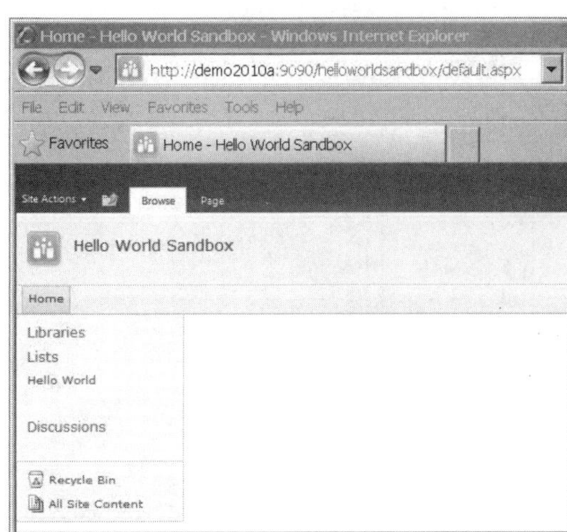

FIGURE 2-7

The URL of your sandbox site can vary. In the book's environment, the sandbox site is located on a server, demo2010a, running on port number 9090. The name of the site is helloworldsandbox.

Next, you need to get to the list's properties. Click the Hello World list, and the ribbon changes in response (see Figure 2-8).

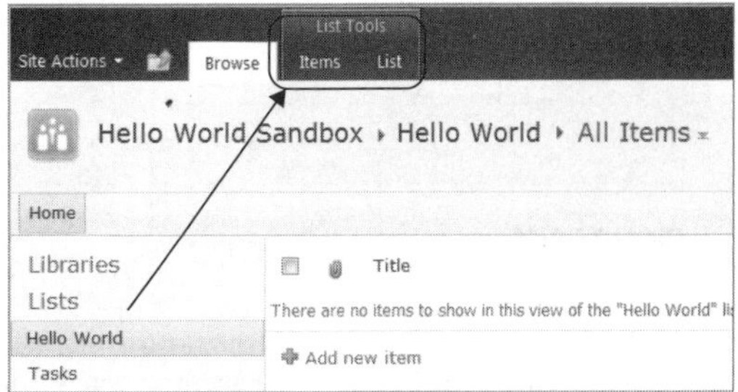

FIGURE 2-8

The new List Tools option reveals itself. Next, click the link labeled List in this new List Tools section. The ribbon transforms into a giant horizontal bar with options galore (see Figure 2-9).

FIGURE 2-9

First, click List. Then, click the arrow to the right of the small Workflow icon. (See the icon on the right side of Figure 2-9.) The ribbon displays a drop- down with four choices. Select Create a Workflow in SharePoint Designer. At this point, SharePoint Designer 2010 fires up, connects to the site, connects to the list, and opens up the Create New Workflow dialog (see Figure 2-10).

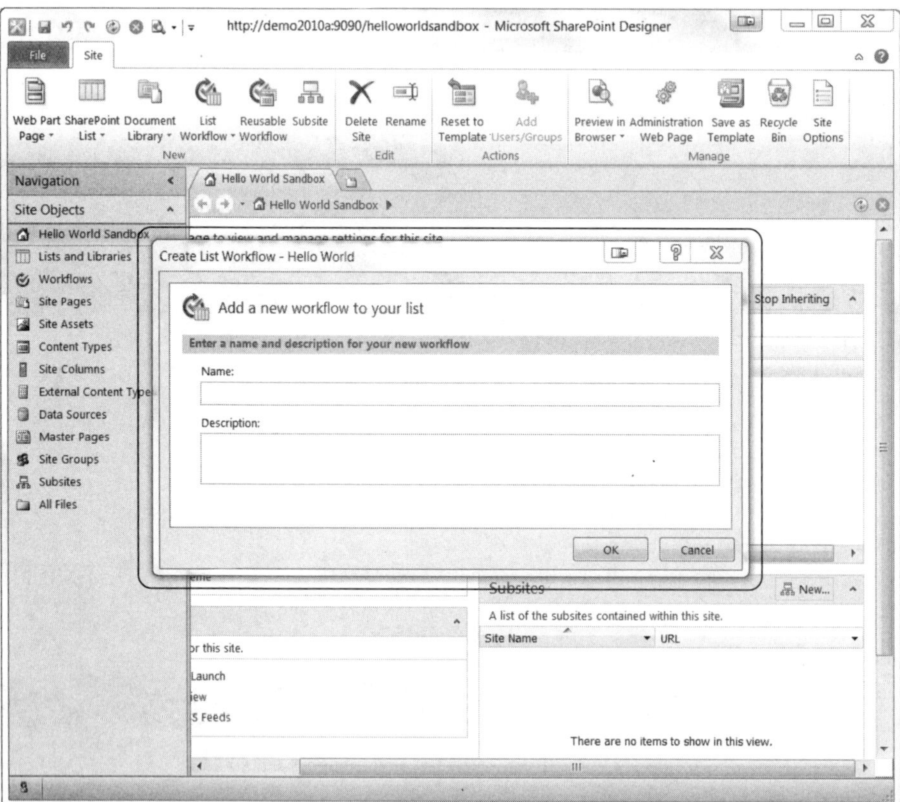

FIGURE 2-10

Provide a name and description, and it's finally time for the main show. Hover your mouse over Start Typing, and click your mouse; type the word `log`, as shown in Figures 2-11 and 2-12.

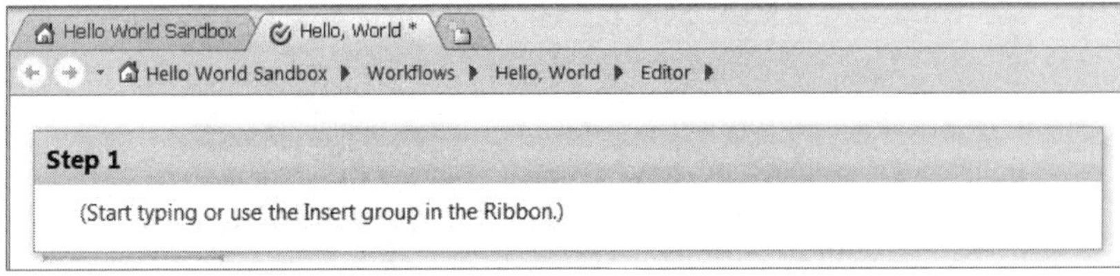

FIGURE 2-11

The large orange/red insertion bar moves directly under the Start Typing message. Begin typing `log`, and SharePoint Designer displays a helpful hint (as shown in Figure 2-12)

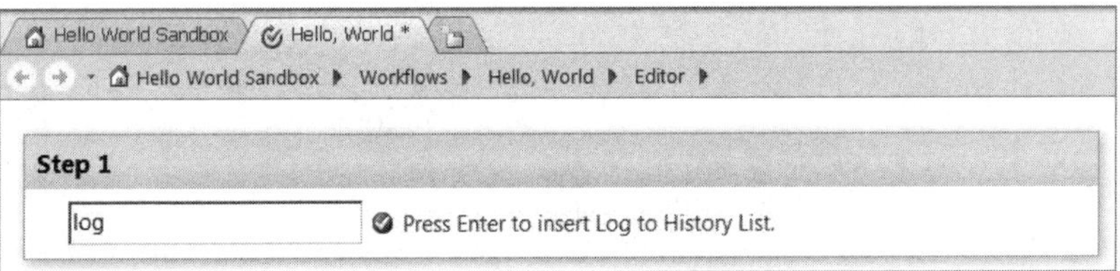

FIGURE 2-12

In marked contrast to SharePoint Designer 2007, SharePoint Designer 2010 enables you (encourages you, even) to type the names of actions and conditions. The precise meaning of *action* and *condition* are covered shortly. As you type letters, SharePoint Designer guesses at potential actions. Because `log` is part and parcel of the Log to History List action and no other action contains the word `log`, you can simply press Return to use that action. Do so. SharePoint Designer displays Log to History List's lone parameter: the message you want to log to history. By now, you can probably guess what that message will be. (See Figure 2-13.)

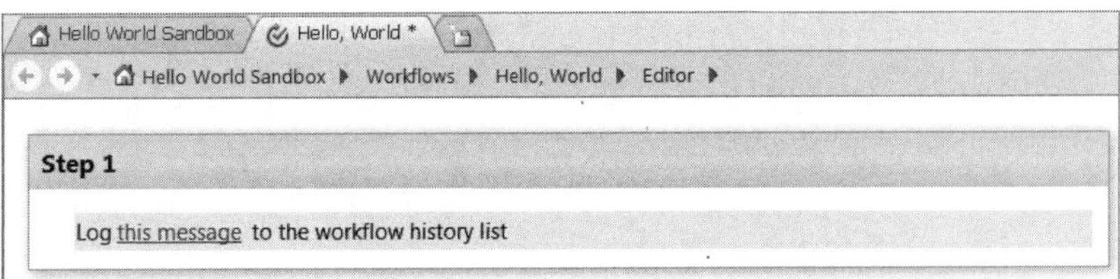

FIGURE 2-13

Click your mouse on This Message and type `Hello, World`. Congratulations; you created your first SharePoint Designer 2010 workflow. (See Figure 2-14.)

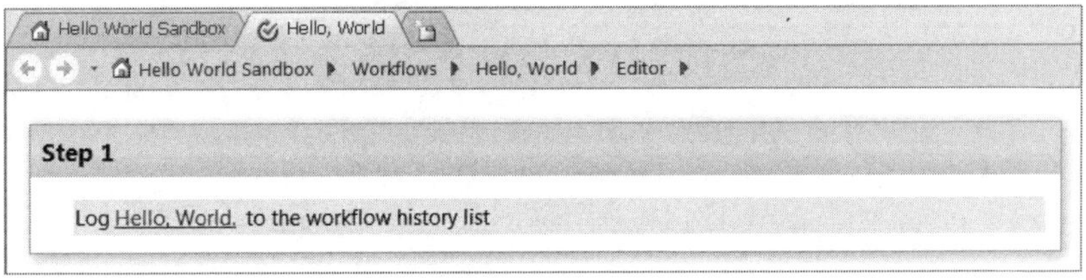

FIGURE 2-14

Save your work by pressing Control-S, or click the Save icon in the upper-left corner to save the workflow.

You're still not finished. So far, you created a workflow that logs a message to a history list. But where? And when? At this point, the Hello, World workflow is in an unpublished state. For end users to access and run the workflow, it must first be published. Do this by clicking the Publish button in the upper-left corner of SharePoint Designer. (See Figure 2-15.)

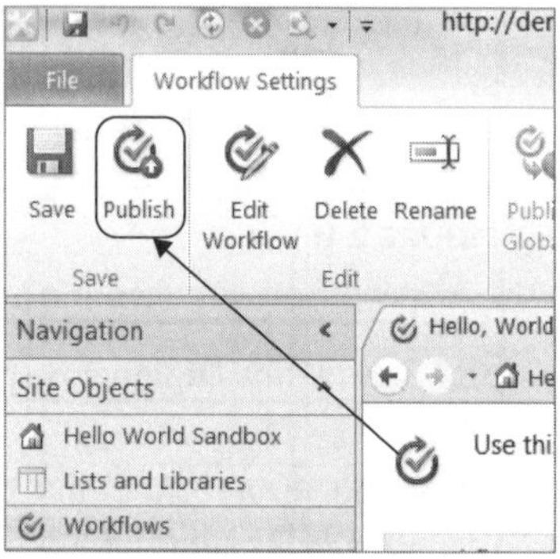

FIGURE 2-15

SharePoint Designer can now publish the workflow. This process can take a few moments, especially the first time you do it in a given session.

Test the Hello, World Workflow

It's finally time to test it out. Return to Internet Explorer and navigate to the Hello, World custom list. Create an item against which you can run the workflow. Then, highlight that row. (Mouse over the row, and click anywhere except on the title of the item.)

Move your mouse over the ribbon, and click Items and then Workflows, as shown in Figure 2-16.

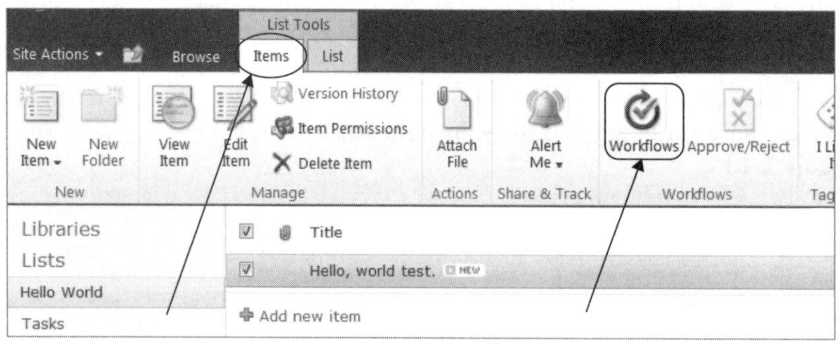

FIGURE 2-16

When you click Items, the ribbon changes to reveal the Workflows button. Click Workflows to get to the Start a New Workflow, as shown in Figure 2-17.

Click the Hello, World link to manually start the workflow. SharePoint responds with a parameters entry screen, as shown in Figure 2-18.

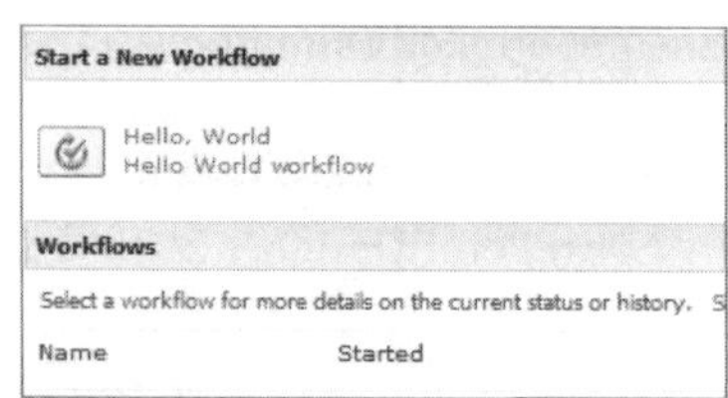

FIGURE 2-17

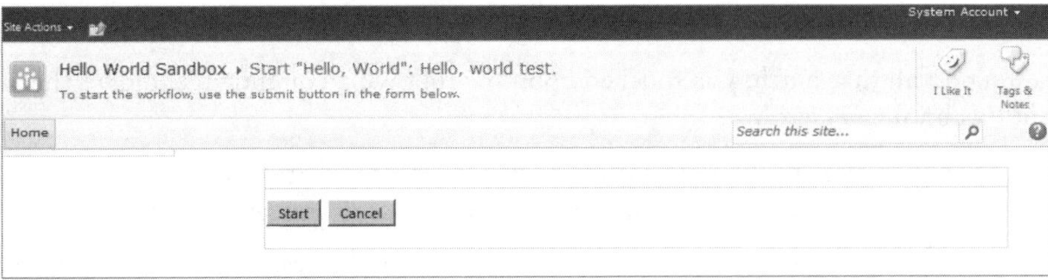

FIGURE 2-18

There are no parameters to this workflow (you add some in future chapters), so click the Start button. SharePoint begins the workflow. As with the earlier publishing step, this may take a few moments, especially the first time around. SharePoint responds by returning you to the main list view. (See Figure 2-19.)

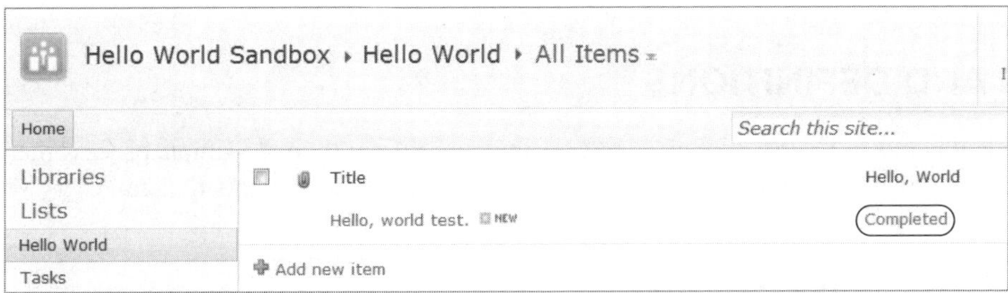

FIGURE 2-19

SharePoint has actually added a new column in your default view named after the workflow. This hyperlink column shows the status of currently running or previously executed workflows. This "helpful" column can turn into a nuisance later because you normally don't want users to access the functionality behind that column. For now, however, it's useful — so leave it at that. Click the Completed link to see the message you worked so hard to create. (See Figure 2-20.) Look for "Hello, World" at the bottom of the figure in the Workflow History section.

Workflow Information

Initiator: System Account **Item:** Hello, world test.
Started: 8/7/2010 7:26 PM **Status:** Completed
Last run: 8/7/2010 7:27 PM

Tasks

The following tasks have been assigned to the participants in this workflow. Click a task to edit it. You can also view these tasks in the list Tasks.

Assigned To	Title	Due Date	Status	Related Content	Outcome

There are no items to show in this view of the "Tasks" list. To add a new item, click "New".

Workflow History

View workflow reports
The following events have occurred in this workflow.

Date Occurred	Event Type	User ID	Description	Outcome
8/7/2010 7:27 PM	Comment	System Account	Hello, World.	

FIGURE 2-20

Your First Workflow: Conclusion

Although you didn't do all that much, you touched upon the following common techniques that are used throughout this book:

- **Creating a sandbox site:** You'll do this often as you learn new SharePoint features (regardless of whether they are related to workflow) and as quick proof of concept exercises.
- **Creating a custom list:** Lists lie at the core of most of the interesting things that SharePoint provides and at the core of most of your business solutions. If a list isn't in the mix, you probably moved left when you should have moved right.
- **Pushing a lot of buttons in SharePoint Designer:** You'll become quite the SharePoint Designer expert over the course of this book.

Future chapters won't provide a blow-by-blow description for creating sandbox sites, custom lists or libraries, and basic workflow technique. Refer back to this section if you feel like you need a refresher.

CONCEPTS AND DEFINITIONS

As you can probably guess, there's a lot more to creating a workflow than the simple process the last section just described. This section touches on the most important concepts that can carry you through the rest of the chapters in the book.

What Is SharePoint Designer?

So far, you installed SharePoint Designer, and you used it to create a workflow solution. What's actually going on, though?

SharePoint Designer is a client tool whose purpose is to connect to and configure SharePoint sites. This includes all the workflow functionality that you build in subsequent chapters, but also out-of-scope features (for this book, at least) including creating entirely new sites, data view web parts, business connectivity services, and a whole array of functionality.

When you use SharePoint Designer to create workflow solutions, you actually do all the following:

1. Launch the client tool.
2. Connect to a site.
3. Create an XML file (XOML, pronounced zommel).
4. Associate the XML file with a list.

This client tool can do a lot of work for you.

SharePoint Designer 2010 creates *declarative* workflows. A declarative workflow is when you say, more or less in English (or your local language) what to do and in what order. SharePoint Designer stores these declarations in the XOML file, and in one key respect, SharePoint Designer is largely an XML editor. There is nothing to stop you from creating your own declarative workflow in Windows Notepad, copying and pasting it into SharePoint Designer, and publishing the workflow (aside from common sense, that is). It is sometimes interesting and useful to edit the XOML file directly. You would take this step for advanced editing scenarios in which you want to do a mass copy/replace of names, text strings, and the like.

Core Workflow Concepts

You created a workflow; you learned the what and how of SharePoint Designer 2010. Now it's time to learn core workflow concepts (as they relate to SharePoint and its workflow capabilities).

Site Workflows Versus List Workflows

With SharePoint Designer, you can create two fundamental types of declarative workflows: site and list. The previous SharePoint platform (WSS 3.0 and MOSS) provided only list workflows. A list workflow is associated with a specific SharePoint list. (Don't forget; document libraries are also lists.) A site workflow is not tied to a list. Over the course of the various workflow solutions, you see when it's appropriate to use one or the other or both in service of a specific business problem.

Workflow Association

List workflows are always tied to a specific list. This tying process is called an *association.*

Starting Workflows

SharePoint Designer 2010 workflows must be started somehow to execute their logic. These workflows can be started automatically or manually. Manual starts are easy enough. Users must access a list of items and run the workflow against that list item.

Workflows may also start automatically. You can configure the workflow to start in response to create and update events. Notably, you cannot start a workflow when an item is *deleted.* This unfortunate lack is the bane of many a comprehensive business solution. It's lack can force you to develop some solution components using Visual Studio and the SharePoint object model, which the later chapters cover.

Steps, Conditions, and Actions

Workflows are composed of steps, conditions, and actions. *Steps* are a collection of conditions and actions. *Conditions* determine whether the step's collection of actions execute. SharePoint executes workflows starting with the first step and continues through every step and its collection of actions provided that the action's conditions are met. Some actions cause the workflow to stop or block. You use a *stop action* when you want a workflow to specifically stop. It halts immediately whether there are any more actions or steps. A *blocking action* causes the workflow to suspend operation until some other condition is met. Following are several ways to cause a block:

- Pause for any duration.
- Assign a task and wait for it to complete.
- Wait for the value of a field to change.

When a workflow is blocked, SharePoint actually saves its state to the database and frees up processor resources. This process is sometimes called *dehydration.* When SharePoint needs to unblock the workflow (because the delay period elapsed or the user completed an assigned task),

SharePoint *hydrates* the previous dehydrated workflow and execution resumes as per its steps, conditions, and actions.

Content Types

You're not supposed to define a word using the word, but content types is a challenge in this regard. Here's the best attempt: A *content type* is a collection of discrete pieces of information that taken as a whole, describe a business concept.

Content types are best described by example. Consider an invoice. An invoice is a demand for payment for products sold or services rendered. A plumber presents you with an invoice when he fixes your leaky faucet. The phone company sends you an invoice (your bill) on a monthly basis. Your company sends invoices to its customers. If you want to use SharePoint as a repository for invoices, you could create a document library called "invoices" and upload invoices to this library. SharePoint enables you to do more than merely provide an online repository, however. You can tell SharePoint that the invoice is more than a document. It is also a collection of important information such as a customer number, invoice number, invoice date, and invoice amount.

Why Use Content Types?

SharePoint content types provide two valuable features. One is logical and the other is technical. Logically, a content type enables you to think in business terms. You can define your business concept of an invoice and then use SharePoint's technical functionality to turn the business concept into something you can use in a workflow.

From a practical perspective, SharePoint Designer workflow can read the content type information of a given item via the workflow's conditions and actions. You do this throughout the solution.

Software Development Life Cycle

SharePoint 2010 provides a set of features that support a robust software development life cycle, typically referred to by its acronym, SDLC, which is a process that reduces a production solution's risk of failure. It supports rapid deployment of both bug fixes and enhancements to the production system.

SDLC starts by defining discrete single-purpose SharePoint environments, which include some or all of the following:

- **Development:** You create your solutions in the development environment. The development environment is normally disconnected from the production environment and locked down so that only developers may access it. It is occasionally refreshed with data from production; although this can be problematic because developers, for testing purposes, often create specific data structures to support specific use cases.
- **Integration:** Frequently called *test*, the integration environment is used to pull together the efforts of multiple different developers, working in multiple different development environments, into a single place. This process often uncovers hidden dependencies or unexpected interactions between developers' work product. These problems are corrected when discovered during integration testing.

- **User Acceptance Testing environment (UAT):** In an ideal world, UAT models production both in farm infrastructure and data. (That is, it is frequently refreshed with production data on a weekly or even daily basis.) Solutions are ported from the integration server to the UAT server. Users then perform their mysterious end user testing, report bugs, and eventually sign off on the solution, signaling that it's ready to be deployed to production.
- **Production:** This is the real enchilada. Production is often locked down by system administrators. Many times, developers cannot make any change of any kind directly in the production server. Instead, they must provide a solution package to administrators who deploy it to production.

These systems represent a fairly by-the-book hardware environment that supports a proper SDLC. By the book is expensive, and it's possible and quite normal to create a pared down version of this ideal. Many times, companies implement just two farms: development and production. This is not ideal and opens you up to a lot of risk.

Features and Solutions

SharePoint provides additional support for a well-defined SDLC by way of the feature and solution framework. This topic is far afield of this book's main topic. However, you need to know about it because you need to leverage this framework in the real world.

Features are collections of bits of different functionality and developers define features.

DESIGNING BUSINESS SOLUTIONS

Successful workflow solutions must be carefully and thoughtfully designed before you ever create a sandbox site or open up SharePoint Designer. There's no shortage of solution design paradigms. Mindful of the audience, this book does not provide or even strongly recommend any particular design process, methodology, or even philosophy. (Although the authors are biased toward Agile.) Instead, we want to provide a practical get-it-done approach that is easy for nondevelopers to follow and adopt but also yields high-quality results. This book propounds a solutions design approach that breaks things down into interviews, swim lanes, prototyping and reusable patterns.

Interviews

There is one fundamental goal for any interview: Understand the business requirements — actually, understand the requirements profoundly. It's easy to sit down with a few business users and have a superficial chat about a business problem. Don't be surprised if you craft a superficial solution that ignores the thorny issues until you're in production, the schedule is compressed, and end users are crying out their frustration.

New solutions designers should keep these three facts in mind:

- **Workflow processes always begin.** This is easy enough to remember.
- **Workflow processes nearly always change.** This simple fact trips up many newly minted solutions designers.
- **Workflow processes occasionally stop before anyone hoped or intended.**

These three facets of solutions design are so common that an acronym, CRUD (Create, Read, Update, and Delete), was coined to describe it. CRUD is described in great detail in the next chapter.

What does this have to do with interviews? Even if it's your solution, go through an "interview." You want someone to challenge you.

Swim Lane Diagrams

Many design paradigms call for extensive and highly regimented documentation steps after interviews have been completed. There's nothing wrong with that, but it can be overkill. Activist users, however, have not been trained in these techniques and won't have a library of standard templates to use. This book proposes that you create swim lane diagrams to describe the behavior of your workflow solutions.

A swim lane diagram breaks the process down into the following:

- **Actors:** Users or system that interact together in the process
- **Actions:** Those steps that actors perform when executing the workflow. Some actions are as simple as pressing a button to approve a request. Some actions may be outside of SharePoint altogether, such as clearing a paper jam.
- **Time:** Sequence and timing of actions taken by actors

A swim lane diagram merges these together in an easy-to-read graph that serves as a road map for your business process.

Actors

Actors, simply put, do "stuff." Actors are the important people or, just as important, *systems*, that cause a workflow process to start, proceed, and complete. In SharePoint, actors typically start a workflow process by uploading a document, creating an item in a custom list, manually launching a workflow, or otherwise touching something important in SharePoint. They push workflows through their paces by doing much the same thing; although, it is usually directed by the workflow process itself. For instance, completing an assigned task by editing and changing the status of the SharePoint task.

You need to recognize that actors are not always human. In fact, no useful workflow process is run entirely by people in your organization. SharePoint itself take on the actor role when, for example, it sends a reminder email to users that they must complete a task. Complex workflow-based solutions may involve entirely separate systems, like your company's ERP or HR system.

Actions

Actors move the workflow process through its paces by filling out forms, sending emails, updating tasks — the list goes on and is dictated by your specific solution. Actions include things such as the following:

- Fill out an InfoPath form, and save it to SharePoint.
- Send an email alert.

- Create a list item and manually start a workflow.
- Pause for 24 hours and send a reminder (if needed).

As you can see, actions do not need to be carried out by a human, and many times, they are not.

Sample Diagram

Now review a swim lane diagram that pulls this all together. Figure 2-21 depicts a simple contract management workflow process.

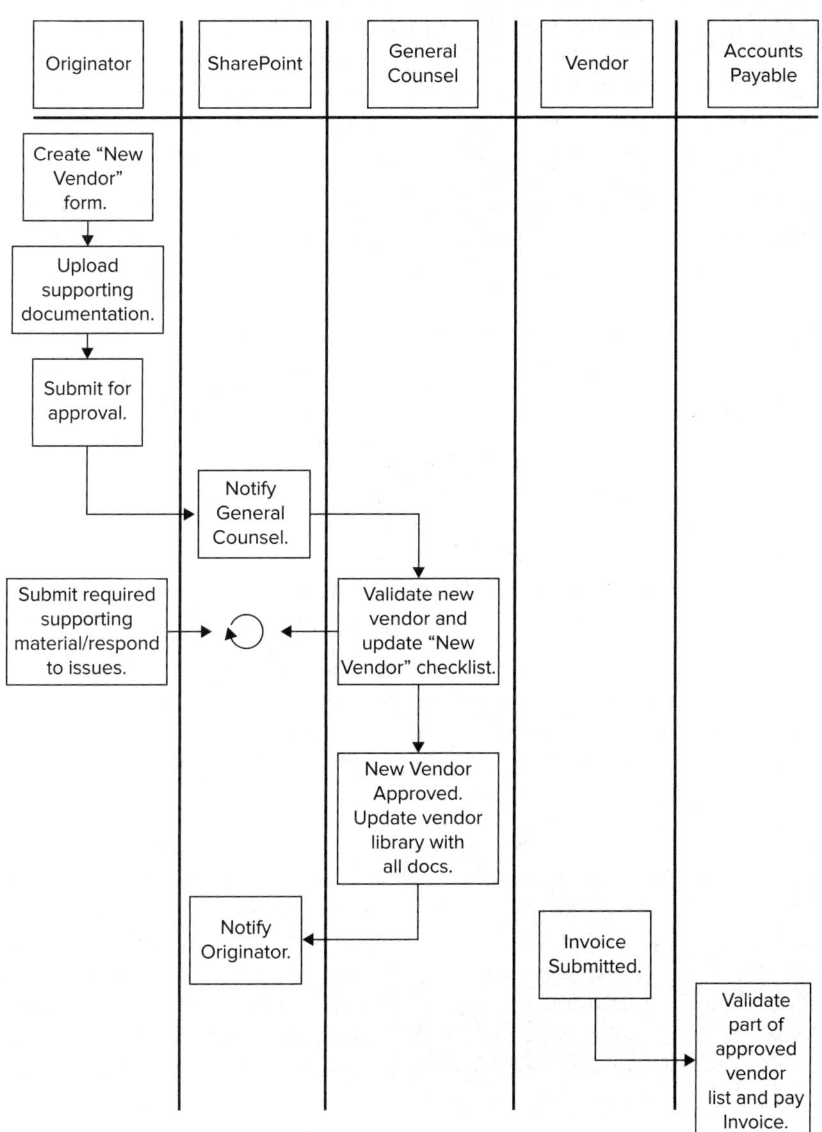

FIGURE 2-21

The contractor process shows that there are five actors altogether:

- Originator
- SharePoint
- General counsel
- Vendor
- Accounts payable

The diagram depicts a workflow process that begins when an originator within the company identifies the need for a new vendor. The originator locates and fills out an online form. (InfoPath might be a good choice.) The originator might upload some supporting documentation (such as proof of insurance and tax paperwork into a shared library), or possibly attach it to the InfoPath form. Don't worry about that level of specific operation at this stage in the game. Eventually the originator believes he has all his ducks in order and submits the new vendor for approval.

SharePoint assigns a task to the general counsel and send an email notifying her that she needs to review the paperwork. The general counsel performs that review and may require some additional paperwork either directly from the originator or indirectly from the vendor, via the originator. The preceding process never shows the general counsel communicating directly with the vendor. If the general counsel were to interact with the vendor, you would want the swim lane diagram to show that.

Eventually the originator and vendor satisfy all the requirements, and the general counsel agrees. Later, the vendor provides some services or sells some product and sends an invoice. Accounts payable looks up the vendor in the approved vendors list. Finding that the vendor is approved, accounts payable cuts a check to the vendor.

Helpful Tips

Microsoft Visio is a good tool for creating swim lane diagrams. If you elect to use it, create several blank swim lane diagrams first. Create an empty three-lane, four-lane, five-lane, and six-lane diagram.

As you'll see in subsequent chapters, you don't want to try and cram everything into a swim lane diagram. If your diagram becomes too complex, break it down into smaller pieces. For instance, if the vendor invoicing/payment process is much more complicated than shown in the diagram (and in the real world, it probably is more complex), it's more appropriate to break that down into its own swim lane diagram.

Finally, when you have a good first version of a swim lane diagram in hand, sit down with the business users (or someone smart upon whom you can rely if *you* are the business user) and game it out. This is to say, talk through the whole process, start to finish, and make sure that the swim lane diagram captures all the actors and actions that take place in the process. Use an actual example for best results. For example, if vendor XYZ was just approved last week, use XYZ as an example, and make sure that the swim lane diagram matches up to the real world of how XYZ was brought on to the company as an approved vendor. Don't forget to talk about what could go wrong. This last point is critical because it's far, far easier to plan for and implement bits of your solution to handle error situations now than it is after the solution is in production.

Reusable Patterns

If you learn only one thing about this book, remember the author's name. If you can learn two things, learn about *patterns*. When solutions architects, developers, and technical wizards use the word pattern, they mean almost exactly what you think. You follow a well-known correct pattern because it makes things easier and guarantees a good result. People use cookie cutters because they want their cookies to look perfect and don't want to be bothered with trying to create them from scratch. This book describes a whole slew of patterns, broken down into business patterns and technical patterns.

Business Patterns

Business patterns are focused on human beings doing real work to achieve a specific goal. For instance, plan for and successfully execute a future event like a birthday party, a new product launch, someone new joining the company. When you think about business patterns, don't think about SharePoint Designer, SharePoint lists, C#, XOML — instead you think about human beings and how they achieve the end result.

Technical Patterns

Technical patterns contrast with business patterns in that they are all about bits and bytes. A technical pattern describes how to do something with SharePoint Designer, or how to create a structured content type appropriate for reuse across multiple applications. For example, this book describes how to use SharePoint Designer workflow to create a well-formatted email message. After you create an email message once, you can create it over and over again.

KNOWING SHAREPOINT DESIGNER'S LIMITS

You can get a lot of mileage out of SharePoint Designer. SharePoint Designer can help you solve a dozen or more common business problems. That said, SharePoint Designer is far from perfect and is not the right tool for many real-world problems. Just as you shouldn't use a straight-edge screwdriver on a Philips head screw, you should avoid using SharePoint Designer when it's just not the right tool. You might get it done, but no one is happy with the result. Keep these limitations in mind as you imagine business problems and solutions:

- **SharePoint Designer workflow cannot loop:** SharePoint Designer does not provide any feature that enables you to iterate over multiple items in a custom list or document library.
- **State machines:** In a certain sense, all workflows are state machine workflows. That said, SharePoint Designer is good at creating sequential workflows and not so good at state machine workflows. This book does offer some options for emulating some generic state machine behavior, but if you need a full-blown state machine engine, look to Visual Studio instead.
- **Complex lookups:** You cannot do a multikey lookup on a list. If you need to implement a complex lookup of this sort, you need to use a nonobvious technique, which is discussed later.

These may seem a little esoteric at this point, but subsequent chapters call these situations out and suggest alternative approaches.

SUMMARY

This chapter introduced two bedrock components that you'll re-use throughout the book. First, it walked you through the process of creating your first actual workflow using SharePoint Designer to create the classic "Hello, World" application. By now, you've installed and/or obtained all of the minimum server and applications you need to create real solutions. This is important hands-on work that will help you out in all of the chapters that follow.

More importantly, the chapter discussed the overall approach you should take when designing and creating these solutions. If you do things correctly, you'll spend more than half your time identifying the business drivers and requirements before you ever crack open SharePoint Designer. The chapters that follow, starting with the next one on HR On-Boarding, emphasize this approach.

3

HR On-Boarding

WHAT'S IN THIS CHAPTER?

- Your first real-world workflow solution
- Learning about the world's oldest business pattern - CRUD
- Creating tasks
- Using workflow parameters

Nothing is more frustrating to a company and its new employees (or contractors) than showing up to for the first big day at work just to get stuck at the front door sitting around for hours and twiddling thumbs while people figure out what to do. How many times have you seen this happen? Probably too many times to count. This kind of future event is not hard to understand conceptually, and everyone agrees that it's important to execute properly. Yet, something manages to go wrong with frustrating regularity. If you've left a new hire cooling her heels in the lobby while people scramble to locate a desk, you're not alone.

The HR on-boarding process provides you with an opportunity to solve this easily preventable problem using some automation via workflow and exception management via dashboards. Workflow can ensure that everyone knows what they are supposed to do and when they are supposed to do it. Dashboards enable the HR managers to follow up and actively manage the process when needed. This way, when new employees walk up to the door, they can not only go straight to their desk, but also be assured that they have a network ID set up, a waiting laptop, new employee orientation scheduled, and so on.

This is the first hands-on chapter of the book, which covers certain steps in greater detail than in future chapters. For instance, you create a custom list to create a lookup site column for the model company's office locations (for example, New York, London, and such). This is a common technique that won't be explained in detail elsewhere.

Before you dive into the solution, consider how to arrive at a true and clear definition of the problem (via interviews) and validate that discovered business knowledge with a swim lane diagram. After this critical planning step is successfully concluded, you crack open SharePoint and build the solution, step by step. This chapter emphasizes the full life cycle of the process, including creating, updating, and deleting operations and how to meet those requirements using SharePoint and workflow.

WHAT IS THE HR ON-BOARDING PROCESS?

The HR on-boarding process is straightforward, which is a big reason why it's the first hands-on chapter in the book. You know that a new person will be joining the company at a future date. That person might be a new full -time employee or might be a contractor. When the new hire arrives in the parking lot, certain things need to be completed for that first day to go smoothly:

- Security access to the physical premises
- Laptop or desktop procurement
- Office space and location
- Phone configuration
- Network credentials
- Payroll
- Scheduling day-one activities (new employee orientation)

The list goes on and on. Every company has a different set of day-zero activities that must be completed, and different employees may have different day-zero activities as well. For instance, sales reps may be issued a light-weight laptop suitable for traveling the country whereas a developer is issued a heavy-duty laptop with more horsepower.

The company is not the only responsible party. The new hires have responsibilities, too. They typically need to fill out some paperwork (acknowledge receipt of employee handbook), make some benefits selections and take a security course. It's not a one-way street, and SharePoint can help you to manage this part of the process as well.

The on-boarding process encapsulates all the activities that both the company and its new employees must complete. These activities start before the new hires walk in the door for the big day and doesn't end until the new hires complete all the "newbie" stuff.

PROBLEM CLASS

HR on-boarding exemplifies the "future event" class of business problems. You know that something important is going to happen at a future date. For that future event to proceed smoothly, a variety of people and business groups need to coordinate their activities and complete tasks before the event takes place. Otherwise, the event won't run smoothly and may even fail altogether!

After you solve this HR on-boarding problem, you have implemented a pattern that you can reuse later with minor variations. These other problems include the following:

- Event planning
- New store opening

- Product launch (marketing event)
- Webinar

TECHNICAL PATTERNS

While solving the HR on-boarding problem, you can implement the following technical patterns:

- **Basic CRUD:** This chapter talks a lot about CRUD (Create, Read, Update, and Delete), which is the core technical pattern for almost every imaginable business process. Job offers are made and accepted, but sometimes, plans change (that is, they are created and updated). Start dates may change or new hires may turn down previously accepted offers and go to work somewhere else (that is, deleted). HR managers need to view the status of new hire activities (that is, read).
- **Delegation:** You have lots of people involved. You can assign tasks to them until you're blue in the face, but what happens if they are on vacation?
- **Dashboard feeder:** The bedrock beneath manage-by-exception principles, dashboards show just the right information in an easily digestible format that requires little or no interpretation. Dashboards represent a snapshot in time of an entire set of processes, and to display that snapshot, the data must be available. The dashboard feeder pattern ensures that your workflows provide appropriate status information so that you can provide meaningful dashboards to the people entrusted and responsible for making sure the business process works smoothly.

BUSINESS PATTERNS

While solving the HR on-boarding problem, you need to implement the following business patterns:

- **Routing:** Who is assigned these tasks?
- **Calendars:** Who is doing what and when?
- **Delegation:** Similar to the technical pattern of the same namesake, delegation enables users to meet their obligations by identifying a responsible team member to handle their responsibilities while they are away. If I'm the guy on the IT team responsible to provision a network security account for a new hire and I'm going to be on vacation, I need to have someone take care of that while I'm away. Delegation enables me to do that.

BUSINESS PROBLEM DESCRIPTION

You can arrive at this via a standard process and pattern that the chapters of this book generally follow. For HR on-boarding, you need to identify the core problem, who are the actors (people and systems) and what actions they need to take to ensure a successful outcome. You identify and dispose of any obvious or not-so-obvious problems.

Requirements Discussion

This section is named "Requirements Discussion" not just because it's going to discuss the requirements (which it does), but also because it's important to actually discuss, out loud, the requirements with all affected users. This is the interview process that Chapter 2, "Workflow Basics," laid out for you.

When you start to analyze the requirements around this process, you need to first figure out who you are going to meet. Different groups of people have different goals, hopes, and dreams in mind. If you don't talk to the right people, you might get a skewed set of requirements. If you talk to too many people, you'll never finish talking. Neither leads to a good outcome.

Imagine that you're meeting with the HR department and a hiring manager. Be prepared for some finger pointing and frustration during the initial meeting. If your company doesn't have an automated process in place today, there's a good chance that things don't work well when new employees join, and as a result, more than once people have done a bit of yelling.

The goal of this initial interview session is to find out several pieces of information:

- Which departments need to be involved in the new hire process?
- What role does the new hire's manager have?
- Who is the watchdog? Who pays attention to the process to make sure that it goes smoothly and cracks the whip when necessary?
- How often does the process change?

When you know who's involved, you can schedule additional interviews. For example, an on-boarding process is almost certainly going to involve the IT department. With that list of departments, schedule additional in-person meetings to cover topics such as the following:

- What information does the group need to prepare for the new employee?
- Does it matter if this employee is in sales, technology, administration, or some other group? If so, what is the impact? For instance, your company typically provides a laptop to a new sales rep but may provide a heavy-duty desktop for on-site development staff.
- Does it matter if this is a contractor and not an employee? Does the department need to be notified about certain types of employees or contractors?
- How much time does the group need to complete these preparations? It may need two weeks to procure and provision a laptop, whereas security may need just a few days to update its employee database.
- Who takes the lead within the group and is primarily responsible to ensure that the group performs its new-hire tasks on time and accurately?
- Does the group have a proper delegation process if the primary responsible person is on vacation?
- Which systems do they need to interface with for the new employee? For instance, IT needs to create an account in Active Directory.

These questions may prompt some soul-searching. For instance, the group may not have any kind of official delegation process; merely asking the question may prompt them to create one.

This chapter makes some assumptions using a model of a company that includes the following departments:

- Human resources department
- IT department
- Accounts payable
- Security

Each of them and their role in the process is discussed next.

Actors

The model on which this hands-on chapter is built coordinates activities between the following departments and individuals:

- **Human resources:** At least one member of the HR department needs to be responsible to launch the process, change start dates, and monitor the dashboard.
- **New hire:** This is the new employee or contractor. You might frequently think in terms of new employees, but many organizations treat temporary contractors in a similar way as new full-time employees. After all, contractors still need an email address, a place to work, and so forth.
- **Hiring manager:** The hiring manager is effectively the HR department's customer. As a customer, the hiring manager wants to be kept in the loop and be involved only if there are issues that require direct intervention.
- **Information technology department (IT):** Procuring hardware, setting up internal network accounts, and access.
- **Accounts Payable:** Setting up payroll.
- **Security:** Providing physical access to the work area.

Different companies can have a varying number of groups involved in making sure that the on-boarding process is successful. This model isn't meant to be exhaustive but does represent a fair cross section of responsible parties.

Actions

Who does what and when do they do it? Now walk through this in detail so that you understand your eventual automated workflow process.

To begin, you can assume that the new hire has a defined and expected start date. Someone needs to enter that information into the system to begin the process. The HR manager fulfills this role.

SharePoint is an actor. SharePoint is often referred to more dryly as "the system." SharePoint creates tasks, alerts people that a new person is beginning on some future date (or changes to the start date) and feeds the dashboard so that the HR manager can exercise control. The IT Department needs to provision hardware and create network credentials for the new hire. Accounts payable sets up the new hire in the payroll system.

In this model, the hiring manager doesn't actively participate. However, the hiring manager is clearly interested in what's happening with the new hire, so the system sends alerts to the hiring manager.

Challenges

If you take a simple view of this problem, it's not all that hard to solve. However, you need to solve three key challenges for this to be a high-quality solution. This chapter discusses two of these but leaves the last (delegation) for Chapter 4, "Helpdesk Ticketing."

First, plans change. Someone may accept a job offer but actually end up taking an entirely different job offer with another firm. Sometimes, people plan to start on a specific date, but for some reason they need to change that start date. In both cases, you need to manage two exceptional conditions: delete and change. These are three of the four pillars in your CRUD requirements. (Create, Update, and Delete; Read is managed via a dashboard.)

Second, a complex process like this involves many different people, some of whom cannot always be available when they are needed. Sometimes it's difficult to predict but many times (for example, scheduled vacation time), it's entirely predictable. Your solution needs to address these cases. You acknowledge this problem here (it's called delegation) in this chapter but wait for Chapter 4, "Helpdesk Ticketing," to see a detailed walk-through of the solution.

Lastly, you have a technical challenge. Company dates don't follow calendar dates. You need realistic due date assignments. For this, you need to calculate due dates that don't fall on weekends or company holidays. You can't solve this easily out-of-the-box, but you can via a custom action. Chapter 12 discusses custom activities.

HIGH-LEVEL SOLUTION

This section describes the high-level solution of the problem upon which the detailed walk-through is built. This section outlines the overall solution, provides a visualization of the workflow by way of a swim lane, and defines the necessary content types and their purpose.

Solution Overview

Kick off the process when an HR manager accesses the system and says in simple terms, "Hey, here's a new hire starting on future date [x]." HR's action triggers task assignments to the departments in the model (IT, AP and security). To this end, you need a custom list to manage the new hire (name, start date, and so on) and three different types of logical task lists, one for each department in the model. You create three logical task lists but implement this as one physical task list with the aid of four site content types.

The new hire custom list and related task list provides the cornerstone of the solution's dashboard. The HR manager (and other authorized and interested parties) use the dashboard to obtain a single unified view of everything that's happening and can manage unusual situations (primarily, when the tasks are overdue). Because the dashboard is driven off tasks and the new hire list, any changes to the underlying data result in an immediate update to the dashboard, providing a real-time view into the state of every new hire on-boarding process in the company.

You meet the CRUD requirements via three distinct physical workflows, all of which are started manually by the HR manager:

- **Launch new hire process:** After the new start date is known, the HR manager creates the new hire entry in the custom list and starts the process.
- **Change new hire start date:** If the new hire's start date changes, HR to provides the new expected start date and updates the workflow for all associated tasks as needed.
- **Cancel new hire:** Notify all the interested parties that the new hire won't be starting.

Swim Lane Diagrams

The swim lane diagram shows the workflow visually (recall that you learned about swim lane diagrams in Chapter 2). (See Figure 3-1.)

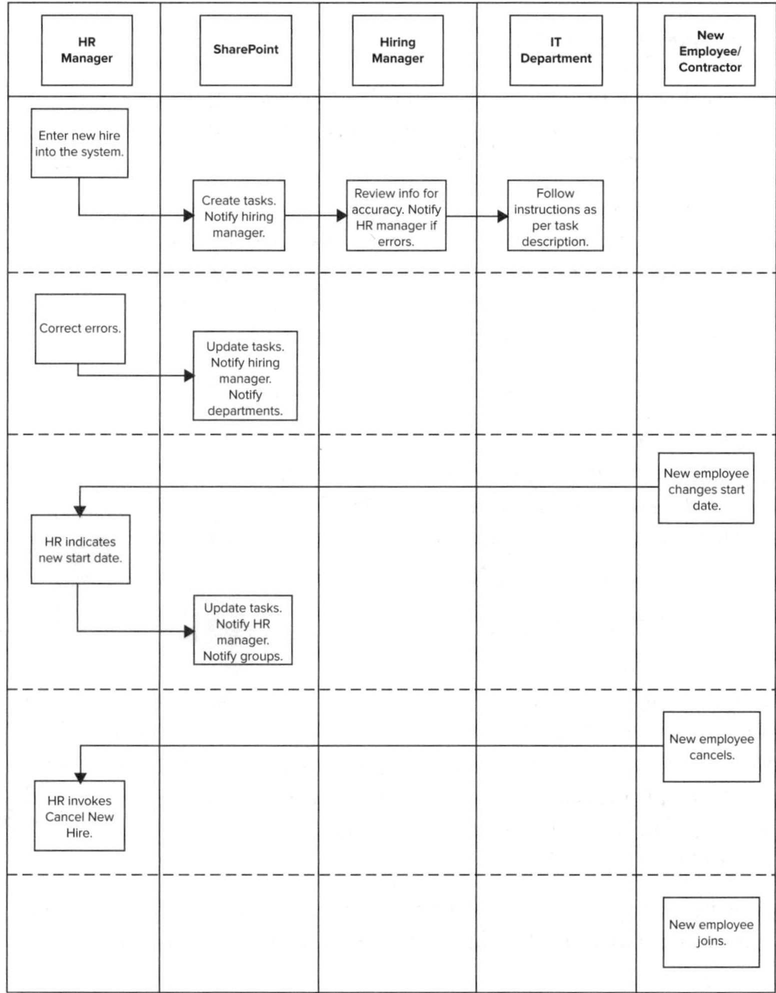

FIGURE 3-1

The swim lane diagram depicts four variations of the new hire process:

1. Entering a new hire
2. Correcting errors
3. Changing the employee's start date
4. Canceling the process

Each variation is separated from the others by way of the heavy dashed line.

The swim lane depicts the actors, actions they may take, and the sequence in which they occur. The diagram shows only the IT department because it can represent all the departments involved in the solution. (All departments take the same actions.)

The technical implementation takes this diagram into account as it describes the actual SharePoint configurations that you need make to create this solution.

Technical Implementation Overview

The technical implementation of this solution relies upon SharePoint content types. To meet the requirements of this solution, you create six content types: one for the new hire, four for tasks, and one final content type for a user experience purpose.

You create several different workflows to support the preceding swim lanes. The first workflow kicks off the grand process. Because this process is all about new hires, you need to provide some way for HR managers to create a new hire in the system. Define a content type for this purpose and allow the new hire custom list to manage it. This provides your basic data entry function and starting point. Workflows that support your various CRUD processes hang off that list.

Developers use a lot of jargon in their daily routine. The idea of a workflow "hanging off a list" is just a colorful way to say that a workflow is defined and attached to a specific list. In this case, the workflows that you create to support this solution will all be associated with the New Hire list itself. More on that as the chapter progresses.

Multiple departments need to work off task lists. Not only do they guide those departments and help to keep everyone accountable, they will also serve as core components to the dashboards. You could use the default SharePoint task list for this purpose, but instead you create a custom list tailored to the specific needs of this business process (and follow best practices to boot). As with the new hire list, you create a content type and associate it with the list. This time, you create four different types (one base type and three specialized per department).

Lastly, you want to build some flexibility into your solution. In particular, you assign tasks to IT, accounts payable, and the good people in security. The description for each department task is quite different from the next and may change over time. You could hard-code these descriptions in the workflow, but instead you separate them into a custom list. This way, if they change, the department owners can update the description.

Content Types

The on-boarding solution uses the following content types:

- **New Hire:** Name, start date, title, and so on
- **New Hire Base Task:** Generic task that defines the most important elements of all the tasks in the system
- **New Hire IT Task:** A specialized form of the new hire base task for the IT department
- **New Hire AP Task:** Specialized task for the AP department
- **New Hire Security Task:** Specialized task for the security group
- **New Hire Task Description:** A simple content type that enables departments to control the description of tasks assigned to them. For instance, a specific set of instructions for IT is distinct and separate from instructions to accounts payable.

What is a content type? If you're relatively new to the SharePoint world, this is a word you will quickly become familiar with. In SharePoint, a content type is similar to a header row you might create in an Excel document. Each column is labeled, and each row in that column normally contains the same kind of data (for example, a number, hyperlink, date, and so on). After you define a content type, you can use it to quickly and easily create items in custom lists (such as your New Hire list or department tasks). SharePoint provides a handy default user interface for this purpose. If you want to learn more about content types, check out Microsoft's introduction here at `http://office.microsoft.com/en-us/windows-sharepoint-services-help/introduction-to-content-types-HA010121570.aspx`.

Custom Lists

The solution builds upon the following key custom lists:

- **New Hire:** The core list in the solution, holding all key new hire information
- **New Hire Tasks:** Workflows create and update items in this list, assigning tasks to the three corporate departments in the model.
- **New Hire Task Descriptions:** A supporting list that enables you to avoid hard-coding the task descriptions

> Hard-coding *is more technical jargon best explained by example. Your workflow assigns tasks to the IT department, and that task has a detailed description of what the IT department must accomplish. You can embed those instructions directly into the workflow. When you take that route, you* hard-code *the instructions into the workflow. Hard-coding is generally considered a bad thing because if you want to change those instructions in the future, you need to change the "code" (in this case, the workflow) directly. Any time you touch a functioning application, you risk introducing an error. Use the New Hire Task Descriptions custom list to avoid hard-coding descriptions. Instead of embedding instructions directly into the workflow, look up the instructions from this list. If you need to change instructions in the future, you can go to the list and update it instead of risking making changes to an existing and tested workflow. In this way, you create data-driven descriptions. Data-driven configuration is almost always preferable to hard-coded configuration. This is an important technical pattern used throughout the book.*

Workflows

It may feel like it took quite a while to get to this point, but you've finally arrived at the root of things. Although people might think of HR on-boarding as one unified process, you can't actually implement it that way in SharePoint using SharePoint Designer. Although it's true that there is one logical process, you need to break that up into several smaller physical processes to fully automate the solution. Three physical workflow processes suffice:

- **Confirm New Hire Start Date:** Launches the workflow process, assigning tasks to the departments
- **Change New Hire Start Date:** If the new hire's start date changes, you need to update the due date on the tasks and notify the appropriate people.
- **Cancel New Hire:** Similar to the change start date workflow, you need to notify the departments that the new hire won't be starting. However, you should also delete the tasks and clean up after yourself.

To start automatically or manually — that is the question. You run these manually. In general you don't want end users to have to learn the relatively complicated set of steps to launch it manually. However, this is a good example of when you should do it that way. First, the HR folks want to exert specific controls over the process, and there are not normally that many of them. This reduces the scope of the training effort. Second, you can get into a real mess if you start workflows automatically for this process. Each of the preceding three workflow solutions need to decide whether it's actually supposed to run this time. There are times when you want to go to that trouble, but this is not one of them. Finally, these three workflows map to a straightforward and real scenario. New hires plan to start on a certain date; events intrude, forcing start dates to change; and occasionally, new hires never actually start.

Dashboard

Your dashboard strives to meet one primary and one secondary goal. The primary goal is to allow the HR manager to quickly identify problems, which you accomplish this way:

- Defining views on the task list that filter by department and task status
- Creating a web part page
- Adding the task list to the web part page, taking advantage of the views you just created

You frequently create dashboards using this technique. Create views on the primary lists or libraries involved and then add the lists/libraries to a web part page.

DETAILED TECHNICAL IMPLEMENTATION

It's now time to create your first moderately complex workflow solution in SharePoint 2010. The following sections walk you through the process step by step.

Setup

The setup process for the HR on-boarding process follows the same pattern as for any other technical workflow implementation. First, create any custom lists you need to support lookup type site columns. In this case, you create one custom list to provide lookups for the new hire's office location. With supporting lists in place, you create site columns and then organize them into site content types. Lastly, you create the last batch of custom lists and bind them to these content types.

Supporting Lists

There is one supporting list for this workflow: the office lookup. This particular list couldn't be simpler because it's an out-of-the-box SharePoint custom list. Create a standard custom list named "Locations" in your sandbox site using SharePoint Designer. Populate the title field with a handful of office locations, as shown in Figure 3-2.

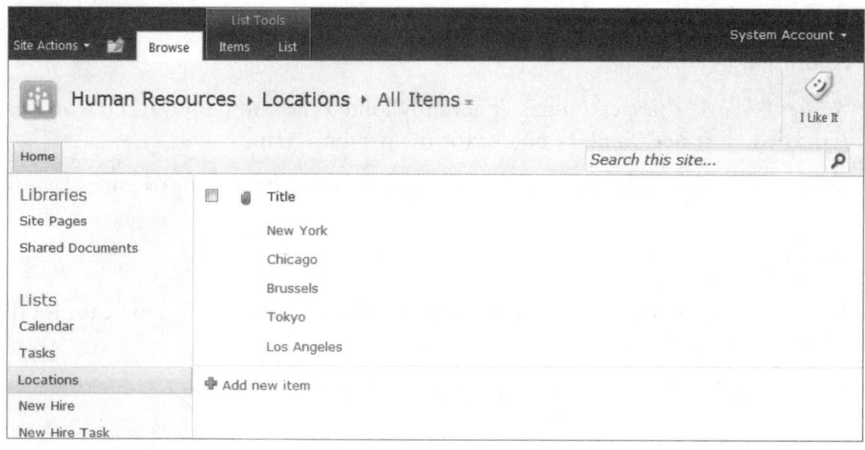

FIGURE 3-2

Content Types

Content types play a critical role in any good SharePoint business solution. As discussed in the high-level overview, you need to create a half dozen content types to support the business process.

When building content types, always begin with the site columns and build up from there. Further consider technical versus business site columns. A technical site column is never (or rarely) intentionally displayed to end users. Technical columns enable the workflow to maintain key information about the process or serve some technical purpose that is of great interest to developers but of no interest to end users (and indeed, would be quite confusing). A business column is, of course, the opposite. In some cases, a site column may play both roles. In such cases, consider it to be a business column so that you don't forget that end users can view and edit this column.

To create a site column, navigate to your sandbox site in which you are developing this solution. Click the Site Actions button in the upper right corner and select Site Actions (typically the last option in the list). SharePoint responds with the site settings page broken into a major sections including Users and Permissions, Galleries, Site Administration, and so forth. The first sub-choice underneath Galleries is Site Columns. Click Site Columns and SharePoint responds with a list of all the site columns defined and/or available to your sandbox site. Create a site column by clicking Create (the upper left hand corner of the main site column display area).

Because the HR on-boarding process begins with the New Hire, start with that.

In the halcyon days of MOSS and WSS, the SharePoint community often searched out some way to implement column-level security. It would be helpful if you could prevent end users from viewing (and especially editing) your technical site columns. There wasn't any surefire way to handle this in MOSS or WSS and sadly, there's no good way to solve this problem in SP2010.

New Hire Content Type

The new hire content type requires the following site columns. You can break this down into business level information and technical information for use by the workflow.

Business columns:

- **New Hire Name:** Because this person hasn't actually joined the company yet, he won't have a network ID, so you just need a place holder for the person's name.
- **New Hire Office:** This is the new hire's office location. It may affect things such as security procedures.
- **New Hire Job Title:** Self-evident
- **New Hire Manager:** The manager will have a network ID, and as a result, you can use the person or group column type.
- **New Hire Start Date:** The date the new hire is expected to walk in the door

Technical columns:

- **Instance Count***:* In general, it's helpful to know how many times a given workflow process has run. In this specific case, you use it to prevent workflows from running more than once.
- **[X] Task ID:** Assign tasks to multiple departments. When you assign that task, record its ID so that you can easily cross reference it later. These columns are critical to change a start date or handle the case when an employee doesn't join the company .

Table 3-1 lists site columns.

TABLE 3-1: New Hire Site Columns

COLUMN NAME	COLUMN TYPE	ADDITIONAL SETTINGS
New Hire Name	Single Line of Text	None
New Hire Home Office	Lookup	Source this from the Office custom list ("locations") you previously created.
New Hire Start Date	Date and Time	Date Only
New Hire Manager	Person or Group	Accept default values
New Hire Title	Single line of Text	None
New Hire IT Task ID	Number	None
New Hire AP Task ID	Number	None
New Hire Security Task ID	Number	None
GP Instance Run Count	Number	Create in group

Following are important notes:

- Excepting the last Column Name (GP Instance Run Count), attach them to the group Hr.Onboarding. You can select any group name that you want, but select a meaningful label that helps you organize this content type, along with all the many other site columns and site content types that you create in your environment.
- Associate GP Instance Run Count with the group *General Purpose WF Technical.*
- It may seem awkward to pre-fix every field with New Hire. This is necessary, however, because a site column's name must be unique with a site collection. Don't worry — SharePoint enables you to relabel these fields later.
- The purpose of the various Task ID site columns becomes clear as you proceed through the rest of the solution. They are crucial to supporting the U and D in CRUD.
- Add a helpful description to the business columns. Your end users will thank you.
- Add each column to a group named "HR.Onboarding".

After creating the New Hire site columns, group them together into a site content type. Figure 3-3 shows the end result.

Create the new content type based off the item content type. Recall that the SharePoint content type named "Item" is part of the "list" content types. Help yourself and add columns in the sequence shown (refer to Figure 3-3). It's not strictly necessary to add them in sequence, but it helps to do that because they show up on the default data entry form that way. You can always correct it later if you make a mistake.

FIGURE 3-3

Lastly, hide the technical columns. Humans won't be editing those values directly. (At least when things are running normally — you might want to leverage them for debugging purposes at some point.) These are there for the workflow process. Click the Title column (refer to Figure 3-3) and mark it as hidden, as shown in Figure 3-4.

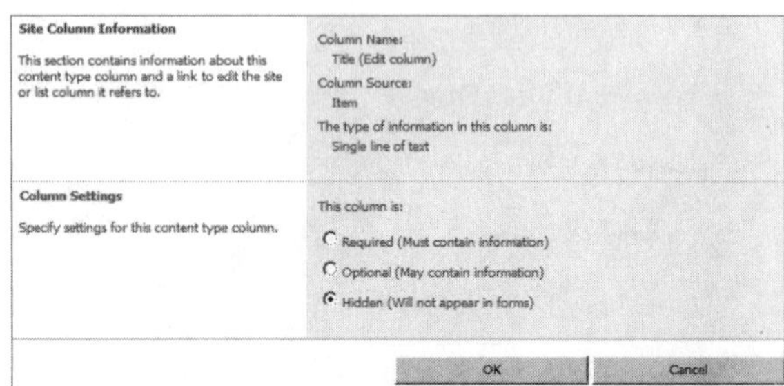

FIGURE 3-4

Next up: tasks.

New Hire Tasks

As per your design, when a new hire joins, the system should assign tasks to the appropriate person in each of the three departments in your model. Because these tasks are in the service or business process, you create them entirely from scratch. In other words, you won't use the out-of-the-box SharePoint task but instead create a new HR New Hire Task. This task includes the following site columns:

- All the business fields of the New Hire content type
- **New Hire Task Due Date:** The task should be completed by this date. This drives your dashboard and supports the design objective of managing by exception.
- **New Hire Task Status**

It also includes one technical column:

- **New Hire Master ID:** The workflow updates this ID with the ID of the New Hire record. This enables you to connect individual tasks back to the new hire record that spawned them in the first place. See Table 3-2, which shows the New Hire Site columns.

TABLE 3-2: New Hire Site Columns

COLUMN NAME	COLUMN TYPE	ADDITIONAL SETTINGS
New Hire Name	Single Line of Text	Added from existing column
New Hire Home Office	Lookup	Added from existing column
New Hire Start Date	Date and Time	Added from existing column
New Hire Manager	Person or Group	Added from existing column
New Hire Title	Single line of Text	Added from existing column
New Hire IT Task ID	Number	Added from existing column
New Hire AP Task ID	Number	Added from existing column
New Hire Security Task ID	Number	Added from existing column
GP Instance Run Count	Number	Added from existing column
New Hire Task Status	Lookup	Sourced from the New Hire Task Statuses custom list created earlier
New Hire Task Due Date	Date	Date Only

This time, you create an inheritance structure. Create a base task that uses all the preceding site columns. Then create three separate task content types that inherit from the base. Figure 3-5 shows the base content type.

When you have your base content type, create the three task list types needed to support the model. Figure 3-6 shows what this look like.

FIGURE 3-5

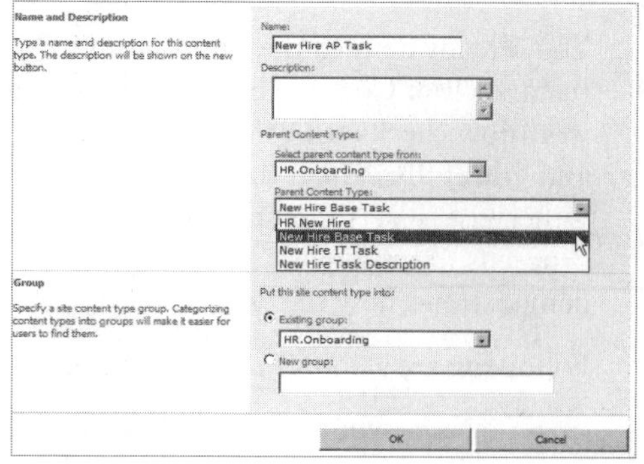

FIGURE 3-6

Create Workflows

As is nearly always the case, it takes multiple physical SharePoint Designer workflows to implement a single logical business process. In this case, three distinct SharePoint Designer workflows operate together to support the HR on-boarding process.

Given the managerial nature of these workflows, each will be configured to start manually.

These three workflows follow:

- **Confirm New Hire Start Date:** This is the master workflow that starts the whole process. It has several features, including creating tasks, sending emails, instance management, and others.
- **Change New Hire Start Date:** Plans change and when that happens, so you need to let everyone know. This is a little tricky because you have all these tasks hanging out there. They need to be updated right along with the new hire master.
- **Cancel New Hire:** HR managers fire off this workflow if the previously expected new hire will not be joining the company.

Confirm New Hire Start Date

The Confirm New Hire Start Date workflow consists of four steps:

1. Determine whether the workflow should run.
2. Perform initializations.
3. Create the tasks.
4. Remember the Unique ID.

Determine Whether It Should Run

The first thing you need to do is make sure that you didn't already run this workflow for the same new hire more than once. You leverage the singleton pattern to accomplish this. To implement the singleton pattern, use a technical site column on the main list (New Hire in this case) that is implemented as a number. Every time the workflow runs, it checks the value of the counter. If it's >= 1 then you know you've run it at least once.

You already defined the site column GP Instance Run Count. The first step in your workflow checks the value of the counter and gracefully exits if the value is >= 1. Otherwise, it sets the value to 1 and proceeds to subsequent steps. Figure 3-7 demonstrates how this works.

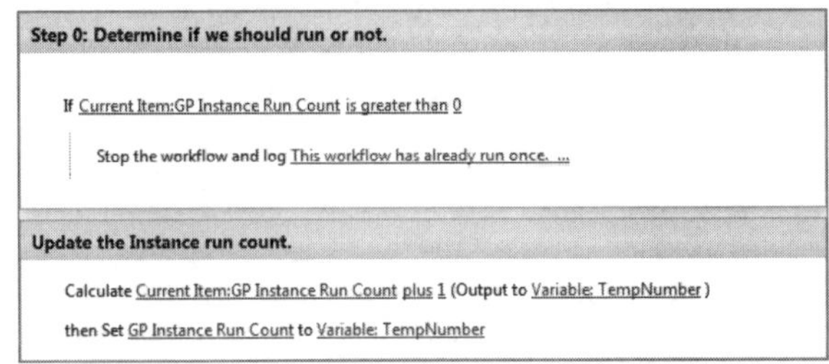

FIGURE 3-7

Following are a couple important notes:

- **Name your steps.** By default, SharePoint assigns a generic label to the step (Step 1, Step 2, Step 3, and so on). It's usually a good idea to keep the numbering intact, but take care to add some additional description so that you and your colleagues understand the objective of that step.

- **Always provide clear explanations when stopping.** This workflow always stops immediately if it has been run before because of the combination of GP Instance Run Count and the Stop action. Some users may find this confusing, so be sure to provide some explanation in the text of the stop action.

Now that you're secure in the knowledge that you won't run this workflow multiple times, go ahead to perform some initializations.

Perform Initializations

The first order of business is to obtain the appropriate descriptions of the tasks. Assign IT's task description to the value from the custom list you defined previously (thereby avoiding a hard-coded description) by way of a workflow variable named IT Task Description. Walk through this step by step.

1. Define the variable. Select Local Variables from the SharePoint Designer tool bar, as shown in Figure 3-8.
2. Click the Add button. Name the variable IT Task Description, and specify its type as String.

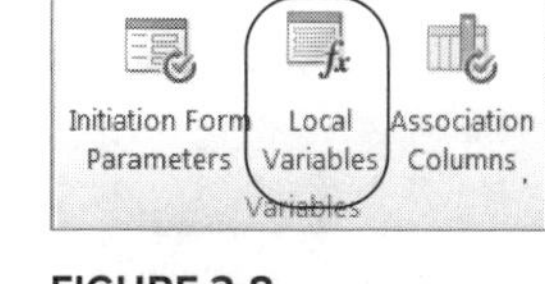

FIGURE 3-8

3. Look up the string value from the task descriptions list. Use the Set Workflow Variable action. SPD enables you to specify the workflow variable and the value to which you want to assign it. The latter part is tricky. Start with the end result and work your way backward. (See Figure 3-9.)

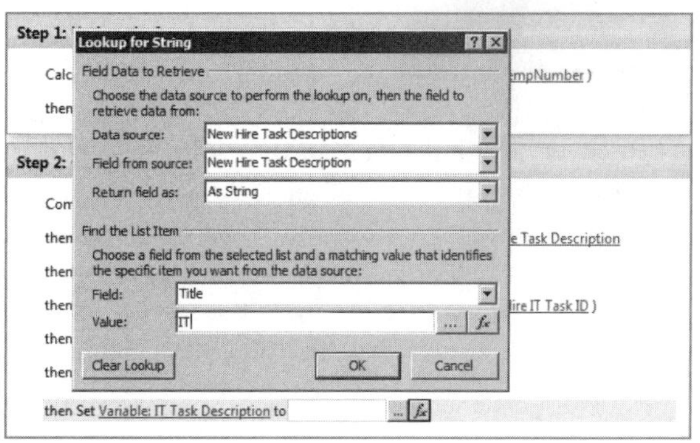

FIGURE 3-9

The dialog box in Figure 3-9 boils down to the following simple English:

- Find the New Hire Task Descriptions row in the list, where the Title is equal to the literal value IT.
- Return back to the New Hire Task Description column in that list.

This dialog box is common and used frequently in SharePoint Designer workflow solutions. Refer to Chapter 2 two for a refresher on how to manage this dialog box.

You can now repeat this process for the AP and security tasks that you create next.

Create the Tasks

It's now time for the big moment, and it's bound to be a little disappointing because you spent so much time preparing for it. Creating the task is a simple Create Item action, as shown in Figure 3-10.

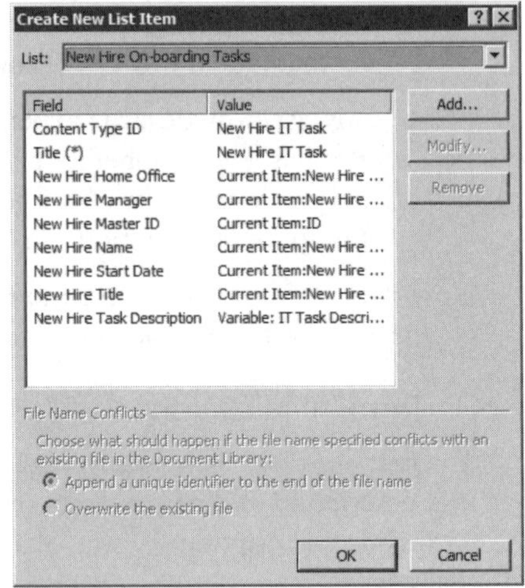

FIGURE 3-10

Tell SharePoint Workflow to create an entry in the New Hire On-Boarding Tasks list you previously created, and assign the values as previously shown. Most of the data comes directly from the new hire with three exceptions:

- **Content Type ID:** Specify this for each of the three tasks: IT, AP, and Security.
- **Title:** You won't actually use the title for anything; however, it's a required field on custom lists, and it's easier to go with the flow instead of fighting.
- **New Hire Task Description:** Assigned from the workflow variable you populated in the prior section "Perform Initializations."

Remember the Unique ID

At this point, you have one final step to perform to finalize this workflow. Going back to CRUD, this workflow represents the C. At some point, for some new hire, the start date will change, or the new hire will never actually join the company. The next sections walk through these kinds of updates. For them to succeed, they need to access the specific tasks associated with the new hire. The Create Item action returns to you the ID of the item that it created. Every row in a SharePoint custom list has one unique ID. You take that ID and then store it into the New Hire custom list. Later, when you need to update a start date or a delete a task entirely, you have the ID on hand. Figure 3-11 shows how SharePoint Designer handles it:

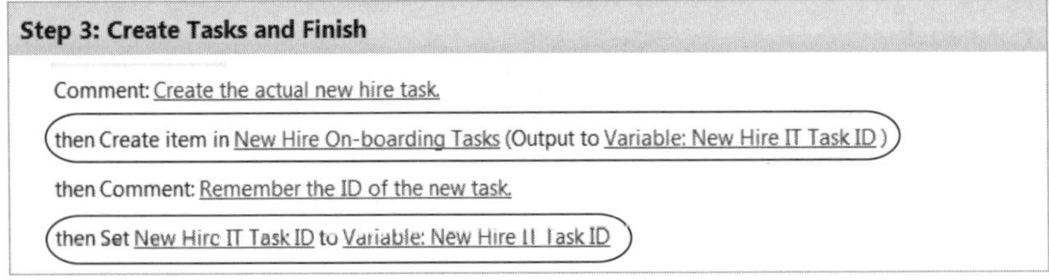

FIGURE 3-11

Figure 3-11 shows that first, you created the new item in New Hire On-Boarding Tasks and saved the ID of the new task into a workflow variable named New Hire IT Task ID. You then set the current item's site column named New Hire IT Task ID to the value of this workflow variable. It's now saved as part of the New Hire record and is available for updates and deletes.

Figure 3-12 shows the final result of this workflow.

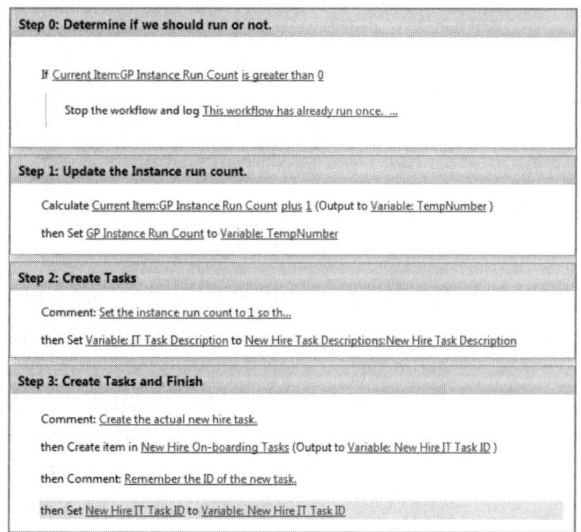

FIGURE 3-12

Change Start Date

Changing the start date is a straightforward process. You add a slight twist to your previous work by way of an initiation parameter. When the HR manager needs to indicate that a new hire's start date has changed, how can she do that? It may be tempting to simply open up the new hire and directly change the start date. It is better to use an initiation parameter. SharePoint prompts the HR manager for the new start date when she runs the Change Start Date workflow, as shown in Figure 3-13.

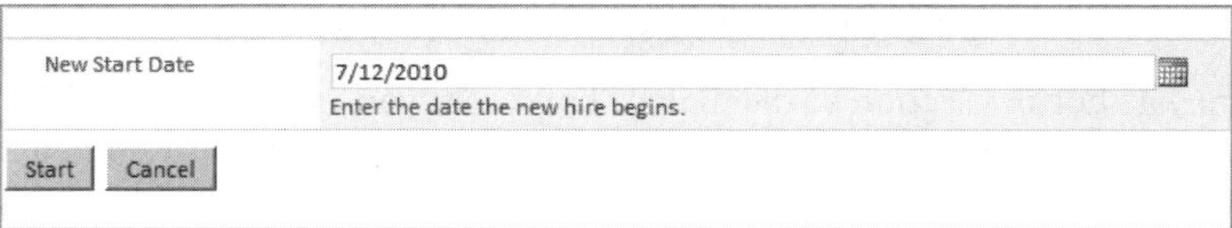

FIGURE 3-13

The initiation parameter approach provides a sensible and easy-to-understand user interface. SharePoint automatically prompts for the new start data, and it's unambiguous to the end user.

SharePoint displays only initiation parameters when users start workflows manually. Your design calls for a manual launch, but you should keep this in mind for future scenarios. It's not uncommon for new SharePoint Designer users to assume that their initiation parameters work the same way when their associated workflow starts automatically.

Follow these steps to define the initiation parameter:

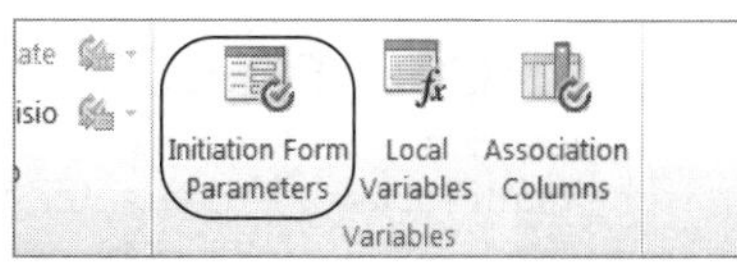

FIGURE 3-14

1. Access the initiation form parameter dialog via the Ribbon menu, as shown in Figure 3-14.
2. Add a new parameter named `New Start Date`.
3. Select Date and Time as the Information Type.
4. Leave default values for the rest.

Now that you have your initiation parameter, you can create the workflow. This is a simple workflow that locates each of the three tasks you originally created and changes their associated start date. Use the Update Item workflow action to accomplish this, as shown in Figure 3-15.

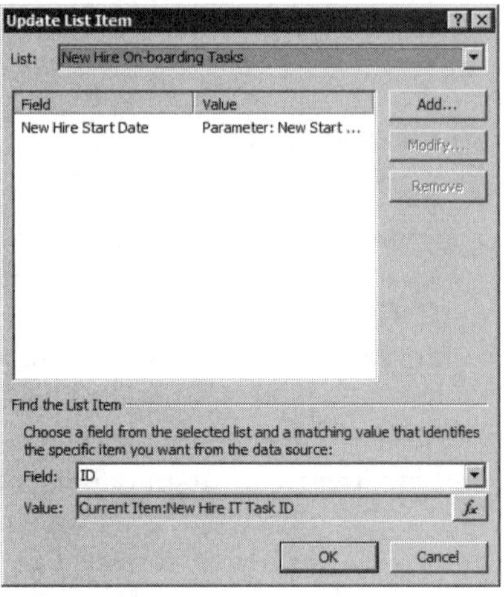

FIGURE 3-15

Figure 3-15 shows that the Update Item activity is broken down into three chunks:

- **The List:** In this case, it's the New Hire On-Boarding Tasks list. An important take-away from this is that you update items in the New Hire On-Boarding Tasks SharePoint custom list from a workflow running on an altogether different custom list (New Hires). Keep this in mind for the future because it's a handy capability.
- **What to Update:** You can update any column in the target list (New Hire On-Boarding Tasks) so long as the column is not a read-only column. Figure 3-15 shows you updating the new hire start date, but you could also update the new hire's name, title, and so on.
- **Find the List Item:** The bottom section of the dialog shows that you can find a specific row in New Hire On-Boarding Tasks whose ID is equal to the value of the current item's column, New Hire IT Task ID.

Cancel Start Date

Last but not least, you need to handle the D in CRUD. This workflow is implemented almost identically to the change start date workflow, so we won't go into great detail. Consider the following:

- Use an initiation parameter for are-you-sure logic. The Cancel New Hire Workflow is a potentially dangerous workflow because it can delete tasks assigned to IT, AP, and Security. This is what you want, but take care to avoid mistakes. Use the initiation parameter to get the users to confirm they mean to cancel the new hire start date. Then, test this value in the first step of your workflow, and stop if the users don't check the Yes box.
- The delete item workflow activity works similar to the update item activity. The only difference is that you don't specify the fields to update. You do specify the list and how to find the specific row you want to delete.

ADVANCED TOPICS

The main focus of this chapter has been on the CRUD pattern that you see in virtually every workflow solution you create. The HR on-boarding process cannot be considered complete until you address three common business and technical issues:

- Dashboards
- Delegation
- Data cleanup

The following chapters in the book delve into each of these areas in detail. This closing section of the HR on-boarding chapter outlines high level solutions to these issues. Come back when you're ready to implement them.

Dashboards

This HR process is begging for two different kinds of dashboards. First, it would be nice to see new hires and their start date superimposed over a calendar. This is straightforward to accomplish. Because all the pertinent new hire data is stored in one custom list, you can create a SharePoint view on the list based off the default calendar view.

Beyond calendars, the solution is also calling out for a more complex dashboard that enables HR to manage exceptional conditions. You can put together a comprehensive dashboard by creating three different views on the New Hire Tasks List: Overdue IT, Overdue AP, and Overdue Security. When you have these tasks, you can create a web part page, add the web part three times, and configure each of these three instances to use the "overdue" view. Whenever a task shows up on this dashboard, HR knows there's a risk that the new hires won't be ready to hit the ground running (through no fault of their own). HR can take steps to try and solve or mitigate the problems.

Delegation

Delegation can be complex, especially in financial approval style workflows. A more simple approach can work for most HR on-boarding scenarios. Recall that you use a custom list to manage the actual descriptions of tasks that workflow assigns to IT, AP, and Security. This technique enables you to avoid hard-coding these descriptions and provides more overall flexibility in the solution. You can use the same technique to specify task owners. When workflow creates a task, instead of hard-coding the user in the workflow, look up the user from another custom list. This now affords you the same flexibility that you baked into the workflow vis-à-vis task descriptions but also allows a simple delegation process to boot. If the primary task owner is going on vacation, simply update the task owner list with the new temporary owner, and all tasks will be assigned to that temporary owner until it is changed.

Chapter 4, "Helpdesk Ticketing," addresses this topic in great detail.

Data Cleanup

SharePoint can maintain new hire information and associated tasks forever. This means that you could have July 2010 new hires still in the system three or four years later. Sometimes, you want to hold onto information like this for an extended period of time, but rarely do you want it or need it to stick around, taking up system resources.

Sadly, SharePoint doesn't provide a good cleanup mechanism for things such as the New Hire custom list or the on-boarding tasks list. This chapter does not take up the challenge. However, Chapter 12, "Custom Activities," does provide a solution (albeit requiring custom coding). Look ahead if you need this problem solved sooner rather than later. There are some issues here that weren't addressed in detail.

SUMMARY

This chapter introduced a number of bedrock SharePoint designer workflow principles and techniques focusing primarily on the requirements for a vigorous and comprehensive CRUD solution. The HR on-boarding process developed in this chapter enables you to create, update, and operate in a clean manner and via a pattern you follow throughout this book.

Helpdesk Ticketing

WHAT'S IN THIS CHAPTER?

- Allowing users to submit new problems issues or requests
- Enabling helpdesk employees and managers to respond to and resolve those problems
- Providing end users with a view into current problem status
- Providing metrics for analysis
- Helping to facilitate and grow institutional knowledge by creating a memory bank of solved problems, organized for easy categorization and retrieval

You don't always need to dive deeply into SharePoint Designer to create a workflow solution. End users and helpdesk managers can manage a workflow process quite well with little more than the clever use of a status field on a key custom SharePoint list.

WHAT IS THE HELPDESK TICKETING PROCESS?

As anyone that works in the IT department of a company of any size knows, technology fails outright on occasion, or end users find creative ways to cause problems for themselves. It often falls to the IT department to unravel these problems and get end users back up on their feet, happy and productive. The goal of a helpdesk ticketing process is to help the IT department manage end user reported problems efficiently, with high quality and with high satisfaction. At the same time, a good solution helps end users figure out things on their own, and when they can't, report the problem and receive updates as IT addresses it for them.

The helpdesk ticketing process loosely follows the pattern you see in crowded delicatessens. You pull a numbered ticket from the ticket machine and wait for someone to call your number. This is where the "ticket" part enters the picture. Unlike at a deli, however, you're not placing an order, you're reporting a problem or requesting action.

Lastly, the helpdesk system helps your organization build a durable base and repository of knowledge from which your team can leverage past effort. The solution that took hours to research this month should be next month's easy answer. You can do this by marking closed tickets with an eye to building an easily searchable knowledge base.

Tickets start with end users. They can't get a printer to work or have lost an important document and need someone to retrieve it from the long-term backup storage. The helpdesk isn't just for problems' it can be the launching point for ordinary business processes. For instance, a hiring manager could create a ticket, requesting that HR begin searching for a new hire. For example, assume the manager lost an important file.

The manager logs into the intranet to find the helpdesk link and clicks Report a Problem. SharePoint opens up an online form for the manager to fill out. The form prompts for information such as the following:

- Short description
- Longer description
- Problem category and subcategory
- Urgency

A smart form (using InfoPath, for instance) would also prefill certain fields of information, including the name of the user reporting the problem and the date the problem was logged and set some kind of initial status on the ticket. Smart forms are beyond scope for this book, but see the sidebar for more on InfoPath and Chapter 11 for a section describing InfoPath in enough detail to get you started. When you begin to solve this problem, the ticket's status is important because it drives list views and enables management by exception (MBE) principles.

InfoPath is a Microsoft office product that works much the same as Excel or Word. InfoPath enables you to create a form by dragging and dropping fields onto the screen. This form is then published to SharePoint, and providing you have the correct edition (Enterprise), SharePoint renders the form in a web browser. InfoPath enables you to create interactive forms that include such things as cascading drop-downs, a conditional display of information, additional buttons beyond OK and Delete, and overall, goes a long way to create a smart online data entry form. This book does not describe using InfoPath much beyond these few sentences because it does not, by itself, necessarily address workflow problems that you can't manage without it. However, InfoPath can provide much better data entry forms, and you should plan to use it for that purpose in your solutions. Chapter 11 covers InfoPath in more detail and should be enough to get you started using that tool.

After the user submits the ticket (the originator), SharePoint sends an email to the default owner. Who is the default owner? The category helps you to identify that individual. For example, the director of HR may handle new hire requests whereas a designated helpdesk manager solves printer problems. Real-life complicates this otherwise simple activity because the usual (default) owner may be on vacation. You need to implement a delegation solution to account for this. When you figure out this owner, the system assigns the ticket to him.

The assignee receives an email (or as you see later, works off a dashboard). The assignee researches the issue, perhaps goes back to the originator for more information and ultimately solves the problem. The assignee then changes the status, which triggers an email back to the originator stating the problem is solved.

You're not quite finished yet. Say that the problem is actually complicated and took up a lot of research time. If it happens again, you hardly want to spend another dozen hours on the same problem. Instead, the system saves the solved ticket and provides enough metadata so that it's easy to locate in the future.

With SharePoint you can to design a full-blown ticket management system. That's what this chapter provides.

PROBLEM CLASS

The helpdesk ticketing problem falls into the real-time response problem class. Random events occur (who can tell when an end user will report a problem?) and someone needs to fix that problem or respond to the request as quickly as possible.

All problems are not created equal. Some problems truly must be resolved ASAP. For example, a sales representative deleted his PowerPoint presentation and needs it restored for a critical sales presentation later that afternoon. These can be time-sensitive issues with dollars (and jobs!) on the line. On the other hand, some helpdesk tickets don't represent problems, but rather a request to start a process, for instance, the new employee on-boarding process described in Chapter 3, "HR On-Boarding." The on-boarding process itself can take some time and is managed with its own workflow. However, it has to be started in a timely manner.

The ticketing process also produces durable information. Helpdesk problems, when resolved, become a history of validated solutions. Over time, the helpdesk ticketing system becomes a treasure trove of institutional problem-solving knowledge.

TECHNICAL PATTERNS

While solving the helpdesk ticketing problem, you implement the following technical patterns:

- **Basic CRUD** (Create/Read/Update/Delete): Tickets are created, they are updated (many times in this case) and they are "deleted." Deleted is in quotes because the system shouldn't normally delete ticket requests but instead archive them. This is a critical component to the long-term repository aspect of the problem. One thing to take away is that the CRUD pattern which was explained in such detail in Chapter 3 shouldn't be taken literally; the "D" in CRUD could just as easily be an "A" for Archive.

  Why save them? Helpdesk metrics can be valuable. Keeping the tickets helps with metrics, as you see later in the chapter.

- **Long-lived data:** Some tickets stick around for a long time. Not all tickets are valuable, so you want to save valuable tickets to a long-term knowledge storehouse. The long-lived data pattern identifies when those items should be moved to long-term storage or instead marked for early archiving.
- **Assignment and delegation:** When tickets arrive into the system, someone has to look at them. The assignment and delegation pattern ensures that 1) tickets never languish because they are always assigned properly and 2) if the usual assignee is on vacation, the system understands that fact and takes the appropriate action in response.
- **Dashboard feeder:** The bedrock of manage by exception (MBE) dashboards show just the right information in an easily digestible format that requires little or no interpretation. Dashboards represent multiple business processes as a snapshot in time. The dashboard feeder pattern ensures that your solution provides appropriate status information so that you can provide meaningful dashboards to the people entrusted and responsible for making sure the business process works smoothly.

BUSINESS PATTERNS

While solving the helpdesk ticketing problem, you need to implement the following business patterns:

- **Routing:** Who is assigned any given ticket when it arrives in the system? This pattern provides for both a default and fallback assignee.
- **Delegation:** Similar to the technical pattern of the same namesake, delegation enables users to meet their obligations by identifying a responsible team member to handle their responsibilities while they are away. If I'm the guy on the IT team responsible to provision a network security account for a new hire and I'm going to be on vacation, I need to have someone take care of that while I'm away. Delegation lets me do that.
- **Knowledge builder:** Routine issues, such as printer paper jams, probably don't merit special attention. After all, there are only so many ways to unjam a printer. Other issues, however, do warrant careful consideration, require a lot of effort to solve, and may come up again in future. It would be a shame to duplicate that investigative effort again if it it's reported a second time. Follow the knowledge builder pattern to implement a solution that helps prevent wasted effort.
- **Metrics:** Management loves metrics, and the helpdesk solution is a perfect place to leverage this pattern. How many helpdesk calls are placed? How long does it take to resolve them? What systems are most affected?

BUSINESS PROBLEM DESCRIPTION

You cannot define the technical solution without first delving into the details behind the business problem. To do that, you begin by discussing requirements with all the potential stakeholders in the solution. You then identify actors and the actions they take. Follow this process to craft a suitable solution. Let's begin with the requirements.

Requirements Discussion

In many cases, organizations already have some kind of helpdesk ticketing system in place. If they don't, odds are good that someone in the IT support department has worked with such systems in the past. In both cases, your company probably has one or a few helpdesk "super stars" (who you can probably name without thinking as you read this). All these are good sources for business requirements.

Helpdesk systems serve the needs of the IT department: printer problems, email issues, security setup, and so on. However, this is a limiting view. The facilities group could and should use a specialized helpdesk system to manage facilities requests, ranging from "change my light bulb" to "move my office." HR could use a helpdesk system to manage information requests on benefits and launch new hire processes.

The point of this discussion is that you should cast a wide net when thinking through the potential users (as always). If you narrow your focus to pure IT interests, you can miss an opportunity to extend the solution outward and drive more value for your company and prestige for yourself as a "big thinker." When you canvass other departments for potential helpdesk needs, keep in mind that a department may tell you on Monday that it is not interested, but a change in leadership or edict from high may change situations. In which case, you want to plan for it in advance.

A helpdesk solution needs to provide certain fundamental services to end users:

- Simple and quick entry
- Answer the question, "What's the status of my problem?"
- Notify the end user when important events occur, such as when the issue is assigned, when the issue is resolved, if additional information is required to solve it, and so on
- Self-help: A quick-and-easy way to look up the issue and solve it before a ticket is created

As important as they are, end users are just part of the picture. The helpdesk system also supports its managers:

- Notification when a new issue is created
- Dashboard to view and manage
- Gathering raw data for metrics
- Delegation

If you can meet these requirements, you have a solid solution.

With these basic requirements in mind, schedule meetings with the end user community to conduct the all-important end user interviews. Consider the following questions:

- Which department within the company could use a helpdesk system to manage department-specific requests?
- What kinds of processes make sense to include within the helpdesk universe? They may launch other workflow processes. For instance, it could make a lot of sense to integrate this process with the HR on-boarding process from Chapter 3, "HR On-Boarding," because that could be a separate ticket.

- Do you want to use this support for both internal and external user communities?
- What are security requirements? Should issues be kept secret, and should they be protected from other users' prying eyes?
- What kind of metrics do you want this solution to produce? Total tickets entered? How many tickets opened and closed on a daily basis? What else?
- What will it take to convince the end user community to use it?

This last question is particularly interesting and should be asked of any solution you plan to deliver in SharePoint. Helpdesk issues can be tricky, particularly if you don't already have a helpdesk process live and operational today. End users tend to follow old patterns rather than embrace a new solution. It's almost always easier to pick up the phone and ask for assistance rather than fill in an online form. This can lead to a troublesome disconnect between the "official" system (the helpdesk solution) and reality (what people are actually doing). The best way to solve this problem is to publish a rule: "If a problem isn't in the helpdesk ticketing system, the problem will not be solved." It can cause short-term pain, but your organization can realize a great deal of value from this harsh stance.

For the purposes of this chapter, the helpdesk solution needs to meet the following high-level requirements:

- Any validated user can enter a helpdesk ticket.
- Only employees are considered "valid" users. In other words, you aren't going to allow customers to enter helpdesk tickets.
- Users can see their own tickets but no other users' tickets.
- Helpdesk administrators may see any ticket.
- Users can see the status of their outstanding and closed helpdesk tickets at any time via a convenient dashboard.
- The helpdesk system automatically assigns tickets to a member of the helpdesk administrator based on ticket data whenever possible.
- The helpdesk system supports delegation.
- The helpdesk system supports and enables MBE.
- The helpdesk system generates a database of metrics — not that the requirement is to generate metrics, but to not necessarily report against them. You learn about this distinction later.

Actors

The model for this solution that meets the requirements includes the following actors:

- An end user who has a problem or wants to kick off a business process.
- One or more users identified as helpdesk administrators. These users work on tickets with an eye toward solving whatever problem prompted the ticket in the first place.
- SharePoint, providing self-service dashboards, email notification, and the automated workflow.

Actions

The helpdesk solution responds to the actions on behalf of its supported actors. These actions include the following:

- Create a helpdesk ticket.
- Manage existing helpdesk tickets to closure.
- View ticket status.
- Mark valuable solved tickets as such.

Challenges

This chapter doesn't provide great details on how to address certain nice-to-have functions, including the following:

- **Duplicate tickets:** Two common scenarios arise leading to duplicate tickets (two or more tickets for the same issue). First, end users are simply confused, and they enter the same issue twice. Sometimes, they enter it twice by mistake; sometimes they enter it twice because they feel like the first ticket was "lost." Second, systemwide failures might prompt many different users to enter the same issue. The former issue is easier to detect and manage automatically. However, this chapter does not walk through a solution to either situation. It does suggest an approach to solving them in the conclusion.
- **Urgency:** Most of the time, end users believe their issue is urgent. In practice, if you allow users to specify priority or urgency, they almost always mark their ticket with the highest available priority. This is a social issue more than a technical issue and is not addressed technically.
- **Self-service:** You would like your end users to check out previous solutions in the knowledge base first. Failing that, it would be nice to analyze the ticket programmatically and email the end user potential solutions before the helpdesk administrator starts working on the issue.

HIGH-LEVEL SOLUTION

The high-level solution is your first attempt to match up SharePoint features and capabilities against the identified business requirements. This solution continues the pattern set from the last chapter where you use content types and custom lists to define data entry screens and the backend data that your workflow process uses to meet the process requirements. A swim lane diagram organizes these different elements into a cohesive picture that you can bring back to the business for validation.

Solution Overview

To implement the helpdesk application, create a solution that leverages a number of out-of-the-box SharePoint components. In the end, the helpdesk solution is rather light on the workflow side of things and rather heavier on lists for dashboard management. Workflow is a critical component. However, workflow provides interesting utility functions instead of managing the entire process.

The solution begins with a SharePoint custom list backed by a content type. In combination, these represent a helpdesk ticket. SharePoint's default Create/Update/Delete forms for custom lists provide the user with an interface. This custom list, with some judicious list views, also provides a handy data source for dashboards built using web part pages.

SharePoint's content approval function meets the security needs of the application. You can configure the list to require content approval, and you can create a SharePoint group, Helpdesk Administrators. You can configure helpdesk administrators as approvers on the list. This enables users to create items (helpdesk tickets) in the list but have read-access only to those items they create. Because helpdesk administrators can approve items in the list, they can also view all items in the list.

SharePoint workflow assigns helpdesk tickets automatically based on list metadata. It can do so by looking up values in another SharePoint list that matches ticket types to appropriate helpdesk administrators (experts in the type of issue the user reported). This workflow is smart enough to account for vacations or other planned absences (that is, delegation).

Helpdesk administrators review and take ownership of tickets. As they work on the ticket, they set the status of the ticket. This status mechanism drives where the ticket shows up on dashboards provided for both end users and administrators alike.

Lastly, the solution marks certain closed tickets to provide a knowledge base of previously solved problems. This solution envisions creating a SharePoint Search Scope on that list (see sidebar for information on scope).

What is a custom search scope in SharePoint? The entire body of information in SharePoint is called the corpus, *which includes all documents, all pages, all list items — anything and everything in SharePoint. If you think of the corpus as a pizza pie, a scope is a slice of pizza. SharePoint search administrators define scopes via a series of rules, and you can create a custom scope that includes only closed helpdesk ticket items. Search scopes help you to meet the knowledge base requirements of the helpdesk solution.*

Swim Lane Diagrams

The swim lane shown in Figure 4-1 depicts the actors and actions they take in a typical request/response cycle.

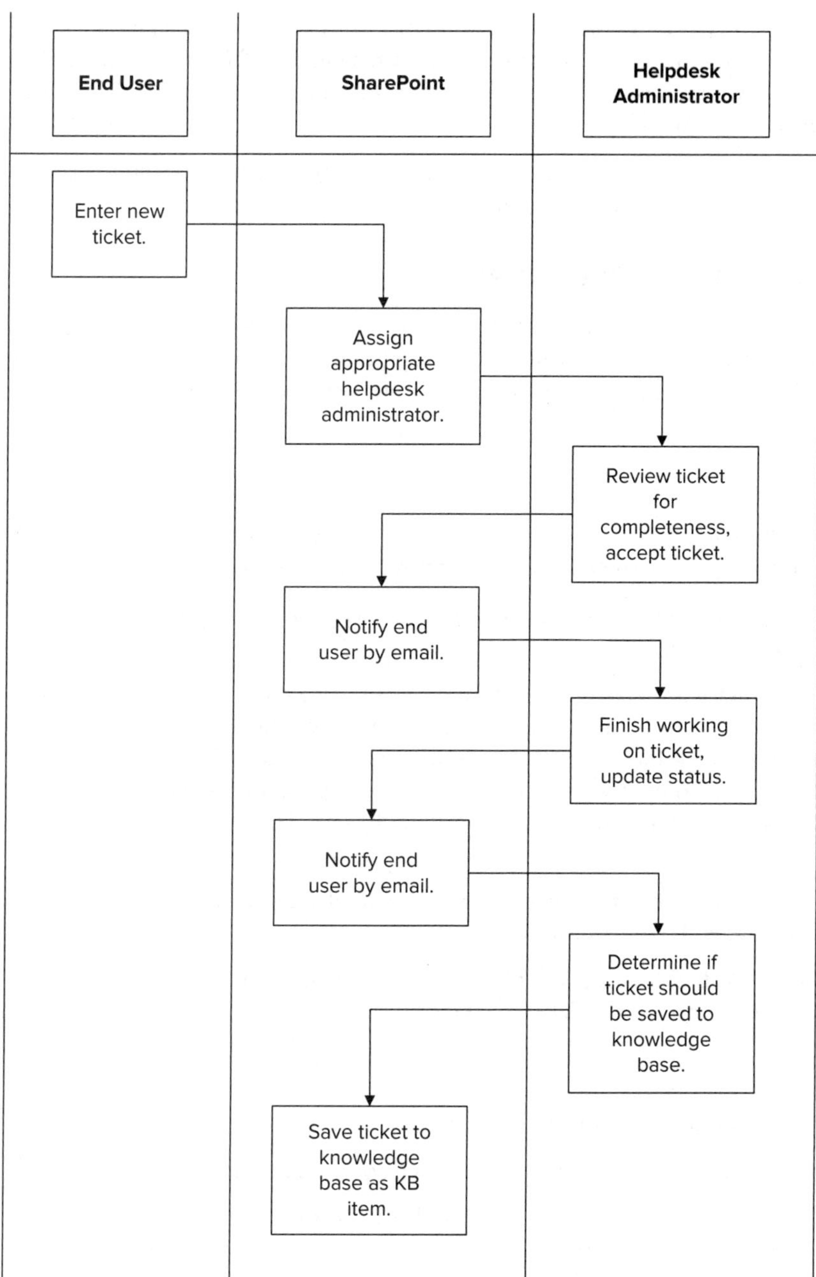

FIGURE 4-1

The process begins when an end user enters a new ticket. SharePoint routes the ticket to the appropriate helpdesk administrator who reviews the ticket for completeness. End users commonly fail to provide enough information for the assigned helpdesk administrator, who can send the ticket back to the end user for this additional information.

After the ticket is accepted, SharePoint notifies the end user of this fact, and the helpdesk administrator begins to research the issue. The administrator may update the ticket with additional information and research notes. Eventually, the ticket is resolved, and SharePoint emails the end user that it's time to open up the Bubbly.

Lastly, the helpdesk administrator decides whether this ticket and its documented solution should be marked as a knowledge base item for future reference.

Technical Implementation Overview

Now that the solution framework is well understood, it's time to get into the weeds and start designing the SharePoint solution. Begin by identifying content types and their lists for the general solution. Beyond that, you'll implement a delegation framework that you'll re-use over and over again in the future.

Content Types

Like all your solutions, site columns and content types lie at the core of the solution. To meet the helpdesk system requirements, you need content types that represent the following:

- **A helpdesk ticket:** This content type has columns such as Short Description, Long Description, and Category.
- **A general purpose delegation content type:** This content type provides the foundation upon which you'll build a delegation model that recognizes the fact that people take vacations or don't show up for work for one reason or another (e.g. sick days). In such cases, the system can't be sitting around waiting for someone to complete an assigned task. Instead, the task must be delegated to another user or group of users. This content type supports that process.
- **Categories:** A list of categories from which the user can select. Categories include items such as Hardware, Software, Email, and so on.
- **Assignment mapping:** Based on a given helpdesk category, determine which helpdesk administrator should work on the ticket by default.

Custom Lists

Use the following custom lists to implement the solution:

- **Helpdesk ticket:** A list associated with a content type of the same name.
- **Helpdesk ticket categories:** A simple one-column list for managing categories of problems/issues on helpdesk tickets.
- **Solved tickets:** When helpdesk administrators determine that a specific helpdesk ticket reflects a problem that could reasonably arise in the future, they create a "solved ticket." These solved tickets support self-service objectives.
- **Delegate mapping:** Much like assignment matching, delegate matching enables administrators to tell SharePoint how to delegate support requests.

Delegation

This chapter introduces a technical solution to manage delegation, which helps to create a seamless transition when the regular assignee is unavailable. Consider this scenario:

- Paul typically handles all requests that have anything to do with email.
- The system automatically assigns email requests to Paul. (You see how shortly.)
- Paul begins a one-week vacation on Monday.

If the system goes ahead and blindly assigns the task to Paul, it obviously won't be looked at until Paul returns. That is a problem. Use delegation to solve this.

The delegation problem is easy to understand. The technical solution is also easy to understand at a high level, although as you see, SharePoint does its best to make the actual solution fairly challenging. Now tackle the easy part first.

The delegation solution has at its root a simple custom list with three columns. The first column represents the specific function. Using the preceding example, this might be called Helpdesk Email. The next two columns represent the usual assignee and his delegate. So, if the usual assignee is Paul and Samantha is Paul's backup, you'd have tuple like this:

- **Function:** Helpdesk Email
- **Default Assignee:** Paul
- **Delegate Assignee:** Samantha

This table structure serves the business purpose well. Any time the usual assignee for a given helpdesk specialty is out sick or on holiday, you can simply add them to this list. Obviously, you need to do something in the workflow itself. This is where it becomes challenging.

The challenge arises due to SharePoint Designer workflow's ability (or lack, really) to look up information in lists. SharePoint Designer is perfectly capable of looking up items with a unique key. This wouldn't be a problem if there were only possible delegates for all helpdesk functions. In this case, you'd have a simpler table structure with just two columns: the default assignee and the delegate. Whenever you need to find a delegate, just look up the default assignee and find his/her delegate. This approach may be sufficient in many cases. However, this chapter deliberately complicates matter by adding that third column. This provides a more general-purpose solution that you can use in other business scenarios and to introduce a useful technical technique.

Dashboard

This chapter introduces the first process dashboard. The dashboard provides a one-stop shopping experience for all matters related to the helpdesk. There are many approaches to creating dashboards. In this chapter, you create a dashboard that leverages a web part page to present views into the overall process.

DETAILED TECHNICAL IMPLEMENTATION

In this detailed walk-through, you'll finally get your hands dirty. You'll create the content types and lists required to support the workflow. You'll create four different SharePoint Designer workflows, including the relatively complex delegation management workflow. You'll begin with the setup tasks.

Setup

To implement the helpdesk solution, you need to create content types, SharePoint custom lists that use those content types and feed your dashboard and, of course, SharePoint Designer workflows to glue it all together.

Supporting Lists

The helpdesk solution is built upon the following set of custom lists:

- **Helpdesk Tickets:** The core list around which the rest of the solution is built.
- **Helpdesk Categories:** Lookup list that includes values such as Email, Printer, Missing File, and so forth. For each category, it specifies the usual (default) helpdesk administrator assigned to solve these kinds of problems.
- **Helpdesk Status Codes:** A list of helpdesk status codes and corresponding descriptions of each. These codes include, for instance, Open, Assigned, In Process, and Closed.
- **General Purpose Delegates:** This list supports delegation, mapping default assignees to their delegate. This list benefits from its own SharePoint Designer workflow to solve the compound key problem previously mentioned.

Content Types

Every supporting list is backed by a content type. As with every other content type in each solution, it consists of two broad types of site columns: business and technical. End users enter data directly into business columns, which appear on dashboards. Technical columns, on the other hand, do not generally appear to end users and instead support the technical needs of the solution. This solution calls for the following content types:

- Helpdesk Status Codes
- Helpdesk Category Codes
- Helpdesk Ticket
- General Purpose Delegates

Helpdesk Status Codes

This simple content type contains two site columns. Both are business columns.

Business columns:

- **Status Code:** Status code.
- **Status Code Description:** A longer textual description of the code. This text appears in list views and displays when the end user clicks the status code.

Table 4-1 shows the helpdesk status site columns.

TABLE 4-1: Helpdesk Status Site Columns

COLUMN NAME	COLUMN TYPE	ADDITIONAL SETTING
HD_StatusCode	Single Line of Text	None
HD_StatusCodeDescription	Single Line of Text	None

Having created the site columns, add them to a new content type named Helpdesk Status Codes.

Helpdesk Category Codes

This simple content type contains four site columns. Three columns are business level columns, and there is one lone technical column. They follow:

Business columns:

- **Category Code:** A short code that describes the category of the helpdesk ticket.
- **Category Code Description:** A longer textual description of the code. This text should help end users accurately select the correct category. The category drives automatic assignment to a specific helpdesk support person, and this description ensures that automatic assignment works as best as it can.
- **Default Assignee:** This is a specific helpdesk support person to whom all tickets in this category are assigned by default.

Technical columns:

- **Category Unique Key:** You need a unique key even for categories. A utility workflow updates this column at run-time, and the helpdesk assignee workflow (described soon) uses it to find the assignee.

Table 4-2 shows the helpdesk categories site columns.

TABLE 4-2: Helpdesk Categories Site Columns

COLUMN NAME	COLUMN TYPE	ADDITIONAL SETTING
HD_CategoryCode	Single Line of Text	None.
HD_CategoryCodeDescription	Single Line of Text	None.
HD_CategoryDefaultAssignee	Person or Group	Select just a single user. Not mandatory: Some categories don't have a default assignee.)
HD_CategoryUniqueKey	Single line of text	Technical column that enables to look up this category's default assignee at run-time.

Having created the site columns, add them to a new content type named Helpdesk Category Codes.

Helpdesk Ticket

This is the meat and potatoes of the solution. Despite its central role in the solution, it too contains only business columns. They follow:

- **HD_TicketNumber:** A unique ID that identifies this ticket
- **HD_ShortSummary:** Short summary of the issue reported. This short summary displays on the dashboard and list views.
- **HD_OnBehalfOf:** This column supports the notion that administrative assistants may enter an issue on behalf of their manager or other situations in which the person entering the issue is not actually affected by the issue.
- **HD_AssignedTo:** The actual helpdesk support person assigned to resolve the issue
- **HD_LongDescription:** The full-blown description of the issue. End users should be encourage to provide more, rather than less, information here to help resolve the issue.
- **HD_Category:** The user-supplied category. SharePoint Designer workflow tries to use this category to automatically assign a support person to this ticket. This category links to another list for its values. This is called a lookup column. A detailed explanation is presented next.
- **HD_TicketStatus:** The status of the ticket. This is also a lookup column.

Table 4-3 shows the helpdesk ticket site columns.

TABLE 4-3: Helpdesk Ticket Site Columns

COLUMN NAME	COLUMN TYPE	ADDITIONAL SETTING
HD_TicketNumber	Single Line of Text	None.
HD_ShortSummary	Single Line of Text	None.
HD_LongDescription	Multiple Lines of Text	None.
HD_OnBehalfOf	Person or Group	Not mandatory.
HD_AssignedTo	Person or Group	Not mandatory.
HD_Category	Lookup	Selects values from the Categories custom list. See next for more details.
HD_TicketStatus	Lookup	See next.
HD_ResolutionNotes	Multiple Lines of Text	None.

Having created the site columns, add them to a new content type named Helpdesk Ticket.

GP_Delegate

This is the most complicated content type in the solution, and you spend a lot of time working with it. It is the only content type that contains a technical site column.

Business columns:

- **Delegate Function:** Identifies the specific function to which this delegation applies
- **Delegate From:** This is the person who would normally be assigned the item. For instance, if Paul normally handles all helpdesk tickets where the category is Email, then the Delegate From is Paul.
- **Delegate To:** For the business function, delegates tasks normally assigned to the Delegate From to this user

Technical columns:

- **Delegate Unique Key:** To work around SharePoint Designer's inability to work with compound keys, you need to generate a unique key. This column holds it. Read more about this in the next section.

Table 4-4 shows the general purpose delegate site columns.

TABLE 4-4: General Purpose Delegate Site Columns

COLUMN NAME	COLUMN TYPE	ADDITIONAL SETTING
GP_DelegateFunction	Single Line of Text	None
GP_DelegateFrom	Person or Group	Specify just one user
HD_DelegateTo	Person or Group	Specify just one user
GP_DelegateUniqueKey	Single Line of Text	None

Create Workflows

To implement the solution, create four separate workflows.

- **Update Delegate Key:** A utility workflow that helps to solve SharePoint's lack of multicolumn primary key support.
- **Determine Delegate:** Used on the helpdesk list to determine the delegate.
- **Update Category Unique Key:** Sets the value of the category's unique key column and used by the Assign default owner workflow.
- **Assign Default Owner:** This utility workflow assigns a default helpdesk administrator to own the ticket until it is closed.

Update Delegate Key

This chapter introduces the first utility workflow of the book by way of the delegate management workflow. A utility workflow is similar to a "technical site column." It fills a critical role in the solution, but it's not directly tied to the business process. The delegate management workflow's utility role is to make up for SharePoint's inability to do a multicolumn lookup in a SharePoint Designer workflow. What does that mean? Consider the following example. Paul and Samantha both work for the IT department. Paul normally handles paper jams, and Samantha normally handles lost file recovery. When Paul is on vacation, Aidan takes on Paul's responsibilities, and when Samantha is on vacation, Sydne handle's Samantha's responsibilities. You can see a clear delegation relationship in the Delegate Relationships table, as shown in Table 4-5.

TABLE 4-5: Delegate Relationships

TASK	PRIMARY	DELEGATE
Clear paper jams	Paul	Aidan
Recover lost files	Samantha	Sydne

Things become more complicated, however, when someone else is also responsible for one of Paul's tasks. For example, assume that Peter is also responsible for clearing paper jams. (There are a lot of paper jams at this company.) This time, Martha takes on that responsibility when Paul is on vacation. Now see how Table 4-6 looks.

TABLE 4-6: Delegate Relationships

TASK	PRIMARY	DELEGATE
Clear paper jams	Paul	Aidan
Recover lost files	Samantha	Sydne
Clear Paper Jams	**Peter**	**Martha**

This solves the problem in a business sense. If Paul is on vacation, the helpdesk ticketing workflow simply has to look up Paul's delegate to solves the delegate problem generally. Furthermore, this is easy to model in a SharePoint custom list. SharePoint Designer workflow, however, can't use a table like that directly. Why not and how do you get around this shortcoming?

Now imagine that you defined a custom list as previously shown. To find the delegate for the Clear Paper Jams task, you need to find the row in the list that matches both the task and the primary person responsible for that task. You need both pieces of information to find the specific row in the list. When you find that row, you know the delegate.

SharePoint Designer does enable you to look up information in a list at run-time. However, SharePoint Designer allows you to use only a single column to specify the target row. You can use only a single column to lookup data in a list. Use a *utility workflow* to solve this problem. In this case, a utility workflow creates a unique lookup value in the delegate lookup list. It does this by concatenating the task with the primary. To implement this solution, follow these steps:

1. Fire up SharePoint Designer, and connect to the GP_Delegation list you previously created, as shown in Figure 4-2.

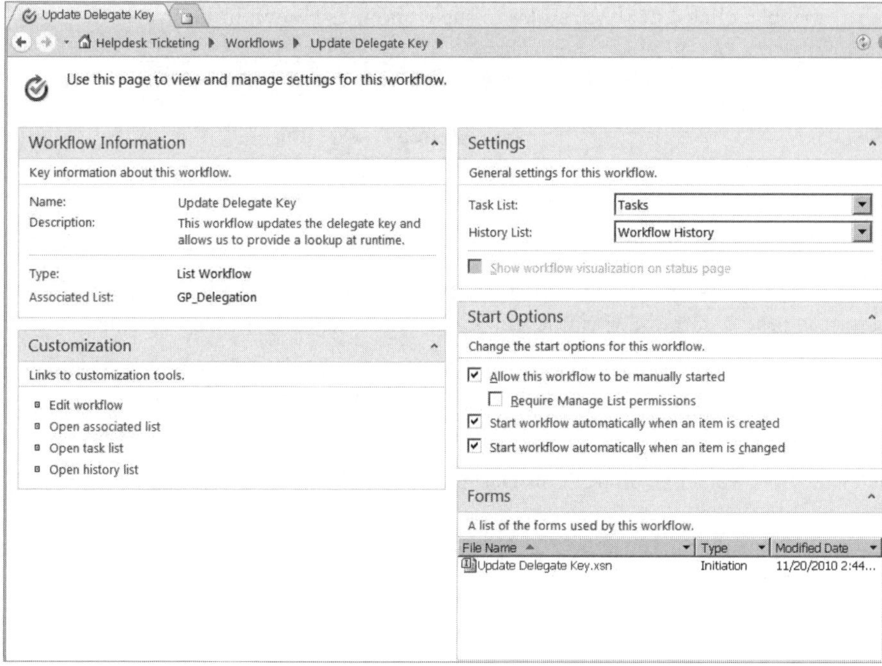

FIGURE 4-2

2. Attach the workflow to the GP_Delegation custom list and name it Update Delegate Key. This workflow should start automatically when an item is created or changed. For testing purposes, it's also handy to allow the workflow to be started manually.

The workflow itself consists of one step. Name the step "Update Delegate Key." This step has the following two simple actions:

1. Assign a variable equal to the task plus the primary (no spaces).
2. Assign that result to the GP_DelegateUniqueKey field.

It looks similar to Figure 4-3 when completed.

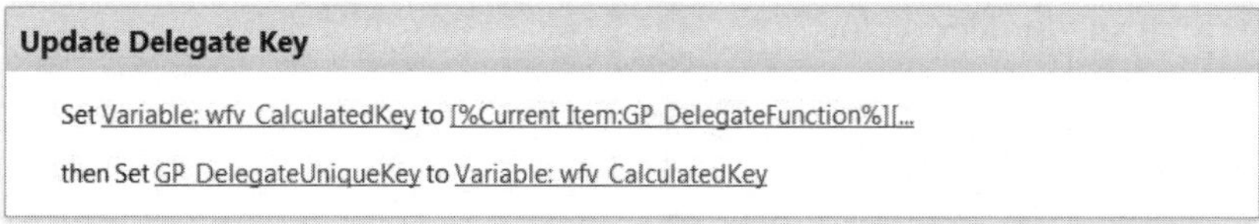

FIGURE 4-3

The first set action is of particular interest. That action creates the unique key and saves it into a workflow variable named `wfv_CalculatedKey`. A workflow variable is the temporary storage place for you to use in your SharePoint Designer workflow.

1. To create a variable, click Local Variables in the ribbon, as shown in Figure 4-4.

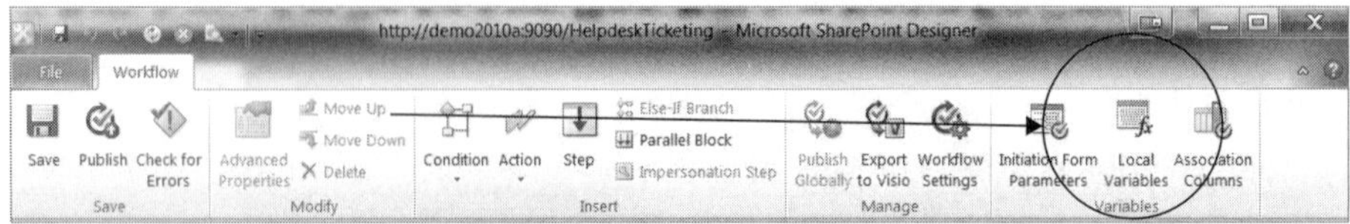

FIGURE 4-4

2. The resulting dialog box enables you to create local variables for use in the workflow. Click the Add button, and create the variable `wfv_CalculatedKey`, as shown in Figure 4-5.
3. With `wfv_CalculatedKey` ready, it's time to calculate the actual unique key. Add a new line to your workflow, and type `set` and press Return. SharePoint Designer responds similar to Figure 4-6.
4. Select Set Workflow Variable. SharePoint Designer displays the set line as shown in Figure 4-7.

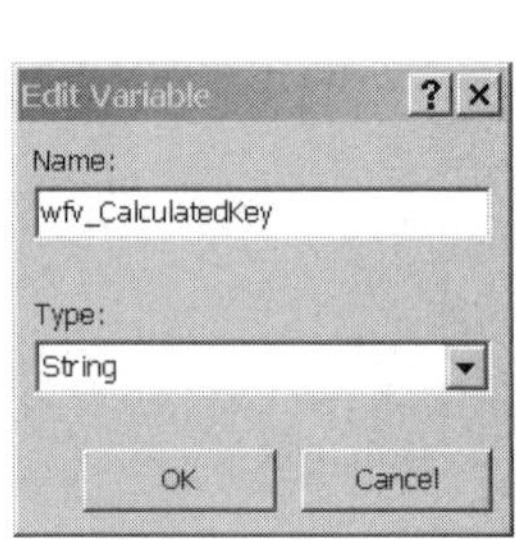

FIGURE 4-5

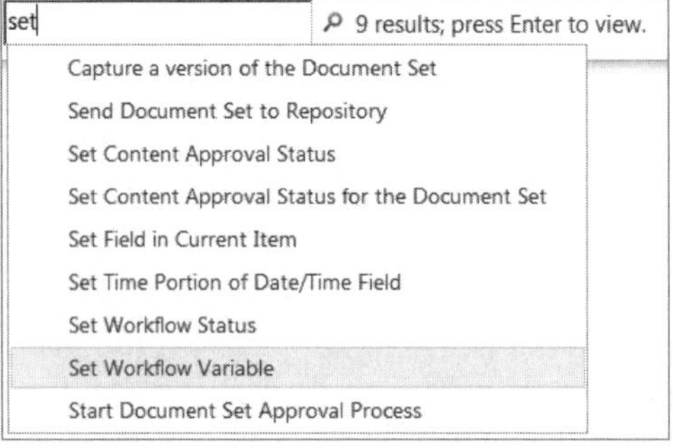

FIGURE 4-6

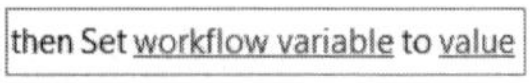

then Set workflow variable to value

FIGURE 4-7

5. Click Workflow Variable, and select `wfv_CalculatedKey` from the drop-down list.
6. Click Value and then the ... button (not the Fx button). SharePoint Designer responds with the String Builder dialog, as shown in Figure 4-8.

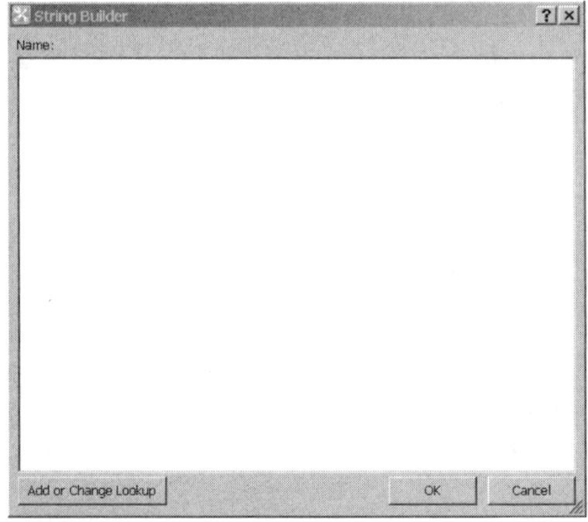

FIGURE 4-8

Figure 4-8 shows SharePoint Designer's general purpose String Builder dialog. You can type any text here that you want, but in this case, you want to build a unique key from the two columns `GP_DelegateFunction` and `GP_DelegateFrom`. To do this, click the button labeled Add or Change

Lookup on the lower-left side of the String Builder dialog. Welcome to SharePoint Designer's general purpose lookup dialog!

SharePoint Designer's general purpose lookup dialog is powerful and useful. It is also a bit tricky to understand for first-time users especially as it changes itself depending on what values you select. Begin by examining the initial dialog, as shown in Figure 4-9.

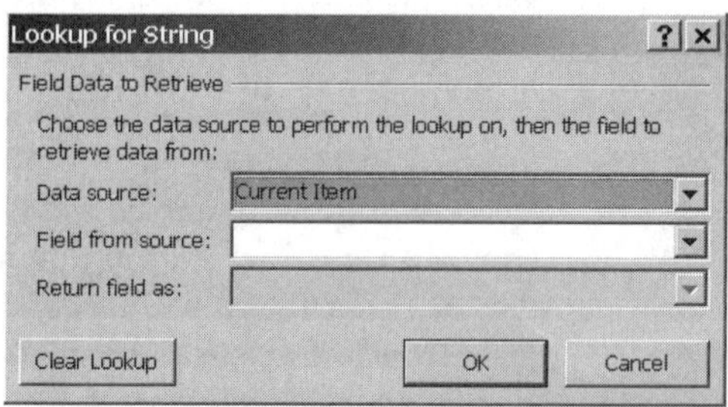

FIGURE 4-9

Use the first two fields as follows (ignore Return field As for the time being):

- **Data Source:** The SharePoint custom list from which you want to retrieve a value. The more general label Data Source is appropriate as you can find data from the other places, including other workflow variables.
- **Field from Source:** The actual field that you want to extract from the source.

In this case, select Current Item as the data source and `GP_DelegateFrom` as the Field from Source. Your screen should look similar to Figure 4-10.

Finally, click the OK button. SharePoint Designer then displays this rather cryptically in the String Builder dialog box, as shown in Figure 4-11.

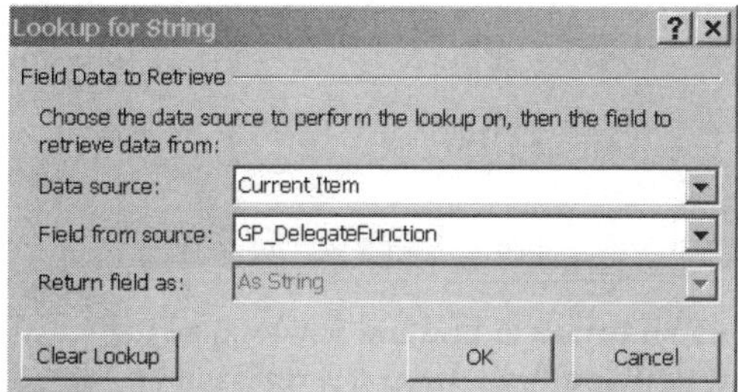

FIGURE 4-10

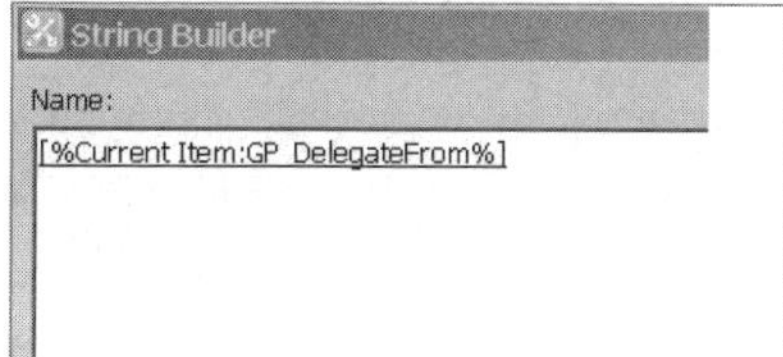

FIGURE 4-11

SharePoint Designer has inserted "[%Current Item:GP_DelegateFrom%]".

Next, repeat the same steps but this time select `GP_DelegateFrom` instead of `GP_DelegateFunction`. In the end, your String Builder dialog box looks like Figure 4-12.

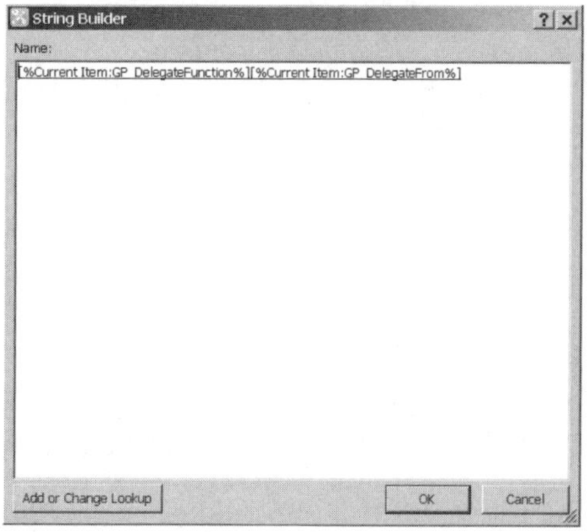

Finally, assign the value of the unique key stored in `wfv_CalculatedKey` to the current item's `GP_DelegateUniqueKey`. Follow these steps to do that:

1. Type `Set` into the Update Delegate Key workflow and press Enter.
2. Select Set Field in Current Item.

FIGURE 4-12

3. Click the underlined word "field," and select `GP_DelegateUniqueKey` from the drop-down.
4. Click the underline word "value," and then the Fx symbol that SharePoint Designer displays in response. You're already familiar with dialog box.
5. Select Workflow Variables and Parameters from the Data Source drop-down and `Variable:wfv_CalculatedKey` from the Field from Source drop-down. You dialog box now looks like Figure 4-13.
6. Press the OK button and you're done with the dialog.
7. Finalize the workflow by clicking the Publish button in the Ribbon and you're finished!

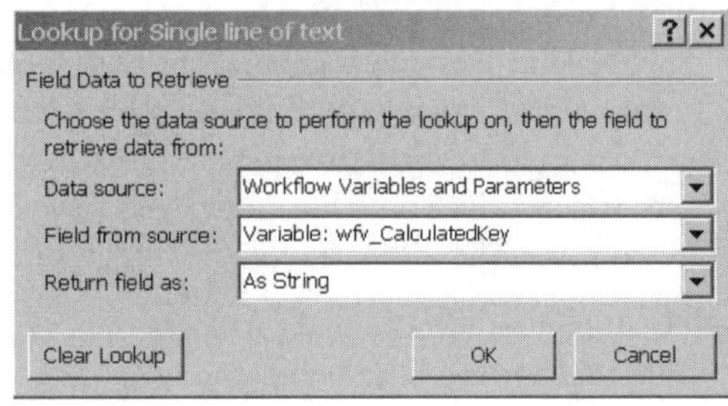

FIGURE 4-13

Delegate Workflow Summary

The Update Delegate Key utility workflow creates a single column that uniquely identifies a row in the list. Consider Table 4-7. You create entries in GP_Delegation. When you do that, you enter values for GP_DelegateFunction, GP_DelegateFrom, and GP_DelegateTo. The workflow runs each time you create a row (three times if you're following along with the book). That workflow populates the site column GP_DelegateUniqueKey as show in in Table 4-7. The values look "funny" because they are mashed together (no spaces). However, this is fine since it's a technical column and only meant to be used by the workflows themselves.

TABLE 4-7: Fully Populated GP_Delegation Custom List

GP_DELEGATEFUNCTION	GP_DELEGATEFROM	GP_DELEGATETO	GP_DELEGATEUNIQUEKEY
Clear paper jams	Paul	Aidan	Clear paper jamsPaul
Recover lost files	Samantha	Sydne	Recover lost filesSamantha
Clear paper jams	Peter	Martha	Clear paper jamsPeter

For the helpdesk workflow to take advantage of this unique key, it must also concatenate the task with the person primarily responsible for that task. When two separate workflows agree on the same definition of a primary key, they are said to cooperate with each other.

You regularly use this technique, both as a utility workflow and an agreed-upon definition of a primary key.

Lookup Delegate

It takes two to tango, and it takes two workflows to demonstrate delegation: one to manage the delegates (previous section) and one to take advantage of delegates. This section covers the latter.

The lookup delegate workflow kicks in when the helpdesk ticket is first created. This is the only workflow guaranteed to run on the helpdesk ticket. Like the Update Delegate workflow, the Lookup

Delegate workflow is also a utility workflow whose only responsibility is to assign the correct person to work on this ticket.

This utility workflow is almost a mirror image of the update Delegate Key workflow. Instead of calculating a key and then saving it to the current item, you calculate the key and look up the delegate. There are a few twists, however, so now walk through it.

1. First, create a workflow variable named `wfv_CalculatedKey`.
2. Using the same technique previously described, assign this variable equal to first `HD_Category` and then `HD_AssignedTo`.
3. With this calculated workflow field, you can now look up the delegate. Use the lookup dialog as previously described. When you finish, your lookup dialog should look similar to Figure 4-14.

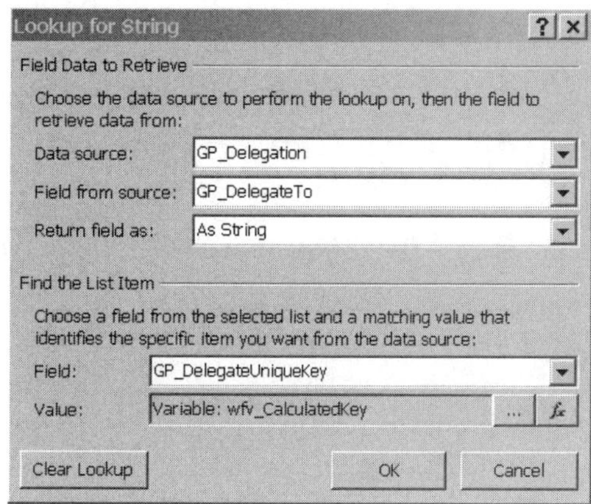

FIGURE 4-14

Figure 4-14 shows that you are looking for `GP_DelegateTo` in the `GP_Delegation` list by finding a row in the `GP_Delegation` list whose column `GP_DelegateUniqueKey` equals the calculated workflow key, `wfv_CalculatedKey`.

Two things can happen at this point. Either the lookup succeeds and it does find a row in `GP_Delegation` or it does not succeed. What happens in the latter case? Quite simply, the value of your workflow variable will be blank. You use this fact to assign the delegate key. You do this using a conditional step in your workflow.

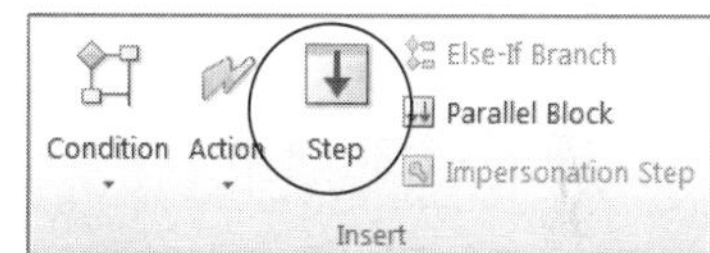

FIGURE 4-15

1. Create a conditional step by clicking the Step button in the Ribbon, as shown in Figure 4-15.

   SharePoint designer responds by adding a new step into the workflow pane, as shown in Figure 4-16.

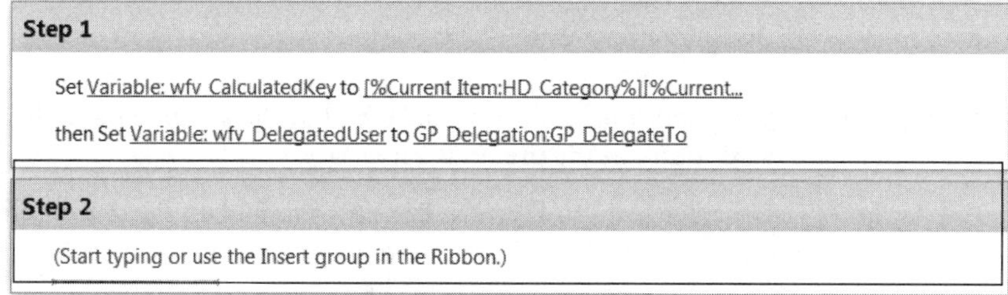

FIGURE 4-16

2. The purpose of creating this conditional step is to assign the delegate you found in the previous list to become the new assigned helpdesk administrator for this ticket. However,

you only want to do that on the condition that SharePoint found a delegate. SharePoint Designer workflow always executes steps in the order in which they display. You can control whether a given step executes by adding conditions. To do so, click the Condition button in the tool bar, as shown in Figure 4-17.

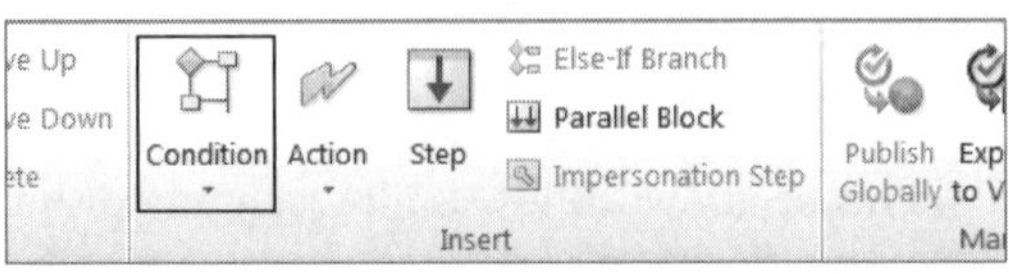

FIGURE 4-17

3. Add a condition to a specific workflow step by clicking the workflow step and then clicking the Condition button. SharePoint Designer responds, as shown in Figure 4-18.

   You use a number of these conditions in later chapters. This time, select If Any Value Equals Value. This brings up the now-familiar lookup dialog.

4. This time the data source is Workflow Variables and Parameters, and the Field from Source is Variable: `wfv_DelegatedUser`.

5. Click Value, and SharePoint Designer responds with the options shown in Figure 4-19.

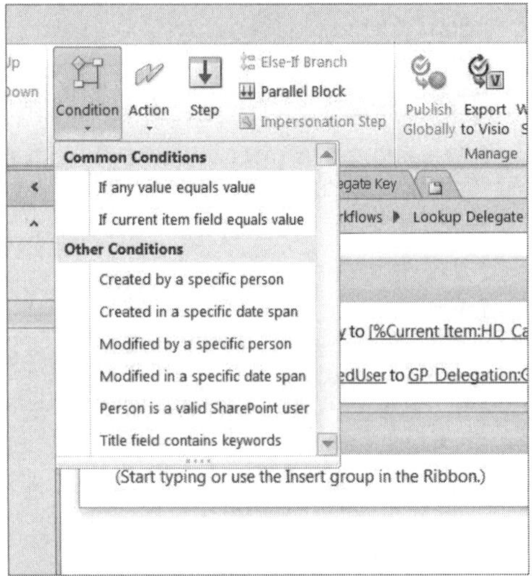

FIGURE 4-18

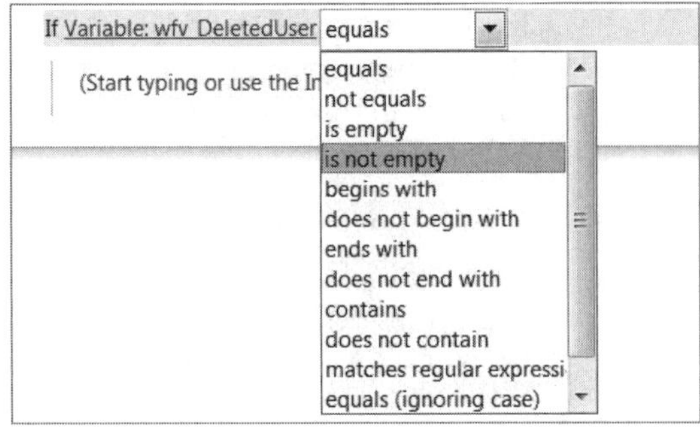

FIGURE 4-19

6. Select Is Not Empty to finalize this condition. This now ensures that the statements in this list will execute only if a delegate were found in the previous series of steps.

7. Finally, assign the delegate. Use the Set Field in Current Item activity. Click Field and select `HD_AssignedTo`. Click Value; then click the Fx button. SharePoint Designer responds with the familiar dialog. Select `wfv_DelegatedUser` from the Workflow Variables and Parameters data source.

Congratulations, you completed the delegation cycle. You can manage delegates and unique keys. You can look up delegates at run-time. Of course, delegation can't kick into drive until you assign the ticket to someone.

Update Category Unique Key

The Update Category Unique Key workflow assigns a value to the `HD_Category`'s site column, `HD_CategoryUniqueKey`. There are often good reasons to assign unique keys, as you just read about vis-à-vis delegates. This time, however, it's for a technical reason that allows you to get around a quirk in how SharePoint represents the value of lookups internally.

Recall that the `HD_Ticket` content type has a site column named `HD_Category`. This site column is backed by the custom list, Helpdesk Categories. When users fill out a helpdesk ticket and pick a category, they are actually picking the category from Helpdesk Categories and saving the selected category into the helpdesk ticket. If you have a category named Lost Files, you'd expect that SharePoint stores the word Lost Files into the `HD_Category` site column. Actually, SharePoint treats lookup columns differently from other columns and stores additional information. Specifically, SharePoint stores both the internal ID of the helpdesk category from the source list and the category itself. Therefore, if the Lost Files category has internal ID 5, then the internal value of the `HD_Category` on the helpdesk ticket list is 5;#Lost Files. (SharePoint inserts the ;# delimiter between the ID and the string value.)

SharePoint is smart enough to strip out the leading characters in list views and elsewhere in SharePoint. However, SharePoint Designer workflows get the internal value, not the display value — therefore, the need for this workflow.

The objective of this workflow is to assign a unique key to the `HD_CategoryUniqueKey` site column so that the Assign Default Owner workflow (described next) can find it.

This is a simple one-line workflow. Create a workflow named Update Category Unique Key with one action, Set Field in Current Item. Click Field and select `HD_CategoryUniqueKey`. Click value and the ... button. SharePoint responds with the String Builder dialog box. Follow these steps:

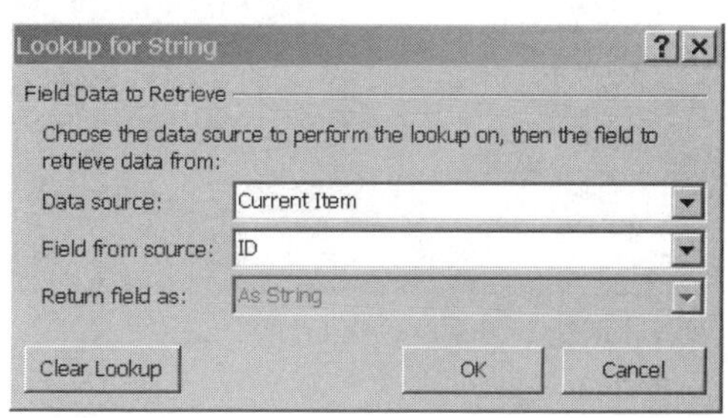

FIGURE 4-20

1. Click Add or Change Lookup.
2. Select ID from the Current Item, as shown in Figure 4-20.
3. Add a ;# character after the [%Current Item:ID%] symbol.
4. Click Add or Change Lookup again.
5. Select `HD_Category` from Current Item.

In the end, your String Builder Dialog will look similar to Figure 4-21.

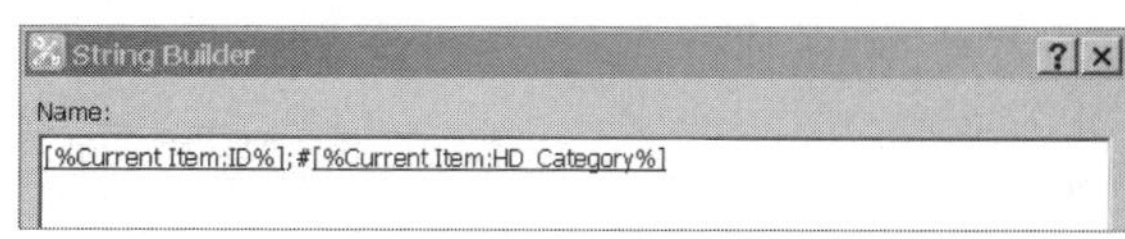

FIGURE 4-21

When this workflow runs, it can now update the unique key column in HD_Categories. This is going to be useful in the next workflow.

Assign Default Owner

The Assign Default Owner workflow leverages the `HD_Categories` list to look up and assign a helpdesk administrator to work on the ticket. This workflow doesn't introduce any new concepts and instead leverages techniques described in the previous two utility functions. This workflow runs on the `HD_Ticket` custom list.

You only want to assign a default owner when no owner has been assigned. Use this by adding a condition that checks to see if the current item's `HD_AssignedTo` is empty.

The one action in this workflow assigns a value to `HD_AssignedTo` by looking at a value in the `HD_Categories` custom list. This lookup function is a little different from the preceding because there are a wider array of possible data sources when user IDs (`HD_AssignedTo`) are added to the equation, as shown in Figure 4-22.

In this case, you want to select a value from the HD_Categories list, so click Workflow Lookup for a User and then Add>>. SharePoint Designer now responds with the same lookup function as before. Use that dialog to select `HD_CategoryDefaultAssignee` from the `HD_Category` custom list. Your dialog will look similar to Figure 4-23.

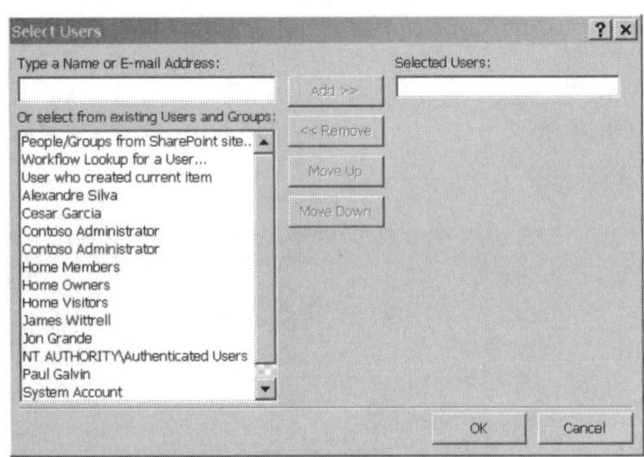

FIGURE 4-22

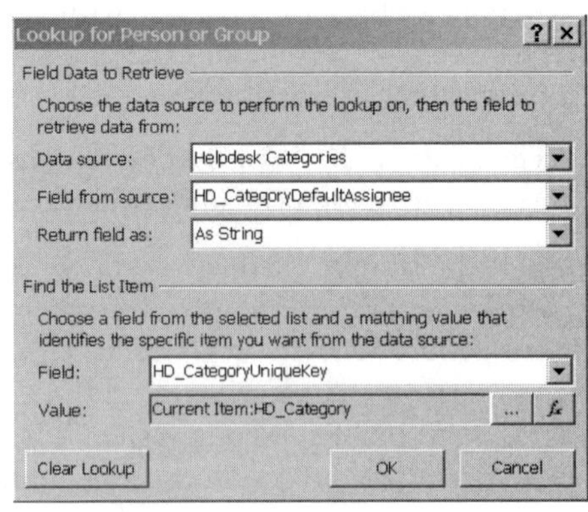

FIGURE 4-23

Click OK and publish the workflow.

Managing the Process

This section glues all the discrete pieces together and walks you through the helpdesk process.

Setup

At this point, you may be wondering how a few content types, custom lists, and some utility workflows make for a comprehensive helpdesk solution. This section describes how these discrete components work together to provide that solution. Begin with a new helpdesk ticket item.

To create a helpdesk ticket, you need to have the supporting data lined up and ready to go. Create several `HD_Categories`, for instance Email and Lost Files. Assign a default owner to each so that you can test this functionality. Figure 4-24 shows an example.

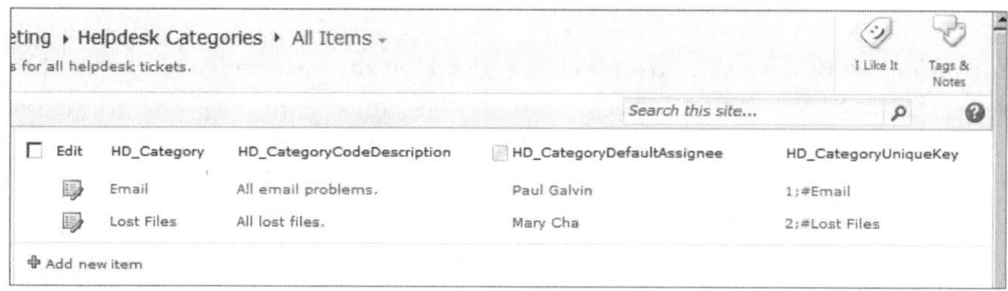

FIGURE 4-24

Figure 4-24 shows two helpdesk problem categories. Email problems are assigned to Paul Galvin and Lost Files are assigned to Mary Cha.

In addition to `HD_Categories`, you need to create Helpdesk Ticket Statuses. These statuses lie at the core of what most people would consider the "workflow" in this solution. Create Helpdesk Status as follows, as shown in Table 4-8.

TABLE 4-8: Helpdesk Status

STATUS CODE	STATUS CODE DESCRIPTION
1. Open	This is the initial value for all helpdesk tickets.
2. In Process	The assigned helpdesk administrator is actively working on the issue.
3. Awaiting Initiator	The helpdesk administrator needs additional information from the helpdesk ticket originator and cannot proceed until he receives it.
4. Closed	The issue is resolved (or closed for some other reason).
5. KB	Indicates that the item should be added to the knowledge base.

You want to prefix status codes with a number to organize helpdesk tickets by status on list views and dashboards. The leading number ensures that tickets sort and group together. This also enables you to create views on the helpdesk list called In Process or Waiting based on status.

Entering Tickets

Now that the setup is out of the way, it's time to create a ticket. End users navigate to the Helpdesk Tickets list, or you can create a link to the list from an appropriate place in you intranet. You should provide instructional content via a wiki or minimally an MS Word document. This content should address topics such as the following:

- How to create tickets
- How to view ticket status

- How to sign up for alerts
- Best practices for tickets (good information helps expedite solutions)

A well-organized document like this can help with adoption because it eliminates mystery and engenders confidence.

Armed with this information, end users should sign up for alerts on the custom list. None of the preceding workflows send emails. Workflow-generated email was omitted on purpose. Alerts on tickets are the best way to handle email communication for a few reasons. First, it's a simple, out-of-the-box approach. Second, alerts go out to end users as helpdesk administrators update the ticket. This helps end users gain confidence that their issue is actually being managed. Lastly, it helps end users learn an important function within SharePoint. Alerting is useful in many other areas, and end users will be the better for it.

Managing Tickets

Helpdesk administrators manage tickets by controlling individual tickets' status. There is nothing automated here and there is no need for automation. Every ticket needs to be looked at by a human being, and that human being can and should change the status as they are worked on.

Administrators know which ticket to work on by way of views on the Helpdesk Ticket custom list. You can probably imagine quite a few useful views. Consider the following:

- **"My Tickets":** A filtered view that lists all tickets sorted by status where HD_AssignedTo = [Me]. Helpdesk administrators use this view to see any tickets assigned to them.
- **"Blocked Tickets":** A list of all tickets that require a response from the end user that originated it.
- **"All Open Tickets":** A filtered view that lists all tickets, grouped by status code. Exclude tickets whose status is "4. Closed" or "5. KB."
- **"Solved Tickets":** A filtered view that shows only tickets whose status is "5. KB" grouped by Helpdesk Category. This view can help to quickly identify tickets that previous helpdesk administrators determined could be useful in the future.

These views can help your helpdesk administrators stay on top of tickets and provide the basis for quick answers to status questions from end users.

Advanced Topics

The techniques and approaches described to this point provide a good basis for a working solution. There are many opportunities to improve upon this. This section describes some of those ideas.

Dashboards

A helpdesk ticket dashboard extends the fairly simple listview-based approach to ticket management. You can create a web part page and add the Helpdesk Ticket custom list to the dashboard. You can add the list multiple times and specify a different view each time. Using this approach, you can quickly have a dashboard that shows all open tickets, all stalled tickets, tickets grouped by assignee, and many others. In the end, you have a dashboard that shows open tickets, in process tickets, and blocked tickets.

Searchable Knowledge Base

Helpdesk administrators decide on a case-by-case basis which helpdesk tickets should be marked as KB, meaning that they are considered valuable references to use when working on future problems. Helpdesk administrators can then use a KB view on the Helpdesk custom list to find these entries. However, this can become ungainly over time as more and more solved helpdesk problems are classified as KB.

SharePoint provides a highly effective search solution out-of-the-box. Use SharePoint search to provide a more powerful solution that can ferret out prior solutions more quickly and with greater fidelity than eyeballing items in a SharePoint list view. SharePoint provides a "free" search tailored to all items in the list. However, you can create a search scope that includes only Helpdesk Ticket items whose status is equal to 5. KB.

SUMMARY

This chapter walked you through the thinking process, technical design, and actual implementation of a simple but effective helpdesk ticketing solution. Following are the key points you should take away from this chapter:

- **Delegation:** How to set up, manage, and use defined delegates for business processes.
- **Utility workflows galore:** Most SharePoint Designer workflow solutions are purely technical. This chapter used technical utility workflows to support delegation and default helpdesk administrator assignments on new tickets.
- **Status-driven manual workflows:** This helpdesk process does not provide a great deal of automation. Instead, it populates statuses and relies upon helpdesk administrators actively managing the issues. This is often good enough.

You can use these techniques for a wide variety of related business problems, some of which are covered by the following chapters and others that you create in the future.

5

Time Off Management

WHAT'S IN THIS CHAPTER?

- Enabling users to request time off
- Enabling users to view their available time (their "time bank")
- Building an audit trail that can recalculate time off buckets, (that is, if a technical glitch occurs)
- Providing a dashboard and calendar view of employee time-off requests
- Implementing sensible validation, such as mandatory four-hour minimums when requesting time
- Implementing a simple one-step approval process (employee direct managers)
- Slicing and dicing time off requests by categories (ordinary vacation time, bereavement, personal days, and so on)

The time off management solution continues to introduce new SharePoint workflow capabilities, building upon previous chapters. It also introduces a couple of new technical and business patterns that you can find valuable in a wide array of circumstances, not just for managing time off processes.

WHAT IS THE TIME OFF MANAGEMENT PROCESS?

Everyone needs to take some time off. In small organizations, it's easy to keep track of who is doing what, and there's not a real need for an automated solution. Large organizations use dedicated HR platforms such as those provided by PeopleSoft or SAP's HR module. Somewhere in between the small and the large are many organizations that could use a

SharePoint-based solution that helps the human resources department track when employees take vacations and provides an automated approval process.

At the core of the time off management system lays the *time bank*. A time bank is much like a bank account; the company deposits time into the bank as you work over the course of a year, and then you can withdraw that time. The banking analogy breaks down because a number of rules constrain how you withdraw time from the bank. For instance, you have a certain number of days that you can use more or less any time — your regular vacation days. On the other hand, you have days such as sick days where you can take that time only when you're sick. This time typically expires, so that if you have five sick days in a year and never use them, they don't carry them forward to the next year.

The time off management process begins with human resources. HR, informed by corporate polices, populates a logical time bank, adding a single entry into the bank for every employee. Each entry in the time bank includes the employee's ID, total available vacation hours, sick time hours, personal hours, bereavement hours, and any other. Employees request time off by way of an online form that launches an approval workflow.

Managers respond to time off requests by approving or rejecting those requests. A calendar overlaid with all the manager's direct reports provides a handy visualization. It enables managers to view their group's vacation coverage as a whole and helps to make the approve/deny decision more scientific.

Lastly, life moves on whether employees use the system. For instance, you can hardly expect employees to dial into the system and request time off in emergency situations. In such cases, time needs to be entered for prior unapproved events. Because the time was already taken, there's no need to go through the approval process, and it should be skipped.

PROBLEM CLASS

The time off management recording and approval problems falls into the "limited resources" problem class. A limited number of resources (hours) can be consumed by various actors (employees). Ideally, the system tightly manages access to these resources (manager approval) even though it's not always possible (unplanned absences that don't or can't require approval).

The limited resources problem class describes a number of real-world scenarios. For instance, access to shared hardware (projectors, loaner laptops, and smart boards) is a business problem applicable to the subject of this chapter. Unlike hours, hardware items are not normally consumed when used, but they must be allocated, and in some cases, approval may be required.

By solving the time off management problem in detail, you solve a specific example of the limited resources problem. You can apply the techniques and approaches outlined in this chapter to similar problems in the future.

TECHNICAL PATTERNS

While solving the time off management problem, you need to implement the following technical patterns:

- **Basic CRUD:** Time off requests are created, periodically updated (vacation plans change) and deleted.

- **Time Bank:** A set of limited and consumable resources manages access to the time bank and removes those vacation days as employees request and their managers approve them.
- **Approvals:** Requires a simple approval process. As employees request time, their managers are alerted and asked to approve or deny the request.
- **Audit Trail:** You could provide a minimally functional solution if you left it a CRUD, Time Bank, and Approvals. However, you need an audit trail to answer the question, "For a given employee, what days did they take and when did they take them?" The audit trail pattern logs every request, approval and denial so that it's easy to answer that question. The audit trail serves another important function; it enables you to manually recalculate time bank summary values. This chapter describes when this is necessary.

Beyond the listed patterns, you can also leverage some patterns discussed in earlier chapters. For instance, the delegation pattern makes sense for manager approvals.

BUSINESS PATTERNS

While solving the time off management problem, you can implement the following business patterns:

- **Time Bank:** Similar to the technical pattern of the same name, this business pattern establishes how you manage access and consumption of limited resources (hours in this case). The time bank business pattern answers questions such as 1) How is time originally entered? 2) Who is allowed to withdraw that time? 3) What rules constrain the use of those hours?
- **Simple Approval:** Provides for a single level of approval and the requirements to support it.
- **Complex Security:** Employee benefits are always private, unless the employee chooses to share them with others. SharePoint certainly should never expose this kind of private information. The complex security pattern can help you identify a process by which 1) You identify when information must be private, 2) How to identify that information in specific SharePoint terms (that is lists, libraries, and so on), and 3) Techniques you can use from a design perspective to ensure that accidents don't happen. In the context of this chapter, you use this pattern to ensure that no employee's information is visible to any other employee except his direct manager and HR administration.

BUSINESS PROBLEM DESCRIPTION

Now dive into the nitty-gritty details of the business problem. First, read about this business problem from a pure requirements perspective and then narrow the discussion down to specific actors and the actions they can take. This section ends by outlining some technical challenges that won't be covered in the detailed walk-through later in the chapter.

Requirements Discussion

One of the things to keep in mind with people's vacation time is this: Everyone is a lawyer. If you have a vague rule such as "time must be requested in ½ day increments," someone is going to assume they can request two hours when you have an official ½ day from work (such as the day before Thanksgiving in the United States). As a result, you need to make sure that time off policies are perfectly and unambiguously clear and that SharePoint supports those rules in a perfect and unambiguous manner. Requirements gathering around any business solution is important, but this topic calls for an even more rigorous discussion than others.

The goal of this process is to enable people to request time off and for the system to ensure that they comply with corporate policies. Different companies implement different corporate policies, which can include some mix of the following (among others):

- Five days or more time must be requested at least two weeks before the requested start date.
- Employees have a maximum amount of time available to them for a given "type" of request.
- There are multiple types of time off requests:
    - Bereavement
    - Vacation time
    - Personal days
    - Sick days
- Time must be requested in minimum increments. (For example, four hours must be requested at a time; employees may not request two hours or 45 minutes off for a doctor's visit.)

The preceding list shows a representative sample of potential corporate policies and is not meant to be exhaustive.

Of course, there has to be some time to take off. Typically, companies provide vacation and time off to employees based on two key factors. These factors normally include seniority (your title) and length of service (how many years you've worked at the firm). Complicating things, some employees break the mold and don't follow the norm. For instance, new employees with some experience under their belt typically negotiate a vacation package that does not conform to the company's standard policies. Your solution needs to recognize and account for this fact. As a practical matter, this means that the system has to treat each employee individually and be aware of corporate policies (such as the four-hour request minimum) while providing flexibility that the new (experienced) employee actually has three weeks of vacation instead of the policy-directed two weeks. The SharePoint solution must support this requirement.

Beyond supporting corporate rules and mechanical needs, the solution must meet the privacy expectations of everyone in the workplace. My vacation perks are no one's business except my own and my manager's. I don't want people to know what sick days I took and what personal days I needed for my personal reasons. The SharePoint solution needs to honor this pact.

In general, employees simply assume the privacy protections are in place, and it's up to you to ensure that trust isn't violated. Another social factor is almost as important — clear and unambiguous status on requests. Setting emergency requests aside, many people plan for their vacations well in advance to lock in discounted airfare and other costs. Smart employees await approval before making those nonrefundable flight reservations. While waiting, their plans are literally on hold, and they want to know what's happening with their request. The solution must provide feedback as soon as possible to keep track of the request's status throughout its lifetime. Not all requests are planned in advance, however.

In the real world, some requests are automatically accepted, and the role of the technical solution is not so much about approval but proper recording. For instance, if an employee's mother passes, no one expects the employee to request time off to attend to matters of such a personal nature. However, the time must be accounted for, and that probably won't happen until the employee is back to work. The system must enable employees or managers to enter time after the fact. In such cases, the manager or employee may enter the time directly and skip the approval process.

Given there's a potential mix of previously approved and unplanned time off, things can become quite confusing. Stressing again that "everyone is a lawyer" when it comes to their corporate perks, you need SharePoint to provide good backup when employees go to HR's office shaking their fist because they think the system cheated them of some time off. To address this, the time off management problem also requires, in some cases, a manual tally and auditing process so that you can identify who used resources and when. It's not always good enough to know the final numbers, but rather all the low-level details behind those numbers. To this end, the solution to this problem creates an audit trail for every request, every approval/denial, and every after-the-fact recording of any employee's day off.

Finally, there's the social aspect of a system like this. As previously stated, a time off system can bring the lawyer out of the most gentle of employees. Throughout history, IT departments have rolled out technical solutions to an enterprise only to find resistance (overt and subvert), frustration, and even anger despite that the designers, implementers, and testers have the highest of motives and professionalism. When you roll out a solution that touches upon employees' perks, you will almost certainly come under fire. The best way to mitigate result is to ensure that you canvass a wider than normal subset of the end user community for the business requirements. If you hear one message from this book, it's "Do a great job on requirements gathering." This kind of business solution calls for twice the usual effort.

In summary, following are the requirements for this business solution:

- Support corporate-wide time off policies, such as four-hour minimum requests.
- Provide for unique vacation time for individual employees. Break this out by category for bereavement, personal, and standard vacation time.
- Ensure clarity; let employees know exactly how much time they have available and provide an accounting for used time to ensure end user community acceptance of the solution. In addition, make each step of the process clear and unambiguous to the employee by clearly communicating when vacation requests are approved or denied.
- Employees must be able to request time off, implying the need for a data entry function that enables them to request time off, specify some dates (start and end), and type of time.

SharePoint provides everything you need to meet these requirements in a purely technical sense. It's up to you to handle the social acceptance aspects of the solution. Take this seriously in cases that touch upon employees in such a personal way.

Actors

This solution is built on a model that includes the following actors:

- HR managers are generally responsible to manage the entire process.
- End users who enter their requests

- Managers who receive and approve or deny individual time off requests
- SharePoint is always an actor in these solutions.

As you can see, a solution like this typically touches all SharePoint users in their organization.

Actions

The helpdesk solution responds to the actions on behalf of its supported actors. Now break these actions down by actor.

HR managers:

- Manage the time bank.
- Review employees' time off requests over time, in detail.

Employee managers:

- Approve or deny time off requests.
- Record after-the-fact time off events (such as emergencies or sloppy book keeping by employees).

Employees:

- Request time.
- Record after-the-fact time off.

SharePoint:

- Notify all parties by email at defined moments.
- Create an audit trail of requests, approvals, and denials.

Challenges

This chapter does not explain in great detail how to address certain nice-to-have functions that a full-fledged time off management solution would implement, such as the following:

- **Automatic time bank population:** You create a time bank (as a custom list) and provide a data entry process. You can expand upon the solution by populating the time bank on a yearly (or other periodic) basis.
- **Delegation:** You can read about delegation in Chapter 4, "Helpdesk Ticketing," so you can reuse those techniques when creating a production quality version of this solution.
- **User interface niceties:** A proper data entry function that employees use to enter their requests would be rather jazzier than what this chapter provides. For instance, it would be better to show immediate validation errors and a more integrated view of the employee's available time in the bank. SharePoint does give you good options to do this, such as using InfoPath (see sidebar for an introduction to InfoPath). However, that's beyond the scope of this chapter.

You can meet some of these challenges on your own using techniques described in prior and following chapters. In other cases, you can look to online resources and other Wrox books for assistance, which are noted as they are warranted.

ABOUT INFOPATH

InfoPath is a Microsoft product that tightly integrates with SharePoint that offers advanced data entry functions. You can think about your options for creating data entry screens as being on a spectrum ranging from easy-to-create versus very-hard-to-create and maintain. The easiest data entry screens are those that SharePoint creates itself. You don't need to do anything special to create them. However, you have limited options to customize that default out-of-the-box user interface. For instance, implementing a four-hour increment validation rule is simply not possible if you stick to what SharePoint gives you out-of-the-box. On the other hand, you can create entirely new data entry screens following the latest state-of-the-art in ASP.Net development if you go the hard-to-create route. You'd go that route to provide a rich user interface. InfoPath lies in the middle of this spectrum.

InfoPath is another application in the Microsoft Office family. It looks and feels a lot like SharePoint Designer or Microsoft Word. You can drag and drop fields around the screen, change layouts, add fonts and interesting colors, and do all that with a user-friendly interface that many end users find easy to learn. Any standard SharePoint data entry form can be customized using InfoPath.

You can learn more about InfoPath from a series of Microsoft-created videos at `http://www.youtube.com/watch?v=VKJ3A12RfE8`.

As of the writing of this book, InfoPath is available in the Microsoft Office 2010 family, so do some Internet searches for "InfoPath 2010" to find a great deal of content.

HIGH-LEVEL SOLUTION

This chapter's solution is based on custom lists, site content types, and SharePoint Designer workflows similar to previous chapters. This time, you'll learn about SharePoint's ability to create list templates (re-usable list definitions) so that you can work around SharePoint Designer workflow's lack of flexibility when it comes to real-world scenarios with multiple and variable numbers of managers.

Solution Overview

To implement the time off solution, leverage a number of out-of-the-box SharePoint components and learn a new type of SharePoint Designer workflow. This business process is, at its core, a workflow solution and leverages some of the more advanced features that SharePoint Designer offers.

Like all good SharePoint solutions, everything begins with lists backed by content types. This solution requires three distinct content types:

- **Time Bank:** Supports a list that has all employees in the system and tracks how much time they have available for each type of request.
- **Time Off Request:** Represents the employee's time off request.

- **Time Off Actions Audit:** Represents any action taken by the system that helps HR answer questions and provides reports on who requested time off, who it was approved or denied by and when, and notifications sent.

Taken together, these content types cover all the bases.

You might be thinking at this point that you'll want three custom lists, one for each of the content types. Actually, there will be at least three custom lists, but for security purposes, you'll more than likely create multiple instances of the time off requests list. Why? You do this because a properly configured out-of-the-box SharePoint list supports much, but not all, of your security needs. You can configure a given list so that only managers can view time off requests from their direct reports. However, if you have multiple managers, it's a lot more difficult to ensure that manager #1 can view only his direct reports' requests, whereas manager #2 can view only his direct reports' requests and no others. It's true that you can implement item level security (see sidebar "About SharePoint Security") but you can't do that using SharePoint Designer workflows. To get around that, use separate lists for each manager. Later, we'll discuss the benefits of this approach over item level security, and its disadvantages and some ideas how to overcome them.

ABOUT SHAREPOINT SECURITY

SharePoint security starts with the notion of "securable objects." A security object is just a general-purpose way of referring to anything that you can secure in SharePoint. The most common secured objects are site collections, sites, lists (including libraries) and ultimately, individual items within libraries.

One of SharePoint's core security features is inheritance. By default, a given securable object automatically inherits the security configuration of its container. So, items inherit security defined for their containing list. Lists inherit from sites and sites inherit from site collections. Items are the most granular level you can configure.

SharePoint provides a straightforward user interface to configure security at these levels. However, SharePoint Designer workflows cannot configure security. SharePoint Designer can be extended with custom actions, which Chapter 12, "Custom Activities," discusses in great detail.

You can override this inheritance feature by specifically configuring security at a given level. However, when you do that, you "own" security at that level and must manually configure it going forward. As this can become a maintenance nuisance and even a nightmare, it's best to avoid if possible.

Just like with helpdesk tickets, SharePoint's content approval function meets the privacy needs for a given list containing time off requests. You create one list for each manager and then assign that manager's ID with the approver security role. The approver security is a standard SharePoint role and is not used for any other purpose except security. This approach ensures that individual employees may only view and edit their own vacation requests, whereas their direct manager may view and approve all his direct reports' requests.

End users fill out requests and then submit them for approval. SharePoint workflow assigns an approval task to the manager. You won't implement it in this chapter, but you would implement the same delegation pattern that the previous chapter described in detail. Assuming the manager approves the request, the workflow can then update the time bank by decrementing the appropriate counters in the time bank.

As the main workflow on time off request runs its course, it also creates audit records in the audit list. This audit list can prove to be a veritable treasure trove of great information against which you can create reports in the future (and provide evidence to end users who challenge the system's record).

Swim Lane Diagrams

The swim lane in Figure 5-1 depicts the three primary actors and their actions for a specific time off request.

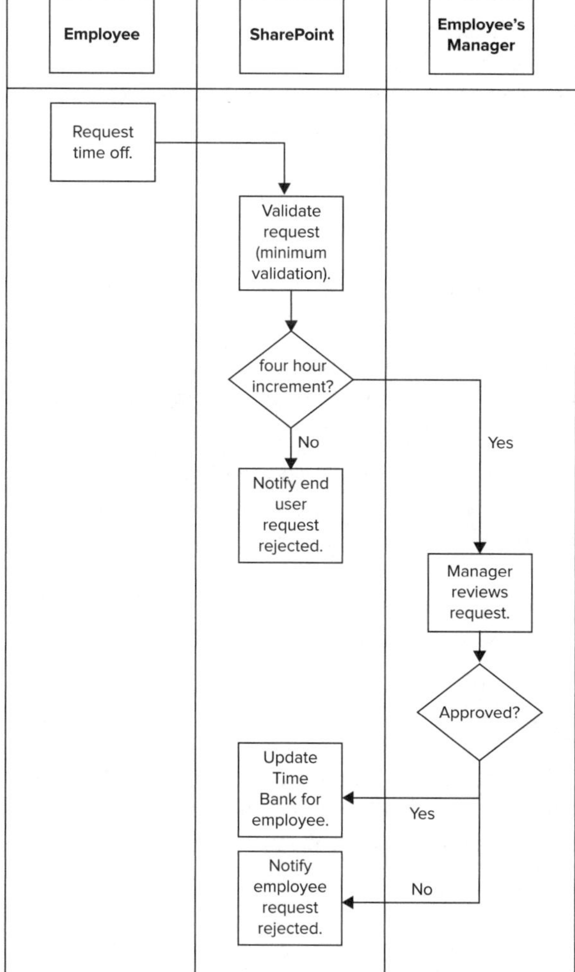

FIGURE 5-1

The process begins with the employee. He requests some time off.

SharePoint receives the request and ensures that is passes some minimal validation rules. For instance, it ensures that the request is within a four-hour increment. If it is not, SharePoint sends an email to the employee rejecting the request and explaining why.

If the request passes the four hour validation rule, it is forwarded to the employee's manager. The manager receives the request by email for notification purposes. Equally important, SharePoint creates a task in a task list. It assigns this task to the manager. The manager reviews the request to ensure that the employee can be absent during that time without unduly affecting the team's ability to do its job.

If the manager approves the request, SharePoint updates the employee's time bank record as needed. In both approval and denial cases, SharePoint notifies the employee of the manager's decision.

Technical Implementation Overview

This solution is based upon three (or more, as you'll see) custom lists backed (as usual) by appropriate site content types. SharePoint Designer workflow manages the business process. This time, SharePoint Designer also populates an audit list. A dashboard pulls it all together for managers and end users alike. As always, you will start with the content types.

Content Types

As described in the previous section, you need content types that represent the following:

- **Time Off Request:** Has all the columns required to manage a time off request, including the person making the request, the type of request, the start and end date, and more.
- **Time Bank Content Type:** The time bank content type provides summary level information for all employees' allocated time, tracking available time, time off pending approval, and approved time.
- **Time Off Audit:** A record of each important activity associated with any given time off request, including the original request, approvals or denials, and any notifications that were sent. Each audit is tied together with a common unique key so that they can be viewed and grouped together by employee.

Custom Lists

Use the following custom lists to implement the solution:

- **Time Bank:** The famous time bank itself
- **Time Off Requests:** This is a list template; you create multiple different time off request lists. The detailed walk-through section explains the reasoning behind this in all the gory detail and explains and demonstrates the notion of a list template.
- **Time Off Audit:** A single list that includes all the audit messages that the SharePoint Designer workflow creates

You may be wondering, "Why isn't there a lookup list and content type for the time off categories?" It's a reasonable question to ask because all the previous chapters followed that pattern. You do want to use lookup columns whenever possible. Unfortunately, SharePoint Designer doesn't provide any way to work with a random number of categories when working with the time bank pattern. This is clear during the detailed walk-through. As a result, you may bake (see sidebar) the time off types directly into a choice column.

WHAT DOES BAKING HAVE TO DO WITH SHAREPOINT?

If you're an end user and begin to work with the IT department or technical consultants, you need to learn some of their lingo. An earlier chapter defined what it means to "hard code" a value. Baking is just developer slang to say the same thing. Something is "baked into" a solution when it can't be changed without a relatively large effort. In this chapter, you're baking the time off request types into a manually edit choice column.

Dashboard

The time off management solution provides a sort of freebie dashboard in the form of the standard list views. The detailed walk-through explains how to create, view, and hammer home the idea that one big part of the art of content definition is thinking about the kinds of list views you want to provide for dashboard purposes.

DETAILED TECHNICAL IMPLEMENTATION

This solution follows the same pattern as previous chapters. First, set up the environment with content types and lists. Then, create the workflow using SharePoint Designer. This time, your workflow does some math and creates entries in an audit list. This detailed walkthrough also explains why you need, and how to create, list templates.

Setup

This section walks you through the detailed process for creating the solution.

Supporting Lists

The time off management solution is built upon the following set of custom lists:

- **Time Bank:** The famous time bank itself
- **Time Off Requests:** This is a list template; you create multiple different time off request lists. A list template is the definition of a type of list. You can create multiple lists from a single list template. List templates are not particularly special — a list and library you

can create in SharePoint is based off a list template. This includes the trusty custom list, document libraries, task lists, calendars, and so on. Learn more about this next.

- **Time Off Audit:** A single list that includes all the audit messages that the SharePoint Designer workflow creates.

Content Types

As with every other content type in each solution, it consists of two broad types of site columns: business and technical. End users enter data directly into business columns, and business columns appear on dashboards. Technical columns, on the other hand, do not generally appear to end users and instead support the technical needs of the solution. This solution calls for the following content types:

- Time Off Request
- Time Bank
- Time Off Audit

Time Off Request

This simple content type contains seven site columns.

Business Columns:

- *Request Type*: The type of request (bereavement, vacation, and so on).
- *Hours Requested*: The number of hours requested. On a business column like this, it's important to use a descriptive help message such as `Enter hours requested.` Note that one week is 40 hours, two weeks is 80 hours, etc. You must enter time in one-half day increments. In other words, two hours or five hours will not be accepted and automatically rejected.
- *Description:* Any notes that the employee things are important for the manager to know when he needs to approve or deny the time off request.
- *Start Date:* The date the vacation begins
- *Return Date:* The date the vacation ends

The dates are important because they feed into a calendar view that the managers can use to view all their direct reports' scheduled time off by day, week, or month.

Technical Columns:

- *Status*: Status code. This is a hybrid column because the workflow uses it for technical purposes while end users use it for business purposes.
- *Audit Link:* Like the status code, this is a sort of hybrid column. The workflow process assigns a value here but the actual value is "technical" in nature because it's a URL constructed to point to a filtered view of the audit custom list. When users views their previously entered time off requests, they can click this link, and SharePoint shows all the audit records associated with this specific time off request, as shown in Table 5-1.

TABLE 5-1: Time Off Request Site Columns

COLUMN NAME	COLUMN TYPE	ADDITIONAL SETTING
TOR_AuditLink	Hyperlink or picture	None
TOR_Description	Multiple lines of text	None
TOR_HoursRequested	Number (1, 1.0, 100)	Set decimals to zero
TOR_RequestType	Choice	Provide values: Bereavement Sick Vacation
TOR_ReturnDate	Date and time	Date only
TOR_StartDate	Date and time	Date only
TOR_Status	Single line of text	None

Note the naming convention of TOR_ with these site columns. As usual, the goal is to differentiate these columns from all the other site columns when you view them in the site column administrative screens.

Create a new site content type named TOR_TimeOffRequest and add the the site columns from Table 5-1.

Time Bank

This represents the time bank. It contains only business columns. Create the following business and technical columns:

Business Columns:

- *Employee:* The user id of the employee. All the time off information in any given item in the list is associated with its employee.
- *Full Name:* The full name of the employee. This is simply for sorting and views on the list.
- *Job Title*: The employee's job title. This is for informational purposes only and helps HR validate that it enters the correct vacation and other time for a given employee.
- *Maximum Vacation Time:* The maximum number of hours that the employee is allowed to take off per year
- *Vacation Requested*: The number of hours that the employee has requested off for the year
- *Vacation Approved*: The amount of time that has been approved year to date
- *Max, Requested Approved Bereavement Time:* Three separate columns mirrored after vacation time

The solution designed in this chapter provides only two types of time-off requests: vacation and bereavement. A real-world solution should include a number of other time off request types as previously described in the requirements discussion.

Use Table 5-2 to create the Time Bank site columns and then the site content type itself.

TABLE 5-2: Time Bank Site Columns

COLUMN NAME	COLUMN TYPE	ADDITIONAL SETTING
TB_Employee	Person or Group	None
TB_FullName	Single Line of Text	None
TB_JobTitle	Single Line of Text	None
TB_VacationMax	Number (1,1.0,100)	Zero decimals
TB_VacationRequested	See TB_VacationMax	
TB_VacationApproved	See TB_VacationMax	
TB_BereavementMax	See TB_VacationMax	
TB_BereavementRequested	See TB_VacationMax	
TB_BereavementApproved	See TB_VacationMax	

Create a site content type named TB_TimeBank and add all the preceding site columns to the site content type.

Time Off Request Audit

This records all the activities of the workflow. It has just three columns that are both system-generated and technical in nature:

- *Request Group Key:* Enables you to create a view on the time off request list that glues multiple different audit records together. Only one list holds all audit records. In the course of a week, several different people may add records to the audit list and multiple different audit requests from multiple different users (the employee, his manager, and possibly HR) are intermixed with time off requests from other employees. This site column groups them together for easy viewing.
- *Event Description*: This is a note of what actually happened, which includes messages such as "Time off request created," or "Time off request denied."
- *Request Link*: A hyperlink (URL) that points back to the original time off request. This enables quick-and-easy clicking between audit records and their parent item.

You would expect an audit to include other important pieces of information, such as when the record was created, who created it, and the length of time between audit entries. Because this information is already part of the standard SharePoint custom list, you don't need to add your site column for this purpose. Every SharePoint list saves the date it was created and who created it.

Table 5-3 shows the Time Off Audit site columns.

TABLE 5-3: Time Off Audit Site Columns

COLUMN NAME	COLUMN TYPE	ADDITIONAL SETTINGS
TOA_RequestGroupKey	Single Line of Text	None
TOA_EventDescription	Single Line of Text	None
TOA_RequestLink	Hyperlink or Picture	

Finally, create a new site content type named TOA_Audit, and add those three site columns to it.

Content Types Summary

If you followed the instructions so far, you created about two dozen site columns and three different content types. The content types follow:

- TB_TimeBank
- TOA_Audit
- TOR_TimeOffRequest

These content types must now be attached to some SharePoint custom lists.

Custom Lists

With the content types out of the way, you need to create some custom lists. This solution requires at least three custom lists:

- **Time Bank:** The actual time bank
- **Audit:** The audit list
- **Time Off Request:** One instance of this list for each manager with direct reports

These custom lists are all you need to implement the solution. The phrase "at least" is important. You create a "master" Time Off Requests list and then save it as a template. After you have that template, create individual Time Off Request lists for each manager with direct reports. As previously discussed, you need to do this because SharePoint Designer workflow solutions cannot configure security on items or lists. As a result, this is necessarily a manual configuration step.

The other two lists, Time Bank and Audit, are just normal lists and no different from any other lists you've created thus far. You create these two custom lists and configure them to use their respective site content types. The next section describes how to treat the Time Off Request custom list itself.

Saving Lists as Templates

Saving lists as templates is simple. First, create the list and configure it *as if you were going to use it*. This point is emphasized because the save template process records all your settings. If you forget to make a configuration setting, the template won't have it. When you create new lists off the template, the new list won't work as expected. This first list you create is called the master list. Note that "master list" is not a SharePoint term but rather used just in this chapter when discussing templates.

The solution calls for one time off request custom list for each manager with direct reports. You can save time and ensure accuracy by defining the Time Off Request list and then saving it as a template. Let's define it first. There are two key configuration steps: assigning a content type and configuring content approval for security. Refer to Chapter 2, "Workflow Basics," for more detailed treatment on these topics. Briefly, to configure security, access the list's settings page and require content approval via the Versioning settings option under General Settings. To add the content type, enable content types via the list's Advanced Settings and then add the TOR_TimeOffRequest content type. While you're fiddling with content types, you should remove the folder and item content types. Your solution will work with them anyway, but they add no value and produce clutter.

After you've configure the master list and it's perfect, it's time to save it as a template. You can do this via the web browser administration interface or SharePoint Designer. To save using SharePoint Designer, access the home page of the list, and the Ribbon lights up the Save a Template button, as shown in Figure 5-2.

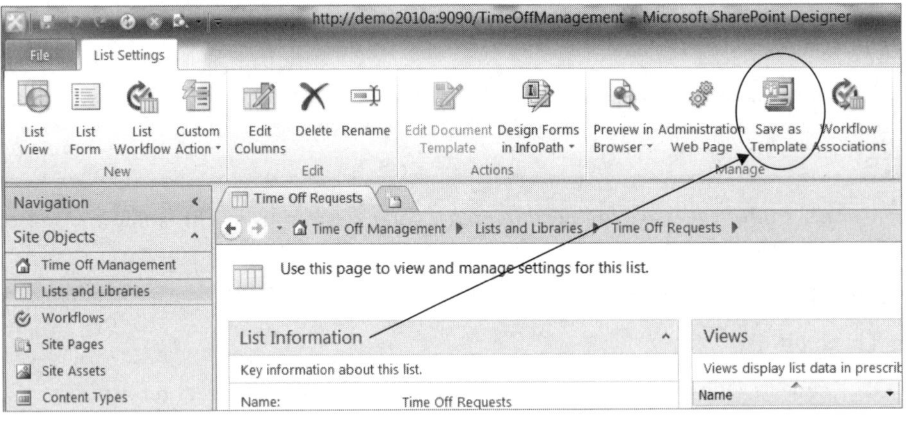

FIGURE 5-2

Strangely enough, SharePoint Designer actually opens up your web browser and brings you to the Save Template function just as if you had been using the web interface all along. When you do you this, you see a data entry screen similar to Figure 5-3.

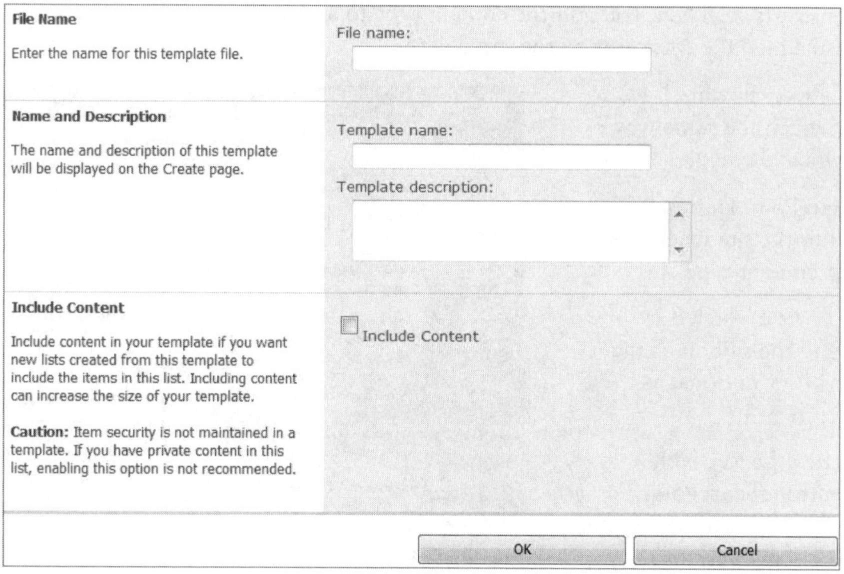

File Name

Enter the name for this template file.

File name:

Name and Description

The name and description of this template will be displayed on the Create page.

Template name:

Template description:

Include Content

Include content in your template if you want new lists created from this template to include the items in this list. Including content can increase the size of your template.

Caution: Item security is not maintained in a template. If you have private content in this list, enabling this option is not recommended.

Include Content

OK Cancel

FIGURE 5-3

When you save a list as a template, SharePoint takes the list's definition (columns, title, security, and so on) and bundles that up into a single file and saves it to a special kind of system-managed document library. Therefore, it asks for a filename first. Pay close attention to the Template name and Template description fields. These appear in the user interface when end users create a list based off this template. As always, take care to provide an appropriate name and description. Otherwise, you leave your end users (and yourself) with a confusing mess down the road. To this end, enter data as shown:

- **File Name:** `TimeOffByManager`
- **Name:** Time Off by Manager
- **Description:** Create one of these templates for each manager who has direct reports.
- **Include Content:** Leave unchecked.

Leave Include Content unchecked because you don't want a prepopulated list when you create a new Time Off List for a given manager.

Create Workflow

Departing from previous chapters, the time off management solution is composed of one monolithic workflow. SharePoint Designer provides all the required functionality (actions and conditions) required to meet the business process automation needs of the solution. Even though you create just one workflow, it's actually the most complex workflow so far. For starters, it's a reusable workflow as opposed to a list workflow.

A reusable workflow is not tied to any specific SharePoint list or document library. Instead, the workflow is tied to a content type. If you mastered or are on the verge of mastering the concept of SharePoint content types, you can see the power of this feature. You define the workflow just once against a specific content type. Then, you add the content type to a SharePoint list or library and voilà — you have also added the workflow to the same list.

You create a reusable workflow in SharePoint Designer much the same way as you create a list workflow.

1. Open up SharePoint Designer and connect to the site where you defined your content types.
2. Click Workflows in the left navigation and the ribbon changes to show workflow options, as shown in Figure 5-4.
3. When you click the Reusable Workflow button, SharePoint Designer responds with the Create Reusable Workflow dialog, as shown in Figure 5-5.

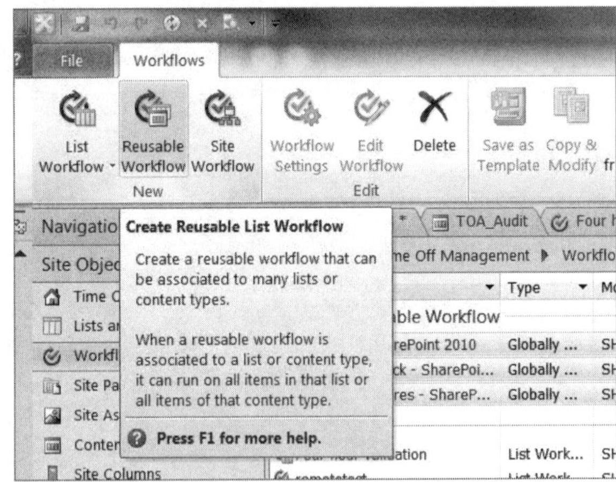

FIGURE 5-4

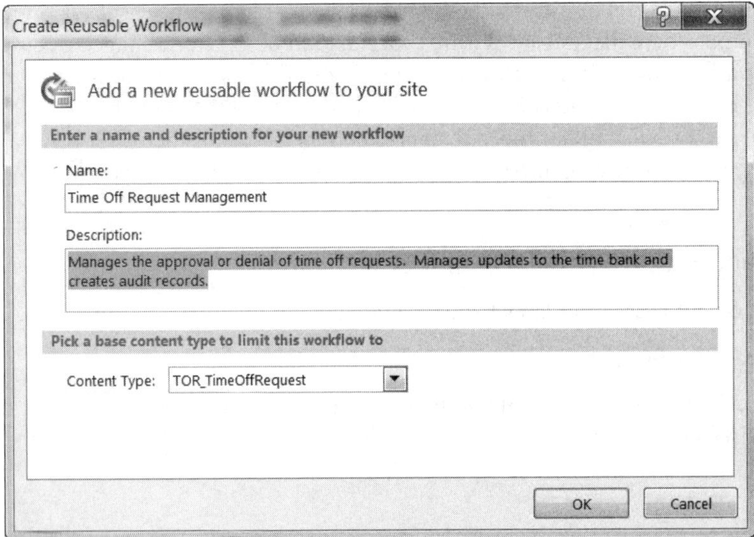

FIGURE 5-5

4. Provide a name that is clear and friendly to your end users.
5. Don't skimp on a description because this also appears to people who view the workflow. It's all too common in the SharePoint world for seasoned developers and enthusiastic power users alike to leave descriptions blank or too light in detail.

6. Lastly, pick the correct content type. In this case, `TOR_TimeOffRequest` (which you created previously).
7. Click OK.

At this point, you have created your first, albeit blank, reusable SharePoint Designer workflow.

This workflow has three major steps:

1. Validate that the time requested is minimally proper.
2. Submit the request for approval.
3. Update the time bank.

Now address each in order.

Validation

The workflow provides only one hard and fast validation: Time must be entered in four increments. To accomplish this, use the modulo function. Modulo is a math function that returns the remainder in division. Following are some examples:

- 4 / 4= 0. (There is no remainder.)
- 5 / 4 = 1 (4 goes into 5 once and then there is 1 left over.)
- 16 / 4= 0 (4 divides into 16 evenly.)

As you can see, you can test the requested number of hours by calculating the requested hour modulo 4. If that result is 0, then it's allowed.

To implement this validation, rename the default Step 1 step to `Validate Hours`. Use the Do Calculation step to calculate the modulo. At the insertion point, type `Do` or select the Do Calculation action from the Ribbon. SharePoint Designer inserts a line similar to Figure 5-6.

then Calculate value plus value (Output to Variable: calc)

FIGURE 5-6

SharePoint Designer gives you a chance to enter two values, an operator, and to save the result to a predefined variable named calc. SharePoint adds that variable calc to your workflow automatically. In this case, it's helpful, but you'll see next that it's not always a great thing.

SharePoint Designer enables you to pick the two values and the operation.

1. Use the familiar lookup dialog to pick the site column.
2. Enter `TOR_HoursRequested` for the first value option.
3. Enter the literal number 4 for the second value. Next, select mod as the operator.
4. Next, add a condition to test if the mod function returned a nonzero and hence, invalid number of hours.

5. Click the insertion point just after the calculate function; type `if` and then select If Any Value Equals Value from the list. You can do the same thing via the Ribbon by clicking the Condition button.
6. Check to see if the workflow variable Calc is not equal to 0.0. If it does not equal zero, then you want to set the status of the request to Rejected and to stop the workflow. Add these two actions to the workflow to finish up the validation logic.
7. Lastly, it's a good idea to log a message at the end of this validation step that shows that the validation passed.

When finished, your Validate Hours step looks like Figure 5-7.

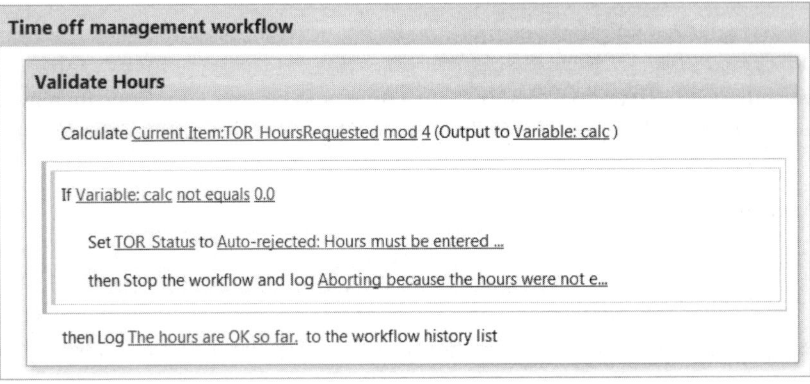

FIGURE 5-7

Seeking Approval

At this point, it's time to obtain approval from the user's manager. SharePoint Designer 2010 provides a much-improved solution to what used to be a thorny and thoroughly unsatisfying experience in the SharePoint 2007 lineup. There is now a single action that provides a tremendous amount of flexibility and depth that the 2007 product lacked.

To use it, create a new step and name it `Obtain Disposition`. This step needs the following actions:

1. Update the time bank to show the time that the user has requested off.
2. Notify the manager and obtain his response (approved or denied).
3. Review the result and act upon it.

Now walk through these actions in detail.

Before you ask the manager to review the request, you want to provide as much context information as possible. This way, the manager has the best and complete information available to make his decision. To this end, you need to look up the requestor's time bank entry, find how much time has already been requested, and increment that amount by the current request's amount. Unfortunately, this is a little tricky, and you're forced into to some awkward clicking to do this correctly. This issue is similar to what you faced in Chapter 4 vis-à-vis delegation. SharePoint Designer's lookup function is quite rigid. This rigidity bites you in this chapter when you figure out what value to update in the time bank. Ideally, you'd like to tell SharePoint Designer to Look Up the Value in the Time Bank Based on the Type of Request.

The user might request vacation time or personal time. SharePoint Designer won't let you do this in a general way because you must always select a specific field to look up. You can't specify a variable field whose value depends upon another. As a practical matter, this means that you need to have one lookup step for each type of time off request. This chapter just provides two (vacation and bereavement) but in a real-world scenario, there would be closer to eight or more types.

Accepting this, follow this approach. Define a general purpose workflow variable named `CurrentRequested`. Create a series of conditional calculations and lookups, one for each type you want to look up. Figure 5-8 shows an example lookup.

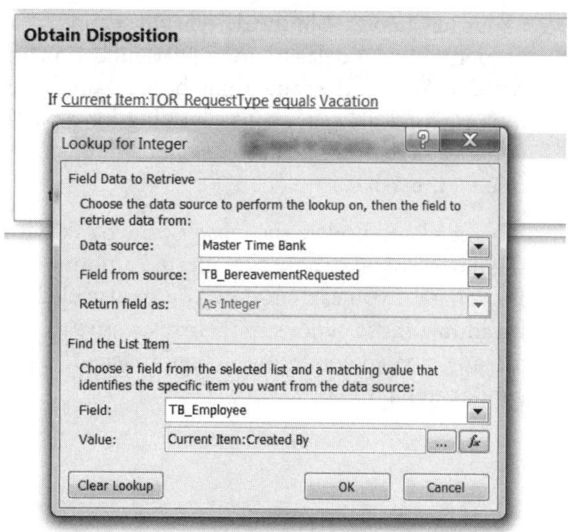

FIGURE 5-8

When finished, you have two conditional calculations, as shown in Figure 5-9.

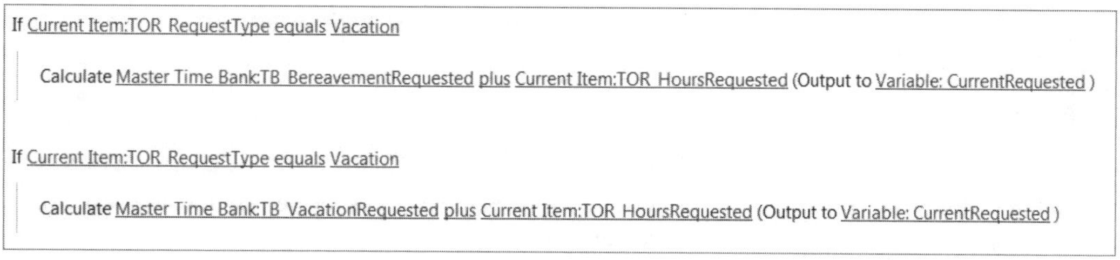

If Current Item:TOR RequestType equals Vacation

Calculate Master Time Bank:TB BereavementRequested plus Current Item:TOR HoursRequested (Output to Variable: CurrentRequested)

If Current Item:TOR RequestType equals Vacation

Calculate Master Time Bank:TB VacationRequested plus Current Item:TOR HoursRequested (Output to Variable: CurrentRequested)

FIGURE 5-9

Regardless of the type of request (bereavement or vacation), you now have the total amount requested, which includes not only the amount on this specific request, but also the summed amount for all the open unapproved requests.

The next step is to actually update the time bank with these values. For the same SharePoint Designer-is-rigid reasons, you need to conditionally execute one Update List Item action for each type of time off request. Update List Item is one of SharePoint Designer's available workflow actions. To use it, you need to know the list ("Master Time Bank") and the how you find the row you want to update. The "find the row" process is the process you learned about in Chapter 4 in the delegation section. You needed to find a delegate for a particular type of request. You do the same thing here except instead of looking for a delegate, you're looking for a particular employee's row in the master time bank custom list (see Figure 5-10).

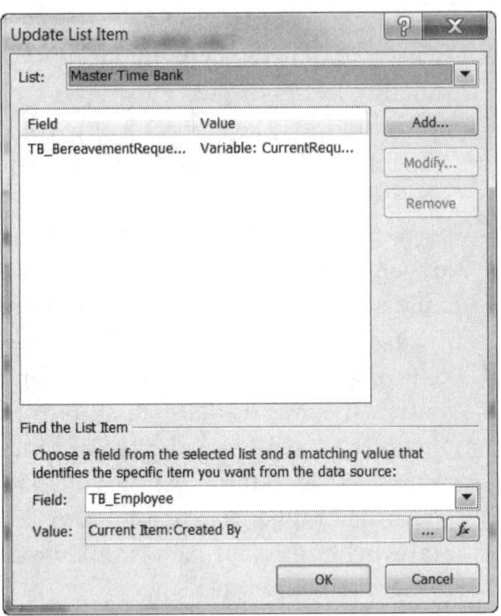

FIGURE 5-10

Go ahead and update the master time bank with the newly calculated total requested amount of time. Fortunately, you can cut down on mouse clicks by adding those actions to their respective already-created conditions. When finished, it looks similar to Figure 5-11.

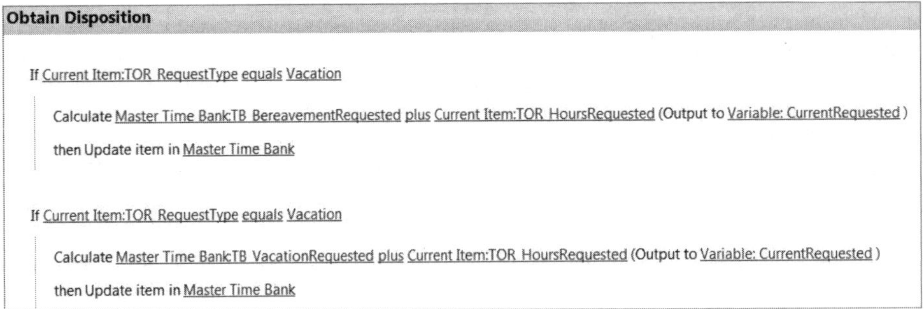

FIGURE 5-11

Figure 5-11 shows that you have two `if` statements that calculate and then update the total amount of requested time for vacation and bereavement times respectively.

With all that out of the way, it's time to obtain the direct manager's decision. In Chapter 3, "HR On-Boarding," you created a workflow that assigned tasks to users. The overall solution relied on a simple dashboard to track whether the assignees were following through on those tasks. You accomplished this by directly creating a task item using the Create Item action in SharePoint Designer. This time, you follow a different path.

SharePoint Designer 2010 workflow introduces a new, much more powerful activity called the Start Approval Process (SAP). The SAP activity is not your grandfather's SharePoint Designer 2007 activity! It effectively begins an entirely separate self-contained workflow whose job is to find out the manager's answer (is the time off approved or denied?), accounting for time limits, whether the record is deleted, pre- and post-activities, and more. Much of this was difficult or impossible to do with SharePoint Designer 2007. In this chapter, you use the barest minimum of what this powerful activity has to offer. Future chapters, most notably Chapter 8, "Enterprise: Authorization for Capital Expenditure", go into greater detail.

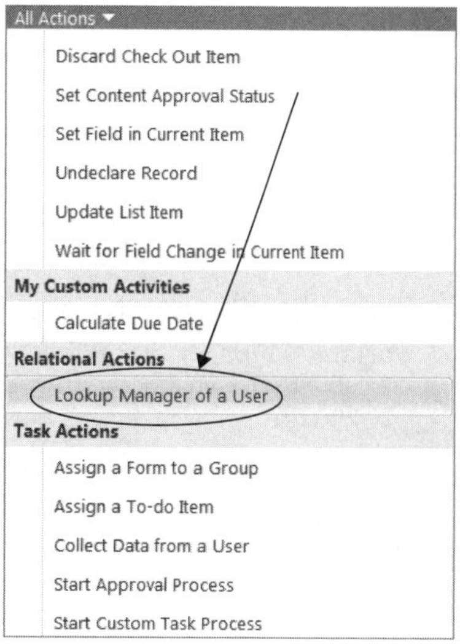

The purpose in using the SAP approval activity is to get the manager's response. Two important technical considerations arise: How do you know the user's manager? and how do you get the answer?

SharePoint Designer 2010 provides another new activity named, easily enough, Lookup Manager of a User. Figure 5-12 shows this activity on the Action drop-down from the SharePoint Designer Ribbon:

All Actions ▾
Discard Check Out Item
Set Content Approval Status
Set Field in Current Item
Undeclare Record
Update List Item
Wait for Field Change in Current Item
My Custom Activities
Calculate Due Date
Relational Actions
Lookup Manager of a User
Task Actions
Assign a Form to a Group
Assign a To-do Item
Collect Data from a User
Start Approval Process
Start Custom Task Process

FIGURE 5-12

Lookup Manager of a User is a general purpose lookup function that can help you find the manager of any given user. (See the sidebar for more background information on how SharePoint can do this.) You need the manager of the employee requesting time off. In this business solution, the employee is the person who created the record in the first place, so use that as input to the activity and get the manager that way.

HOW CAN SHAREPOINT FIGURE OUT YOUR MANAGER?

SharePoint maintains a separate database that profiles every user in your organization. SharePoint terms this the User Profile. SharePoint populates its own user profile database in a couple of ways. First and foremost, it pulls content from your company's Active Directory (AD). It then pulls it from optional secondary sources, such as an enterprisewide HR application, such as PeopleSoft. Lastly, depending on how it's configured, SharePoint enables users to directly update some of their user profile properties. This works well, but there's a garbage-in, garbage-out risk. If your company's AD doesn't have managers populated correctly, then SharePoint can't figure it out. Therefore, you need to have a clean AD or some other authoritative source pushing this information to SharePoint on a regular basis.

Like many SharePoint Designer activities, when you add the action to your workflow, it creates a new workflow variable for you. In this activity's case, it creates a workflow variable named Manager.

Add the activity after the two `if` conditions, and then click This User. From the dialog box, select User Who Created Current Item, and click OK, as shown in Figure 5-13.

With this completed, you now have the user's manager safely tucked away in the manager workflow variable.

Now it's time to ask the manager for his answer. To do this, simply add the task, Start Approval Process, as shown in Figure 5-14.

This inserts the activity at the insertion point. Update the Manager input field with the workflow variable Manager that you just used with the lookup activity.

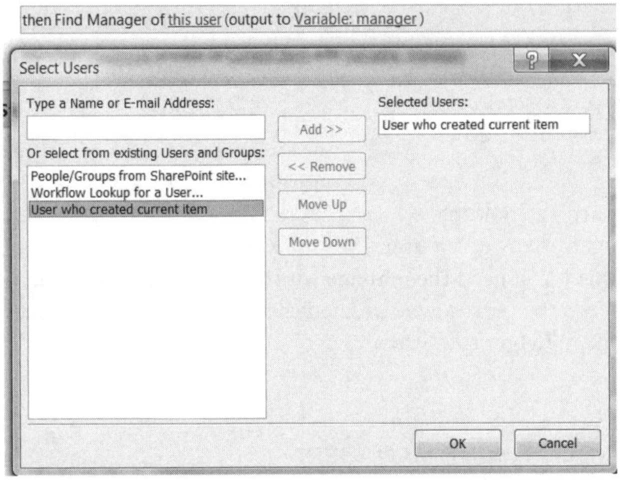

FIGURE 5-13

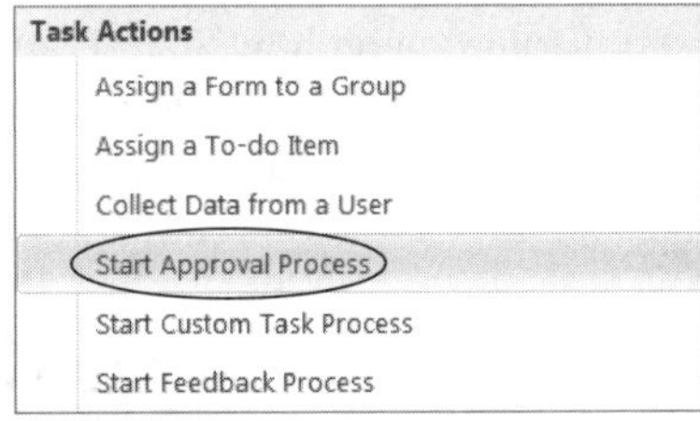

FIGURE 5-14

The SAP activity adds about a dozen workflow variables to your solution. There are a few negative side effects. First, it adds a bunch of undifferentiated workflow variables without any particular naming convention. As a result, it can be confusing when you look at your workflow variables altogether. Second, many of these are not useful most of the time, so it's just a cluttered situation. Lastly, if you delete the action, the workflow variables remain. Worse, if you add it, delete it, and then add another one, you get double the number of workflow variables — one set for the first time you added it and then another for the second (with an unhelpful "1" appended to each variable name this time). Be aware of this. If you do accidentally add too many of these activities to your workflow, there is a slightly easier way to do the clean described at `http://www.mstechblogs.com/paul/manually-edit-spd-xoml-file-to-clean-up-variables`.

For the purposes of this solution and specifically for the scaled down version of the solution in this chapter, that's all you're going to do with that activity.

At runtime, SharePoint assigns a task to the manager, asking for him to approve or deny the request. The manager is notified by email and is given a simple user interface to view the request and decide whether it should be approved. After the manager approves or denies the request, SharePoint Designer workflow continues on to the next defined steps.

When the SharePoint Designer workflow resumes, it's time to figure out what the manager decided to do. This is easy. One of the variables that the SAP activity added is named `isItemApproved`, as shown in Figure 5-15.

The `isItemApproved` variable is set to true if the manager approved it and false if not. Using this fact, you can now move to the final major step in the workflow.

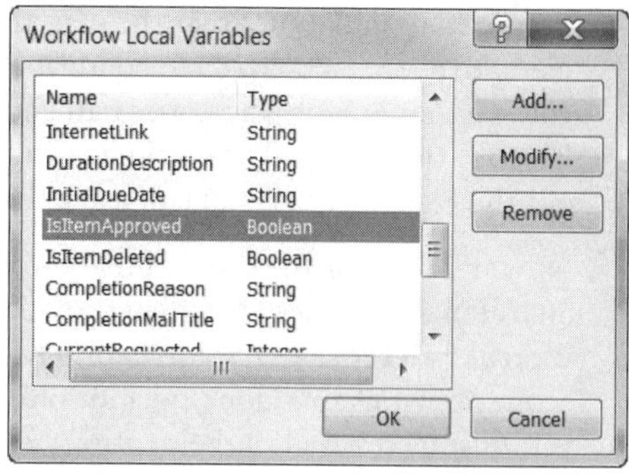

FIGURE 5-15

Update the Time Bank

If the manager approved the request, you need to update the time bank by decrementing the amount requested and incrementing the amount of time that was approved. On the other hand, if the manager denied the time off request, then you want to decrement the amount requested and leave it at that.

This is basically no different from the initial set of `if` conditions that you implemented while setting up the approval request. Because a lot of individual activities are logically grouped together, it makes sense to create new substeps. A substep is just a step within a step. Create a substep by clicking the insertion point where you want to add it; then click the Step button in the Ribbon. Do this now by following these steps:

1. Add a condition, `If Variable:IsItemApproved` equals Yes.
2. Click the insertion point directly after this condition.
3. Click the Step button.

When finished, your SharePoint Designer screen should look Figure 5-16.

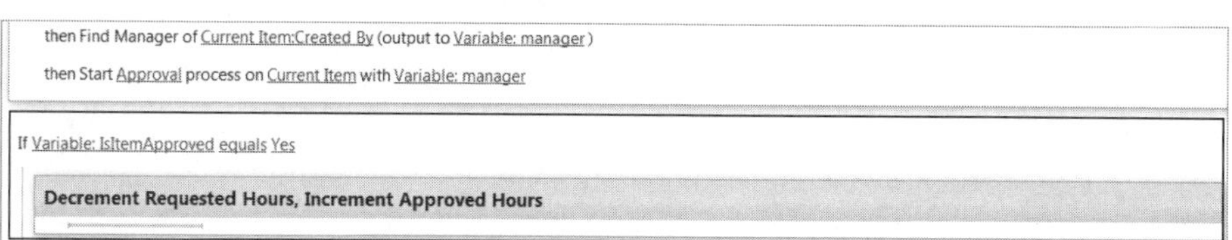

FIGURE 5-16

As always, be sure to provide a meaningful label for your steps (refer to Figure 5-16). Figure 5-16 shows the framework of activities that take place when the item is approved. You also need to have a mirrored structure for the other case, when the manager denied it. This requires a little mousal dexterity. You need to move the mouse to the precise correct location and right-click, as shown in Figure 5-17.

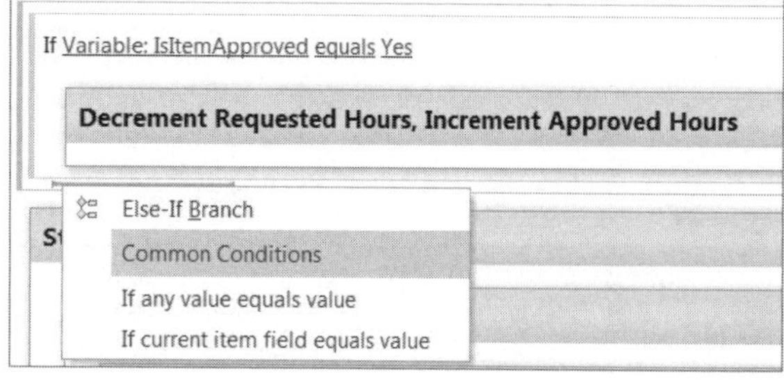

FIGURE 5-17

You need to make sure that the insertion point is in the specific spot just outside of the `If Variable:IsItemApproved` condition. Click `Else-If` Branch, and SharePoint Designer rewards you with an `else` branch. You can chain multiples of these together, each with its own condition. Because there are only two choices in this case (approve or deny) and you've already explicitly called out the approve case, you can leave this as a simple `else` block.

Now it's time for the some of the hardest and most frustrating clicking you'll have to do for a while. SharePoint Designer workflow provides a nice declarative way for creating your workflow. However, it breaks all those declarations into tiny focused steps. As a result, you're forced into a lot of small-scope activities that don't do a lot on their own, or do something nearly identical to another activity yet must be rekeyed in their entirety every time. Now consider the case in which the manager approves a vacation request.

When vacation time is approved, you need to take the following set of discrete steps in SharePoint Designer to properly record changes to the time bank:

1. Calculate the new total approved hours.
2. Calculate the new total of requested hours.
3. Update the time bank with these new totals.

Just as you had to execute a group of nearly identical activities based on type of request (vacation or bereavement), you also do the same with these calculations. Figure 5-18 shows what it looks like when finished.

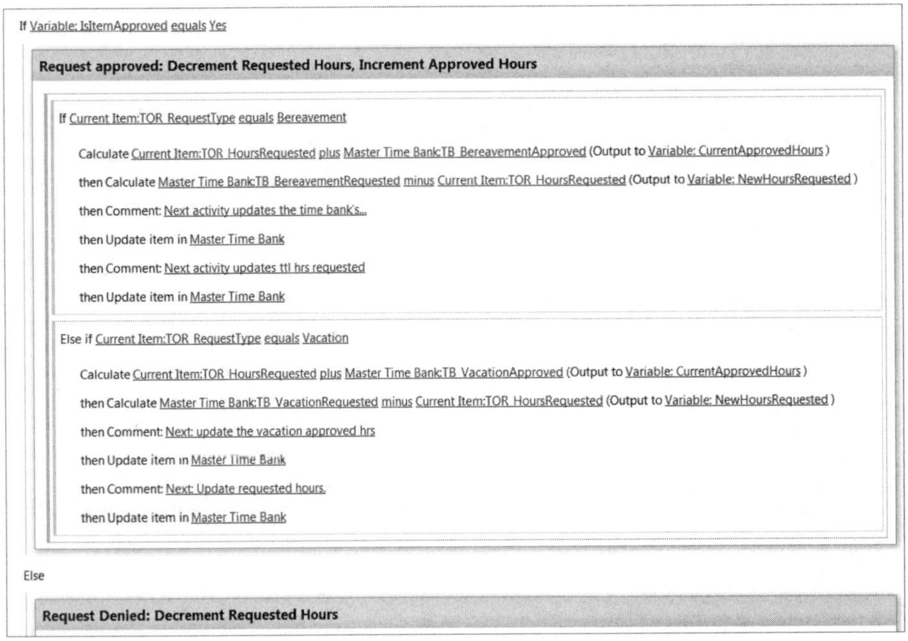

If Variable: IsItemApproved equals Yes

Request approved: Decrement Requested Hours, Increment Approved Hours

If Current Item:TOR RequestType equals Bereavement

Calculate Current Item:TOR HoursRequested plus Master Time Bank:TB BereavementApproved (Output to Variable: CurrentApprovedHours)

then Calculate Master Time Bank:TB BereavementRequested minus Current Item:TOR HoursRequested (Output to Variable: NewHoursRequested)

then Comment: Next activity updates the time bank's...

then Update item in Master Time Bank

then Comment: Next activity updates ttl hrs requested

then Update item in Master Time Bank

Else if Current Item:TOR RequestType equals Vacation

Calculate Current Item:TOR HoursRequested plus Master Time Bank:TB VacationApproved (Output to Variable: CurrentApprovedHours)

then Calculate Master Time Bank:TB VacationRequested minus Current Item:TOR HoursRequested (Output to Variable: NewHoursRequested)

then Comment: Next: update the vacation approved hrs

then Update item in Master Time Bank

then Comment: Next: Update requested hours.

then Update item in Master Time Bank

Else

Request Denied: Decrement Requested Hours

FIGURE 5-18

Note the use of the Comment activity in Figure 5-18. This is particularly useful when using the Update Item activity because it shows so little information in the default SharePoint Designer view.

The Request Denied scenario is nearly identical except that you don't update the approved hours because they were not approved.

Auditing

At this point, you have implemented the workflow process by creating a reusable workflow and attaching it to the time off request content type. One of the goals in this process is to create an audit trail. This is a straightforward thing to do with SharePoint Designer after you've gone to the trouble of creating the audit content type and creating the list that uses it. All you need to do is insert a few Create List Item activities in the main workflow, and you can audit to your heart's content. In this specific scenario, you should insert audit messages into at least the following areas:

- When the workflow first runs
- Just before you send the request to the manager for approval or denial
- Just after you receive the response. Include the actual response
- The final step in the workflow

When you audit at these times, you build an unambiguous history of what happened to the workflow and the overall end user request at every important step. An audit trail like this is a great source of analysis in the future. For instance, you may want to generate a report that shows the average amount of time that it takes for a manager to review these time off requests. That's easy to do with these audit messages; simply load them into Excel and do some Excel magic to get the answer.

The only tricky bit with the audit trail is the hyperlink field. Recall that there's a site column on the audit site content type that contains a link back to the item. This is useful because SharePoint shows this link when users view the audit list. If they click it, they can see the original request — it's a kind of drill down function that end users enjoy.

To this end, you need to craft a URL that accomplishes this. Create a URL that links to the current item by way of `dispform.aspx`, which is an out-of-the-box SharePoint display function that knows how to display list items.

To create a functional hyperlink column in SharePoint Designer, you need two pieces of information: the URL to which you want to link and the description of that URL. Both pieces are saved into the hyperlink column, and you separate them with a comma and a space. For instance, to populate a column that links to `www.wrox.com` with a label, [click here to go to Wrox web site, you would populate the value like this:

```
http://www.wrox.com, [click here…]
```

The space following the comma is important or the whole thing won't work for you.

To create a functioning "display form" URL, you need the ID of the item. Because you run the work on the time off request list, you can get at that via a workflow lookup for ID on current item. Define a variable named `DispFormUrl` as a string. Then, set its value using the Set Worfklow Varible activity. Populate the dialog as shown in Figure 5-19.

You don't need to prefix `dispform.aspx` with `http://...` because SharePoint and your web browser can handle that automatically. You now have everything you need to create good audit messages related to this specific workflow process.

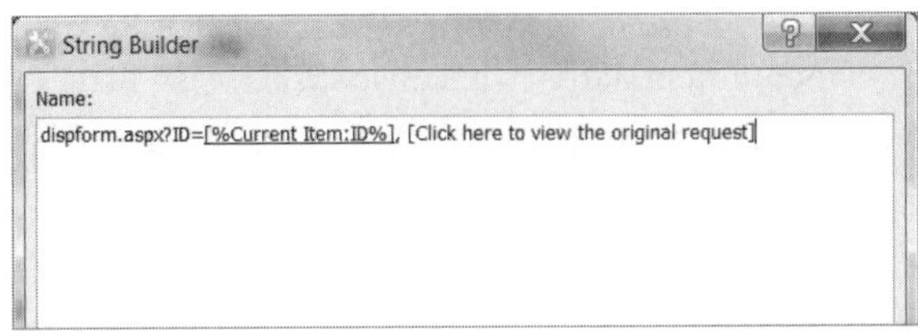

FIGURE 5-19

Managing the Process

This section glues all the discrete pieces together and walks you through the time off request process.

Review

By now, you've created three content types:

- Time bank
- Time off request
- Time off audit

The time bank and time audit content types are each married to a single SharePoint custom list with the same name. The time off request, on the other hand, is a list template. You create a separate time off request list based on that template for each manager. This enables you to secure the list as a whole so that only that manager's employees can access it. This further ensures that the manger can view and manage only his direct reports and not anyone else in the organization.

You create one workflow, and it's the most complex workflow you've created so far. It ensures some minimum validation using the modulo function. It sets up a call to and then seeks an approval decision from the employee's direct manager. It then updates the time bank with the result.

As it works through its paces, the workflow creates audit records. These audit records include some descriptive information and a hyperlink back to the original list item. Consider how these elements all work together.

When you first conceive a need for this solution and prepare to go live, you create the solution and deploy it to your production environment. The first thing you need to do is create one entry in the time bank custom list for each employee. Populate the time bank with that employee's specific information.

Next, you need to create multiple time off request lists. Each of these lists is based off the time off request template that you created earlier. If you have three managers with discrete managers, you would create three separate lists. Use standard SharePoint security to configure contributor access to these lists. For each manager-specific list, grant the contributor access to each of his direct reports.

As employees request time off, the workflow can generate audit messages and notify the direct manager of these requests. When the direct manager approves or denies these requests, the time bank is automatically updated.

Advanced Topics

The techniques and approach described to this point provide a good basis for a production-quality solution. There are many opportunities to improve upon this, ranging from simple to complex. This section describes those ideas.

Dashboards

This chapter did not provide a detailed walk-through to create a good visualization into the process. By their nature, the lists, to a great extent, stand on their own for process-view purposes. The time bank is straightforward, listing every employee's time. It makes sense to create several different views on this list and SharePoint's built-in sorting and filtering capabilities.

SharePoint provides one particularly interesting type of view: the calendar view. Managers can find this kind of view useful because it shows, at a glance, who is taking vacations. It overlays that onto a calendar and integrates multiple different employees' vacations. This provides a useful view for coverage purposes and can help the manager to know when to approve or deny vacation requests on this basis.

Year-End Refresh

Most U.S.-based companies hit the "start over" button on January 1st each year. If you haven't used your vacation, it's lost. In some cases, it must be used up in the first quarter of the following year. This can be a difficult issue to resolve in a programmatic way, and you may spend a lot of time making manual adjustments to the time bank. Use the audit trail in this case to track these kinds of manual changes. There's no reason why an HR administrator can't just go directly to the audit list and manually create a record. It won't be tied to a specific time off request, but that's doesn't matter.

Recording After-the-Fact Time Off Scenarios

Sometimes time is taken before it can be approved. In some cases, it's deliberate and in others it's accidental. In either case, the time bank must be updated to properly reflect it.

You can handle this in a few ways:

1. Go through the normal approval process after-the-fact. The employee fills out a request as normal but adds a comment that it was already taken.
2. HR can simply update the time bank directly. If HR goes that route, it should also manually create an audit record that explains the change.
3. Enhance the workflow to provide a new request type called auto-approve. Using a security technique described Chapter 7, "Facilities Management," allow just HR or employee managers to use this function.

The solution, as described in this chapter, provides a few good options for you. However, you can also extend it and by the time you finish this book, you'll have a number of technical and business patterns to draw upon in solving it your way.

Delegation

Chapter 4, "Helpdesk Ticketing," introduces delegation. Delegation is as relevant for time off management as it is for helpdesk tickets. Employees want to know whether their vacation time is approved.

SUMMARY

This chapter walked you through the thinking process, technical design, and actual implementation of a time off management solution. You learned some new techniques, most notably about reusable workflows and the powerful Start Approval Process activity. You also learned some less momentous technical bits, including the modulo function and how to create URL fields in content types and how to update them via workflow.

Just as important as the technical bits, you should also take away the importance of structuring your workflow process from a visual perspective. Affirmatively name your workflow variable and steps. Don't use SharePoint's nondescript "Step 1" or "calc4" style variable and step names. Sprinkle comments throughout the workflow, especially when a given activity (such as Update Item) is bereft of detail.

You continued to learn about some of SharePoint Designer workflow's limitations. In this solution, you needed to do a lot of clicking to do the calculations needed to update the time bank, and you had to repeat it over and over again for each type of request. This chapter confined itself to just two request types. A real-world solution typically requires eight or more types of time off requests. It's still manageable but the effort required to do this does start to raise the question, "Would it be better to implement this some other way?"

This chapter built upon the Chapter 4's key points. The next chapter ("Interview Scheduling") does the same. You can look forward to an in-depth discussion of the Start Approval Process family of SharePoint Designer workflow activities.

Interview Scheduling

WHAT'S IN THIS CHAPTER?

- Identifying and managing candidates and their multitude of related documents via the SharePoint 2010 document sets
- Arranging phone and face-to-face interviews with candidates and hiring managers
- Providing a scheduling mechanism that feeds into a dashboard
- Building an automated checklist to track important interviewing activities

The interview scheduling solution builds upon concepts from prior chapters, introduces and illustrates a few new technical tips, and provides the first detailed walk-through to create a dashboard.

WHAT IS THE INTERVIEW SCHEDULING PROCESS?

Even in these difficult economic times of high unemployment, companies still interview and hire new staff. Of course, companies might wait until the last possible moment to hire someone, meaning that existing full-time employees are often pushed to the breaking point, overworked, and spending more time than ever trying to get their job done. And even though generally fewer jobs are available, more people than ever apply for them, creating something of a perfect storm for HR departments and hiring managers alike. HR needs to schedule more candidates for fewer jobs and arrange for hiring manager calls and face-to-face meetings when the hiring managers have less time than ever.

The interview scheduling process kicks off after a job has been posted and the company has begun to receive inquiries for the open position. HR typically screens candidates against some kind of rubric that includes such things as education level, years of experience in similar roles, relevant background, and so on. After HR identifies a potential candidate, HR wants to schedule a phone call and/or face-to-face meeting with the appropriate hiring manager. That's where SharePoint comes into the picture.

HR has some notion as to the availability of the hiring managers and can work to schedule meetings with them and the candidate. For one-shot interviews, this is simple enough to do, but the problem becomes more difficult when there are multiple candidates with multiple managers and multiple rounds of interviews required for the same position.

Lastly, hiring managers may meet upward of a dozen candidates for a single position. These interviews may spread out over two or more weeks. With a lot on their mind, hiring managers' and HR's memory may become a little fuzzy when it comes to the older meetings.

The interview scheduling process encompasses some of the key workflow steps involved with interviewing and managing candidates. This chapter explains how to support this kind of process in SharePoint using out-of-the-box features and workflow.

PROBLEM CLASS

The interview scheduling problem represents a class of problems that revolve around, obviously enough, people scheduling. Different employees and nonemployees (hiring managers and interviewees) must meet at mutually convenient times. These people must collaborate (decide if they are mutually appropriate for the job). All parties may change their schedule at any time.

The people scheduling problem represents a class of common business problems that include real-world situations such as performance reviews. Managers must meet with their direct reports to provide performance feedback and set yearly goals.

By solving the interviewing scheduling problem, you can build an intellectual framework around which you can solve similar problems in its problem class as they inevitably arise in the future.

TECHNICAL PATTERNS

While solving the interview scheduling problem, you need to implement the following technical patterns:

- **Checklist:** HR departments establish a standard process by which new employee candidates are treated, evaluated, and ranked. The checklist pattern helps to track and ensure that the HR policy is followed.
- **Dashboard Feeder:** You create a dashboard that shows upcoming interviews and learn how you can extend this chapter's dashboard with additional end-user tools. The dashboard feeder pattern touches upon the design of your lists (they need to be defined with columns that hold onto valuable dashboard data) and the workflows. (They need to update those columns.)
- **Document Sets:** This chapter explains the new SharePoint 2010 document set feature and how to use them in SharePoint Designer workflows.

Beyond the patterns listed here, you can always leverage patterns discussed in earlier chapters.

BUSINESS PATTERNS

While solving the time off management problem, you can implement the following business patterns:

- **Reminders:** The technical pattern is straight-forward, but the business pattern is a little more complicated.
- **Checklist:** This business pattern has wide applicability to many different business processes. The checklist pattern supports business processes by establishing events or tasks that must be completed in total to consider a business process closed. In the example in this chapter, the checklist pattern ensures that the interview scheduling process and all its discrete tasks are clearly identified and tracked as they occur. The checklist pattern is a powerful tool to ensure completeness and correctness of a business process.

BUSINESS PROBLEM DESCRIPTION

The following sections describe the business requirements, list the actors and actions they take, and explain some of the special challenges that this problem and the requirements present to you as a SharePoint workflow developer.

Requirements Discussion

No requirements discussion is complete until you've met with your end users. If you actually build this solution, you'll want to do just that. The framework for those in-person requirements discussions can include the "who, what, and when" that newspaper writers around the world ask every day. That is, identify the actors (the "who") and their actions (the "what and when").

You need to satisfy three major groups of people with this solution: HR (so that they can manage the process), hiring managers (who interview candidates), and job candidates. You should address each of these various groups (actors) separately. This chapter addresses two of them in the walk-through; Chapter 9, "Marketing Contact Management," addresses how to handle external users. It's obviously difficult to interview job candidates (those external users) for this purpose, but you can start with recent hires at your company. After you identify a core set of requirements that satisfy, you merge them together into a grand unified theory of interview scheduling.

The HR department has the hardest job of all (at least as far as scheduling is concerned!). HR needs to match up hiring managers' precious time with the corresponding interviewees'. That's a complex requirement, simply stated. To assist this effort, the system should provide some kind of visual display, such as a calendar, to identify manager availability — a kind of time bank akin to the time off scheduling solution in Chapter 5, "Time Off Management."

While on the topic of visibility, it would also help the HR department to provide some kind of useful view showing the overall status of all the interviewees for a given position. Have they been screened? Have they been scheduled for a meeting? Did they actually take the meeting on schedule? Did they miss any meetings? This leads to one clear need: HR needs a dashboard to help it manage the process in the form of a checklist. As the interviewees and managers do their thing, the checklist should reflect this.

Managers' needs are different. Many managers wait until shortly before an interview to view the candidate's paperwork. (Typically, the resume but also the cover letter and maybe some aptitude tests, if that's the kind of thing your company does.) SharePoint should keep all this information in a convenient, easy-to-find location for your managers so that they have it all at their fingertips when it's time to conduct the actual interview. Lastly, managers should provide some immediate feedback on the interview. SharePoint should capture this information and account for different managerial styles; some will provide deep and voluminous analyses of the candidates they interview, but most will provide relatively little. This is an important requirement to meet because at some point, the manager and others involved in the hiring process need to make a decision. Sometimes, this may take place a week or two after the original interview, and these notes can be invaluable.

Finally, interviewee requirements must be considered. Granted, they are "just" candidates and don't necessarily warrant a great deal of "love and attention." However, if you go the trouble to provide a good solution that meets their needs, you can both impress them, differentiating yourself from the competition while also helping to create a smooth streamlined process that works best for the company, the managers, and the interviewees. Interviewee requirements are relatively light. You should provide some kind of email reminder system to reduce the risk of missed interviews. The chapter wrap-up discusses some advanced ideas, such as enabling direct interviewees access to their information in SharePoint over the public Internet.

Now let's break this discussion down into its component actors and their actions.

Actors

The solution this chapter puts forth is built upon a model that includes the following actors:

- **HR managers:** They initiate and manage the process.
- **Hiring managers:** Aside from the obvious need to conduct interviews, hiring managers must also record feedback.
- **Interviewees:** Naturally, they show up for interviews, but they also provide documentation that is saved into SharePoint by the HR team.
- **SharePoint:** Sends emails and manages the checklist automatically

These actors are relatively sophisticated and as such, you can expect a little more from them in terms of making sure they correctly do things. HR managers are sophisticated in the sense that they are well-trained and can rely upon this process to get their job done. Hiring managers are sophisticated or they wouldn't be managers. (Or at least you hope!)

Actions

All actors have their own set of activities and actions.

HR managers:

- Obtain job candidates' paperwork
- Schedule interviews
- Track the process and ensure that interviews take place on schedule
- Ensure that managers provide feedback
- Manage all direct communication with interviewees

Hiring managers:

- Provide availability for interviews
- Participate in interviews
- Record feedback about interviews

Interviewees:

- Provide documents (employment application, resume, and so on)
- Provide interview availability
- Accept/confirm interview times
- Notify HR if a previously confirmed interview time must change

SharePoint:

- Notify all parties by email at defined moments
- Create an audit trail

Challenges

This chapter won't spell in great detail how to address an obvious nice-to-have function a full-fledged interview scheduling system would implement. Specifically, it won't address direct system access for interviewees. It would be ideal if interviewees could directly apply for jobs, upload their resume, and manage their schedule online. SharePoint does provide all the tools you need to do this, but for scope reasons, you won't learn about that here. Don't worry, because Chapter 9, "Marketing Contact Management," does address these issues. The technical patterns and techniques you learn there can help you solve this problem for interview scheduling.

Requirements Summary

In summary, the requirements for this business solution are

- Set up mutually convenient interviewee and hiring manager meetings.
- Track the status of those meetings and the entire process on an interviewee-by-interviewee basis.
- Provide a single authoritative place for interviewee paperwork that hiring managers may rely upon to find interviewee resumes, cover letters, and the like.
- Remind hiring managers and interviewees about up-coming interviews.
- Provide a mechanism by which the hiring managers can record their impressions and thoughts about the interviewees.

SharePoint provides everything you need to meet these requirements. That said, the requirements summary does not go out of its way to say things such as, "SharePoint will. . . ," "A SharePoint document library will be configured" or "Using an SharePoint Designer workflow. . . ." In other words, the requirements are plain statements of need in straightforward English (or your favorite language). Never lose sight of that fact. If you focus first on the requirements, the better the chance you'll have of crafting a well-suited technical solution.

HIGH-LEVEL SOLUTION

In addition to following previous chapters' patterns (site content types, custom lists and workflow), you'll use a new SharePoint feature called documents sets. Document sets allow you treat a group of documents as a single unit for metadata purposes, which will be quite handy.

Solution Overview

To implement an interview scheduling solution, follow the same pattern described in the previous chapters. First think about the SharePoint content types that you need to hold onto all of your information. Then, you implement the workflow that you need to model the process as per the swim lane diagram.

This chapter adds a few new twists. First, you learn about a new feature in SharePoint 2010: the document set. Document sets enable you to treat a batch of documents as a single unit. This can be helpful in this and future solutions. Second, it provides the most detailed walk-through for a dashboard yet in the book.

This solution begins with content types. You create the following content types to support the workflows:

- **Job candidate:** Defines all the information relevant to the job candidate and can be used by both the manager and HR. This includes the candidate's name, contact information, and the job applied for.
- **Interview:** Tracks all the key activities that take place with this candidate. That includes who screened the candidate, whether the interview took place as scheduled, and whether the manager has written up post-interview notes.
- **Manager feedback:** Marks a document in a document set as being manager feedback (as opposed to any other document in the document set).

As usual, these content types back SharePoint lists, which are next.

The interview scheduling solution can leverage several SharePoint lists. Keep in mind that document library in SharePoint is also a list while you consider the following:

- **Job candidate:** Each job candidate is added to this list. You can use the ID column in this list to glue together all the many job candidates' information, which, in total, can span multiple documents, lists, and libraries.
- **Interview:** HR creates one entry in this list for every interview it schedules between a manager and the candidate.
- **Positions:** A lookup list that lists all the open jobs. The job candidate content type leverages this list.

These lists and their workflow partners comprise the delicate dance that is the interview scheduling solution.

Swim Lane Diagram

Figure 6-1 shows a swim lane diagram depicting the normal interview scheduling and management process flow.

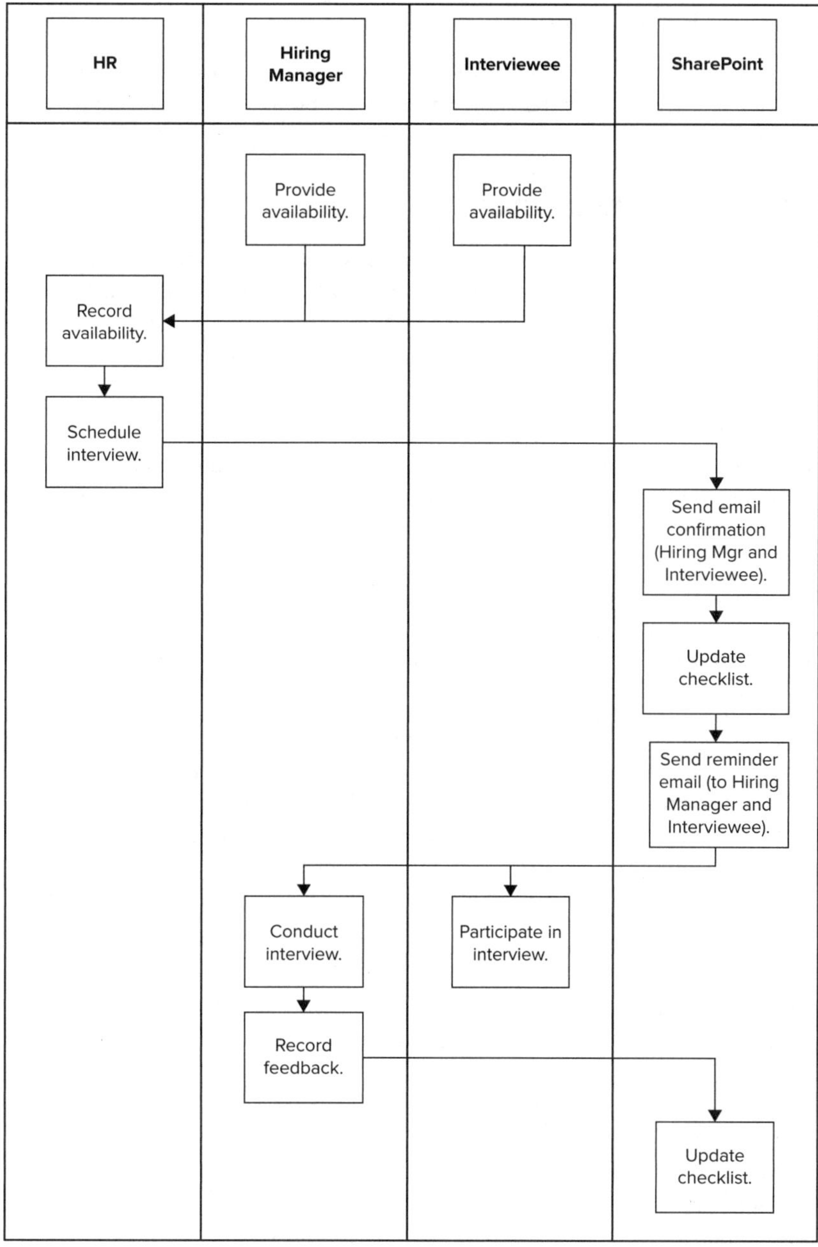

FIGURE 6-1

The idealized process works as follows:

- The hiring manager and the related interviewee provide their availability. HR records their availability and then actually schedules an interview.
- SharePoint sends an email notification to both parties and updates an activities checklist for tracking purposes. SharePoint waits until the day of the actual interview and then sends a reminder email to both the hiring manager and the interviewee.
- The hiring manager and interviewee meet or discuss by phone. The manager updates SharePoint with his feedback on the interview. SharePoint updates this interview process's checklist and you're done.

Technical Implementation Overview

This solution will see you follow the familiar pattern of creating site content types and custom lists. This time, you'll create a new kind of site content type, a Document Set. Your workflow will operate against the document set and provide a convenient single package of related job candidate documents that will help HR and managers track job candidate information.

Introducing Document Sets

A document set is a collection of documents that SharePoint treats as a single document. This means that you can create a document set, add many documents to that set, and yet move it around within SharePoint as if it were just one document. More useful, however, is that you can tag a document set. Before Microsoft introduced document sets with SharePoint 2010, there wasn't any easy way to do this. If you had a handful of identical documents (from a metadata/content type perspective) you had to either sling some awkward C# code or try to use the frequently misunderstood "folder" content type. Neither approach satisfied, for a variety of reasons that are no longer interesting because SharePoint 2010 solves the problem.

This business scenario cries out for document sets. Job candidates present multiple documents. These include resumes, cover letters, letters of recommendation, and so on. You can set up SharePoint to treat each of these as a single document. If you do that, HR will be uploading job candidate documents and entering the same information about that candidate over and over again, once for each document. That's obviously not a great solution, and if that were your only option, you'd be looking to another software platform to meet your goals.

Document sets are not available by default to your typical team site. To make document set functionality available to your site, you need to enable the appropriate-named *Site Collection* feature: Document Sets. (See Figure 6-2.) To do this, go to your site's settings and then navigate to the site collection settings. Under Site Collection Administration, click Site Collection Features (Figure 6-3). Scroll down (if necessary), and click the Activate button next to the Document Sets feature. SharePoint may take a few moments to respond to your click.

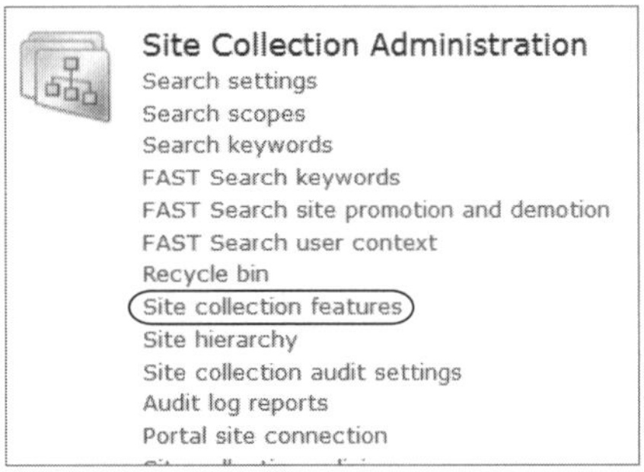

FIGURE 6-2

Document Sets

Provides the content types required for creating and using document sets. Create a document set when you want to manage multiple documents as a single work product.

Deactivate | Active

FIGURE 6-3

When you enable the document set feature, you can create a new kind of content type whose parent is the Document Set, as shown in Figure 6-4.

Name and Description

Type a name and description for this content type. The description will be shown on the new button.

Name:
Interview Candidate

Description:

Parent Content Type:

Select parent content type from:
Document Set Content Types

Parent Content Type:
Document Set

Description:
Create a document set when you want to manage multiple documents as a single work product.

Group

Specify a site content type group. Categorizing content types into groups will make it easier for users to find them.

Put this site content type into:

Existing group:
Custom Content Types

New group:
HR Interview Scheduling

OK | Cancel

FIGURE 6-4

When you have a document set-enabled library, you can create new document sets. To do this, navigate to the library, and click New Document from the Ribbon. If you click Add Document from the main body of the page, SharePoint enables you to directly upload a single document. It doesn't make sense, but it is what it is (see Figure 6-5).

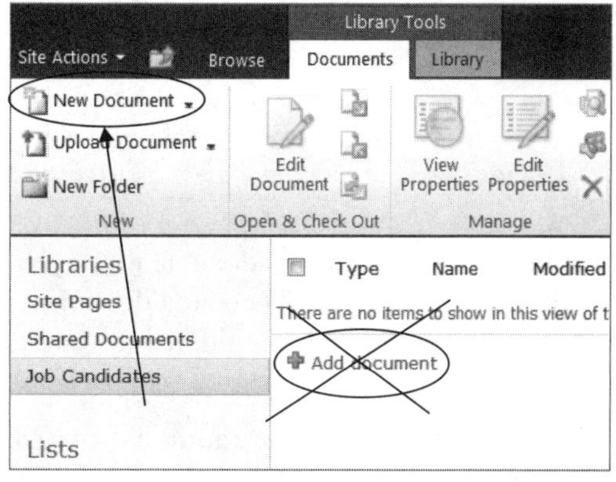

FIGURE 6-5

When you click New Document, SharePoint responds with the familiar metadata entry screen, prompting you for all the site columns associated with your document set. You can take away from this that document sets are quite like any other content type in SharePoint: They have site columns like every other content type and operate the same way. (You create the actual content types for this solution soon.) Figure 6-6 shows a sample data entry screen.

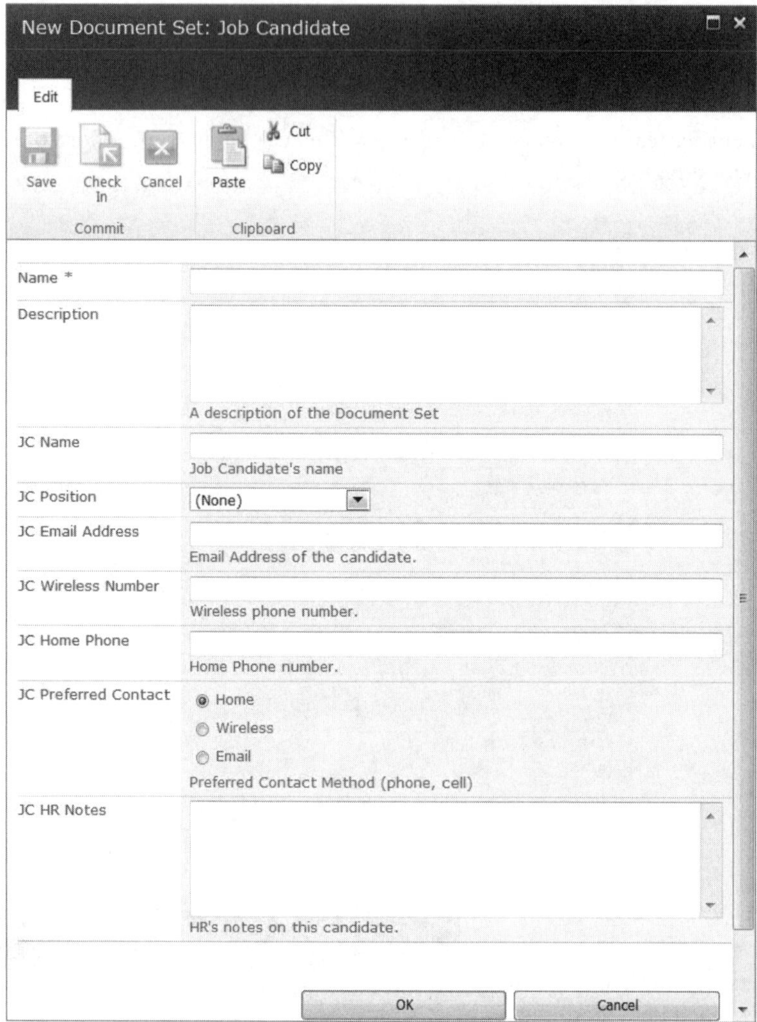

FIGURE 6-6

When you create a new document set, you are basically creating a basket into which you can add new documents. Newly created document sets are empty things. The document sets in this solution are going to hold job candidate information, such as resumes, job applications, manager feedback, and the like.

Document sets get some additional controls, adding a new "tower" named Document Set to the ribbon and some quick links to view/edit the properties. See Figure 6-7 for an example. You can also see that you can quickly run a workflow for the document set via its specific Ribbon.

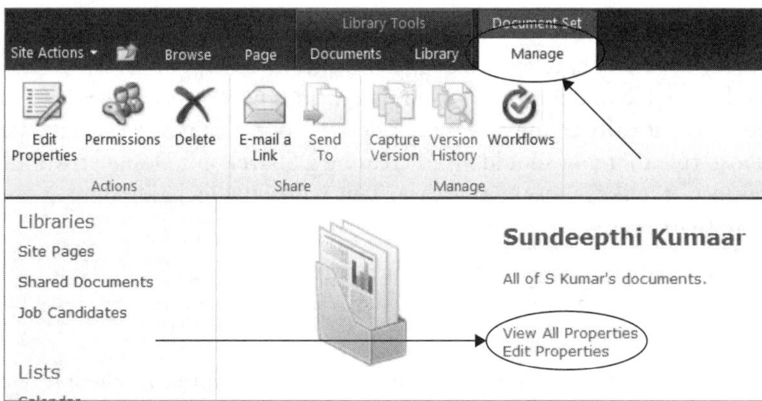

FIGURE 6-7

Content Types

As described in the previous section, you need content types that represent the following:

- **A job candidate:** Defines all the site columns that describe a job candidate. This includes columns for name, phone number, email, and so on. The job candidate content type is derived from the document set content type.
- **An interview checklist:** This serves a dual role. It is both an interview (who does the interview, when is the interview, and how will it be conducted?) and a checklist; did it take place on time? Was it canceled? Did the manager provide feedback?
- **Manager feedback:** An "empty" content type whose only real value is in the content type's name. Managers can provide any kind of feedback they want in any format. When they upload the feedback into the job candidate's document set, they specify the "manager feedback" content type. This makes it clear and easy to distinguish between manager feedback (there could be more than one manager feedback document) and job candidate documents.

Custom Lists and Libraries

Use the following custom lists and libraries to implement the solution:

- **Job candidates:** A document library configured to use the Job Candidate content type.
- **Interviews:** A custom list backed by the interview content type.

Dashboard

This section walks you through the process to create a simple but effective dashboard step by step. Because you know the kind of dashboard you want (a master overall view of upcoming interviews) you need to ensure that the workflows and end users naturally produce the information that drives the dashboard. This is the dashboard feeder concept. For instance, when an interview is scheduled, you create an entry in a list of upcoming interviews. When the interview occurs and manager feedback is required, you set a value on the list indicating that fact. The dashboard then uses that piece of information to provide an appropriate view to the user.

This becomes clearer as this chapter unfolds.

Workflows

The detailed walk-through describes two SharePoint Designer workflows in support of the following assumption: HR won't go to the trouble to define a job candidate who is never interviewed. Therefore, the system should automatically create a new interview as soon as a new job candidate is defined. This breaks the loose rule that you should avoid creating a SharePoint Designer workflow that runs automatically. However, it makes sense in this case. This workflow includes logic to ensure that it doesn't run more than once.

HR runs the second workflow manually. It simply creates a new entry in the interviews list for the candidate. HR can do this in the ordinary business case in which a job candidate is interviewed by more than one manager.

In both cases, these workflows follow the dashboard feeder pattern, making sure that the interviews list is populated with the information required to provide a dashboard.

DETAILED TECHNICAL IMPLEMENTATION

You will follow the usual process of creating site content types and associating them with lists. This time, you'll create a new type of content type based on SharePoint 2010's document set, and you'll use a helpful organizational technique: creating and using a content type that has no site columns. This solution's workflow component uses both automatically and manually scheduled workflows. Lastly, you'll create a detailed dashboard using SharePoint 2010 web part pages.

Setup

Like most SharePoint Designer-based solutions, you follow the same familiar pattern: Create content types and lists.

Supporting Lists

You will create three custom lists in this solution:

- **Job Candidates:** The core list around which the workflow and dashboards are built.
- **Interviews:** Represents an actual scheduled interview between a manager and an a job candidate.
- **Job Positions:** Job for which a job candidate can apply.

Each of these lists is backed by a content type as described in the next section.

Content Types

As with every other content type in each solution, it consists of two broad types of site columns: business and technical. End users enter data directly into business columns, and business columns appear on dashboards. Technical columns, on the other hand, do not generally appear to end users and instead support the technical needs of the solution. This solution calls for the following content types:

- Job candidate
- Manager feedback
- Interview

Job Candidate

This simple content type contains eight site columns, which are explored further in Table 6-1.

Business Columns:

- Name of the Candidate
- Email Address
- Home Phone
- Wireless Phone
- Position Applied For: This is a lookup column against a custom list that manages all the open positions
- Preferred Contact: Home, wireless, or email
- HR Notes: Any notes that the HR department adds for the candidate for everyone to see

Technical Columns:

- **Audit Link:** Like the status code, this is a sort of hybrid column. The workflow process assigns a value here, but the actual value is "technical" in nature because it's a URL constructed to point to a filtered view of the audit custom list. The idea is that HR or management can see all the stuff that happened with this candidate. This chapter doesn't actually build out the audit functionality. Instead, it provides the framework for you to do so yourself. Review Chapter 5's treatment on this subject for pointers.

TABLE 6-1: Job Candidates Columns

COLUMN NAME	COLUMN TYPE	ADDITIONAL SETTINGS
JC Email Address	Single Line of Text	None
JC HR Notes	Multiple Lines of Text	Append text. See note.
JC Home Phone	Single Line of Text	None
JC Name	Single Line of Text	None
JC Position	Lookup	Create a new list called "Positions" with no columns. Map this site column to that lookup and its Title column.
JC Preferred Contact	Choice	Enter choices: Home Phone Wireless Phone Email
JC Wireless Number	Single Line of Text	None
JC Audit Link	Hyperlink or Picture	Format URL as Hyperlink

Figure 6-8 shows the completed content type. Note the naming convention of "JC_" with these site columns. As usual, the goal is to differentiate these columns from all the other site columns when you view them in the site column administrative screens. This naming convention is actually different from previous chapters, which is deliberate. The most important points about a naming convention are that it exists and is applied consistently.

Next, create a new site content type with these columns. For the first time, you'll use a new base content type — the document set. (Remember, you may need to enable document sets via your site's features; see "Introducing Document Sets" earlier in this chapter.) Figure 6-9 shows how.

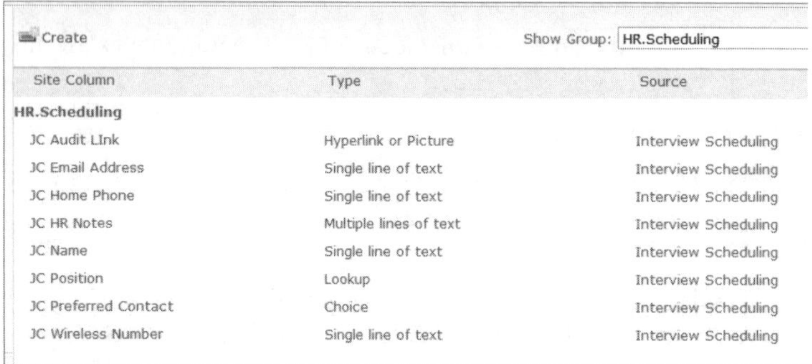

Create   Show Group: HR.Scheduling

Site Column	Type	Source
HR.Scheduling		
JC Audit LInk	Hyperlink or Picture	Interview Scheduling
JC Email Address	Single line of text	Interview Scheduling
JC Home Phone	Single line of text	Interview Scheduling
JC HR Notes	Multiple lines of text	Interview Scheduling
JC Name	Single line of text	Interview Scheduling
JC Position	Lookup	Interview Scheduling
JC Preferred Contact	Choice	Interview Scheduling
JC Wireless Number	Single line of text	Interview Scheduling

FIGURE 6-8

Name and Description

Type a name and description for this content type. The description will be shown on the new button.

Name: Job Candidate

Description:

Parent Content Type:

Select parent content type from: Document Set Content Types

Parent Content Type: Document Set

Description: Create a document set when you want to manage multiple documents as a single work product.

Group

Specify a site content type group. Categorizing content types into groups will make it easier for users to find them.

Put this site content type into:

Existing group: HR Interview Scheduling

New group: HR.InterviewScheduling

OK   Cancel

FIGURE 6-9

Interview

Next, you need a content type for the interviews. There may be multiple interviews for a given candidate. This content type is going to define a lookup content type with a twist; instead of the usual lookup against a boring list, it's actually going to do a lookup against the job candidates. This shows that lookup site columns can also be sourced document libraries, not just custom lists like you've used in the book so far. Because you can't create a lookup site column in a vacuum, you first need to create the job candidate library.

Create a new document library named Job Candidates. Enable content types via its advanced settings, and then add the JC Candidate content type to it.

With that out of the way, create the following business columns, using the information included in Table 6-2.

- **Candidate:** Lookup column for the candidate
- **The Position:** Provides a simple reference point for managers and HR when they viewing the full list
- **Assigned to Manager:** The manager who conducts the interview
- **Type of Interview:** Phone, video conference, or in person
- **Date and Time of Interview:** When is the interview?
- **Interview Took Place?:** Indicates whether the interview took place as planned. This is a key piece of data for the dashboard.
- **Manager Feedback Captured?:** Did the manager feedback happen? This is also a key piece of information for the dashboard.

TABLE 6-2: Interview Columns

COLUMN NAME	COLUMN TYPE	ADDITIONAL SETTINGS
Candidate Name	Lookup	Lookup against the Job Candidate's document library.
Position	Lookup	Backed by the Positions custom list
Type of Interview	Choice	Values: Phone, Video Conference, In Person
Interviewing With	Person or Group	None
Date Time Scheduled	Date and Time	Enable both date and time for this column
Interview Took Place?	Yes/No	Default to No
Manager Feedback Captures?	Yes/No	Default to No

Create a site content type named Interview, and add the above site columns. Remember, choose them in the order you want them to appear on data entry screens because that is the default display order.

Manager Feedback

The manager feedback content type will be added to the candidate's document set. When managers upload their feedback, be it a Microsoft Word document, a recommended format provided by HR, or a simple .txt file, they tag it as manager feedback. This is a useful technique, helping you organize content, create views, and enhance SharePoint's search capabilities.

Content Types Summary

If you followed the instructions so far, you just created about a dozen or more site columns and three content types. The content types are:

- Job Candidate
- Interview
- Manager Feedback

These content types must now be attached to some SharePoint custom lists.

Create Workflows

In this walk-through, you create two workflows: one that executes automatically when a job candidate is created in the job candidate list. The second workflow is run manually by HR when a particular job candidate will be interviewed by more than one manager.

Create Initial Interview

You learn two new techniques while you create this workflow: 1) How to determine whether an item exists in a list and 2) Important facts about lookup columns in workflows.

The initial interview workflow is designed to be run automatically and creates the first interview for the candidate. Actually, it creates a placeholder item for an interview; HR still needs to work with the manager on an available time slot.

Fire up SharePoint Designer, and connect to your SharePoint development site. Create a new list workflow on the library, Job Candidates, that you created in the previous section. Give your workflow a name: Set Up First Interview. When you finish this initial setup, SharePoint Designer should look similar to Figure 6-10.

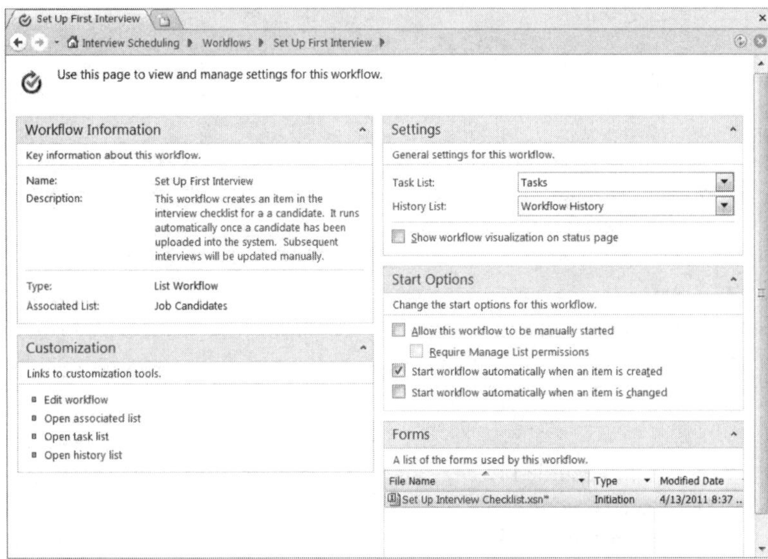

FIGURE 6-10

This workflow has three steps:

1. Determine whether the initial interview has been scheduled.
2. Abort the interview if it were previously scheduled.
3. Create the actual initial interview.

Now go through these one by one.

Determine if Already Scheduled

This step introduces a new technique: how to determine whether an item in a list already exists. This workflow should create only the initial interview. You don't want it creating multiple "first" interviews. To prevent this, you need to look to see if there's any existing interview for the current job candidate. How do you do that?

The answer is simple. Attempt to find a row with that candidate in the interview list. If you find it, you know the candidate already has an interview scheduled. Otherwise, they don't. SharePoint doesn't have a Check if List Item Exists function. Instead, you do this indirectly. Start by defining a new workflow variable named `ExistingScheduledInterviewID` whose type is `List Item Id` (see Figure 6-11). You attempt to assign this variable to the ID of the interview list in which the interview's candidate name matches the candidate's name on the current item. See Figure 6-12 for this lookup. At runtime, if SharePoint can't find that row, it assigns a value of zero to your workflow variable. You can test for the value and voilà! You now know whether an interview exists.

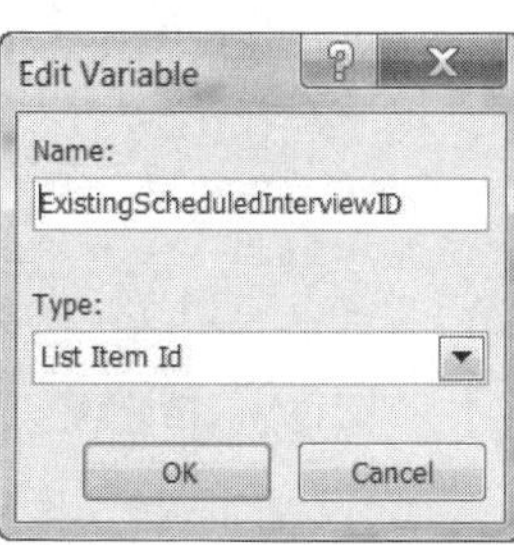

FIGURE 6-11

The next part is easy. You either abort the workflow or you create that initial interview. The latter introduces a new and interesting fact. Let's dig into it a bit.

> **COMMENTS IN WORKFLOWS**
>
> Look at Figure 6-12. The first action in the workflow is a Comment. Preceding chapters discuss Comments. Comments are very, very valuable, and you should pick up the habit of inserting them into all your workflows. Maintenance (the on-going and never-ending support, updates, and enhancements to technical solutions you and teammates create) comprises the largest part of a given solution's real lifetime. Helpful comments make this maintenance much easier and ultimately enables you and your team to spend more time on interesting new work and less time on boring maintenance work. (In most cases, Comments are stripped from the book's examples to help focus on the key part of the discussion).
>
> *(continues)*

(continued)

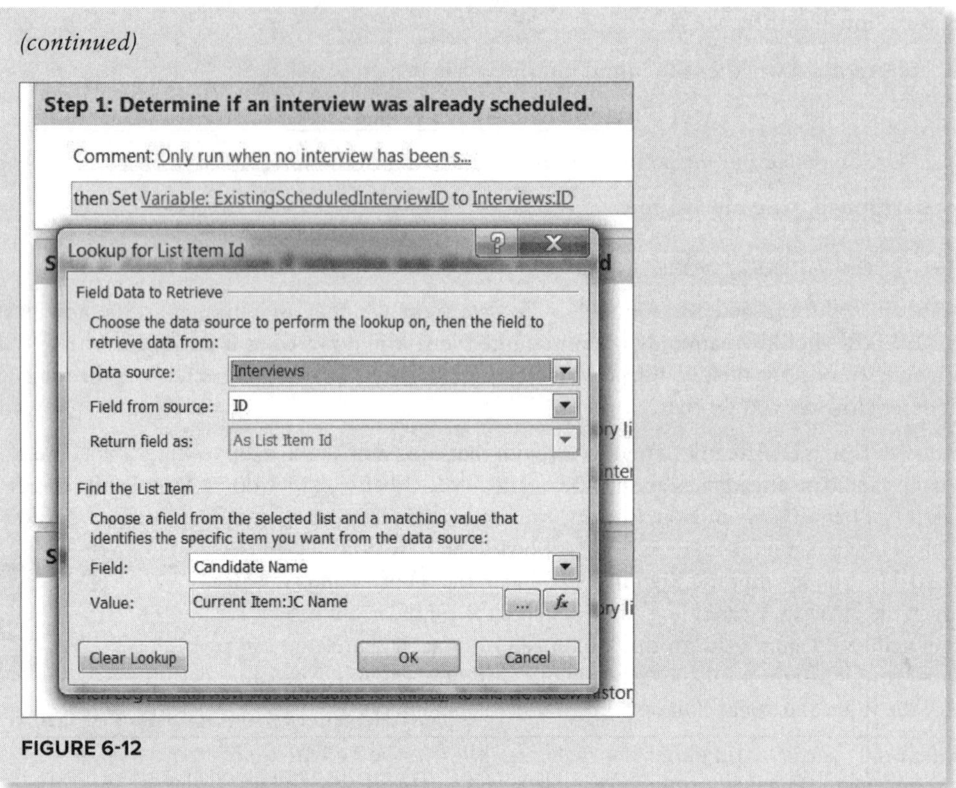

FIGURE 6-12

Create New Interview Item

You've created items before, going all the way back to the HR on-boarding solution. You do it again here. The only difference this time is that you update a couple of lookup columns; and although the process has a "natural" feel to it, it's a good time to explain the concept of a list ID in a little more detail. Before that, look at Figure 6-13, which shows this relatively simple step that has comment, create item, and log activities.

Figure 6-14 drills down into the activity that creates the initial interview record. Note the two columns, Position and Candidate Name. Both of these are IDs. In SharePoint, every list (and remember, document libraries are just another kind of list) has an ID column. IDs are numeric and start with the number 1 and always increment. If you allow users to delete items from lists, you will get gaps in the ID sequence.

Even though "under the covers," the Position and Candidate Name are IDs, SharePoint is smart enough to display the friendly value of that column in lists and list views. See Figure 6-15 for an example.

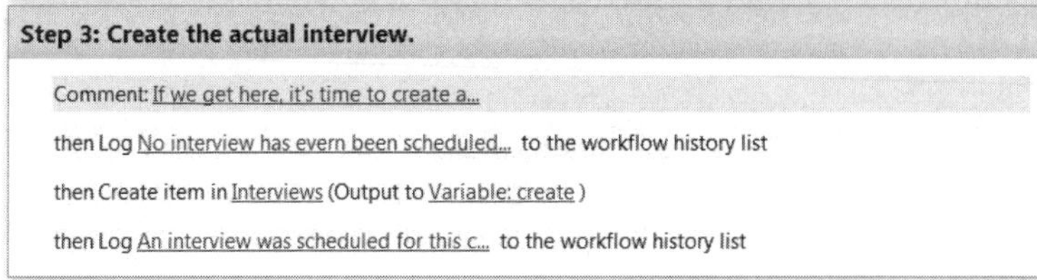

FIGURE 6-13

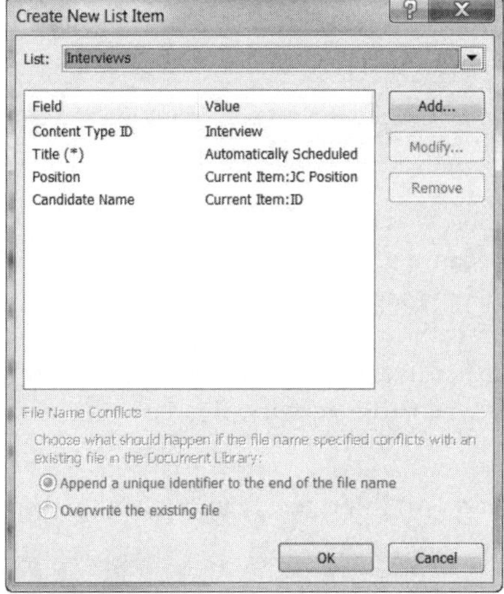

FIGURE 6-14

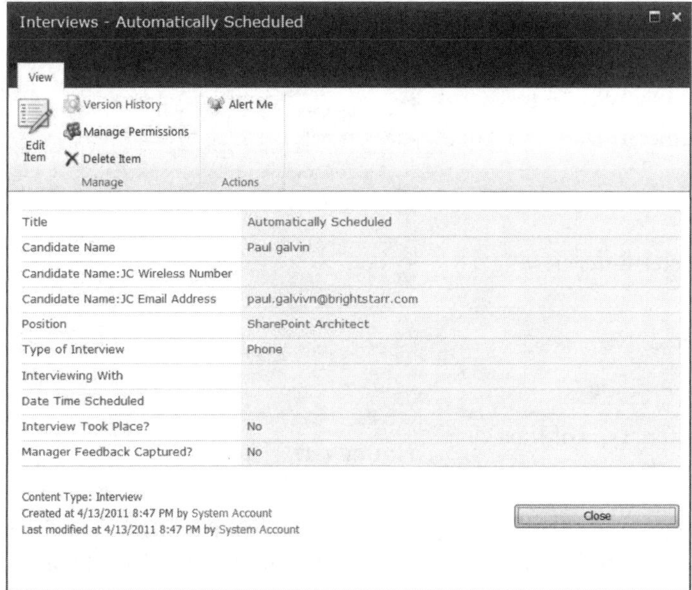

FIGURE 6-15

Manually Set Up an Interview

HR invokes this workflow manually when it knows it needs to set up a second interview (or more) for a job candidate. Because it runs manually, you have the opportunity to prompt HR for some additional information. Create three workflow initiation parameters:

- Date and time (see Figure 6-16)
- Name of the manager
- Type of interview (Phone, Video Conference or In Person)

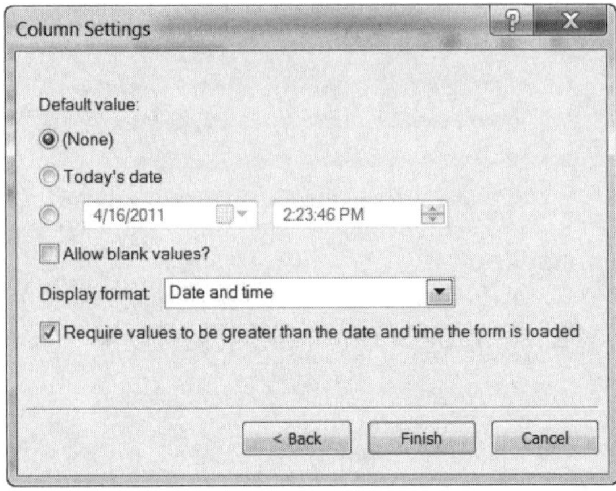

FIGURE 6-16

When you define the initiation parameter for the "Name of the manager," resist the temptation to enable multiple users. You may be tempted because group interviews are common, and it makes sense to create one interview but select multiple managers for the same time slot. Designer workflows won't let you iterate through lists like this, however, so don't paint yourself into a corner. If you find a need for this kind of iteration, either live with the limitation, give up on SharePoint Designer, or extend SharePoint Designer with a custom activity. Read about custom activities in Chapter 13.

What does this manual workflow accomplish? It simply creates an interview item. Create the list items as follows:

- **Content Type ID:** Leave as default value, Interview
- **Title:** Manually scheduled interview for [[%Current Item:JC Name%]]
- **Candidate Name:** Current Item: JC Name
- **Date time Scheduled:** Parameter: Date and Time of Interview
- **Interview Took Place:** No
- **Interviewing With:** Parameter: Interviewing Manager
- **Manager Feedback Captured:** No
- **Position:** Current Item: JC Position
- **Type of Interview:** Parameter: Type of Interview

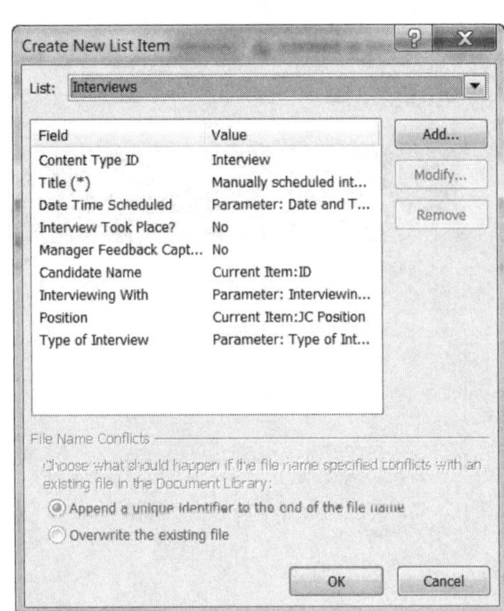

FIGURE 6-17

It can look similar to Figure 6-17.

When you assign a value to Interviewing With, you need to specify how SharePoint Designer should treat the value. All site columns have an internal representation and "natural" way of working. Text works with text, numbers work with numbers, and so on. However, some can be represented in more than one way. People and groups are one such item. SharePoint Designer enables you to do this kind of conversion via the Return Field As option (see Figure 6-18). Unfortunately, SharePoint Designer enables you to create a workflow and specify a return-as type that will fail at run-time. To avoid that in this case, specify the return as User Ids, Semicolon Delimited.

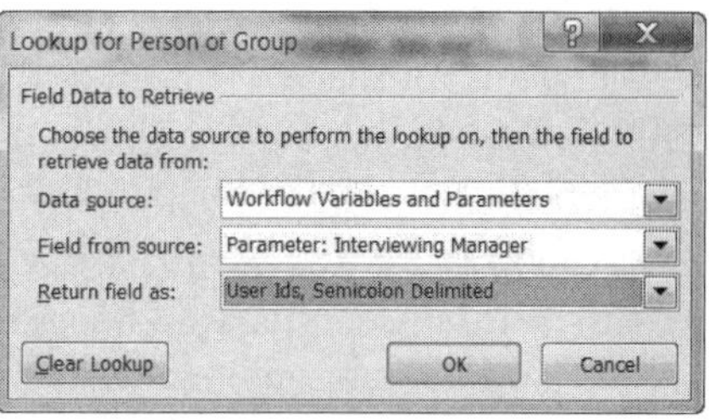

FIGURE 6-18

IDENTIFY AND CORRECT "RETURN AS" PROBLEMS

If you select the value As String from the Return Field As options, SharePoint presents you with one of its classically infuriating run-time errors. First, it simply tells you Error Occurred if you keep the status on the view (see Figure 6-19). When you click the error status, SharePoint tells you: "The workflow could not update the item, possibly because one or more columns for the item require a different type of information." See Figure 6-20. Could Microsoft have come up with a more vague and confusing error message? Probably not. This speaks once again to develop a cyclical attitude toward implementing these solutions. If you had added a bunch more actions to this workflow, you may not know what caused the issue. Because the workflow has only one action at this point, it's easy to pinpoint the error.

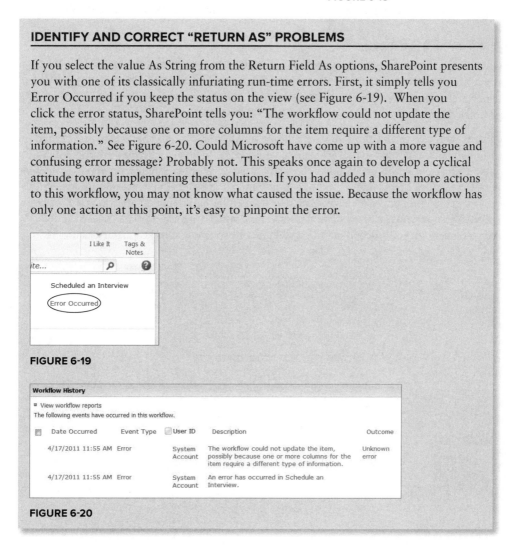

I Like It
Tags & Notes
ite...
Scheduled an Interview
Error Occurred

FIGURE 6-19

Workflow History

- View workflow reports

The following events have occurred in this workflow.

Date Occurred	Event Type	User ID	Description	Outcome
4/17/2011 11:55 AM	Error	System Account	The workflow could not update the item, possibly because one or more columns for the item require a different type of information.	Unknown error
4/17/2011 11:55 AM	Error	System Account	An error has occurred in Schedule an Interview.	

FIGURE 6-20

Create the Dashboard

The introduction to this chapter discussed the dashboard feeder and checklist technical pattern. The workflows in this solution cooperate together to update the Interviews list. These updates enable you to create a go-to dashboard that HR can use to manage the overall process. To build the dashboard, create a new kind of SharePoint artifact: the web part page. You add several new views to the interviews list and then add the interviews list to the web part page. The page, working with the interviews list and its views provides everything you need to create a simple yet highly effective dashboard.

Dashboards thrive on data. When you work on defining requirements for a solution, always make sure to discuss dashboards' hopes and needs. With a dashboard in mind, define your content types and workflows by adding site columns and additional workflow steps to populate them.

This solution's dashboard consists of a web part page, some content editor and list web parts, and list views. Start by creating a web part page to hold the dashboard's display elements.

Create a Web Part Page

Create a web part page much like you do for a custom list. Go to Site Actions, and click More Options. SharePoint responds with the usual selection dialog box. This time, click Page in the left filter pane. SharePoint presents you with at least two options: a Page and a Web Part Page. Click the latter. Click Create.

From here, you need to give the web part page a name. Enter Job Candidates Dashboard, and then select a layout template. It doesn't matter which one you select, and you should play around with different layouts to figure out which one you like the best for any given situation. If you follow along with the book, select Header, Left Column, Body, as shown in Figure 6-21. Finally, be sure to save it in the right place. You actually create a new .aspx page that needs to be saved into an appropriate library. SharePoint will probably show you the default Site Assets library, which isn't appropriate. Select Site Pages instead, or even consider creating a document library whose only purpose is to keep your dashboards.

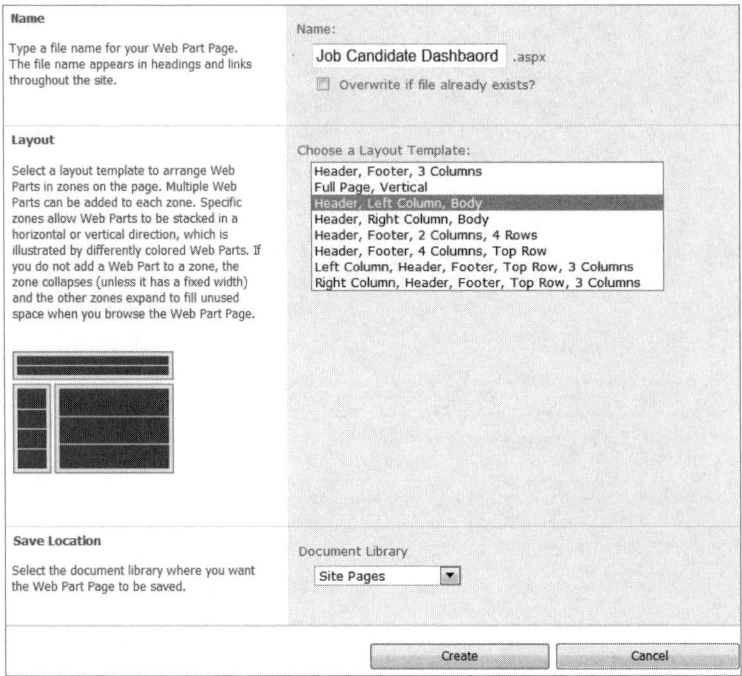

FIGURE 6-21

When you click the Create button, SharePoint provides you with a blank canvas upon which you can draw the dashboard daVinci always wanted (or would have wanted, if he used SharePoint). More on that after you create your views.

Create Views

A dashboard is only as useful as the information it provides, and the kind of dashboard you create in this chapter provides information by way of list views. The SharePoint Designer workflows have been carefully crafted so that they feed the Interviews custom list, which has all the important information that a dashboard should present.

Creating views is simple; although, it varies from the old days in MOSS and WSS. Access the view create/edit function via the breadcrumb. Click the view name, and SharePoint displays a drop-down menu, as shown in Figure 6-22.

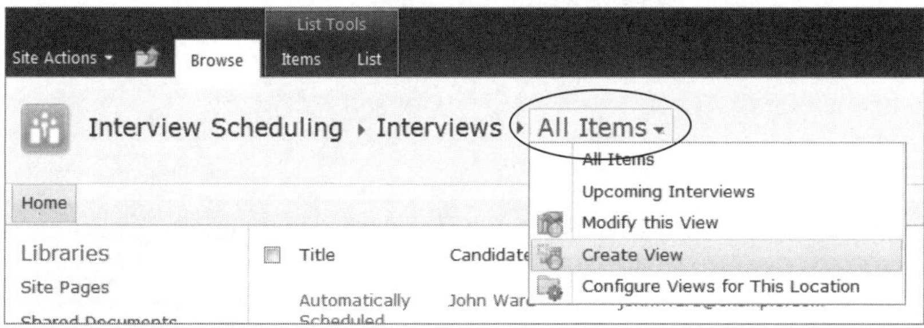

FIGURE 6-22

SharePoint enables you to create many views. For now, you create just one view so that you can see how all these glue together. In the summary, you can read about some other potential views that may appeal to your end users.

Create a view as described next.

View Name

Name the view Upcoming Interviews.

Columns

- Display the following columns:
    - Interviewing With
    - Position
    - Type of Interview
    - Date Time Scheduled

See Figure 6-23 to see what both Name and Columns look like when this configuration step finishes.

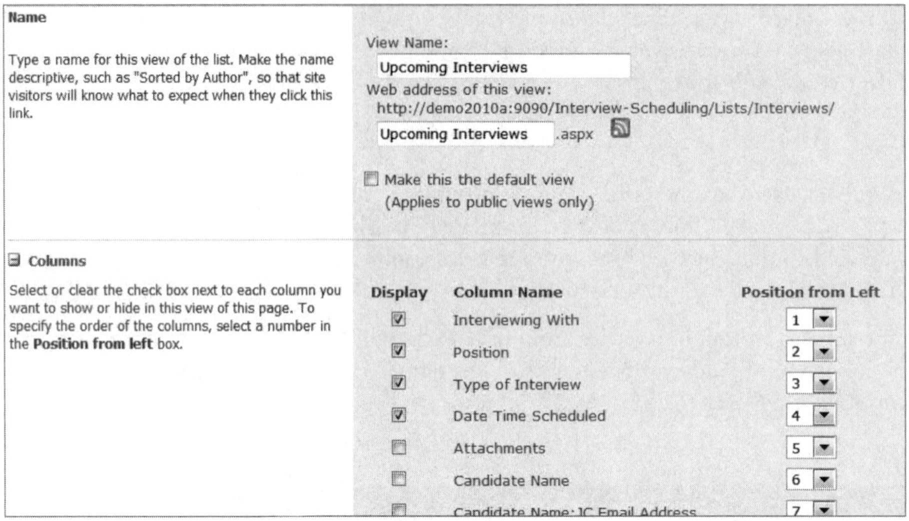

FIGURE 6-23

Sort

First sort by Candidate Name. Next, sort by Date Time Scheduled (see Figure 6-24).

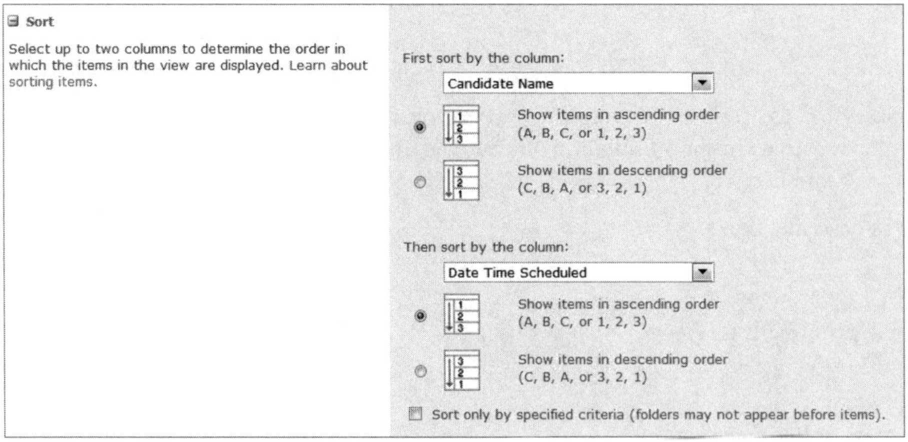

FIGURE 6-24

Filter

Next, specify how to filter the view. As its name implies, you want to show only future interviews, not past interviews. Select "Show Items Only When the Following is True, and then select Date Time Scheduled from the drop-down list labeled Show the Items When Column. Pick Is Greater Than or Equal To from the conditional drop-down, and enter [Today] in the Fill-in Field. Note that there are literally brackets around the word Today. See Figure 6-25 for help.

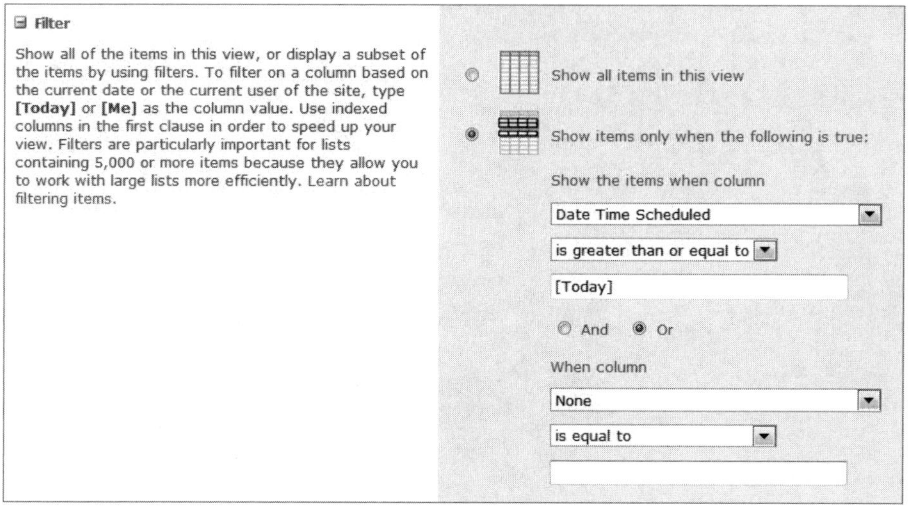

Filter

Show all of the items in this view, or display a subset of the items by using filters. To filter on a column based on the current date or the current user of the site, type **[Today]** or **[Me]** as the column value. Use indexed columns in the first clause in order to speed up your view. Filters are particularly important for lists containing 5,000 or more items because they allow you to work with large lists more efficiently. Learn about filtering items.

Show all items in this view
Show items only when the following is true:
Show the items when column
Date Time Scheduled
is greater than or equal to
[Today]
And Or
When column
None
is equal to

FIGURE 6-25

Group By

Finally, you want the dashboard to group interviews by job candidate. The grouping function has the side effect of showing the group by column, so you don't need to select from the columns list like you did when you first created the view. In the field, First Group by the Column, select Candidate Name. Down near the bottom of the section, click the word Expanded in the subsection, By Default, Show Groupings. See Figure 6-26 for a guide.

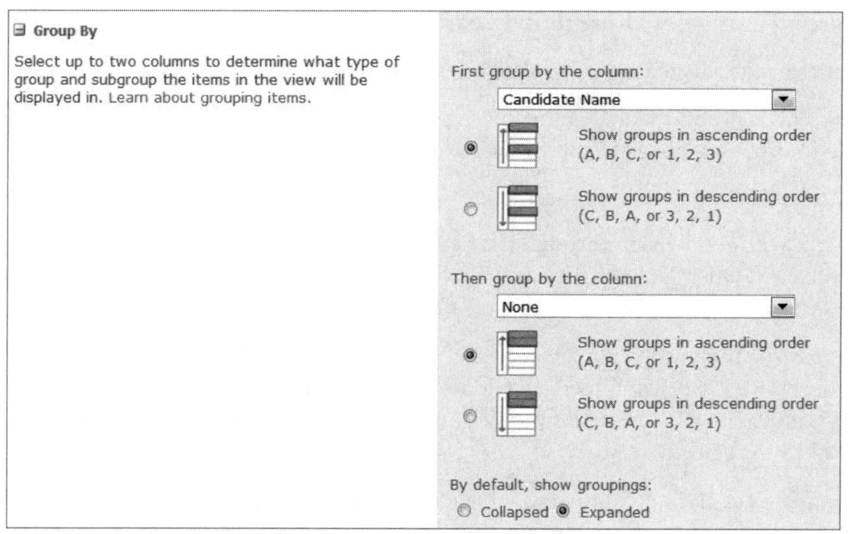

FIGURE 6-26

When you finish, SharePoint shows you the list with your new view. It should look something like Figure 6-27.

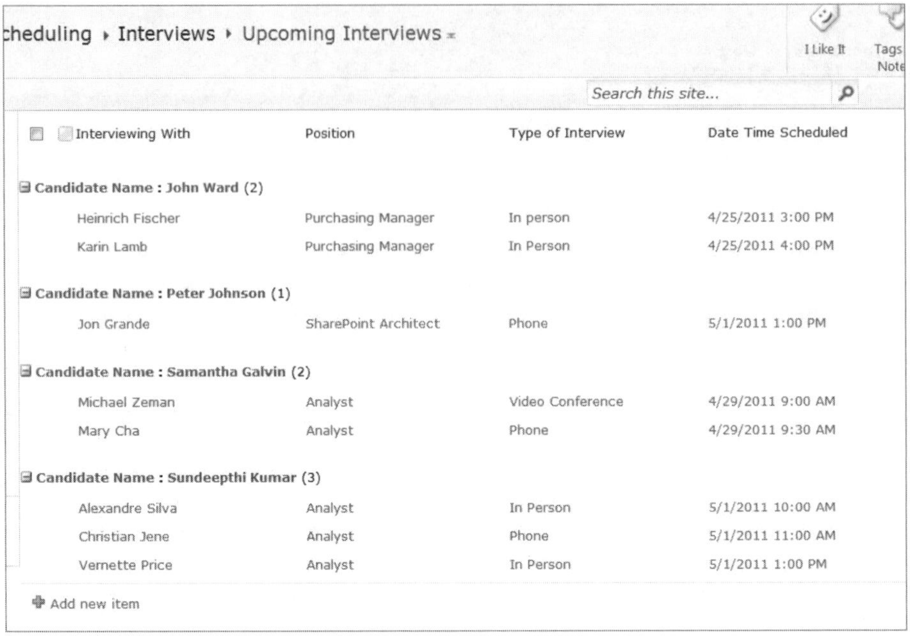

cheduling ▸ Interviews ▸ Upcoming Interviews

I Like It Tags Notes

Search this site...

Interviewing With	Position	Type of Interview	Date Time Scheduled
Candidate Name : John Ward (2)			
Heinrich Fischer	Purchasing Manager	In person	4/25/2011 3:00 PM
Karin Lamb	Purchasing Manager	In Person	4/25/2011 4:00 PM
Candidate Name : Peter Johnson (1)			
Jon Grande	SharePoint Architect	Phone	5/1/2011 1:00 PM
Candidate Name : Samantha Galvin (2)			
Michael Zeman	Analyst	Video Conference	4/29/2011 9:00 AM
Mary Cha	Analyst	Phone	4/29/2011 9:30 AM
Candidate Name : Sundeepthi Kumar (3)			
Alexandre Silva	Analyst	In Person	5/1/2011 10:00 AM
Christian Jene	Analyst	Phone	5/1/2011 11:00 AM
Vernette Price	Analyst	In Person	5/1/2011 1:00 PM

Add new item

FIGURE 6-27

Create the Dashboard

Now it's time to create the actual dashboard. Navigate to the site pages library (or wherever you saved your dashboard page). Click it and then, using the Ribbon, go into edit mode. For this particular page layout, it's customary to use the web part zones as follows:

- **Header:** Content editor web part with some brief statement of the dashboard's purpose
- **Left Column:** Navigation links (via a links web part or another content editor web part) that navigate to other dashboards and the site's landing page
- **Body:** The individual web parts that include the valuable stuff: the views on the interviews list

This section won't walk you step by step through the header and left column on the dashboard because these are quite easy. (Just add content editor web parts and add what you want.) Now focus instead on the Body section.

Click Add a Web Part in the body web part zone. SharePoint responds with a web part selection function on the top of the page but just under the Ribbon. Select Lists and Libraries in Categories and Interviews from Web Parts. Click the Add button, and SharePoint deposits the web part onto the page. See Figure 6-28 for help.

By default, SharePoint uses the list's default view. This won't be suitable for the dashboard. Instead, edit the web part by clicking its title; then from the drop-down list, select Edit Web Part. SharePoint displays the web part properties pane on the right side in response. In the List Views section (which opens by default), from the Selected Views field, select Upcoming Interviews. Change the Toolbar Type to No Toolbar. Your web part property pane should look similar to Figure 6-29. Click OK, and SharePoint shows you a dashboard similar to Figure 6-30.

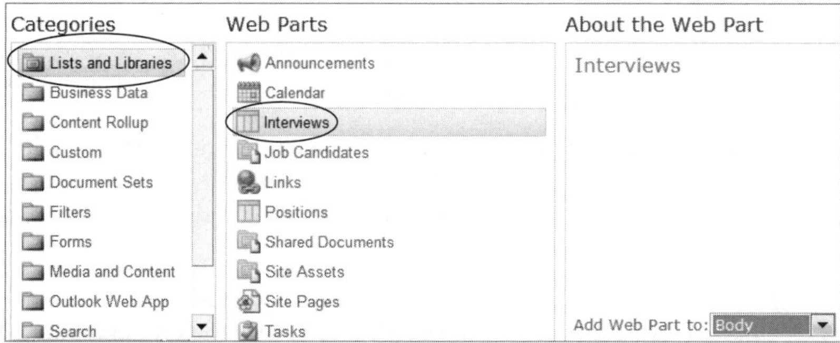

FIGURE 6-28

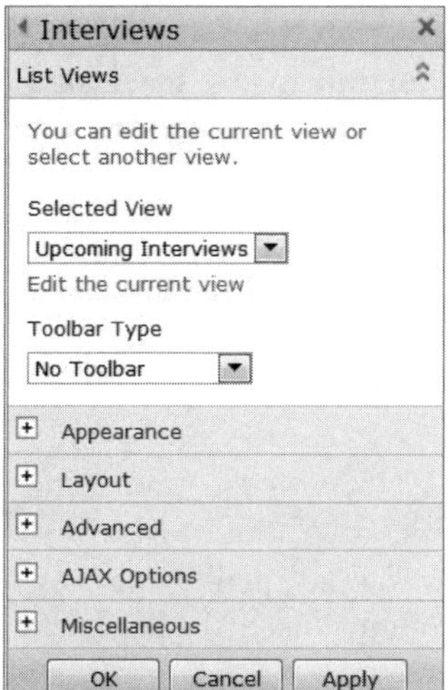

FIGURE 6-29

Upcoming Interviews

Dashbaord Navigation

Site Home Page

Interviews

Interviewing With	Position	Type of Interview	Date Time Scheduled
Candidate Name : John Ward (2)			
Heinrich Fischer	Purchasing Manager	In person	4/25/2011 3:00 PM
Karin Lamb	Purchasing Manager	In Person	4/25/2011 4:00 PM
Candidate Name : Peter Johnson (1)			
Jon Grande	SharePoint Architect	Phone	5/1/2011 1:00 PM
Candidate Name : Samantha Galvin (2)			
Michael Zeman	Analyst	Video Conference	4/29/2011 9:00 AM
Mary Cha	Analyst	Phone	4/29/2011 9:30 AM
Candidate Name : Sundeepthi Kumar (3)			
Alexandre Silva	Analyst	In Person	5/1/2011 10:00 AM
Christian Jene	Analyst	Phone	5/1/2011 11:00 AM
Vernette Price	Analyst	In Person	5/1/2011 1:00 PM

FIGURE 6-30

Extending the Dashboard

This is a simple dashboard that, nevertheless, shows some useful and helpful information. There are several good ways to extend the functionality of this dashboard page:

- Create more views for the dashboard. The view you previously created is helpful, but your workflows are actually feeding more information than you use. For instance, you could create a view called Awaiting Feedback and show only past interviews that are still awaiting manager feedback.
- Connect the web parts. Using SharePoint's web part connections features, you can add leverage to your Positions list and connect it to the interviews list. SharePoint automatically filters interviewees based on the position that you select.

Extending the Solution

The detailed walk-through glossed over a couple of important points (mainly to give space for a more full treatment of dashboards). The following sections list them and offer some guidance on how to solve them.

Auditing

In Chapter 5, you learned about an auditing technique whereby you create entries in a separate custom list. Auditing could be useful for this solution as well. You can use Chapter 5's approach with minor changes.

Emails

Probably the most obvious omission, the solution doesn't explain how to send emails. The next chapter does address this in great detail. If you can't wait and want to immediately begin integrating email, try the Send Email activity in your workflow.

Reminders

The system should send email reminders or instant messages to managers and job candidates. The solution doesn't outline how to do this, but rest assured, there are several techniques available to meet this need. You learn about this in great detail in Chapter 8.

Direct Job Candidate Access

It would be useful to allow job candidates to directly upload their documents to your SharePoint site. This is technically challenging, but it's not a strange or odd thing to do. SharePoint provides a set of platform features that can help you meet this requirement. It starts with SharePoint's farm architecture and its capability to have dedicated and secured web front end servers. It's buttressed with SharePoint's claims-based and forms-based authentication. These features enable you to define job candidates in a user profile database that lives outside of your company's Active Directory. It's not a trivial configuration, but a properly trained and skilled developer can do this without any trouble.

Security: As you can recall, in the last chapter you created multiple different lists. You could do that for this solution if you want. However, we're not going to focus on security. If you do it for this solution, you are doing this for the purpose of security. Have one list per manager.

Metrics

You may want to extend this solution by capturing some metrics. For instance, track the number of interviews conducted per manager or the number of interviews taking place on a weekly and monthly basis. If you think about it, the kinds of calculations you learned for the time bank pattern in Chapter 5 can show you a path to this end.

SUMMARY

This chapter described the requirements and detailed solution to the interview scheduling problem. You learned about SharePoint 2010 document sets feature and how this feature enables you to apply metadata to a set of related documents in masse, rather than on a document-by-document basis. Document sets are even more functionally useful because you can attach a workflow to the document set.

You learned a new technique in this workflow: how to determine if an item exists in a list. You attempted to locate it to see if you did by testing the resulting search value to zero. Nonzero values mean that the item exists; otherwise it does not.

The document set, its content type, and the workflow together worked to implement the dashboard feeder pattern. You created the first detailed dashboard in this book. Before moving on to the next chapter, spend some time exploring the extensibility options of this chapter's dashboard and indeed, the overall solution. It can come in handy in the following chapters.

7

Facilities Management

WHAT'S IN THIS CHAPTER?

- Understanding the classic four-phase workflow
- Using a "brute force" approach to column level security
- Working with SharePoint's mobile interface capabilities

This chapter introduces the facilities management business problem and solution. Consider your workspace for more than 30 seconds, and you quickly realize that you take a lot for granted. Someone had to move that desk into the room. The heat and air conditioning work as you expect. Every now and then, someone comes in to clean the place. Beyond this kind of ordinary on-going maintenance, someone is always around to fix things when they break. This can be as simple as replacing one of those super-long fluorescent light bulbs or can be more complicated such as solving a persistently leaky faucet in the men's room. Your company's facilities group does more than maintenance and repairs. They also improve the place or execute other special projects, such as moving people from one office to another. This final point is where SharePoint comes into play.

This chapter explains how you can use SharePoint to create a solution that helps the facilities group accept work requests, manage those requests, and generate some useful reports. You learn how to create an approval tree, learn about queues (not lines, but sequenced work orders) and dabble with SharePoint's mobile interface. Begin as you always do, with a detailed description of the problem.

WHAT IS THE FACILITIES MANAGEMENT PROCESS?

The facilities management process is a classic four phase generic workflow:

1. Request something.
2. Approve or deny that request.

3. If approved, execute the request.
4. Report the results.

For facilities management, those generic requests turn into the following:

1. Request that facilities do something (such as move your office from one building to another).
2. Determine who needs to approve this request, and obtain an approval or a denial.
3. If approved, assign the work to a person who does the actual office move, or whatever else is required.
4. As work starts and completes, notify all involved parties of the status. After the work is completed, report the actual time and money spent.

This facilities management process is a clear cut example of the classic workflow problem. SharePoint and SharePoint Designer workflows are well suited to this kind of problem — and indeed, all similar business problems in this problem class.

PROBLEM CLASS

The facilities management problem is a first-class example of the four-phase request/approve/execute/report family of business problems. One thing that differentiates this kind of business problem from others is the execute link in the chain. These steps often include activities that happen in the "real world" or other external systems. They take place outside of SharePoint's direct control.

Other business problems in this class include the following:

- **Travel arrangements:** I'm a sales person and I want to travel to a show in Las Vegas. I request that the travel team makes arrangements for me. My manager will approve or deny that request. Assuming it's approved, the travel team obtains my airline tickets, reserves a hotel, and so on. They update me throughout the process and in the end report the actual costs to me and my manager.
- **Ordering lunch for a business meeting:** I expect a client to visit the office next week, and I want to have great food. I request that the department assistant order food for delivery. He obtains approval, arranges for the delivery, and then reports the actual cost when it arrives.

As you can see, the solution you learn about in this chapter is well represented in the business world.

TECHNICAL PATTERNS

While solving the helpdesk ticketing problem, you need to implement the following technical patterns:

- **Basic CRUD:** It almost goes without saying, but this solution, like most every other, follows the create/update/delete technical pattern.

- **Approval trees:** End users make many requests. Some of them may be automatically approved. Some may require just one manager's approval. Others require several. The approval tree technical pattern sets up this tree with SharePoint Designer. You also learn how SharePoint Designer limits your options in this area, too.
- **Queues:** You read more about queues in a minute, but in short, you use a queue to ensure that a "fair" prioritization work assignment is used when you have more than one request to handle at a time.
- **Hierarchical content types:** You've learned a lot about content types so far. You soon learn that content types have even more capability than previously discussed.
- **Mobile users:** Although not strictly a workflow issue, this chapter explains and walks you through SharePoint's capability to provide a useful mobile interface for a change.
- **Waiting:** Some workflow activities, such as Assign a Task or Start Approval Process can cause your workflow to "block" or sleep until the assignees completes their work. You learn that you have another more explicit option available to you and when it makes sense to use it.

This chapter also covers several new powerful business patterns.

BUSINESS PATTERNS

While solving the facilities management problem, you can implement several new business patterns. In many respects, these are just the flip side of their corresponding technical patterns. It's important for you, as a solution designer, to wear two hats and personalities. Which hat/personality depends upon your audience and what you're doing at the time. Consider the following business patterns:

- **Approval trees and routing:** How do you decide who is responsible to approve or deny requests? How do you decide if more than one person needs to approve the request (routing)? This business pattern answers these questions.
- **Queues and prioritization:** As requests come in, how do you decide which is addressed first? There is only so much work the facilities team can execute, no matter how many requests are approved. This business pattern addresses the problem of prioritization by means of a default ("fair") model that enables emergency or privileged requests to jump to the front of the line.
- **Mobile Interface:** When does it make sense to use SharePoint's mobile capability? When it does make sense, what should you do to ensure it's done correctly?
- **Brokers:** Some business processes have a single person playing a gatekeeper role for all the related work activities. You learn how the facilities manager plays that role and how SharePoint supports it.

These business patterns provide useful models for you to follow when designing your own four-phase workflow solutions.

BUSINESS PROBLEM DESCRIPTION

This chapter's requirements discussion starts by asking a number of "seed" questions to get everyone talking. It focuses on four major phases of the problem and its solution, identifying each step, its role and its peculiar set of needs.

Requirements Discussion

As always, schedule meetings with the users most affected by the business process. In this case, the facilities team tends to take primacy because it is the most affected by the solution. You also want to include at least one representative from executive management because she will have strong opinions on reporting. It's much easier to accommodate reporting requirements at this stage than it will be after you've gone live with the solution. Additionally, select a couple of end users so that you can white-board and game-out some real-world scenarios with a wide array of interests. In this way, you have the best chance to identify appropriate business requirements. Consider using these "seed" questions:

- What does the universe of valid requests look like? For instance, if you assume that changing a light bulb is a valid request, what about installing a space heater?
- Should some jobs be done only off hours (nights or weekends)? Does that affect the cost? Should these kinds of jobs be tracked and reported separately from others?
- What kind of mobile interfaces are required?
- How do you decide the sequence to act upon approved requests?
- Do all requests require approval?
- What kind of reporting does executive management expect and require from this solution?

These questions can help you start and should lead to an effective requirements discussion. The following paragraphs walk you through a sample end result of a theoretical requirements gathering meeting.

The requirements discussion for the facilities management process breaks down, predictably, to the four major phases of the workflow process. Start with the request.

Broadly speaking, the solution should account for two different types of requests: simple quick-fix style requests and more complex requests that may merit a project plan. The requestor may have an option for this, but it's actually up to the facilities team to make that determination. Therefore, you want end users to describe the need and submit it for approval. Simple or complex is determined by someone else.

After the submission, the facilities manager plays a broker role. He receives the requests and needs to determine whether it's simple or complex. He can automatically approve simple requests and trigger a more complex approval process for complex requests. For instance, it's one thing to replace an old desk with a new one. It's another thing to move an office from one building to another. The best and most useful measure of complexity is cost. Hence, the facilities manager should estimate the cost of any given request. This can tell the workflow what it needs to assign the appropriate approver or approvers. The workflow should not proceed until the facilities manager supplies this cost. (Otherwise, how would it know the approver or approvers?)

As soon as the workflow process identifies these approvers, it should obviously seek their approval and act upon their decision. SharePoint should log all these activities.

After the request is approved, it's time to move into phase 3, "execution." Again, it's time to turn to the facilities manager. He leads a team of facilities workers who do the actual office move, change the light bulb, or whatever is requested. The facilities manager selects those people and assigns them the work task. How does he do that? SharePoint should suggest an open task by means of a fair process. Common sense tells us that the most fair process is this: Whoever got in line first should get to go first. If Paul, Sally, and Vivek sequentially request that facilities fix a broken light bulb, facilities should fix those bulbs in the order in which they were approved. This kind of fair selection process is based on a computer science principal called a queue or first in, first out (FIFO).

Of course, paraphrasing that famous *Animal Farm* line, "All requests are equal, but some requests are more equal than others." A given request may legitimately jump to the front of the line because of its emergency nature. Other times, a given request can jump ahead because the requestor is higher on the totem pole than anyone else. (Who's going to make the VP of finance wait for his new desk? I'm not.) These exceptions to the "fair" rule tell you that the facilities manager should not be constrained by the system, but rather advised by the system. SharePoint should display the tasks in "fair" order but enable the facilities manager to implement his own prioritization.

Eventually the facilities team finally changes that pesky light bulb. Now you've entered phase 4: reporting.

Now, to a great extent, your solution should be "reporting" status changes throughout. When the request is accepted, the originator should be notified. When the request is approved or denied, the requestor should be notified. When work begins, the requestor should be notified. You get the picture. Notification is not the same as reporting, however.

Reporting occurs when the facilities team "trues up" the work request and updates the system with actuals. That includes the actual work completed. It includes the actual amount of time spent on the task. It includes the actual money spent on consumables, such as paint and wire tape. This kind of reporting could be done by paper or via a SharePoint data entry screen directly by the facilities team. However, this problem is one of the relatively rare cases in which SharePoint's mobile interface meets the real-world requirement of accuracy. If the team can enter these actual values on the spot, they will tend to be more accurate. Why not let them do that on their mobile device? For that matter, why not *require* it?

The reporting phase is required because your company needs metrics. Your executive management team will want to know things like the following:

- How many requests are placed a month?
- What constitute the majority of requests?
- How much is all this costing us?

These questions are the hallmark of the four-phase workflow. Business outcomes from the processes in this problem class must all stand ready to answer these management questions.

In summary, the business requirements are as follows:

- Employees should enter both simple and complex facilities' requests.
- Simple requests should be approved automatically.
- Complex requests should be approved on the basis of their estimated cost.

- The facilities manager should have full and complete control of when approved requests are assigned to the facilities team members who does the actual work. However, SharePoint should suggest a fair approach.
- Facilities team members must report their work by means of a mobile interface.
- Throughout, the business process should notify the requestor of key events, including whether the request was approved or denied, when it's scheduled to be completed, and how much it cost overall.

Actors

The model for this solution that meets the requirements includes the following actors:

- **An employee or contractor that needs some work done:** Note that contractors need functional light bulbs, too. This chapter makes an important assumption about contractors. Namely, it assumes that you've added them to your active directory and that they are treated, from a SharePoint perspective, just like anyone else.
- **Facilities manager:** The facilities manager has two distinct roles in the business process (aside from managing the workforce, of course). First, the facilities manager must estimate the cost of the work request. Second, the facilities manager must assign the work to someone on the team.
- **Various approvers:** When approval is required, the approvers obviously signal approval or deny requests.
- **Facilities work staff:** These team members don't have an office with a laptop and docking station. Instead, they have a mobile device with which they can update actuals.

Actions

The facilities management solution responds to the actions on behalf of its supported actors. These actions include the following:

- Create a work request. End users fill out an online form describing the type of request and other important information about the request.
- The facilities manager estimates the work effort (thus, dictating a certain approval tree).
- Managers receive approval requests and act upon them.
- The facilities manager assigns approved work requests to his team.
- Facilities team members use their mobile devices to provide actual effort for the job.

Challenges

This chapter doesn't spell out in great detail how to address certain nice-to-have functions, including the following:

- **Abusive users:** It may not be on the top of your worry list, but some users may abuse a system like this. You can reduce that risk by identifying users who have placed an extraordinary number of requests and flag their requests for additional scrutiny.

- **Time-sensitive requests:** The detailed walk-through meets the requirements but it doesn't allow for the requestor to specify whether the request is urgent or whether it should be done only off hours or while the requestor is on vacation.
- **Unexpected delays:** Sometimes, a job is far more complex than anticipated or delayed for something simple, such as a broken tool. This could cause a ripple effect in the schedule.
- **Unequal treatment of contractors:** Contractors are people, too, but they are not full-time staff. As a result, the types of requests they make should be constrained by the system. For instance, most contractors can never move their office, so why even offer the choice?
- **Justifying costs:** Sometimes, the facilities manager may estimate a cost that is simply too high to justify the effort. It would be helpful to provide some additional details to the requestor as to the reason for that cost.

HIGH-LEVEL SOLUTION

This chapter's solution is the most complex covered so far in the book and blends human control (a broker) with automated processing (SharePoint Designer workflow). In addition, it addresses one of SharePoint's more significant security holes: the lack of column-level security.

Solution Overview

To implement the facilities management application, you must create a solution that leverages a number of out-of-the-box SharePoint components and create a fairly complex SharePoint Designer workflow.

The solution starts with a facilities request. Someone (a requestor) needs some work done. The requestor fills out a simple form and submits the request. This implies the need for a content type and a custom list.

After the requestor submits the request, it is routed to the facilities manager. The facilities manager analyzes the request and estimates the cost. He then enters the cost onto the request. This now allows the workflow to build an approval tree. You don't want to allow requestors to enter the estimated cost. Up until this point in the book, when you've had a security requirement, it generally centered upon an entire library or a list item as a whole. This is the first time you've had a requirement for securing individual columns.

As it turns out, SharePoint doesn't provide column-level security. It doesn't provide it in data entry, and it doesn't provide it in views. You'll learn a technique in the technical overview and walk-through that addresses this in detail.

SharePoint workflow builds an approval tree by determining the requestor's direct manager. Based on that manager's approval level and the estimated cost, the request may be routed to the manager's manager. The SharePoint Designer workflow won't build an approval tree that has more than the manager and the manager's manager in the tree. This is because SharePoint Designer workflow is limited and cannot dynamically build a tree. As you'll see in the walk-through, SharePoint Designer workflow steps must be explicitly declared. SharePoint Designer workflow cannot dynamically "walk up the tree." If you truly require that level of flexibility, you need to use a more complex tool such as Visual Studio, or you need a custom activity. See Chapter 12, "Custom Activities," for more details.

When the cost is entered, the system figures out who needs to approve it. It may be auto-approved or it may go to someone else. Maybe it is automatically rejected? Maybe the facilities manager can reject it.

Of course, in some cases, no approval is required. To make auto-approve decisions, the workflow needs some kind of identifier. This can be done in several ways. In this case, the facilities manager is responsible to make this determination. You revisit this in the "Advanced Topics" section.

When the work request is approved, the facilities manager assigns it to someone or a team. They will do the required work and use a mobile interface to indicate when they begin and when they finish. When they finish, they should also enter in any notes, actual time spent, and actual cost. SharePoint's default mobile interface is not the most exciting thing ever, but it's available out-of-the-box.

Swim Lane Diagrams

Figure 7-1 depicts these actors and their actions in a swim lane diagram. This simplified view of the process assumes that a single request runs through to completion and is not aborted somewhere along the way.

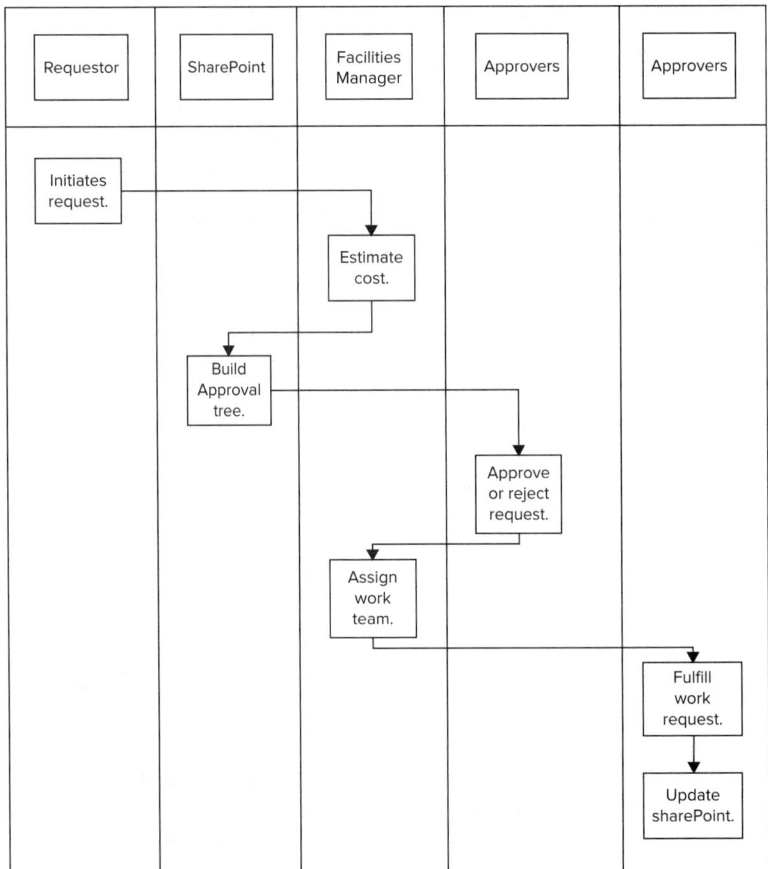

FIGURE 7-1

The diagram shows the five actors in this solution: the initiator, the facilities manager, approvers (there could be more than one), the work team, and SharePoint itself. The process begins when someone requests some work. The facilities manager estimates the total cost and this tells SharePoint what it needs in order to create the approval tree. It then routes the request to the required managers. Once approved, the facilities manager determines the correct team of people to implement the work. They do the job and record their results.

Technical Implementation Overview

The facilities management technical solution follows the same pattern everywhere else: content types backing lists and SharePoint Designer workflow controlling activity and feeding a dashboard. This time, you'll use content types and their associated lists to implement a brute-force type of column-level security.

Content Types

Like all of the solutions, site columns and content types are at the core of the solution. To meet the facilities management solution requirements, you need content types that represent the following:

- **Work order request:** This content type has columns such as Description and Requested Work Date.
- **Secured work order request:** As its name implies, this is a secured custom list and the core of the primary SharePoint Designer workflow in this solution. This list, along with SharePoint Designer's capability to temporarily elevate a user's security privilege, is the cornerstone of this solution's capability to simulate column-level security. More on this shortly.

These two content types share a common set of site columns. The secured work order request needs the same site columns as the original (unsecured) work order request plus a number of additional columns. SharePoint enables you to build a hierarchy of site content types. You've been doing this all along. Every custom content type is based upon a pre-existing content type. You've been creating custom content types that extend out-of-the-box content types such as Item and Document. In this case, you do the same when you create the work order request content type. However, you use this unsecured work request content type as the basis for the secured content.

Custom Lists

Use the following custom lists to implement the solution:

- **End user maintenance request:** A list backed by the unsecured maintenance request content type. A workflow on this list can create an entry in the second secured maintenance request list.
- **Secured request:** A separate list containing secured requests and containing all the site columns to which you want to restrict most users to read-access only.

Column-Level Security

This solution calls for column-level security. Before proceeding, you should know that there is no column-level security in SharePoint 2010. Microsoft didn't provide column-level security in the prior version either. Microsoft will almost certainly exclude this from the next major version as well. That said, you can simulate it and provide an effective solution that implements, for all intents and purposes, column level security.

To simulate column-level security, you create two lists just like you do in this solution. The first list contains just those columns to which you want to grant contribute access. You create a second list and secure it by restricting access to those same users. In this case, everyone has contributor access to the unsecured maintenance request, but only members of the facilities team have contributor access to the secured list. Everyone else is granted read access to the secured list. That's one half of the solution.

The other half relies upon SharePoint Designer workflow's capability to impersonate another user at run-time. Your SharePoint Designer workflow can temporarily execute a group of activities and conditions the privileges of the user who created the workflow itself. Therefore, grant contributor access to the workflow creator. Create an entry in the secured list using impersonation.

In the end, a low-privileged user creates an entry in the unsecured request list, workflow creates an entry in the secured list, and the facilities manager has the appropriate level of access.

That's a lot of work to implement a simulated column level security. However, it's not that hard in practice, and in this solution's case, it's a good and appropriate technique. You'll find it useful in many other scenarios.

Workflow

This solution's primary SharePoint Designer workflow is a relatively complex multistep solution. It reuses several techniques from previous chapters and introduces the wait-for-field change activity. First, it sets status and waits for the facilities manager to estimate the cost. The facilities manager also decides whether manager approval is required. If manager approval is required, the workflow identifies those managers. It then starts an approval process for each of them. Assuming the request is ultimately approved, the workflow waits for the facilities manager to assign a team (either an individual user or SharePoint group).

At this point, the automated workflow is finished, and the work team executes the request. The work team uses SharePoint's mobile interface to record its work.

DETAILED TECHNICAL IMPLEMENTATION

Follow the detailed instructions in the following sections to build the solution. Pay close attention to the column-level security solution and carefully consider how you might use it to solve some of your company's current business problems.

Setup

To implement the helpdesk solution, you need to create content types, create SharePoint custom lists that use those content types, and implement column-level security. Of course, you create SharePoint designer workflows to glue it all together.

Supporting Lists

Two custom lists are at the core of this solution:

- **Initial Request:** End users create maintenance requests by adding an item to this list.
- **Secured Work Request:** Facilities managers and the SharePoint workflow work off a secured copy of the initial request.

You back these two lists with distinct content types, one of which is a child to the other.

Content Types

You need to create two content types:

- **Maintenance Request:** End users create maintenance requests. This is a simple content type composed of just a couple site columns.
- **Secured Maintenance Request:** Used by the facilities manager and his team, this site content type defines all other relevant site columns required by the solution.

Maintenance Request

This simple content type contains two business site columns.

Business Columns:

- **Description:** The end user's request, in detail
- **Requested Work Date:** The end user's preferred date for this maintenance to be conducted

Create these columns with the names and configuration options described in Table 7-1.

TABLE 7-1: Maintenance Request Site Columns

COLUMN NAME	COLUMN TYPE	ADDITIONAL SETTINGS
MR_Description	Multiple Lines of Text	None
MR_RequestedWorkDate	Date and Time	None

After creating the previous two site columns, add them to a new content type named Maintenance Request and a group called Maintenance Requests. See Figure 7-2 to validate your effort.

FIGURE 7-2

Secured Maintenance Request

This content type extends the end user's maintenance request with all the business and technical columns required to manage the facilities management process. This content type includes all the site columns from the maintenance request and adds several more.

Technical Columns:

- **MR_Status:** This represents the overall status of the maintenance request process.
- **MR_ApprovalStatus:** A specialized status for approvals.
- **MR_Originator:** As you'll see when you create the workflow itself, workflow can create an entry in the secured list by means of an impersonation step. This impersonation step is the key to implementing column-level security. However, it has the drawback that the newly created item's Created site column is assigned to the impersonator. You still want the original end user's ID, and this technical column serves that purpose.

Why use two different status site columns? You do this because you want to both increase the granularity of the business process's overall status and provide some additional metrics for reporting. Consider the following values for MR_Status:

- **Open:** Submitted but not processing as started. This is the initial status of the request.
- **Awaiting Estimation:** The request is on hold until the facilities manager estimates the cost.
- **Estimated:** The facilities manager has provided the request.
- **Awaiting Manager 1 Approval:** The request has been routed to the first manager in the approval tree (typically the end user's direct manager).
- **Manager 1 Approved:** The first manager has approved the request.

- **Awaiting Manager 2 Approval and Manager 2 Approved:** Similar to the previous bullet point except that they are for the manager's manager.
- **Awaiting Work Assignment:** For approved requests, waiting for the facilities manager to submit the request for approval.
- **Assigned:** The facilities manager assigned the work request to a team.
- **Work in Process:** The work team has started and is actively working on the request.
- **Work Completed:** The work team finished the job.

These status codes provide a great deal of information to end users, facilities managers, and anyone else that wants to know about the these work requests. Contrast that with the status code values for the MR_ApprovalStatus site column:

1. Pending
2. Approved
3. Declined

These three status codes tell the user about the approval status in specific detail. Two separate status codes enable you to answer questions such as "How many closed work requests were declined?" The second status site column enables you to answer that question.

With all that out of the way, go ahead and create the following technical columns, as shown in Table 7-2.

TABLE 7-2: Secured Maintenance Request Technical Site Columns

COLUMN NAME	COLUMN TYPE	ADDITIONAL SETTINGS
MR_Status	Single Line of Text	None
MR_ApprovalStatus	Choice	Values: 1. Pending 2. Approved 3. Declined
MR_Originator	Person or Group	None

Notice the Prefix MR_ApprovalStatus values with the numbers as shown. This can help you to created sorted views in the sequence as shown. If you don't prefix the codes with a number, SharePoint always displays status codes in alphabetical order, which would result in an awkward list view.

Business Columns:

The facilities management requires another 1/2 dozen site columns to support itself. They include the following:

- **Estimated cost:** Provided by the facilities manager and dictates which approvals are required.
- **Actual cost:** When the work is finished, the facilities manager updates the actual cost, which can be used in reports for analysis purposes.
- **Actual hours:** The amount of the time the maintenance team spent on this request.
- **Notes:** Any notes that the maintenance team wanted to capture about this work request.
- **Work Team:** The user or group of users assigned the work by the facilities manager.
- **Auto-approve:** The facilities manager can determine that some requests can skip the normal approval process. This would be for items such as "change a light bulb."

Create the business columns, as shown in Table 7-3.

TABLE 7-3: Secured Maintenance Request Technical Site Columns

COLUMN NAME	COLUMN TYPE	ADDITIONAL SETTINGS
MR_EstimatedCost	Currency	None
MR_ActualCost	Currency	None
MR_ActualHours	Number	None
MR_Notes	Multiple lines of text	Set as "plain text"
MR_WorkTeam	Person or Group	None
MR_IsAutoApproved	Yes/No	Default is "no"

When finished with technical and business columns, your SharePoint definition will look like Figure 7-3.

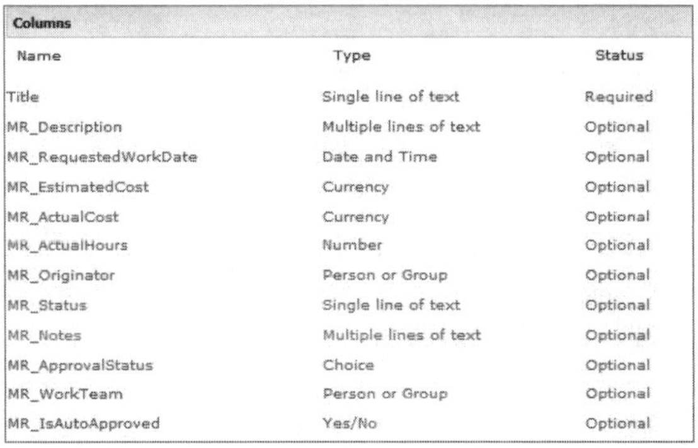

As usual, these site columns need to be added to a site content type. Create a new site content type named Secured Maintenance Request. However, this time select a different base content type. Up to this point in the book, every time you create a site content type, you pick a base content type, and you've been picking "item" or "document." This time, base the new secured maintenance request from the Maintenance Request content type you just previously created, as shown in Figure 7-4.

Columns

Name	Type	Status
Title	Single line of text	Required
MR_Description	Multiple lines of text	Optional
MR_RequestedWorkDate	Date and Time	Optional
MR_EstimatedCost	Currency	Optional
MR_ActualCost	Currency	Optional
MR_ActualHours	Number	Optional
MR_Originator	Person or Group	Optional
MR_Status	Single line of text	Optional
MR_Notes	Multiple lines of text	Optional
MR_ApprovalStatus	Choice	Optional
MR_WorkTeam	Person or Group	Optional
MR_IsAutoApproved	Yes/No	Optional

FIGURE 7-3

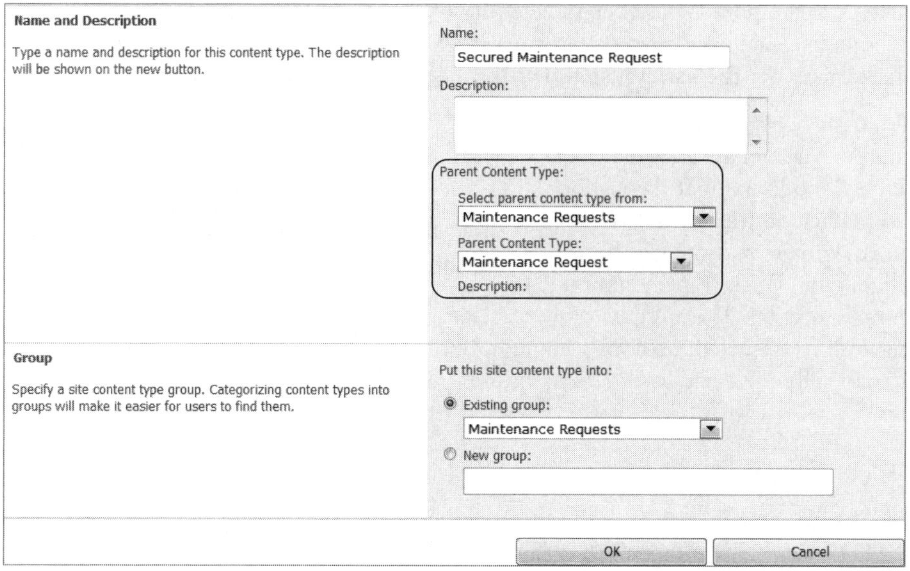

FIGURE 7-4

Custom Lists

You've created two site columns, and now it's time to create custom lists to use them. These two custom lists work together to implement site column-level security, to the extent that you can do that in SharePoint. End users create entries in the first list. This first list, named Maintenance Requests, is backed by the Maintenance Request site content type. You've done this several times by now, so there's nothing special about it.

The second list is a little more complex. When the end user submits the work request, SharePoint Designer workflow copies that request into the secured list by means of an impersonation step. As a result, you need to do what you normally do: Create a custom list and back it with a content type. In addition, you need to secure the list. Chapter 5, "Time Off Management," walked you through this process, so consult there for details.

Create Workflows

This solution uses two workflows to meet its requirements. The first simply copies end user's request to a secured list. The second workflow is far more complex and walks the request through all its stages until complete.

Create a Secured Request

This simple workflow introduces you to the concept of an impersonation step. In SharePoint Designer workflow, impersonation defines a group of conditions and activities that execute as if the person who created the workflow in SharePoint Designer is the person running the workflow. Normally, when you run a SharePoint Designer workflow, it executes with the security rights of the user who started it. This means that if the workflow tries to create an entry in a custom list, that user must have access to the custom list. If the user does not have access, the workflow fails. Use impersonation steps to temporarily assume the identity of the workflow creator. Give that creator access to the custom list, and now anyone that runs the workflow can update the list. This does not give the user direct access to the list, it just allows the workflow's steps to access the list.

Fire up SharePoint Designer, and create a new list workflow on the Maintenance Request list. Click default Step 1 and look up at the ribbon. (You don't need to click Step 1 to do this, but it guarantees that the Impersonation Step button on the ribbon lights up.) Click Impersonation Step, as shown in Figure 7-5. This adds a new step to the workflow labeled, obviously enough, Impersonation Step. Create a list item in the Secured Maintenance Request list, as shown in Figure 7-6.

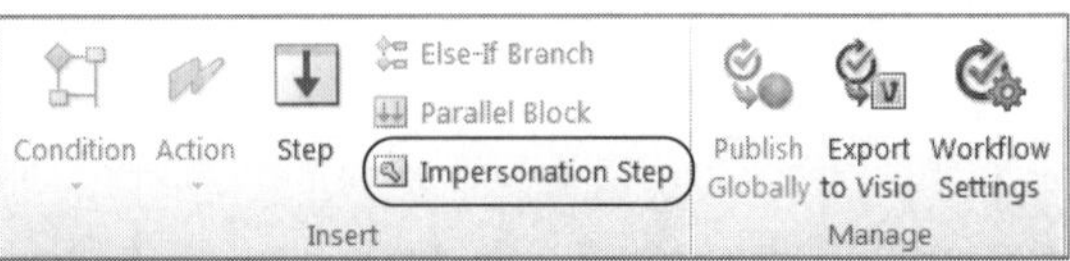

FIGURE 7-5

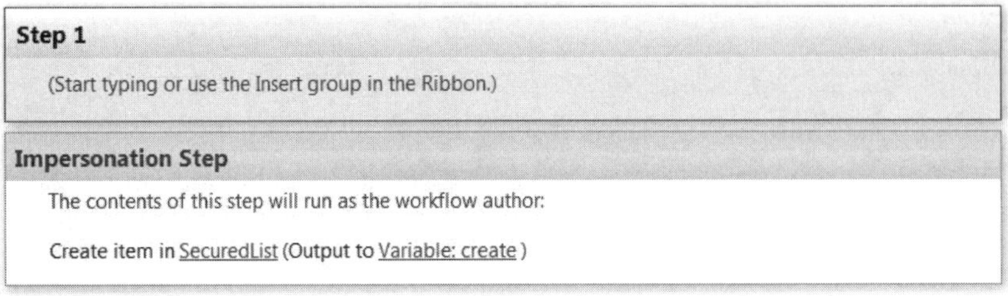

Step 1

(Start typing or use the Insert group in the Ribbon.)

Impersonation Step

The contents of this step will run as the workflow author:

Create item in SecuredList (Output to Variable: create)

FIGURE 7-6

You can safely delete Step 1 — and you should for clarity's sake.

You'll use impersonation again in Chapter 10, "R&D Gateway."

That's it for this workflow.

Process Maintenance Request

Now it's time for the big show. This workflow introduces some new concepts and enhances a few techniques you've used before. It includes five steps.

Step 1 — Initialization

The initialization step sets the initial value for status fields and a "magic value" into Estimated Cost. In this case the magic value is negative one, and it's "magic" because it's not a real-world business value. (Nothing costs negative dollars.) Instead, the workflow uses it to indicate that the facilities manager hasn't entered a real estimated cost yet, as shown in Figure 7-7.

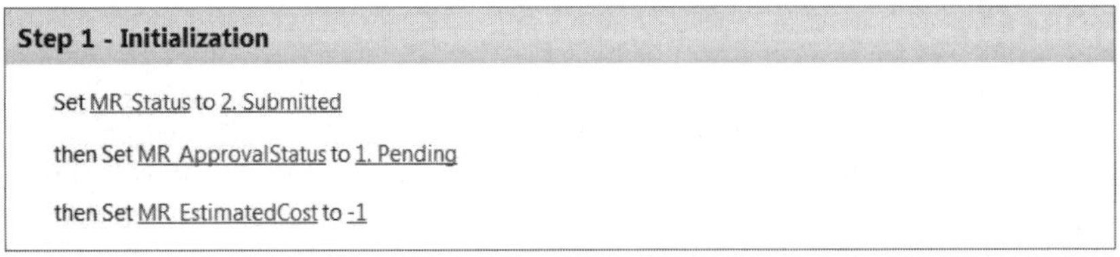

Step 1 - Initialization

Set MR Status to 2. Submitted

then Set MR ApprovalStatus to 1. Pending

then Set MR EstimatedCost to -1

FIGURE 7-7

Step 2 — Wait for Estimation

This chapter introduces a new "blocking" activity: Wait for Field Change in Current Item. This activity tells SharePoint Designer to stop running and go to sleep until the value of a field on the list changes. This is where the magic negative one number from the initialization step comes into play. You can proceed until the facilities manager provides a cost estimate. You'll know that he did when the value changes from negative one to some other value. Go ahead and add the wait-for step. When you finish, it should look like Figure 7-8.

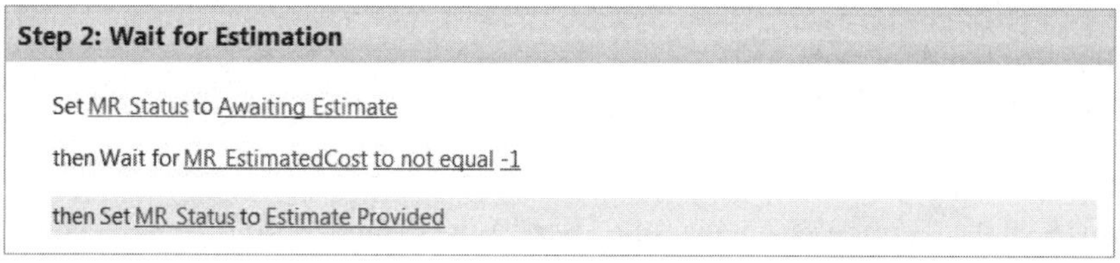

Step 2: Wait for Estimation

Set MR Status to Awaiting Estimate

then Wait for MR EstimatedCost to not equal -1

then Set MR Status to Estimate Provided

FIGURE 7-8

Refer to Figure 7-8 to see that its first activity is to set the MR_Status field to Awaiting Estimate. Now refer to Figure 7-7 to see that MR_Status is set to Submitted. You may be asking yourself, "Why bother setting these statuses because they will just overwrite each other. There are two reasons to do so.

First, there is a possibility that something will break in SharePoint while this workflow is operating, and it could happen in the small slice of time that passes between Step 1 and Step 2. This is unlikely, but if it does, it can help you reconstruct the status of things later when SharePoint has been fixed. Another reason is akin to "muscle memory." If you pick up the habit to assign a status, you'll have picked up a good habit. Always assign statuses; you'll never regret having it, and you will regret not having it if you need it.

Step 3 — Check for Automatic Approval

This third step determines whether the facilities manager set the IsAutoApproved site column value to Yes. This means that it's a simple request and doesn't access and run through the approval tree. First, it sets the MR_Status site column to Checking auto-approval. It then looks at the MR_IsAutoApproved column and if set to Yes, workflow assigns the MR_ApprovalStatus and MR_Status to appropriate values. See Figure 7-9 for a full view into this.

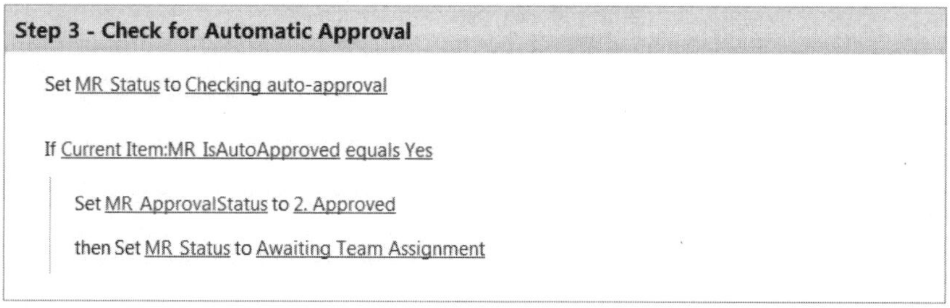

Step 3 - Check for Automatic Approval

Set MR Status to Checking auto-approval

If Current Item:MR IsAutoApproved equals Yes

Set MR ApprovalStatus to 2. Approved

then Set MR Status to Awaiting Team Assignment

FIGURE 7-9

Step 4 — Approval Tree Processing

Step 4 is where things get interesting. This step builds up the approval tree and then obtains approvals as needed. You use the Lookup Manager of a User activity to find the manager and the manager's manager. Use the Start Approval Request activity to notify the manager and obtain his response. You then analyze the response, update various status codes, and stop the workflow if the request is denied. Now get into the details.

First, encapsulate all of Step 4 inside an If condition. If the facilities manager approved this step, there's no need to do any of this.

The first major logic step is to build the approval tree. Create a new step named Step 4a: Determine Approvers. Create two workflow variables named wfv_RequestApprover1 and wfv_RequestApprover2. Add two new activities to this Step 4a, "Lookup Manager of a User." When you first do this, SharePoint Designer responds with a new activity, as shown in Figure 7-10.

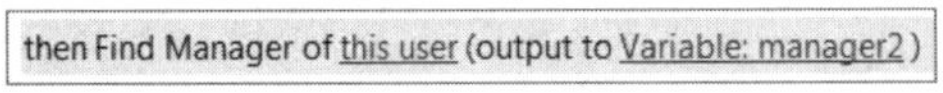

then Find Manager of this user (output to Variable: manager2)

FIGURE 7-10

Click this user to access SharePoint Designer's Select Users dialog (see Figure 7-11).

The first of these paired Lookup activities looks up the manager of the originator. Highlight Workflow Lookup for a User, and then click the Add>> button. SharePoint Designer presents you with the familiar site column picker dialog. Navigate to MR_Originator in the current list, and click OK. When finished, your Select Users dialog will look similar to Figure 7-12.

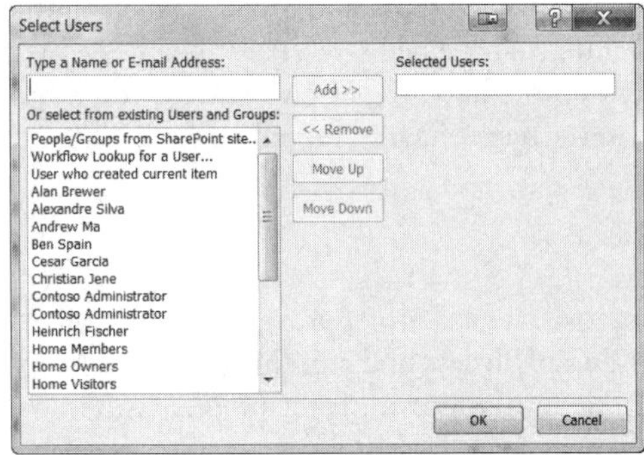

FIGURE 7-11

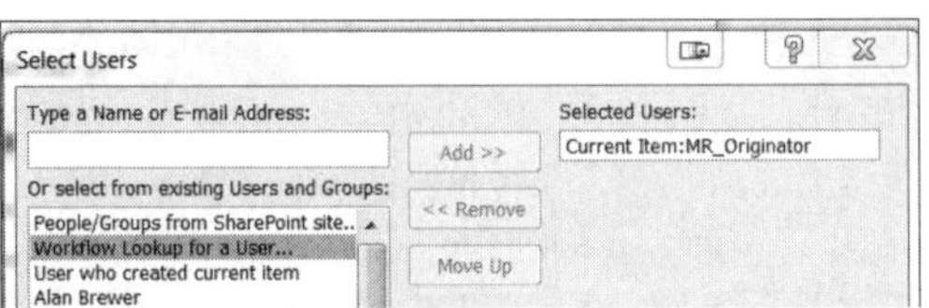

FIGURE 7-12

Lastly, set the output to Variable: wfv_RequestApprover1.

The second activity is nearly the same as the first with the exception that you find the manager of wfv_RequestApprover1 instead of MR_Originator. (See Figure 7-13.)

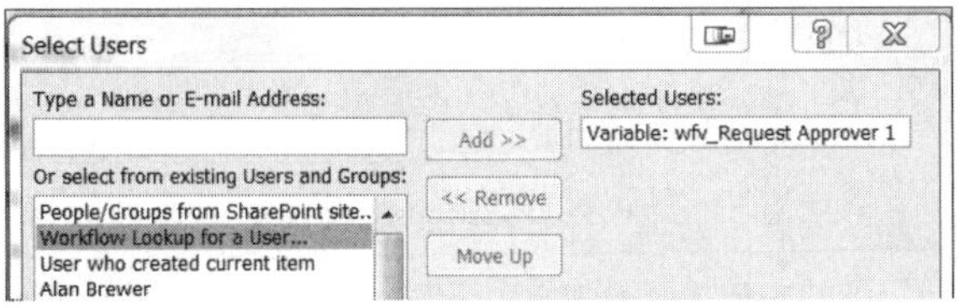

Select Users
Type a Name or E-mail Address:
Selected Users:
Add >>
Variable: wfv_Request Approver 1
Or select from existing Users and Groups:
<< Remove
People/Groups from SharePoint site..
Workflow Lookup for a User...
User who created current item
Alan Brewer
Move Up

FIGURE 7-13

In the end, Step 4a looks like Figure 7-14.

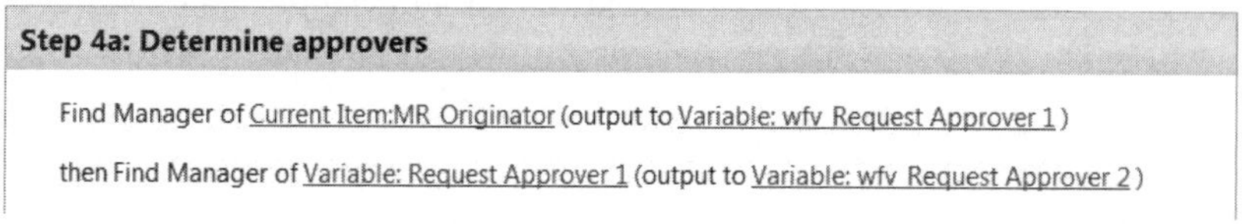

Step 4a: Determine approvers

Find Manager of Current Item:MR Originator (output to Variable: wfv Request Approver 1)

then Find Manager of Variable: Request Approver 1 (output to Variable: wfv Request Approver 2)

FIGURE 7-14

Now that you know the approvers, it's time to solicit their approval. You use the Start Approval Status activity, and in this case, you want to assign this request to the workflow variable wfv_RequestApprover1. When SharePoint Designer hits this activity at runtime, it assigns a task to the manager and then waits for his response. After he responds, the workflow continues.

Inspect the manager's decision by checking the value of the IsItemApproved workflow variable. If it's been set to No, the manager rejected the request. In this case, you need to set your two status fields and stop the workflow. Otherwise, set the status and move on to seek manager two's approval. See Figure 7-15 for all of Step 4b.

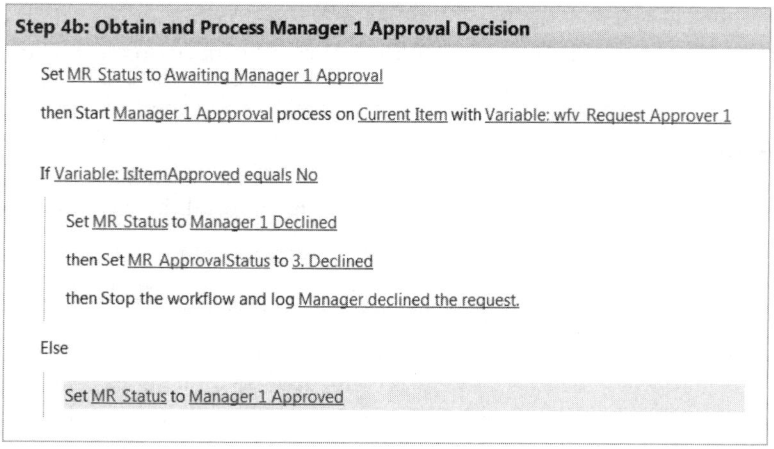

Step 4b: Obtain and Process Manager 1 Approval Decision

Set MR Status to Awaiting Manager 1 Approval

then Start Manager 1 Appproval process on Current Item with Variable: wfv Request Approver 1

If Variable: IsItemApproved equals No

Set MR Status to Manager 1 Declined

then Set MR ApprovalStatus to 3. Declined

then Stop the workflow and log Manager declined the request.

Else

Set MR Status to Manager 1 Approved

FIGURE 7-15

Round out the approval process by adding a Step 4c for the second manager.

That's it for Step 4 and now you can move to Step 5.

Step 5 — Assign a Team to This Request

The goal of this final step is to wait for the manager to assign a team to do the work required for this approved work request. Do the usual status setting here, and use another wait-for activity while the facilities manager determines the most appropriate person or people for the job. More interesting, you need to use another technique to identify the condition that ends the wait-for activity.

Recall that last time, you used a "magic value" to determine whether the facilities manager had entered an estimate. You could do something similar here, but it feels awkward putting in a magic value into a Person or Group field. After all, you need to assign an actual person to that field. How do you pick a magic value for a field like that? It's just not appropriate. Instead, use a workflow variable to help.

Create a workflow variable named wfv_WorkTeam of type String. Set its value to the MR_WorkTeam site column in the current item. Then, use the wait activity, and tell your workflow to wait for MR_WorkTeam to not equal wfv_WorkTeam. This ensures that the workflow pauses until the facilities manager enters an actual person or group into the field.

That's it for the SharePoint Designer workflow component to the solution. It may seem like it ends a bit abruptly, but don't worry, all is explained shortly in the "Managing the Process" section.

Workflow Summary

That's it for the two workflows. The first workflow creates an entry in the secured request list by means of an impersonation step. This enables you to provide a method that meets the security requirements of the solution: End users can enter requests but cannot edit many of the key data elements of the request, such as the estimated cost, actual cost, and so forth.

The second workflow uses the wait-for activity and two different techniques to identify ending conditions. It uses the magic value technique (estimated cost of negative one) to pause until the facilities manager supplies an estimated cost. It uses the workflow variable comparison technique to detect when the facilities manager assigns a work team.

Managing the Process

This concluding section summarizes the solution and walks you through how all these components work together to provide a comprehensive facilities request solution.

Initiating a Request

End users can navigate to your SharePoint site to create a request. To do that, they need to add an item to the Maintenance Request list. This list's security is configured to grant all valid users "contributor" access. The list is backed by the simple Maintenance Request content type; therefore, the users enter just a few fields: Title, Description, and the date they would like the work completed.

Using impersonation, SharePoint Designer workflow creates an entry in the secured maintenance request list. This secured list is configured to grant read access to authorized users. However, only facilities managers and the facilities team are granted contributor access. This is one way to simulate column-level security in SharePoint. End users feel like they are entering data into one list, but actually they cause the data to load into a second list to which they don't have contributor access. This prevents them from tampering with estimated costs and gaming the system.

Managing Facilities Requests

When SharePoint Designer workflow creates a secured request, the "process request" workflow kicks in. It sets status values throughout all its steps that will be useful for building a dashboard (see more on that in the "Advanced Topics" section).

The first thing it does is await an estimate. The facilities manager must provide this estimate and mark whether the request is automatically approved and can avoid manager approval. This is a manual decision, but look at the "Advanced Topics" section for more ideas about automatic approvals.

Assuming approval is required, the end user's direct manager is asked to approve it. Then, the manager's manager is asked to approve it. These steps are hard-coded into the workflow. As discussed in the "High Level Solution" section, SharePoint Designer does not provide much flexibility around this. This workflow envisions up to two approvers. If your workflow process requires more than that, say four, you need to create four separate approval steps. You do have the flexibility to short circuit the number of approval requests. So, if you have a workflow that may require two approvers for one request and four for another, you can, relatively easily, obtain just the two approvals you need. However, you need to account for the maximum number of possible approvers. SharePoint Designer can't support a random number of approvers.

When approved, the request's status changes, and again workflow waits for the facilities manager to identify and assign a team to do the actual work. After he does that, the workflow ends. How can that be, you ask? That is OK because the facilities team is going to update the status directly via a mobile interface.

Mobile Interfaces in SharePoint

SharePoint 2010, for the first time, provides real hope for a mobile interface. It's not perfect, but you have a real shot now at providing one for your end users. In this solution's case, the team to which your facilities manager assigned a work task will use their mobile device to update status and actual hours spent.

SharePoint 2010 provides a mobile interface to sites and lists. You can access the mobile view of a site or list from your desktop by using the correct URL. Simply append a "/m" to the URL of the site. For instance, if your facilities site is located here

```
http://demo2010a:9090/FacilitiesManagement/default.aspx
```

simply append "/m" as shown:

```
http://demo2010a:9090/FacilitiesManagement/m
```

SharePoint shows a mobile-friendly view of the page (see Figure 7-16).

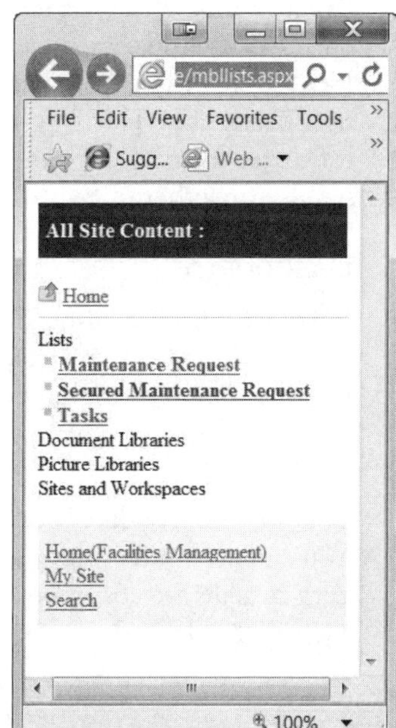

FIGURE 7-16

It's not the prettiest view, but it's workable.

The work team conducts its work and uses the mobile interface to record its results.

You could extend the SharePoint Designer workflow to wait for the facilities team to update SharePoint. You can do that following the patterns presented in the chapter.

Advanced Topics

This chapter took something of a bull-in-the-china-shop approach to this solution, and you can add finesse to the solution in several ways.

Changing Requests

What happens if a user changes his mind? As it now stands, this workflow fires off a request and begins an approval process for a request in a fire-and-forget kind of manner. If the end user changes his mind, he has to directly contact the facilities manager.

To manage change requests, use the techniques you learned in Chapter 5. The maintenance request list should maintain a pointer to the secured request list. Provide a manual workflow that enables the user to edit the description, change the requested work date, or outright cancel the request. This workflow locates the secured request and via impersonation updates it or even deletes it.

Improved Auto Approve

It would be nice to have the system automatically approve requests. Right now, "auto approve" means that the facilities manager decided that a more formal approval is not required.

To make this better, add another custom list with two columns: Request Type and Auto Approve. Create a new site column named MR_RequestType of the lookup type that is backed by this new custom list. Add the column to the Maintenance Request list. In the Process Request workflow, look up this value from the Request Type list, and set MR_IsAutoApproved to Yes based on the user's selection. This way, the value is set to a correct default value when the facilities manager estimates the cost. He can accept the decision or override it. Or you could take it out of his hands altogether.

Dashboards

Every workflow solution should have a dashboard, and this one is no different. Just follow the patterns from previous chapters to create a list-based dashboard. This is a status-rich workflow process, and as a result, you can create more list views than some of the other solutions.

Reporting

This solution produces a rich set of raw data from which you can derive some interesting reports. You can do this as simply as exporting the list to Excel and use Excel for analysis. You have enough data to generate cost reports and variance reports. You can also generate some time-based reports, such as the elapsed time between the request and completion.

SUMMARY

You created a fairly complex workflow solution in this chapter that introduced some new techniques and borrowed from patterns in previous chapters, such as an approach to site column security, building approval trees, waiting for changes to an item, and leveraging SharePoint's mobile interface.

The key points you should take away from this chapter include the following:

- **Site column security:** There is no site column security in SharePoint. That said, you can use SharePoint Designer workflow and impersonation steps, combined with content type hierarchies, to simulate it.
- **Wait-for events:** You can pause your workflow and wait for events to occur, such as when the facilities manager updates an estimate. You learned two techniques for this purpose: magic values and workflow variable comparisons.
- **Mobile interface:** You were introduced to SharePoint 2010's mobile interface and read about how this can support the facilities' management process.

You'll build upon these and more in the following chapters.

Enterprise: Authorization for Capital Expenditure

WHAT'S IN THIS CHAPTER?

- Understanding how users submit CAPEX expenditure authorizations for approval
- Using the decision making and approval processes for CAPEX purchases
- Enabling approvers and requesters to respond to purchases and make comments
- Routing capital expenditure forms for approval based on project codes
- Understanding how to change and add approvers and project codes to an authorization
- Implementing validation to fields
- Providing metrics for analysis
- Maintaining a solid financial control on costs to the business
- Understanding the complexities of CAPEX expenditure purchases to an organization

This chapter describes how to implement a capital expenditure (CAPEX) authorization workflow solution that is designed to allocate approved capital budget funds to projects. In this chapter you learn that intelligent workflow routing decisions can automatically occur depending on the project codes and the status of a CAPEX form.

WHAT IS AUTHORIZATION FOR CAPITAL EXPENDITURE?

CAPEX refers to any capital expenditures used to acquire physical assets in an organization such as land or buildings, and equipment for an office or to set up a manufacturing floor. Along with being related to the acquisition of new assets, CAPEX can also be associated with the decision to upgrade physical assets by making improvements or otherwise refurbishing the property or equipment.

CAPEX decisions, therefore, ultimately form a foundation for the future profitability of a company and normally have two distinct processes: (1) making the decision and (2) receiving and implementing it, which may include performing a post-appraisal. This chapter mainly deals with the first process within the scope of SharePoint technology. The second post-appraisal process normally involves an Enterprise Resource Planning (ERP) software, such as Microsoft GP/AX. There is normally considerable integration of information between the deployed SharePoint technology and your company's ERP system.

This section outlines the procedures to follow in making CAPEX decisions. The CAPEX process is almost a universal process in most organizations but may vary depending on the industry. For simplicity, you can break up procedures into two sections:

- Estimates
- Decision-making process

Estimates

Reliable estimates and forecasts are vital to the capital investment decision. A sophisticated process to analyze financial information and manage decisions related to a project is of little value if you take an informal approach to develop these estimates. The foundation for good capital planning is reliable forecasts and timely decisions. The estimate of the costs and benefits of a capital project should show the *differential principle*, which is the difference that result from making the investment and the change in cash flows as a result of undertaking the project.

The degree of precision necessary for the estimates related to the CAPEX decision depends on the stage of evaluation of the project, the sensitivity of the project's economics to the level of accuracy and timing of each of the elements within the estimates, and if there is similarity of this expenditure to others already undertaken within the organization or industry.

If the investment is of a fixed nature such as equipment costs, installation, training, commissioning, initial spoilage and spare parts inventory, the CAPEX investment can usually be estimated with greater precision because capital investments occur in the near future, whereas operating costs and revenues are incurred over the life of the project. Bids from suppliers' quick estimates can often be obtained because the values are often published and freely available.

If the CAPEX is the result of the replacement of existing equipment and/or the net cash inflows or outflows from the removal and disposal of that equipment, you need to take into account tax.

If the CAPEX involves working capital estimates, any analysis should include estimates of all investments required for a project, such as increases (or decreases) in cash, accounts receivable, accounts payable, or inventory. Include these changes in working capital and the changes at the end of the economic life of the project in your calculations.

Every CAPEX purchase has an economic life (planning horizon), which is difficult to estimate because you need to understand when the purchase is completely worn out or technically dated. Depending on the organization and industry, it can affect the optimism of this planning horizon.

Some organizations set an arbitrary limit on the planning horizon to be used in the analysis and are shorter than the estimated economic life of the project. Other organizations apply an arbitrary estimate of value for the benefits beyond the planning horizon.

With most CAPEX purchases there are operating costs. When estimating, consider the following:

- Only cash costs after the payment of tax on income are relevant; noncash expenses such as depreciation are excluded except to the extent they affect taxable income.
- Only future costs are relevant. Historical costs may be useful to provide a basis for prediction, but they do not represent the future costs.
- Only consider the difference in cash operating costs between implementing or not implementing a proposal.
- Include overtime or savings in the labor costs.

Decision-Making Process

After you gather the relevant information for an estimate, a financial decision needs to be made on whether to make the purchase. Numerous techniques are available, such as the net present value method, the internal rate of return method, the discounted, or the payback method.

The internal rate of return, discounted payback, and net present value use discounted cash flows (DCF), which considers the time value of money in making investment decisions, whereas the payback method does not.

The payback method is useful when preliminary screening of many proposals is necessary; a weak cash position has an important bearing on the selection of projects; or when the project is extremely risky.

If you use this method, the required payback period should be consistent with that developed by applying the required rate of return on projects with similar characteristics. When you establish the financial rate of return, this CAPEX project may be competing with other proposed CAPEX projects in the organization; therefore, a ranking process may occur. The process is normally based on the required rate of return and calculates the net present value of each project. Often an organization has a profitability index of each CAPEX project. A project may be canceled, delayed, or reassessed during this decision-making process.

The estimating process is a complicated process of information gathering from multiple parties both internal and external to the organization, and adhering to company policy with these kinds of purchases. This complex process of information gathering, presenting, and decision making does make this business process ideal for SharePoint because information is captured in a single repository, and relevant people can be notified that their decision is required.

PROBLEM CLASS

This chapter's problem falls into the "complex approvals" problem class. This is a business problem that contains multiple levels of approval and steep dashboarding requirements as befits such a process that plays such a central role in a company's major expense processes.

TECHNICAL PATTERNS

While solving the CAPEX approval problem, you need to implement the following technical patterns:

- **Basic CRUD:** Approvals are created, updated (many times in this case) and deleted (archived).
- **Approval and delegation:** When approvals are submitted, they are assigned to managers for information. This ownership process encourages appropriate actions on an approval.
- **Security:** Some users require access to review, edit, and approve approvals; whereas others require access only to review their own approvals. Some users have no access to this business process.
- **Dashboard:** With multiple approvals in different approval staging, dashboards provide considerable value to provide one source of the "What," "Where," and "Who" of an approval.
- **Outlook integration:** Most end users are familiar with the Outlook interface because they work in this application for most of the day.

BUSINESS PATTERNS

To establish CAPEX authorization, you need to implement the following business patterns:

- **Approvals:** The person(s) who approves the submitted authorizations, which then progress to the next step in the submission life cycle
- **Reviewers:** Personnel who provide content to the submission and assist in the decision-making process
- **Approval matrix:** All approvals have a workflow life cycle, and at each stage, different actions are required by different users. The assignment of an approver (user) should be a simple look up and if possible automatic and based on a business rule, without manual input.
- **Metrics:** The mantra in finance is "What gets seen gets measured." You need to view authorizations in progress and to understand which projects they effect and the amounts, time, and costs, which is essential for forecasting and decision making.

- **Form capturing:** The ability to capture the required information with an InfoPath form.
- **Notifications:** During the submission life cycle, email notifications need to be sent out to the appropriate personnel to review and approve.

BUSINESS PROBLEM DESCRIPTION

There is a lot involved with CAPEX purchases. You can manage these types of purchases with Enterprise Resource Planning (ERP) software such as Microsoft Dynamics GP because these applications already have built-in accounting and reporting processes. However, typical ERP systems do not have sophisticated workflow capabilities or are deployed across an enterprise for approvals and information gathering to occur.

The approval process of these CAPEX items can be difficult to understand and implement within a business because of the following:

- Complex Vendor selection processes; official Request For Proposal (RFP) submission and concomitant evaluations
- Differences in corporate policies based on expenditure type, location, and business unit
- Integration of budgeted and approved information
- Multilevel dollar and quality amount approvals
- Review of the documents from vendors such quotes, RFP responses, comparisons, and blanket purchase orders

The impact of any of the preceding points can lead to approvals delays, under- or over-utilization of budgets, absence of an audit trail especially in case of exceptions, or lack of standardization.

The key to using SharePoint is to implement a standard process to capture the information stated in the preceding bullet points.

Requirements Discussion

A CAPEX authorization tool built within SharePoint should complement your company's ERP system and not replace it. If anything, the SharePoint solution should formalize the current business processes and not reinvent them. Most organizations are already performing this business authorization process through email, saved attachments, and of course, plenty of face-to-face meetings.

You need to identify where the business process in SharePoint starts and ends and where your organization's ERP should be used. There is little value in building out an existing ERP functionality in SharePoint when it already exists in software that you already own. Therefore, you need to understand your current ERP functionality and processes to have agreement within the business for the data integration points to and from SharePoint to the ERP system.

A CAPEX solution needs to provide certain fundamental services to end users:

- Simple and quick entry
- An intuitive interface where users know what to do with the authorization at different stages. This requires clear instructions with defined fields.
- A status of the authorization — what is the next step and who will perform this step?
- Notification to the end user when important events occur, such as when an approval occurs and to whom it is assigned
- Self-help: A quick-and-easy way to look up previous authorizations and understand the business process for the type of capital expenditure project
- A repository of project-related documentation

The CAPEX authorization process also supports users from finance, purchasing, and stakeholders and provides the following:

- Notification when a new authorization is created or flagged for further input or completed
- Dashboard to view and manage in-progress approvals and complete approvals; submissions that require no further action from the user or information transfer to the ERP application
- Metrics based on raw data gathered

If these requirements can be met, you have a solid solution to add value to a CAPEX authorization process.

With these basic requirements in mind, schedule meetings with the end-user community such as finance, purchasing, and project management teams to identify the approval process, information that needs to be captured, and the integration points to the ERP system. Conduct the requirements gathering process with face-to-face interviews to address the following data requirements:

- **Information managed:** Budgets, actual costs, project status, revisions, supplements, tolerances, multistream approvals, attachments, and audit history
- **Processes:** Audit history, work flow automation, actual versus budget variance, accruals, revisions, multiple, user base internal or external dry and completion budgets, security, gross or net calculations, and reclassification of work-in-progress journal entries
- **Deliverables:** Timely approvals, required attachments, online review capability, approval signatures, and detail budget to actual variance reports
- **Input data:** Budgets, expenditures, Active directory integration, approval authorization, project progress, and supplemental budgets
- **Output data:** Ad-hoc inquiries, journal entries (GL), ERP integration, and reports

Often during the data requirement gathering process, users are not fully aware of the capabilities of SharePoint, such as the workflow, eform (InfoPath), field capture, and reporting capabilities. These functionalities should be demonstrated to the end users, so they are aware of what is possible in a SharePoint solution.

The high-level requirements of the business process and SharePoint capabilities for a CAPEX authorization solution follow:

- An approved user can submit or approve a CAPEX project request.
- Submitters may see their submissions.
- Designated users can see relevant submissions.
- A power user or administrator of the process may see any submission.
- The approval process is based on the project type, project code, and value. This process is a matrix process.
- A submission can generate a GRID ID.
- The system can generate a database of metrics, based in project codes and the value to the business and time frames.

Actors

The solution includes the following actors:

- An end user who has a CAPEX submission.
- Approvers: These are based on the project codes and types of projects.
- Finance and project manager's users who add content to the submission throughout its lifecycle. This content includes variance totals, vendors' quotes, forecasting, costs, explanations, and policies.
- Power users of the process. These users identify submissions stuck in a certain stage, change matrix approvers, and soft-coded variables.
- Finance: These users have the task to develop the internal controls in an enterprise and also have the responsibility to coordinate the input of the various functional groups and obtain authorization approval.
- Proposal Review Committee SharePoint group: This group of people will be notified at the appropriate stage of the workflow life cycle.

Actions

The required actions for the CAPEX authorization process to work follow:

1. Create a submission.
2. Manage existing submission to closure.
3. View submission status.
4. Report.
5. Integrate to the ERP.
6. Be a repository for the documentation related to the submission.

Challenges

A CAPEX authorization process is unique to an organization and its culture and can often be tailored to the users involved in the process. Therefore, you can architect a solution that is one-size-fits-all. Certain functions have been omitted from this chapter, which include the following:

- **Integration points from SharePoint to the ERP system:** For example, the Read Write process to the ERP system may not be at the end of the approval process with a single Write. It may be incremental at different approval stages. When the approval is first submitted, a record number in the ERP system may need to be assigned. Given that variation in the ERP systems that companies deploy, it is impossible to detail this functionality without devoting a book or numerous chapters for each system.
- **This chapter's approach:** Write values from SharePoint to a separate SQL database, which can act as a staging database for information to be written to the ERP application.
- **Field values:** For example, project and budget codes are updated or referenced by the user. This could be in the ERP system or a SharePoint list.
- **Approval process:** Does this match the business process and accommodate wanted variations?
- **Validation:** Which fields are validated and at what stages are they validated?
- **Calculations:** Are these correct and can these accommodate extreme values?
- **Delegation:** Because the submission cycle does not require an instantaneous response from this user base, delegation is not required in this solution.

HIGH-LEVEL SOLUTION

The following sections describe the solution you'll craft to meet this problem's business requirements. This will include a now familiar swim lane diagram to show the relationship between actors and the actions they take. This discussion leads directly to the eventual solution.

Solution Overview

A cost-effective CAPEX authorization must leverage as much out-of-the-box functionality as possible to aid the speed of deployment. This out-of-the-box functionality should include workflow, document repository, eforms, and data integration to and from the ERP. Therefore, allowing users to submit a CAPEX authorization form for approval, and during this approval process, documentation, comments, and calculations can be uploaded and performed on this eform.

You can manage the entire authorization process within the SharePoint environment, integrating data elements to an ERP application. The submitted form is a web-based InfoPath form (eform) stored in a forms library. Approvals (electronic signatures) can be appended to the form as it progresses those the authorization life cycle.

CAPEX Expenditure Decision Swim Lane Diagrams

Figure 8-1 shows the decision progress, up until the final approval of CAPEX in an organization.

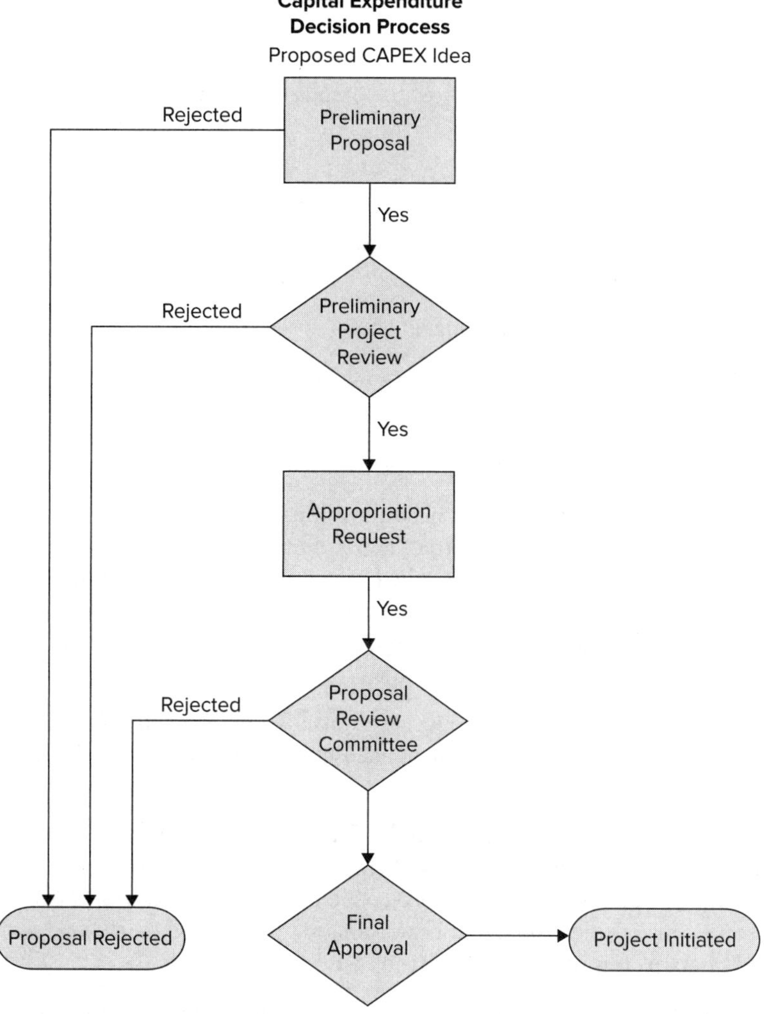

FIGURE 8-1

Each CAPEX authorization expenditure competes for limited resources that are available and needs to be justified. Figure 8-1 outlines formal procedures and rules to ensure that all proposals are reviewed fairly and consistently. Managers and supervisors who submit an authorization need to know what the organization expects the proposals to contain, and on what basis their proposed projects will be judged and assessed, so fields to capture information and uploaded Word templates are essential. Those managers who have the authority to approve specific submissions need to respond to workflow approval requests, which exercise that responsibility in the context of an overall organizational capital expenditure policy and be aware of other submissions.

When the user creates the CAPEX form and completes the initial information requirement, it should include the following:

- Purpose with a brief description of the project
- Timing and amount of the operating cash flows expected
- Timing and amount of the investment required
- Any major assumptions that affect the accuracy of the cash flow estimates
- Economic desirability of the project
- Budget code
- Forecast information
- Funding details
- Appraisal method(s) used to evaluate submission
- Minimum acceptable rate(s) of return on the project and various risks
- Project sponsor
- Review of the alternatives to the project, if appropriate

This information may take some time to gather, so you need the ability to save the form as a *Draft*, prior to submitting it. After the project is submitted, a Preliminary Project Review process should provide an early consideration of and guidance to the project, which could result in an appropriation request and provide an early indication of the value of the project, lead time to implement the project, and visibility of required resources so that activities associated with the project can be scheduled.

Upon submission, the selected Project Sponsor should receive a notification; typically the Project Sponsor is responsible for all the required documentation needed for a decision to be made during the *Preliminary Project Review* stage.

The Project Sponsor reviews the submission and then formally declares this project is approved to progress to the next stage. At this next stage, reviewers of the project, which include project managers, finance, and accountants, are assigned to the project. This stage requires workflow notification. Assigning personnel for notification could be automatic if it is based on the budget code. For the purpose of this chapter, it is assumed this is the case.

During the *Appropriation Request* stage, the information gathered during this step is critical because the ultimate decision by senior personnel is made during this process.

Management accounting personnel are usually responsible for coordinating and compiling information with the aim of prompt completion and address the issue of the appropriation request. The marketing, technical, production, and engineering staff and others may make a considerable contribution. Although Project Sponsors must take the ultimate responsibility for preparation of the appropriation request, the responsibility for development of the report on their behalf should be defined on the InfoPath form.

The benefits of gathering formal procedures and documenting information at this stage include the following:

- Standard terminology, estimating techniques, and methods of appraisal enhance the comparability of appropriations originating in different parts of the organization and are associated with a single business process.
- Decision-making process to be made in the same manner throughout the organization for all CAPEX authorization is encouraged, and authorities for approving expenditures can be delegated with greater confidence.
- Standardization of appraisals enables senior management to concentrate on the strategic and intangible aspects of major expenditures because it is these aspects that often have the greatest impact on the long-term future of the organization.
- When this task is complete, the submission is reviewed by the Proposal Review Committee. In a perfect SharePoint world, this review process would be done with the click of a mouse, but senior management normally meets to review the submitted documentation face to face.
- A decision is made and the submission's status is marked as the Final Approval, and the project can be initiated.

During each stage (including rejection) of the authorization life cycle, notifications should be sent to the submitter, Project Sponsor, and other contributors. This is essential to provide visibility to the process to the user community.

Technical Implementation Overview

The technical implementation begins with content types. These back custom lists and then you finish with a four-step SharePoint Designer workflow.

Content Types

As explained in previous chapters, site columns and content types are a foundation to CAPEX authorization and other solutions. You need content types that represent the following:

- **An InfoPath CAPEX authorization form:** This content type has columns such as Short Description, Long Description, and Category.
- **Approver content type:** Reuse this content type in future chapters (and revisit Chapter 3, "HR On-Boarding," to implement proper delegation.).
- **Project type:** A list of categories from which the user can select
- **Budgeting criteria:** A list of categories such as Internal Rate of Return, Profitability Index, Payback Period, and Return on book Value
- **Approvers and reviews:** Users who would be notified of the submission

Custom Lists

Following are custom lists to use to implement the solution:

- **CAPEX authorization:** A list associated with a content type of the same name
- **Budget codes:** A simple one-column list of budget codes. These codes should correspond the ERP system.
- **Project Sponsors, Proposal Committee members, and final approvers:** A single list of names in the organization. These should be in the Active Directory field.
- **Audit History:** Tracks all relevant business activities for this CAPEX process

ERP Integration

As discussed earlier in this chapter, information on a CAPEX authorization normally resides in an ERP system. Despite common belief, ERP integration does not occur in most authorization life-cycle processes.

To access data external to SharePoint and data within a SharePoint list, you need to understand SOAP.

WHAT IS SOAP?

A SOAP service is a web service that returns XML from a procedural query using the HTTP or HTTPS. SharePoint exposes its data as a SOAP service, enabling you to create, for example, a list of announcements from the current site and its child sites, known as a rollup of announcements. SharePoint can both retrieve data from a third-party source such as an ERP system and act as a data repository using a Data View for an ERP system to request XML data, instructions (known as methods), parameters, and values to the XML. The methods and parameters that a SOAP service supports are described in a Web Service Description Language (WSDL) file. If the SOAP service supports data manipulation, you can select, insert, update, or delete data on the XML Web service provider by using the Data Source Properties dialog box to configure each command.

An ASP.NET page can also act as a SOAP service provider to expose XML data to other sources. This can be deployed using SharePoint Designer, by creating an ASP.NET page to request data stored externally to SharePoint.

This data integration method, can all be done in SharePoint Designer without the skill set of a .Net developer.

Content Providers, Reviewers, and Approvers

When a project submission progresses through the approval process, personnel associated with this submission should have the ability to add content and review it, and if users have the security rights, they can approve it. In doing so, it helps to create a single source of information and review cycle with a seamless transition.

Consider this scenario:

Monis is a project manager and completes a CAPEX form, with Adolfo as the Project Sponsor. Adolfo is the only user who has the authority to either approve or reject this submission but requires other resources to add content to the submission.

These may include, but are not limited to, the following:

- **Finance:** Dawn
- **Project manager:** Jim
- **PMO office:** Mitra

The InfoPath form has the capability to security trim the form, so users can add content but cannot approve and submit the project to the next level. This is a great example of team collaboration. *Security trim* is a SharePoint term of art that you will come across from time to time. SharePoint "trims" objects from end users who are not allowed to see them. Those objects can include search results, menu options, documents, and so forth. The goal behind security trimming is not just to secure an object, but to prevent a scenario where an unauthorized user is even aware that the object exists. There's nothing more frustrating to an end user than clicking on a link just to get SharePoint's generic "not authorized" error message.

At the end of the workflow life cycle, the submission has all the related information stored in a single location, and the relevant parties have reviewed it.

Dashboard

Other chapters have introduced dashboard viewing of the information. The concept of a dashboard is to have a single screen with targeted information for reviewers and the submitter.

DETAILED TECHNICAL IMPLEMENTATION

This chapter's walk-through provides a simple and straightforward implementation of this complex business problem. It is necessarily incomplete as much of the value of this business problem lies within its integration to your company's ERP system. That level of detailed walk-through is beyond the scope of the book.

Setup

To implement the CAPEX authorization solution, you need to create an InfoPath form content type. This is the placeholder for each authorization because each form holds the files and information for the CAPEX project. A SharePoint custom list that uses this content type can feed any required dashboards. All the workflow and integration with the Business Data Catalogue can be implemented with SharePoint designer.

Supporting Lists

The helpdesk solution is built upon the following set of custom lists:

- **CAPEX submissions:** The core list around which the rest of the solution is built
- **Budget codes:** A list of budge codes and corresponding budget descriptions of each
- **Project codes:** A list of project codes and corresponding project titles of each
- **Reviewers:** This is a list of users such as the Project Sponsor, Proposal Review Committee, and final approvers. This is a list of a key component for workflow notification
- **Audit history:** Each time a submission is edited a log entry is created in this list.

Content Types

Every supporting list is backed by a content type. As with every other content type in each solution, it consists of two broad types of site columns: business and technical. End users enter data directly into business columns, and business columns appear on dashboards. Technical columns, on the other hand, do not generally appear to end users and instead support the technical needs of the solution. This solution calls for the following content types:

- Authorization Status Codes
- Project Codes
- Budget Codes
- Reviewers

Authorization Status Codes

This simple content type contains two site columns. Both are business columns:

Business Columns:

- Status code: Status code.
- Status code description: A longer textual description of the code. This text appears in list views and displays when the end user clicks the status code in the InfoPath form.

Create the business columns, as shown in Table 8-1.

TABLE 8-1: CAPEX Authorization Status Site Columns

COLUMN NAME	COLUMN TYPE	ADDITIONAL SETTING
CAPEX_StatusCode	Single Line of Text	None
CAPEX_StatusCodeDescription	Single Line of Text	None

After you create the site columns, you can add them to a new content type named CAPEX Status Codes, as shown in Figure 8-2.

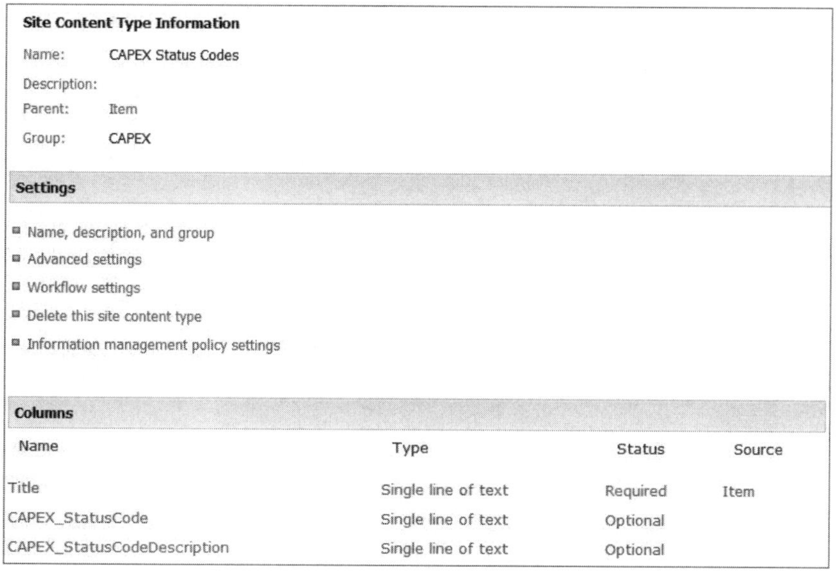

Site Content Type Information

Name: CAPEX Status Codes

Description:

Parent: Item

Group: CAPEX

Settings

- Name, description, and group
- Advanced settings
- Workflow settings
- Delete this site content type
- Information management policy settings

Columns

Name	Type	Status	Source
Title	Single line of text	Required	Item
CAPEX_StatusCode	Single line of text	Optional	
CAPEX_StatusCodeDescription	Single line of text	Optional	

FIGURE 8-2

Project Codes

Another simple content type contains two site columns. Both are Business Columns:

Business Columns:

- **Project code:** Status code.
- **Project code description:** A longer textual description of the code. This text appears in list views and displays when the end user clicks the status code in the InfoPath form.

Create the business columns, as shown in Table 8-2.

TABLE 8-2: CAPEX Project Codes Site Columns

COLUMN NAME	COLUMN TYPE	ADDITIONAL SETTING
PROJECT_Code	Single Line of Text	None
PROJECT _CodeDescription	Single Line of Text	None

After you create the site columns, you can add them to a new content type named Project Codes, as shown in Figure 8-3.

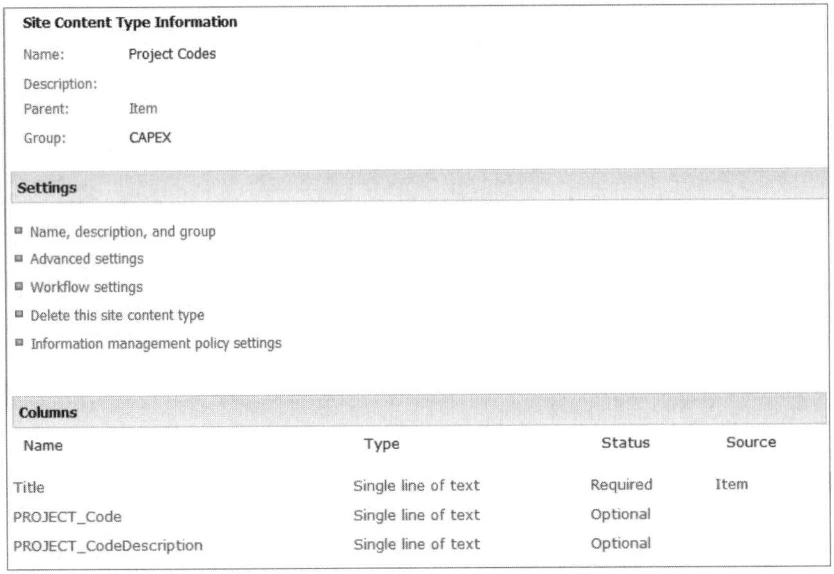

Site Content Type Information

Name: Project Codes

Description:

Parent: Item

Group: CAPEX

Settings

- Name, description, and group
- Advanced settings
- Workflow settings
- Delete this site content type
- Information management policy settings

Columns

Name	Type	Status	Source
Title	Single line of text	Required	Item
PROJECT_Code	Single line of text	Optional	
PROJECT_CodeDescription	Single line of text	Optional	

FIGURE 8-3

Budget Codes

Another simple content type contains two site columns. Both are Business Columns:

Business Columns:

- **Budget code:** The funding code of the project.
- **Budget code description:** A longer textual description of the code. This text appears in list views and displays when the end user clicks the status code in the InfoPath form.

Create the business columns, as shown in Table 8-3.

TABLE 8-3: CAPEX Budget Codes Site Columns

COLUMN NAME	COLUMN TYPE	ADDITIONAL SETTING
BUDGET_StatusCode	Single Line of Text	None
BUDGET_CodeDescription	Single Line of Text	None

After you create the site columns, you can add them to a new content type named CAPEX Budget Codes, as shown in Figure 8-4.

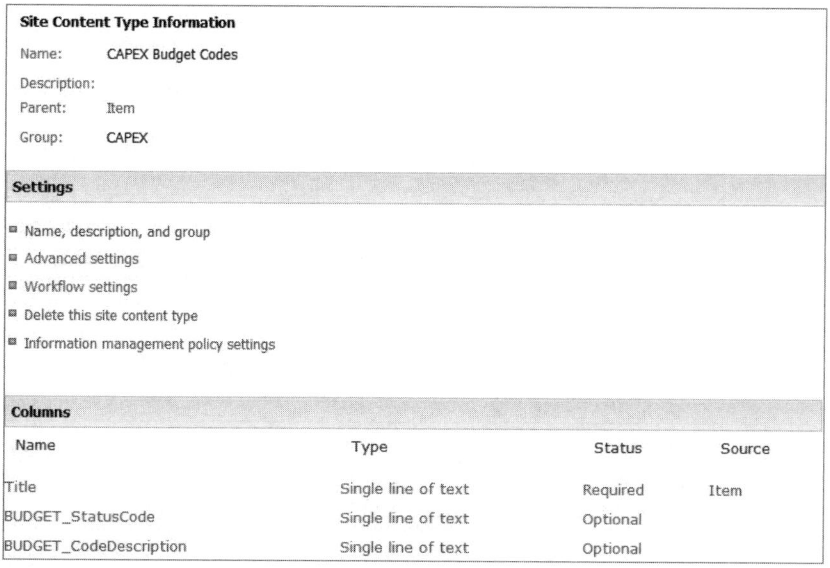

Site Content Type Information

Name: CAPEX Budget Codes

Description:

Parent: Item

Group: CAPEX

Settings

- Name, description, and group
- Advanced settings
- Workflow settings
- Delete this site content type
- Information management policy settings

Columns

Name	Type	Status	Source
Title	Single line of text	Required	Item
BUDGET_StatusCode	Single line of text	Optional	
BUDGET_CodeDescription	Single line of text	Optional	

FIGURE 8-4

Reviewers

Another simple content type contains three site columns. They are Business Columns.

Business Columns:

- **Full name:** Full name of the user.
- **Email address:** The email address of the user. This text appears in list views and displays when the end user clicks the full name in the InfoPath form. In a large organization it is often difficult to identify personnel by just an email address.
- **Project code:** A project code that this reviewer is associated with.

Create a site content type named "CAPEX Reviewers" using the information provided in Table 8-4.

TABLE 8-4: CAPEX Reviewers Site Columns

COLUMN NAME	COLUMN TYPE	ADDITIONAL SETTING
CAPEX_FullNAME	Single Line of Text	None
CAPEX_Email	Person/Group	None
CAPEX_Project	Lookup (information already on this site)	Choose the list of the Project Codes. Allow multiple values.

After you create the site columns, you can add them to a new content type named CAPEX Reviewers, as shown in Figure 8-5.

Site Content Type Information

Name: CAPEX Reviewers

Description:

Parent: Item

Group: CAPEX

Settings

- Name, description, and group
- Advanced settings
- Workflow settings
- Delete this site content type
- Information management policy settings

Columns

Name	Type	Status	Source
Title	Single line of text	Required	Item
CAPEX_FullName	Single line of text	Optional	
CAPEX_Email	Person or Group	Optional	
CAPEX_Project	Lookup	Optional	

FIGURE 8-5

CAPEX Submission

This is the engine of the CAPEX authorization solution. This contains multiple business columns, which need to include the following:

- **CAPEX_Number:** A unique ID that identifies this ticket
- **CAPEX_ShortDescription:** Short summary of the project, which displays on the dashboard, list views, and email notification
- **CAPEX_Reviewers:** Based on the Project Code, supplied by the user. SharePoint Designer workflow uses this value to automatically assign reviewers to this a submission. This field links to another list for its values. This is called a lookup column
- **CAPEX_ProjectSponsor:** The actual sponsor of the proposed project
- **CAPEX_Submitter:** User who created the submission
- **CAPEX _LongDescription:** A detailed description of the project
- **CAPEX_BudgetCode:** The user-supplied category. This is a lookup value to another list
- **CAPEX_ProjectCode:** The project code associated with the submission. This field is user-generated and looks up it values in another list
- **CAPEX_Desirability:** The economic desirability of the project
- **CAPEX_FundingDetails:** Timing and amount of the investment required

- **CAPEX_ReviwerComments:** Long description for comments and feedback on the submission
- **CAPEX_Assumptions:** Any major assumptions that bear on the accuracy of the cash flow estimates
- **CAPEX_AppraisalMethod:** Appraisal method(s) to be used to evaluate submission
- **CAPEX_MinRates:** Minimum acceptable rate(s) of return on projects of various risks
- **CAPEX_ForecastInfo:** Forecast information for the submission
- **CAPEX_Status:** The status of the submission. This is also a lookup column
- **CAPEX_ProfitablilityIndex:** A list of values from 1 to 10 used for ranking the proposed expenditure

Create the business columns, as shown in Table 8-5.

TABLE 8-5: CAPEX Submission Site Columns

COLUMN NAME	COLUMN TYPE	ADDITIONAL SETTING
CAPEX_Number	Single Line of Text	None
CAPEX_ShortDescription	Single Line of Text	None
CAPEX_Reviewers	Person or Group	None
CAPEX _ProjectSponsor	Person or Group	None
CAPEX _LongDescription	Multiple Lines of Text	Selects values from the Categories custom list
CAPEX_ProjectCode	Lookup	Selects values from the Project Codes custom list
CAPEX _BudgetCode	Lookup	Selects values from the Budge Codes custom list
CAPEX_Desirability	Multiple Lines of Text	None
CAPEX_ReviewerComments	Multiple Lines of Text	None
CAPEX_Assumptions	Multiple Lines of Text	None
CAPEX_AppraisalMethod	Multiple Lines of Text	None
CAPEX_MinRates	Multiple Lines of Text	None
CAPEX_ForecastInfo	Multiple Lines of Text	None
CAPEX_Status	Lookup	Selects values from the authorization Status Codes custom list
CAPEX_ProfitablilityIndex	Number	Min. Value 1 and max. value as 10

Technical Columns:

Email sent: For a workflow to run multiple times on a submission without the status changing since it was last saved, this particular setting is required. The default value should be 0.

After you create the site columns, you can add them to a new content type named CAPEX Submissions, as shown in Figure 8-6.

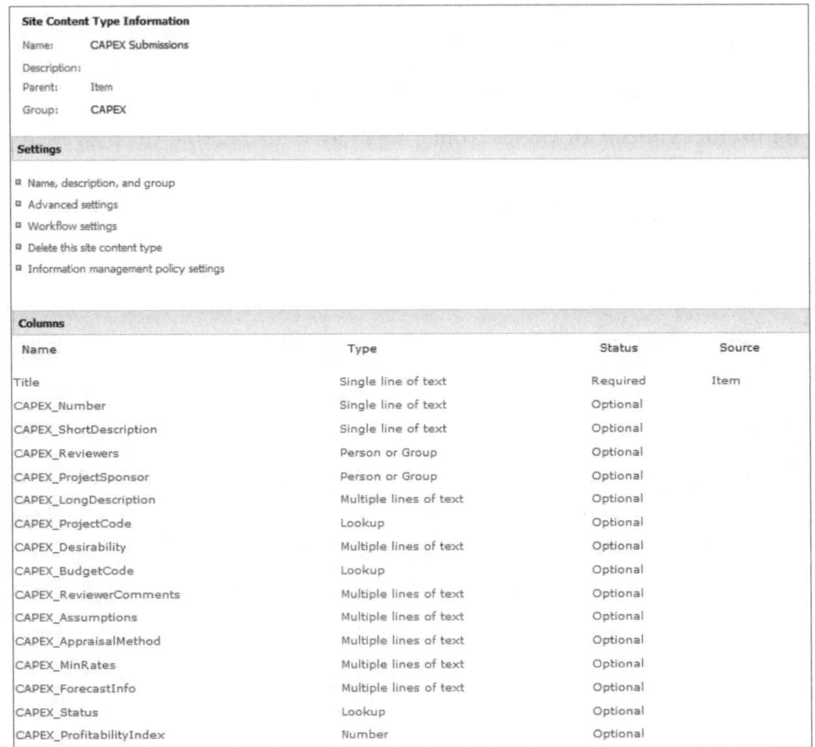

Site Content Type Information

Name: CAPEX Submissions

Description:

Parent: Item

Group: CAPEX

Settings

- Name, description, and group
- Advanced settings
- Workflow settings
- Delete this site content type
- Information management policy settings

Columns

Name	Type	Status	Source
Title	Single line of text	Required	Item
CAPEX_Number	Single line of text	Optional	
CAPEX_ShortDescription	Single line of text	Optional	
CAPEX_Reviewers	Person or Group	Optional	
CAPEX_ProjectSponsor	Person or Group	Optional	
CAPEX_LongDescription	Multiple lines of text	Optional	
CAPEX_ProjectCode	Lookup	Optional	
CAPEX_Desirability	Multiple lines of text	Optional	
CAPEX_BudgetCode	Lookup	Optional	
CAPEX_ReviewerComments	Multiple lines of text	Optional	
CAPEX_Assumptions	Multiple lines of text	Optional	
CAPEX_AppraisalMethod	Multiple lines of text	Optional	
CAPEX_MinRates	Multiple lines of text	Optional	
CAPEX_ForecastInfo	Multiple lines of text	Optional	
CAPEX_Status	Lookup	Optional	
CAPEX_ProfitabilityIndex	Number	Optional	

FIGURE 8-6

Create Workflows

To implement the solution, you need to deploy two workflows to notify users of the submission, to track progress and document editing activity of the submission.

Figure 8-7 shows the submission life cycle stages.

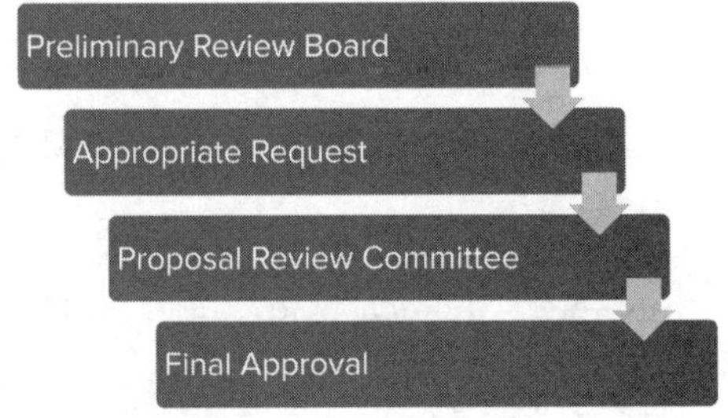

FIGURE 8-7

You need to create two workflows:

- **Assign unique key:** Assigns a unique identification key to the submission
- **Contributor approval:** Notifies the project sponsor and other contributors of the submission at appropriate times of the submissions life cycle

Assign Unique Key

In Chapter 4, "Helpdesk Ticketing," you were introduced to the concept of creating workflows with SharePoint Designer. That chapter also provides an explanation of how to create a unique key to a submission with the *Update Delegate Key* workflow. It provides the information on how to assign a unique key to a submission saved in the `CAPEX_Number` field and should be implemented in this workflow.

The trigger for the workflow should be set to when the item is created (see Figure 8-8) and run only when the item is saved.

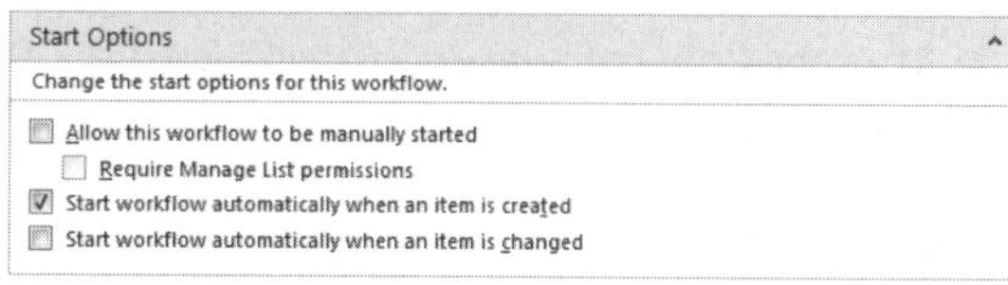

FIGURE 8-8

This unique ID may flow into the company's ERP system, so there should be a company format, such as ProjectCode + BudgetCode + today's date.

Contributor Approval

As the submission progresses through the workflow cycle, it should notify the relevant personnel to take action. The Start Options for this workflow should be set to both Created and Changed, as shown in Figure 8-9.

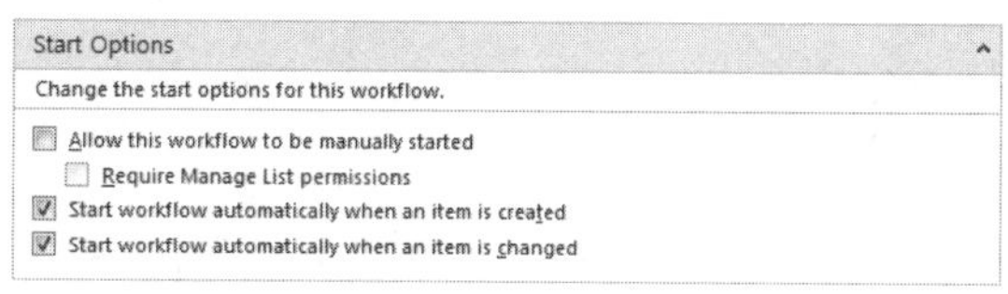

FIGURE 8-9

Every time the submission is changed, this workflow runs and depending on the status of the item, requests the appropriate action. The workflow has to take into account the item being created and then saved as a nondraft item, so the status is set to *Preliminary Review* on the first save.

The SharePoint Designer workflow is designed so that the sequential steps in the workflow are a conditional event, based on the status value. There are basically five steps and a few simple actions in each step.

Four steps should be named for each status choice of the item: Preliminary Review, Appropriate Request, Proposal Review Committee, and Final Approval/ Rejected.

The fifth and final step should be called Audit.

The inner working of each step is outlined next.

Preliminary Review Status

Each step needs to have a parallel condition set on it, indicating the status and if this step has been run before in this instance of the workflow. The conditions and actions are shown in Figure 8-10.

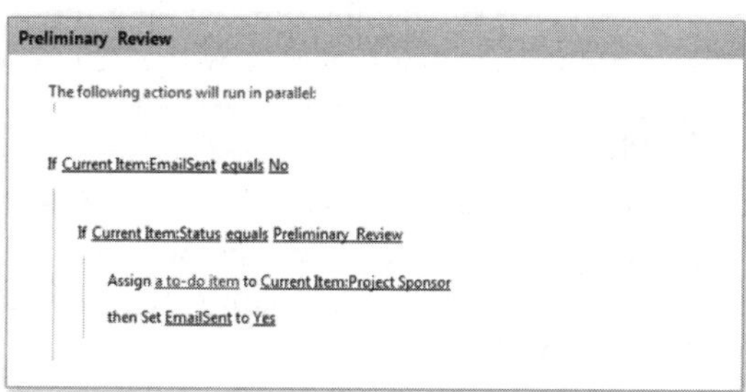

FIGURE 8-10

The following are added to the actions:

- ToDo Task assigned to the Project Sponsor field of the item. The project sponsor will be notified though a Task list associated with this workflow.
- Set the value `EmailSent` to Yes.

After the Project Sponsor has completed the task, he changes the status of the submission to Appropriate Request.

Appropriate Request Status

The condition should be the same as previously outlined but with the status of Appropriate Request. Following are the actions:

- ToDo Task assigned to the Reviewers field of the item. The users in the Reviewers field will be notified through a Task list associated with this workflow.
- Set the value `EmailSent` to Yes.

After the reviewers and Project Sponsor complete the task, they change the status of the submission to Proposal Review Committee.

Proposal Review Committee Status

The condition should be the same as previously outlined but with the status equal to the Proposal Review Committee. Following are the actions:

- Send email to the SharePoint members group Proposal Review Committee. This email notifies the members of the group that a submission is now ready for the proposal review committee, and a date will be set.

After the committee meets with the Project Sponsor, the committee can change the status to Approved or Rejected.

Final Approval Status or Rejected

The condition should be the same as previously outlined but with the status of Final Approval. Following are the actions:

- Send an email that is sent to the SharePoint group Proposal Review Committee, the creator of the submission, Project Sponsor, and reviewers that this CAPEX approval has been Approved or Rejected by the Review Committee.

Audit

There are no conditions with this step of the workflow. Every time the workflow is run, a new item is created in the Audit list, as shown in Figure 8-11.

FIGURE 8-11

The value that should be added to this list item is the Modified By field because this indicates who edited the CAPEX submission.

SUMMARY

This chapter walked you through the business process, technical design, and actual implementation of a CAPEX authorization solution. The key points you should take away from this chapter include the following:

- **Approval:** How to set up, manage, and use notifications
- **Complexities of the business process:** This chapter expands the knowledge of a complex business process, whereas other chapters introduced you to SharePoint Designer and InfoPath.
- **Introduction:** How to use to the ERP integration points

CAPEX authorization approval is a huge win in an organization, but only if it is implemented thoughtfully and strategically and with a thorough understanding of the business processes.

Marketing Contact Management

WHAT'S IN THIS CHAPTER?

- Providing the submitter confidence to actually use the form
- Providing a decision-making framework to route the form to the correct personnel within an organization for them to respond
- Gauging response time to the submitter within the organization
- Providing exceptional user experience for the submitter
- Providing metrics for analysis

This chapter describes how to implement an anonymous form within the SharePoint environment, with specific focus on the most common business example of the infamous Contact Us form on public-facing SharePoint websites. In this chapter you learn that simple workflow routing decisions can automatically route requests from customers and prospects that can ultimately and positively impact bottom-line profits.

WHAT IS CUSTOMER SERVICE?

Dealing with customer's rights? Something that the marketing department down the corridor does? Answering phones? All of these responses are valid. However, in reality, customer service is an activity that everyone in a company provides and unfortunately is something that many organizations fail to meet their customers' or prospects' expectations, which might lead to a loss of business.

Customer service is as an intangible and ad hoc activity, difficult to immediately measure that can lead to an immediate decision by potential customers on whether they do business with an organization, which is why these organizations allocate resources and spend considerable time in trying to perfect this business activity.

So far, this still does not define customer service.

(continues)

(continued)

Consider that customer service is a relationship in which you have a commitment to the other person that is transparent in your activity and availability to that person. In short, you are of service to customers and committed to providing the said service.

If this notion is executed incorrectly by an organization, problems can arise. The reputation and perception of a company can be adversely impacted if the customer service and customer experience is negative. This is evident especially nowadays with faceless ticketing systems and general department voicemail boxes.

THE ANONYMOUS CONTACT US FORM

Most corporate web sites provide a Contact Us submission form. However, they are often very shallow and the site visitor contact us forms often fall into a black hole due to a poorly thought out and poorly implemented workflow process. As a result, most visitors to these sites have little confidence in the Contact Us form functionality.

This is an easy business process to implement, but to implement it so that the website visitor (Visitor) has confidence in using it and for an organization to respond to a submission does require some thought and effort to execute.

You may think that explaining this functionality of a website is obvious and the benefits of the function are marginal compared to other sales and marketing activities that a company could focus on. This is an incorrect assumption. The following section outlines some facts, myths, golden rules, and web functionalities as they relate specifically to the Contact Us form.

Facts

Most users do not have a great deal of confidence with this form because of the lack of transparency and the perception that the submission will end up in an inbox, which is rarely monitored and probably never replied to, so they end up calling the company requesting the information they need. It's often a last resort. It represents an opportunity because if you implement an effective solution here, you can shine even brighter as people have low expectations to begin with.

Most companies have the submission details captured in an email, which, in turn, is directed to an email distribution list. Often, it does work as a process but can be unreliable because the submission is not monitored, and emails can get lost in the designated persons' email inboxes. Thus it ultimately reinforces a submitter's perception of the execution of this form.

Website Myths

Even if the submission form has a rock solid workflow process built in SharePoint, there is no guarantee that a submitter will have the confidence to use it.

Just because a website has the functionality, it does not mean that the functionality is used. This is not just with anonymous forms but also other pages of the business processes.

Some organization may think the Contact Us business process has marginal value. This is incorrect. Companies who spend tons of marketing dollars on branding, messaging, and a cool website have fully functional Contact Us processes.

Golden Rules

This section outlines the golden rules that you need to apply to website submission forms so that the submitter has confidence in using the form knowing that the information is captured, correctly routed, and managed properly. By following this approach, the contact form not only adds value to an organization's website, but also to the submitter's experience.

Visitor Confidence

For the submitter to have confidence with the form, a statement must clearly indicate how long it will take for the organization to respond to the submission on the Contact Us page. This manages the submitter's expectations and builds confidence in the process.

The submitter's confidence can be further reinforced with instructions for the organization out-of-office response voice messaging service stating something like the following:

> "For quicker responses use the Contact Us form. We always monitor form submissions and respond to the submission promptly."

After the submission, the sender should receive an acknowledgment email that states the details of the submission and the title of the person who is handling it. Figure 9-1 is an excellent example of an acknowledgment email from the hosting company Site 5.

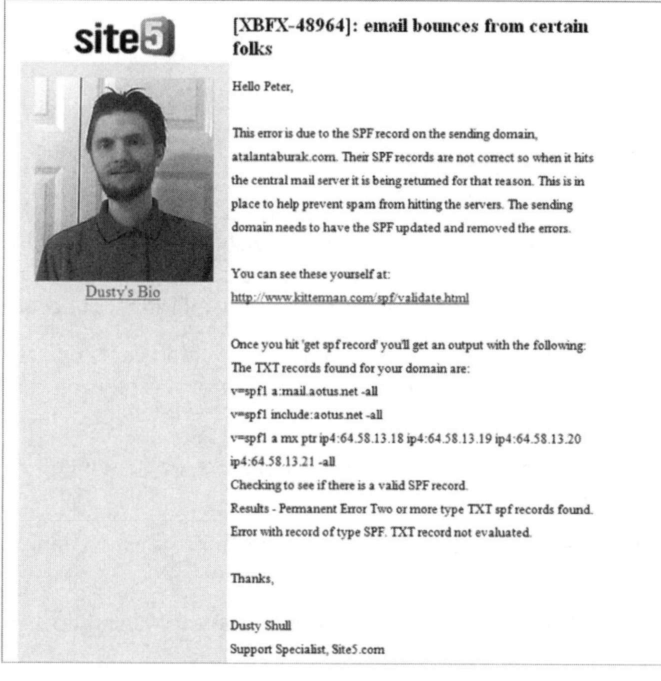

site5

Dusty's Bio

[XBFX-48964]: email bounces from certain folks

Hello Peter,

This error is due to the SPF record on the sending domain, atalantaburak.com. Their SPF records are not correct so when it hits the central mail server it is being returned for that reason. This is in place to help prevent spam from hitting the servers. The sending domain needs to have the SPF updated and removed the errors.

You can see these yourself at:
http://www.kitterman.com/spf/validate.html

Once you hit 'get spf record' you'll get an output with the following:
The TXT records found for your domain are:
v=spf1 a:mail.aotus.net -all
v=spf1 include:aotus.net -all
v=spf1 a mx ptr ip4:64.58.13.18 ip4:64.58.13.19 ip4:64.58.13.20 ip4:64.58.13.21 -all
Checking to see if there is a valid SPF record.
Results - Permanent Error Two or more type TXT spf records found.
Error with record of type SPF. TXT record not evaluated.

Thanks,

Dusty Shull
Support Specialist, Site5.com

FIGURE 9-1

This acknowledgment email shows the person who is handling the submission, what he looks like, that he exists, and a link to his bio, so the sender has visibility and confidence with the person's skill set. There is now an associated ticket number, which can be referenced, and the email is formatted with the company logo.

Even though this is a standard boilerplate, there are some nice features to the content, which re-enforces the submitter's confidence in the process.

Routing

When the form is submitted, it needs to be routed to the correct person within the organization. This should be an automatic process based on field values selected by the submitter, such as a department or category.

If a response time is slow, there should be an escalation process, or if the submission requires management response, submissions need to be a flagged for its attention.

Process Management

In any business process there needs to be someone accountable for it. This is normally the Webmaster, or someone closely associated with updating the content of the site. This person needs to have the authorization to follow up with users who are part of this business process and if necessary bring management intervention to the process.

Many anonymous requests fall into broad and common categories, for instance, requests for information on your flagship product or for local sales contacts. Once your organization identifies these patterns, it can create a knowledge base of vetted responses to immediately send to the requestor.

By applying these golden rules, you can implement a professional process — a process that the visitor has confidence to use.

PROBLEM CLASS

Although the Contact Us form is a simple process in concept, people are included both internally and externally to the organization who must be in agreement with the process and understand their roles in this process. The workflow may be simple, but challenges to deploy a solution can occur:

- What information does the form capture? Obviously, the more information captured, the better the routing process and reporting potential, but if too much information is on the form, it will not be used by the visitor.
- Who is the target audience of the form? Prospects, potential employees, or customer support? This affects the routing process.
- The form must be seen as the point of capture for information from a prospect, vendor, or existing customers.
- Does the routing of the form add value to the business process for the users? And does the routing process match the steps on how the submission should be handed?

If these points are not understood or are incorrectly implemented, this submission form has a slim chance of being adopted within an organization.

You can use SharePoint to capture and manage the process and provide a single source of who is managing the submission.

TECHNICAL PATTERNS

While implementing the Anonymous forms Contact Us form, you need to implement the following technical patterns:

- **Basic CRUD:** Submissions are created, updated (many times in this case) and deleted (archived).
- **Responses and delegation:** When forms are submitted, they are assigned to information workers for action. This ownership process encourages responses to be quicker and accountability to the process.
- **Security:** Given the nature of the submission, security is not viewed as an issue to be discussed in this chapter. Also given that response time adds value to the business process, submissions should be editable, and sharing of information should be encouraged.
- **Dashboard:** Understanding what is pending and assigned to whom, with minimal effort is key. That's the classic: "what," "where," and the "who" of a submission.

BUSINESS PATTERNS

To establish this form submission process, you need to implement the following business patterns:

- **Submitter:** The visitor to the website and the submitter of the form.
- **Responders:** The organization's personnel who take ownership of the submission and respond to the submitter or take the appropriate action.
- **Routing matrix:** All submissions must be routed to the correct personnel. This should be based on a field on the form. The assignment of a responder (user) should be a simple look up and based on a business rule and be automated without manual input.
- **Metrics:** As mentioned in previous chapters, understanding where a submission is in the process is key to the effectiveness of the business process.
- **Form capturing:** The capability to capture the required information with a form.
- **Notifications:** During the submission life cycle, email notifications need to be sent to the appropriate personnel to review and take action.

BUSINESS PROBLEM DESCRIPTION

The following sections describe the business requirements, list the actors and actions they take, and explain some of the special challenges that this problem and the requirements present to you as a SharePoint workflow developer.

Requirements Discussion

As discussed earlier, the Anonymous Contact Us is an underused functionality of a website, and valid reasons exist for why this is the case with most organizational websites.

By using SharePoint to the capture this business process, the form should not be over-engineered and should minimize effort from people involved in the process.

To minimize effort a performance methodology to "getting things done" is outlined. You need to focus on the work that has been done for a constant period of time. This is difficult when there is an endless drip feed of messages arriving in your Inbox, which when on arrival, always notify and distract you. It is not uncommon that when you attempt to respond to the unopened emails there can be an overwhelming sense of "Where do I start?"

SharePoint is a perfect tool to manage this performance process methodology by keeping the content outside the user's cluttered Inbox in a structured way, but also managing the timeliness of the notification process, with the end result of the users structuring their day better, by allocating a time of the day to respond to submissions, which are stored in a single place, in a dashboard format.

Email (memo) was designed as a messaging tool for individuals to casually communicate to people, rather than as a tracking tool involving multiple people with escalation procedures.

A SharePoint solution should formalize the business processes with the focus to capture and process submissions, with a focus on keeping this process in SharePoint, so the submitter does not end up following up via phone or another submission, which can be a huge distraction to personnel's other activities.

With some basic requirements and considerations, schedule meetings with personnel from the departments that respond to submissions. This should be at a minimal support, marketing, and sales. The key is to obtain traction with this business process. Ideally this requirements-gathering process should be conducted with face-to-face interviews to address the following data requirements:

- **Information managed:** Submitter's details, detailed description of submission, submission's status, revisions, category, internal category tags, attachments, and version history
- **Processes:** Submission number, organization's assigner, and assigners details
- **Deliverables:** Responders response
- **Output data:** Notifications to submitter, responders, and management.

While discussing this business process with the user community, you should identify how many requests the organization receives for information such as marketing material, product support, directions, and accounting information. It is important to address these issues, rather than how many submissions the organization currently receives through the website because this is not a true gauge to forecast the number of submissions.

Following are the high-level requirements of this business process:

- A submitter can submit a Contact Us form via the corporate website without a user ID or authentication.
- Submitters may see their submissions as an email acknowledgment to them or by typing in the generated ticket number (or reference number) to search the web page.
- Designated users can see all submissions.
- The routing process is based on a selected category that the submitter selects.
- A submission generates a GRID ID.
- The system generates a database of metrics based on category, submissions in process, completion, and time frames to complete the task.

Actors

The requirement includes the following actors:

- Submitter of the form — visitor to the website
- Internal personnel who are part of the business process to respond to submissions
- Management of the departments that respond to the submissions
- Power users of the process. These users identify submissions stuck in a certain stage, change responders, add departments, and manage the soft-coded variables.

Actions

Following are the required actions for the Anonymous form — Contact Us form:

1. Create a submission.
2. Manage existing submission to closure.
3. View submission status.
4. Report.
5. Respond to the submitter.
6. Build a submission repository for personnel to reference.

Challenges

The challenges to a successful deployment to this process include the following:

- The ability to engage with the organization departments so that they see the value of this business process and why it is a bad business practice to delay responses and provide little visibility to how the submission is handled by the organization.
- Capturing enough information on the initial submission. "Enough" tells you whether the submitter is "playing around" or is seriously looking for a response. In addition, a certain minimum amount of information is required in order for your company's responders to properly respond.
- Approval Process. Does this really match the business process and accommodate wanted variations?
- Validation. Which fields are validated and when?
- The submitter does not have the ability to save draft forms.
- Displayed fields. Are these correctly displayed at different stages?
- Is the submitter's inquiry answered and are they satisfied with the response?

HIGH-LEVEL SOLUTION

To implement this solution, use all the bread-and-butter techniques described throughout the book (content types, custom lists, and dashboards implemented as custom list views rendered on web part pages). You dip your toes into InfoPath for the first time to create a more effective end user experience.

Chapter 11, "Enhancing the User Interface," provides a more in-depth introduction to InfoPath. You may want to read that chapter before trying out the detailed walk-through in this chapter.

Solution Overview

This business process is not complicated and using out-of-the-box SharePoint functionality should be more than adequate to provide a satisfactory solution. This out-of-the-box functionality should include a web-based submission form, with input forms and a workflow process. This enables capturing and processing of submissions to be process-driven with satisfactory feedback to the submitter at stages.

The whole submission process can be managed within the SharePoint environment, with the capability to promote submissions to a knowledge base for future reference. This extends the collaboration solutions because in most organizations key valuable information is not written down in large documents, but rather walking around the corridors and going up and down elevators in the organization, so these short responses to submissions captures company information in a written form. This is akin to the knowledge base that you created in Chapter 4, "Helpdesk Ticketing."

You might be wondering why this proposed solution uses an InfoPath form rather than a custom list form, given that this is a simple business process. A custom list may work, but the process requires certain fields to be displayed and certain stages to be either editable or in read mode. This can be done by editing the custom list forms in SharePoint Designer, but it does push the custom form to the limits and is time-consuming to edit in SharePoint Designer. For web-based InfoPath forms to be used, the SharePoint environment needs to be Enterprise, rather than Standard and this is a more expensive IT investment.

CUSTOM LISTS

You can create custom lists either through the web browser or SharePoint Designer. When a custom list is created, you must add every field, with the exception of the Title field into the list. Unlike a discussion list, where there are already predefined fields, in a custom list there are none. A custom list has three forms required to be edited in within SharePoint Designer.

NewForm.aspx: Only visible when the form is created and not saved

EditForm.aspx: Only visible when the form is in edit mode

DispForm.aspx: Only visible when the form is in read mode

An Anonymous Form Submission Process

The process begins when a visitor to the website submits a Contact Us InfoPath form. (See Figure 9-2.) SharePoint routes the submission to the appropriate users in a department that reviews, edits, and marks it to the attention of the submitter.

The submitters are notified that their submission has been responded to and they can either mark it as complete, or resubmit the submission, where the department review process begins again.

If the submitter fails to mark the submission as completed over a given period of time, this will be flagged to be closed by the department.

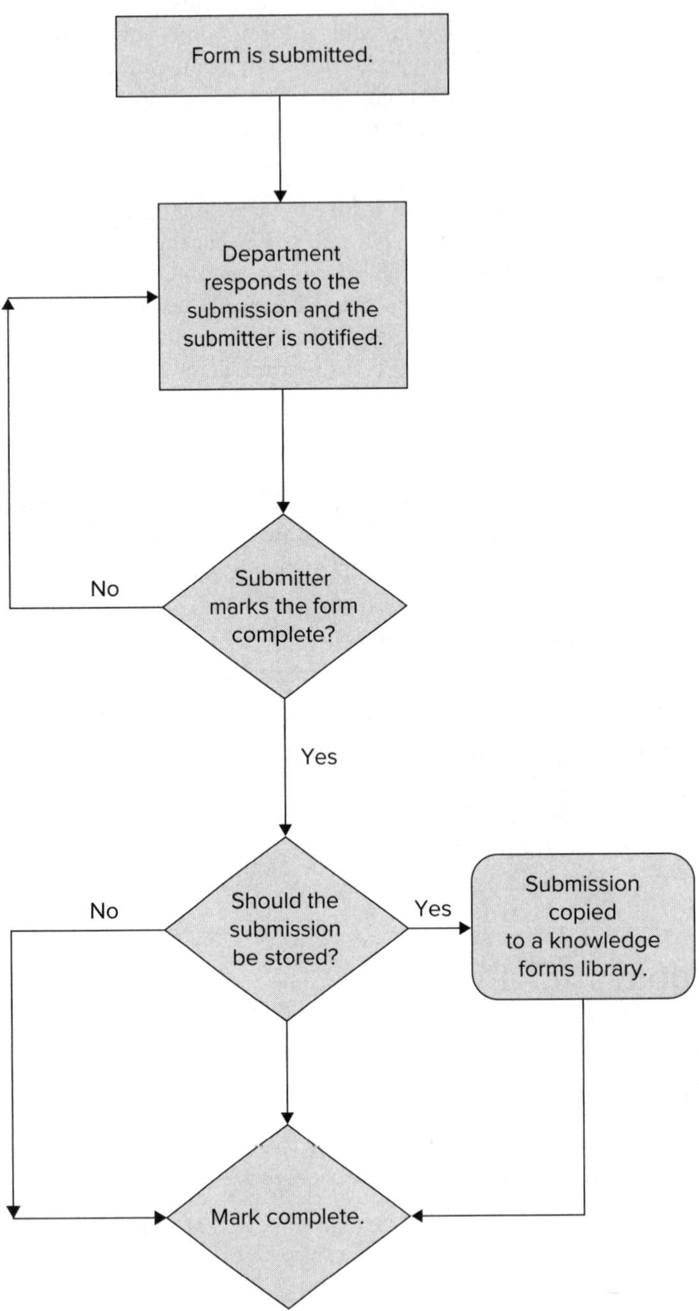
An Anonymous Form Submission Process
Form is submitted.
Department responds to the submission and the submitter is notified.
Submitter marks the form complete?
No
Yes
Should the submission be stored?
No
Yes
Submission copied to a knowledge forms library.
Mark complete.

FIGURE 9-2

Lastly, the department that was assigned the submission decides if this submission should be referenced for future use and tags it to be copied into the knowledge base for future reference.

This process is controlled with the Status field, which changes throughout the life cycle of the form. The status is summarized here:

- **New:** The form has just been opened and has not been saved.
- **Internal Action Required:** The form has just been submitted or resubmitted by the submitter, and the relevant department has been notified. This value is always set when the form is submitted and the form value is New.
- **Submitter Action Required:** Manually set by a user of a department prior to the submission of the form.
- **Pending Internal Review:** Manually set by a user of a department prior to the submission of the form.
- **On Hold:** Manually set by a user of a department prior to the submission of the form.
- **Complete:** Manually set by a user of a department prior to the submission of the form.

The status field is a drop field on the form and can be manually altered only by department users. This is explained further in the "Views" section of an InfoPath form.

TECHNICAL IMPLEMENTATION OVERVIEW

This chapter leverages SharePoint 2010 InfoPath to create a properly branded and rich user interface for your end users. An in-depth explanation of InfoPath is not properly in the scope for this book. If you aren't already familiar with InfoPath or don't want to use InfoPath, you can replace "InfoPath" with "custom list" everywhere in this chapter. In practice, you don't want to ask anonymous users to fill out a standard default SharePoint 2010 edit form. Your web site visitors will be confused and you'll defeat the entire purpose of providing this "contact us" functionality.

Beyond InfoPath, you follow the same patterns as before. Create content types that are designed to back up custom lists. Then, you glue these various elements together using a SharePoint 2010 workflow built using SharePoint Designer.

Content Types

For these solutions you need a single content type that represent an anonymous contact us request. This content type has columns such as Submitter Email Address, Full Name, Submitter Phone Number, Short Description, Long Description, and Response.

SharePoint Lists

Following are SharePoint lists to use in implementing the solution:

- **Submissions:** A list associated with a content type of the same name
- **Knowledge base:** A list identical to the submissions list but stores completed submissions that can be referenced

- **Categories:** A simple one-column list of categories. These should correspond to the type of submission and a department system.
- **Actions:** A simple one-column list of categories. These should correspond to the required action person editing the submission.
- **Photos:** A single list of photograph images of the respondents in the departments that respond to the submission

Responders

When a submission progresses through its life cycle, personnel require the ability to respond to submissions and reassign the submission to the creator of the submission.

Dashboard

Other chapters have introduced dashboard viewing of the information. The concept of a dashboard is to have a single screen with targeted information for Reviewers and the Submitter.

DETAILED TECHNICAL IMPLEMENTATION

This chapter's solution follows well-establish patterns from the book's previous chapters. Set up the solution with lists backed by content types. Create SharePoint Designer workflow to manage the process.

Setup

To implement the Contact Us solution, you need to create a content type for the anonymous submission. This is the placeholder for each submission that stores the details for each request that comes in from the public web site.

Content Types

End users enter data directly into business columns, and business columns appear on dashboards. Technical columns, on the other hand, do not generally appear to end users and instead support the technical needs of the solution. This solution calls for a Submission form content type:

Submission Form

This content type contains both business site columns.

Business Columns:

- **Submitter First Name:** Text field
- **Submitter Last Name:** Text field
- **Submitter Company:** Text field
- **Submitter Email Address:** Text field

- **Submitter Contact Number:** Text field
- **Brief Description:** Text field
- **Long Description:** A longer textual description of the submission. This text appears in list views and displays when the end user clicks the link to the InfoPath form.
- **Status:** The status of the submission
- **Category:** A category of the submission
- **Action:** The required action of the submitter or the person responding to the submission.

Table 9-1 examines the business site columns.

TABLE 9-1: Submissions Business Site Columns

COLUMN NAME	COLUMN TYPE	ADDITIONAL SETTINGS
CONTACTUS_Number	Single Line of Text	Required Field
CONTACTUS_ShortDescription:	Single Line of Text	Required Field
CONTACTUS_LongDescription	Multiple Lines of Text	Required Field
CONTACTUS_Submitteremail	Single Line of Text	Required Field
CONTACTUS_*Category*	Lookup	Selects values from the Categories custom list. See later for more details.
CONTACTUS_SubmitterFirstName	Single Line of Text	Required Field
CONTACTUS_SubmitterLastName	Single Line of Text	Required Field
CONTACTUS_SubmitterPhoneNumber	Single Line of Text.	Required Field
CONTACTUS_Submittercompany	Single Line of Text	Required Field
CONTACTUS_ReviewerComments	Multiple Lines of Text	None
CONTACTUS_Status	Choice	New (Default) Submitter Action Required Internal Action Required Pending Internal Review Complete
CONTACTUS_ActionRequiredby	Multiple Lines of Text	Selects value from the Actions custom list. See later for more details.

continues

TABLE 9-1 *(continued)*

COLUMN NAME	COLUMN TYPE	ADDITIONAL SETTINGS
CONTACTUS_PhotoURL *	PictureURL	URL based on the username of last modifier
CONTACTUS_KnowledgeBase	Radio button	Yes No

* CONTACTUS_PhotoURL is a calculated field. This is Path to the photo library plus the photo of the person who modified the InfoPath form, for example, `http://Servername/sitecollection/site/photolib/pward.jpeg`.

Views

The submission InfoPath form displays a view depending on the value of the status field.

InfoPath views offer users different ways to look at data. For example, you might create a special view that is optimized for printing, or you might create a high-level summary view to eliminate some of the details in a complex form template.

The Views are explained next.

New View

Table 9-2 displays the following fields for this view.

TABLE 9-2: "New" View InfoPath Columns

FIELD NAME	READ/EDIT ABILITY
CONTACTUS_ShortDescription:	Edit
CONTACTUS_LongDescription	Edit
CONTACTUS_Submitteremail	Edit
CONTACT_Category	Edit
CONTACTUS_SubmitterFirstName	Edit
CONTACTUS_SubmitterLastName	Edit
CONTACTUS_SubmitterPhoneNumber	Edit
CONTACTUS_Submittercompany	Edit

Internal Action Required View

Table 9-3 displays the following fields for this view.

TABLE 9-3: "Internal Action" View InfoPath Columns

FIELD NAME	READ/EDIT ABILITY
CONTACTUS_Number	Read
CONTACTUS_ShortDescription:	Edit
CONTACTUS_LongDescription	Edit
CONTACTUS_Submitteremail	Read
CONTACT_Category	Edit
CONTACTUS_SubmitterFirstName	Edit
CONTACTUS_SubmitterLastName	Edit
CONTACTUS_SubmitterPhoneNumber	Edit
CONTACTUS_Submittercompany	Edit
CONTACTUS_Status	Edit
CONTACTUS_ReviewerComments	Edit
CONTACTUS_ActionRequiredby	Edit

Submitter Action Required View

Table 9-4 displays the following fields for this view.

TABLE 9-4: "Submitter Action" View InfoPath Columns

FIELD NAME	READ/EDIT ABILITY
CONTACTUS_Number	Read
CONTACTUS_ShortDescription	Read
CONTACTUS_LongDescription	Edit
CONTACTUS_Submitteremail	Read
CONTACT_Category	Edit
CONTACTUS_SubmitterFirstName	Read

continues

TABLE 9-4 *(continued)*

FIELD NAME	READ/EDIT ABILITY
CONTACTUS_SubmitterLastName	Read
CONTACTUS_SubmitterPhoneNumber	Read
CONTACTUS_Submittercompany	Read
CONTACTUS_Status	Read
CONTACTUS_ReviewerComments	Read
CONTACTUS_ActionRequiredby	Read

On Hold View

Table 9-5 displays the following fields for this view.

TABLE 9-5: "On Hold" View InfoPath Columns

FIELD NAME	READ/EDIT ABILITY
CONTACTUS_Number	Read
CONTACTUS_ShortDescription:	Read
CONTACTUS_LongDescription	Edit
CONTACTUS_Submitteremail	Read
CONTACT_Category	Edit
CONTACTUS_SubmitterFirstName	Edit
CONTACTUS_SubmitterLastName	Edit
CONTACTUS_SubmitterPhoneNumber	Edit
CONTACTUS_Submittercompany	Edit
CONTACTUS_Status	Edit
CONTACTUS_ReviewerComments	Edit
CONTACTUS_ActionRequiredby	Edit

Complete View

Table 9-6 displays the following fields for this view.

TABLE 9-6: "Request Completed" View InfoPath Columns

FIELD NAME	READ/EDIT ABILITY
CONTACTUS_Number	Read
CONTACTUS_ShortDescription:	Read
CONTACTUS_LongDescription	Read
CONTACTUS_Submitteremail	Read
CONTACT_Category	Read
CONTACTUS_SubmitterFirstName	Read
CONTACTUS_SubmitterLastName	Read
CONTACTUS_SubmitterPhoneNumber	Read
CONTACTUS_Submittercompany	Read
CONTACTUS_Status	Read
CONTACTUS_ReviewerComments	Read
CONTACTUS_ActionRequiredby	Read

The value of the form's status field depends on which view displays on the form.

You can create InfoPath views with the InfoPath form Designer client, from within the Page Design tab by selecting New view (Figure 9-3). Each view represents a status of the form.

When the form opens, you want the status set to "New." You can set this initial value via a rule that executes on "Form Load." This rule is also set from the InfoPath designer client, by selecting Form Load, on the Data tab (Figure 9-4).

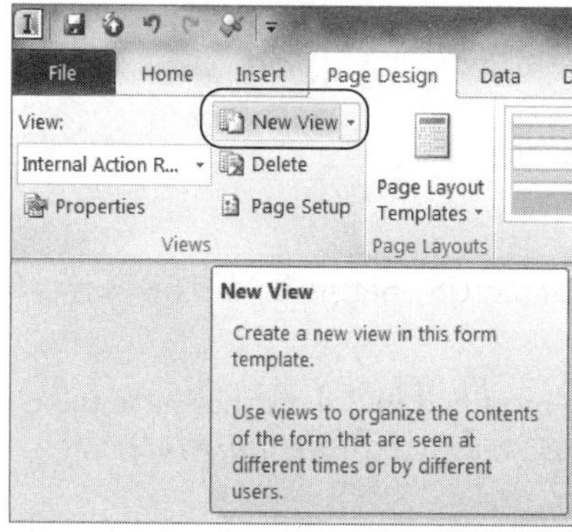

FIGURE 9-3

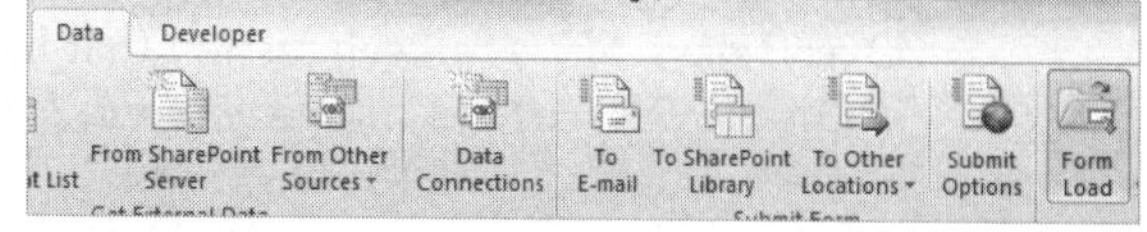

FIGURE 9-4

Then you can create an action, based on a condition of the status field.

Form Buttons

Each view must have two buttons on the form, with a set of actions (see Table 9-7):

- **Save:** Saves the form to the list
- **Close:** Closes the form without saving

TABLE 9-7: InfoPath Buttons and Views Cross Reference

BUTTON LABEL	DESCRIPTION OF ACTIONS	VIEWS
Close	Closes the Infopath form without saving	All views on the form
Submit	Saves the form and changes the status to Internal Action Required	New, Submitter Action Required
Submit	Saves the form	Internal Action Required
Submit	Saves the form	On Hold
Submit	Saves the form	Complete

To add buttons on a form, click on the Home tab in the InfoPath 2010 ribbon and select a button from the menu (Figure 9-5). You can add Actions to Save and close and update fields.

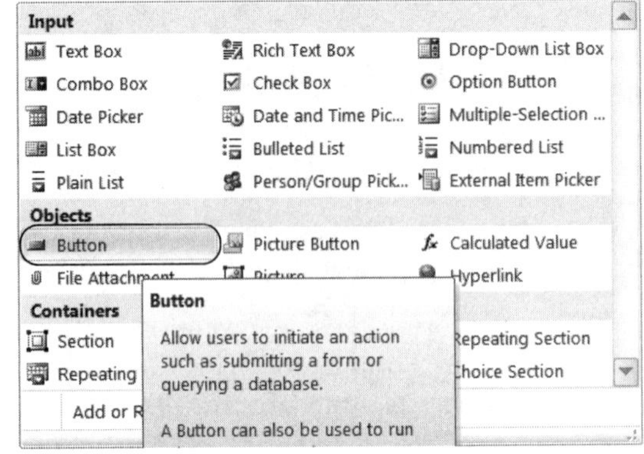

FIGURE 9-5

Lists

This solution relies upon a single custom SharePoint list to manage anonymous requests for information. The list itself leverages a content type with a handful of "lookup" style site columns. This section walks you through each in detail.

Submissions List

The submissions list contains the Contact US Content Type form.

Views in the list follow:

- **Status:** Shows all submissions by the Grouped By – ContactUS_ Status field. This view shows all the submissions that have been submitted.
- **Over 3 days:** Shows all submission that have not been modified in 2 days that have the status of : *Submitter Action Required*, *Internal Action Required*, or *Pending Internal*

Review. The purpose of this view is to highlight submissions that appear to be "stuck" at one of those statuses. If a submission spends more than three days in any of these status codes, then something is wrong and you're probably disappointing your potential customer.

- **Complete:** Shows all submissions with the status Complete

Security

You must configure this list's security. There are two categories of users who can access the site. The first category is the anonymous users who create submissions from the public Internet. The second category includes those users who will actually respond to and process the anonymous users' submissions.

Note that enabling anonymous access to a SharePoint list is typically beyond the administrative capabilities and rights of this book's target audience (which includes "activist users"). Therefore, you will probably need to enlist the support of your IT department. If you're feeling adventurous and you have access to your own isolated SharePoint with full administrative rights, try following the steps outlined here: `http://www.topsharepoint.com/enable-anonymous-access-in-sharepoint-2010`.

Once anonymous access is enabled, you should configure the SharePoint list's security as follows:

- Anonymous Users: Contributor access
- All users of the site: Contributor access

In effect, you're allowing everyone to create and update entries in these lists. In the real world, you would fine-tune permissions to this list by restricting employee access to the list to just those groups who have a legitimate need to view and respond to anonymous user submissions.

Alerts

Alerts are applied to Contact Us submissions; the alerts should include the following:

- **Over 3 days:** The owner of the business process should subscribe a daily alert to the view *Over 3 Days* to identify delays or bottlenecks in the business process.
- **Complete:** All the department SharePoint groups should subscribe a weekly alert to the view *Complete*. The purpose of this alert is an FYI notification to the team members that a submission has been marked complete.

To set up Alerts, for notifications, go to the view. In this case it is the Complete view (see Figure 9-6).

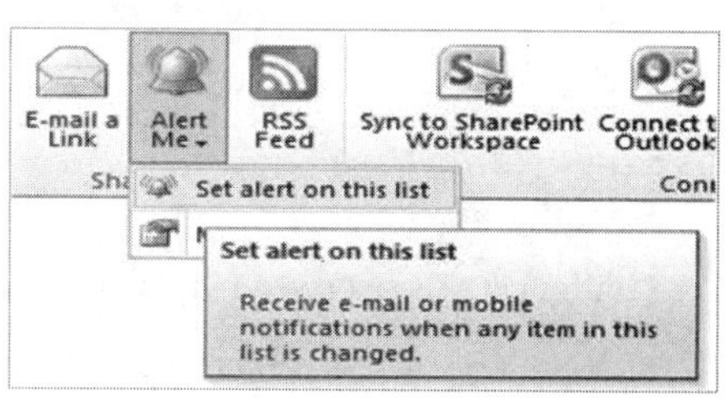

FIGURE 9-6

Set the alert as weekly and for the user's choice as the relevant Active Directory group. By default, the title of the alert's email is the library's name. This is not particularly intuitive. Therefore, you should change the title to something more useful, such as "Weekly alert - Completed Submissions." You should also train your users to this effect.

Categories List

This list contain two business columns (see Table 9-8):

Business Columns:

- **Category:** Category of the submission form. Used for routing purposes.
- **Responders: SharePoint group field:** This contacts a SharePoint group of users to respond to the submission.

TABLE 9-8: Categories List Site Columns

COLUMN NAME	COLUMN TYPE	ADDITIONAL SETTINGS
CATEGORIES_Category	Single Line of Text	Required field
CATEGORIES_Group	Person or Group	SharePoint Group. Note this group needs to exist in the Site collection.

Security

After you create the list, you should set its security as follows:

- **Anonymous Access:** Reader. Anonymous users must be able to read from this list. Otherwise, they won't be able to select a category when they fill out the form.
- **All users of the site:** Read access.

Alerts

Only a single alert is applied to the Categories List. All of the department SharePoint groups should subscribe a weekly alert on this list. It should be configured to show all new items added to the list in the last week. The purpose of this alert is an FYI notification to the team members that additional categories have been added.

Knowledgebase List

This list contains the same field values as the submission list, with the anonymous form content type. Chapter 5, "Time Off Management," explains how to create a list template. This should be used to create a Knowledgebase List.

Security

Configure this list's security as follows:

- **Anonymous Access:** No Access. Anonymous users won't be accessing this list directly. Instead, when individual responders respond to the submitter, they will copy/paste the content of individual Knowledge Base articles into the email.
- **All users of the site:** Read access.

Alerts

Only a single alert is applied to the Knowledgebase List. All department SharePoint groups should subscribe to a weekly alert to show all new items added to the list. Like the Categories list, the purpose of this alert is an FYI notification to the team members that a Contact Us submission has been added to this.

Photo Library

This is a standard picture library. This list contains an additional business column (see Table 9-9).

Business Columns:

- **Responder:** A person field used for lookup purposes

TABLE 9-9: Site Columns

COLUMN NAME	COLUMN TYPE	ADDITIONAL SETTINGS
PHOTOLIB_Responder	Person Text	Single value

Each image in this library represents a department member. The SharePoint Designer workflow looks up the field PHOTOLIB_Responder value, based on the last user who edited the submission form and displays the image on the form and in a receiving email.

Security

Configure this list's security in the same way as you did for Categories:

- **Anonymous Access:** Read
- **All users of the site:** Read

Alerts

Only a single alert is applied to the Photo library List and it follows the same pattern for these simple master table lists. Department groups should sign up for a weekly alert for that useful FYI notification.

Actions List

A simple custom list with a single a site column (see Table 9-10).

Business Columns:

- **Submission Action:** The actions of the submission form

TABLE 9-10: Contact Us Site Columns

COLUMN NAME	COLUMN TYPE	ADDITIONAL SETTINGS
ACTIONS_Description	Text	Compulsory

The ACTIONS_Description is referenced from the Submission form in the form of a Look Up field.

Security

Follow the familiar pattern and configure this list's security as follows:

- **Anonymous Access:** Read access
- **All users of the site:** Read access

SharePoint Groups

There should a SharePoint group for each department that has an assigned category. This group should be listed in the Categories List.

Create Workflows

To implement the solution, you need to deploy two workflows to notify users of the submission and perform wanted actions:

- **Assign Unique Key:** Assigns a unique identification key to the submission
- **Anonymous Submission:** If the business criteria is met, users are notified each time the form is saved. Most notification are related to the value of the Status field, which is outlined earlier in this chapter.

Assign Unique Key Workflow

In Chapter 4, "Helpdesk Ticketing," you were introduced to the concept of creating workflows with SharePoint Designer with the ability to create a unique key to be associated with the submission. This workflow should use the same functionality to create the unique key and be triggered only when the submission is created.

This workflow should send an acknowledgment email to the submitter with the following values, as shown in Table 9-11.

TABLE 9-11: Email Fields

FIELD NAME
CONTACTUS_ShortDescription
CONTACTUS_LongDescription
CONTACTUS_Submitteremail
CONTACT_Category
CONTACTUS_SubmitterFirstName
CONTACTUS_Submittercompany
CONTACTUS_Status

Refer to Figure 9-1 for an example.

Anonymous Submission Workflow

As the submission progresses through the workflow cycle, it should notify the relevant personnel to take action.

The Start Options for this workflow should be set to both Created and Changed (see Figure 9-7).

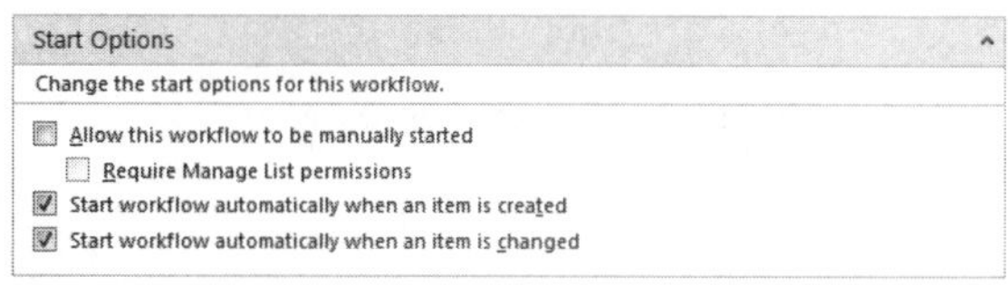

FIGURE 9-7

Every time the submission is changed, this workflow runs and depending on the status of the item requests the appropriate action.

The workflow needs five steps that should be named after each status field value: New, Internal Action Required, Submitter Action Required, On Hold, and Complete

The inner working of each step is outlined next.

Value Initialization

This step identifies which internal department will be notified by the workflow. It does this by referring to the CATEGORY field, in the Category list and returning the value of the RESPONDERS field, which is a SharePoint group containing department members. See Figure 9-8.

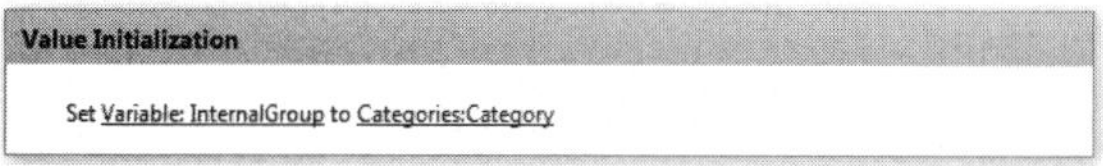

FIGURE 9-8

New

This step sends an acknowledgment email to the submitter and changes the status of the submission (see Figure 9-9).

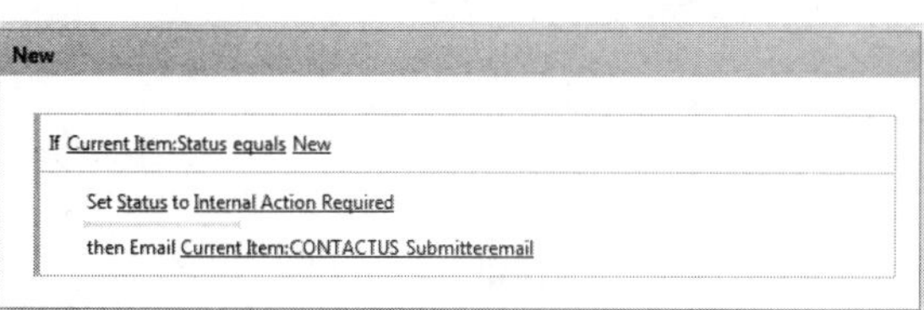

FIGURE 9-9

In the body of the email, the fields presented in Table 9-12 should be displayed.

TABLE 9-12: Internal Email - New Submissions

FIELD NAME	OTHER DETAILS
CONTACTUS_Number	None
CONTACTUS_ShortDescription:	None
CONTACTUS_LongDescription	None
CONTACTUS_Submitteremail	None

continues

TABLE 9-12 *(continued)*

FIELD NAME	OTHER DETAILS
CONTACT_Category	None
CONTACTUS_SubmitterFirstName	None
CONTACTUS_SubmitterLastName	None
CONTACTUS_SubmitterPhoneNumber	None
CONTACTUS_Submittercompany	None
CONTACTUS_Status	None
URL link to submission form	A link to the submission form

Internal Action Required

This step sends an email to the department handling this submission (see Figure 9-10).

In the body of the email, the fields should be displayed that are shown in Table 9-13.

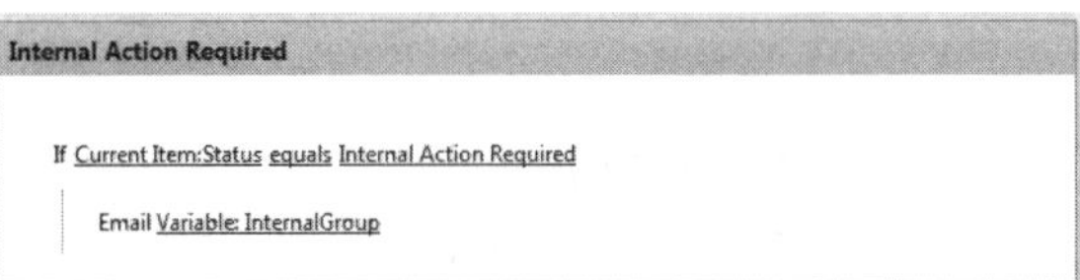

FIGURE 9-10

TABLE 9-13: Internal Email - Change in Status

FIELD NAME	OTHER DETAILS
CONTACTUS_Number	None
CONTACTUS_ShortDescription:	None
CONTACTUS_LongDescription	None
CONTACTUS_Submitteremail	None
CONTACT_Category	None
CONTACTUS_SubmitterFirstName	None
CONTACTUS_SubmitterLastName	None
CONTACTUS_SubmitterPhoneNumber	None
CONTACTUS_Submittercompany	None
CONTACTUS_Status	None
URL link to submission form	A link to the submission form

FIELD NAME	OTHER DETAILS
CONTACTUS_ActionRequiredby	None
CONTACTUS_PhotoURL	A photo of the modifier. This was described earlier in the chapter.
CONTACTUS_ReviewerComments	None

Submitter Action Required

This step sends an email to the submitter requesting action from them (see Figure 9-11).

In the body of the email, the fields in Table 9-14 should be displayed.

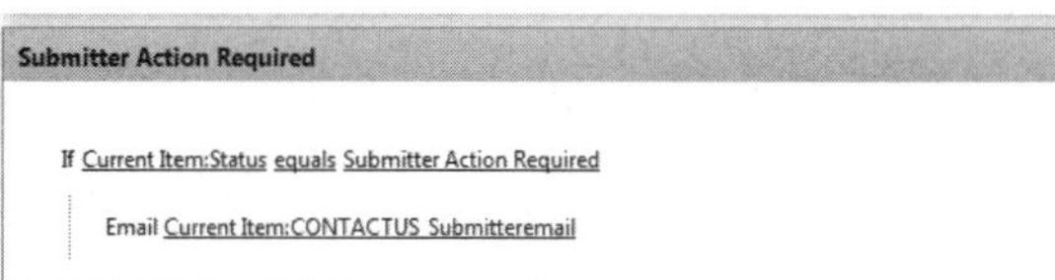

FIGURE 9-11

TABLE 9-14: External Email - Submitter Response Required

FIELD NAME	OTHER DETAILS
CONTACTUS_Number	None
CONTACTUS_ShortDescription:	None
CONTACTUS_LongDescription	None
CONTACTUS_Submitteremail	None
CONTACT_Category	None
CONTACTUS_SubmitterFirstName	None
CONTACTUS_SubmitterLastName	None
CONTACTUS_SubmitterPhoneNumber	None
CONTACTUS_Submittercompany	None
CONTACTUS_Status	None
URL link to submission form	A link to the submission form
CONTACTUS_ActionRequiredby	None
CONTACTUS_PhotoURL	A photo of the modifier. This was described earlier in the chapter.
CONTACTUS_ReviewerComments	None

On Hold

This step sends an email to the submitter stating the submission is on hold (see Figure 9-12).

In the body of the email, the fields shown in Table 9-15 should be displayed.

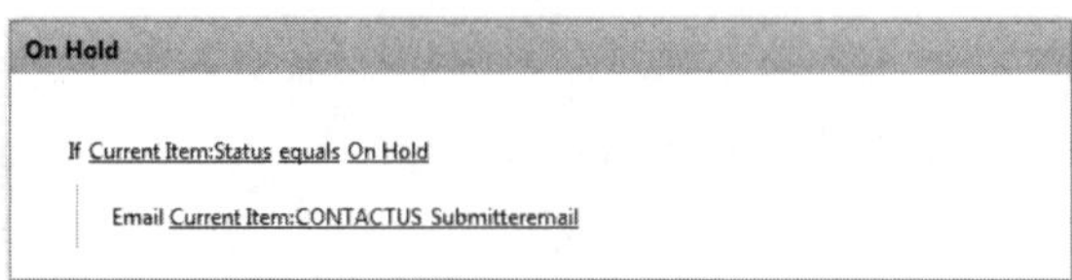

FIGURE 9-12

TABLE 9-15: Internal Email - On Hold

FIELD NAME	OTHER DETAILS
CONTACTUS_Number	None
CONTACTUS_ShortDescription:	None
CONTACTUS_LongDescription	None
CONTACTUS_Submitteremail	None
CONTACT_Category	None
CONTACTUS_SubmitterFirstName	None
CONTACTUS_SubmitterLastName	None
CONTACTUS_SubmitterPhoneNumber	None
CONTACTUS_Submittercompany	None
CONTACTUS_Status	None
URL link to submission form	A link to the submission form

Complete

This step sends an email to the submitter and copies the submission to the Knowledgebase list if appropriate (see Figure 9-13).

In the body of the email, the fields shown in Table 9-16 should be displayed.

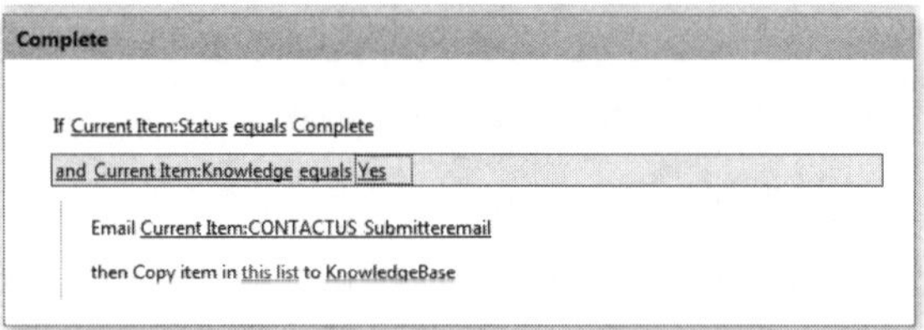

FIGURE 9-13

TABLE 9-16: External Email - Your Submission Was Completed

FIELD NAME	OTHER DETAILS
CONTACTUS_Number	None
CONTACTUS_ShortDescription:	None
CONTACTUS_LongDescription	None
CONTACTUS_Submitteremail	None
CONTACT_Category	None
CONTACTUS_SubmitterFirstName	None
CONTACTUS_SubmitterLastName	None
CONTACTUS_SubmitterPhoneNumber	None
CONTACTUS_Submittercompany	None
CONTACTUS_Status	None
URL link to submission form	A link to the submission form

In some cases the multiple steps run each time this workflow runs.

SUMMARY

This chapter walked you through the business process of an anonymous Contact Us submission form for a website. The key points you should take away from this chapter include the following:

- Notification of all parties involved
- The capability for a knowledge base to be built up over time, further enhancing the value of the business process

10

R&D Gateway Process

WHAT'S IN THIS CHAPTER?

- Coordinating activity streams that need to be accomplished across multiple teams
- Implementing a Master workflow process that coordinates inputs and outputs across multiple child workflows
- Aggregating results of multiple activity streams and providing users or management with a consolidated view of data collected
- Applying a scoring strategy to define objective weighted measurements to knowledge worker activities

This chapter demonstrates how SharePoint workflows can cooperate to solve more complex business problems, and how to enable communication between workflows. This capability enables some new technical and business patterns that you can use to address more complex business processes without making the technology solution difficult to maintain.

WHAT IS THE R&D (RESEARCH AND DEVELOPMENT) GATEWAY?

Successful organizations recognize that to remain competitive, they must continuously innovate. Ideas to improve or create new products and services can come from many sources: social media, customer relationships, and competitive analyses, and internally from managers and employees.

Management faces the challenge of having limited resources to invest in new ideas. It is not enough that an idea be "good"; often too many good ideas exist to match available resources. Management must have a repeatable process to measure the viability of new ideas and enable them to easily identify the best ideas that can produce results for the company.

Measuring ideas for innovation is not easily accomplished. Often a variety of competing perspectives require a wide variety of subject-matter expertise to properly ascertain. Considerations that need to be evaluated and measured may include the following:

- What are the legal exposures to the company?
- How well does the product or service align with the current company client base?
- Does the company have the financial and other resources required to develop and deliver the product or service?
- Can the new product or service be manufactured or delivered profitably and safely?
- Does the product or service leverage existing company competitive advantages?
- Can the new product or service be researched and developed on a timeline that matches the market opportunity?

This is just a short list of what could be a very long list of criteria to properly evaluate ideas for innovation. The expertise required to evaluate and measure the various criteria can cross many lines of responsibility within the organization, such as legal, finance, manufacturing, research and development, sales and marketing, logistics, and customer service.

A number of specific challenges are associated with implementing this process. Each area of expertise must define and manage the specific criteria and weighting within their subject area. Think of "area of expertise" as being the marketing department, the legal review team within your company, and so on. It is also likely that the specific criterion and the weighting measurements may be refined and changed over time for each independent subject area. For instance, the legal review team may change its criteria on the basis of new U.S. Supreme Court decisions. To accommodate for this, the workflow should try to abstract the specifics of each subject area from the overall workflow design. That way, if one group changes its criteria, the overall process remains intact.

PROBLEM CLASS

The Innovation Pipeline represents an example of a decision matrix problem class. Also known as an opportunity analysis, criteria-based matrix, decision grid, or problem selection matrix, a decision matrix evaluates and prioritizes a list of options using weighted criteria.

You can use a decision matrix when a list of options must be narrowed on the basis of a set of criteria. It is most often used when only one solution or problem-solving approach can be implemented, or to narrow and prioritize a list of choices based on a calculated score.

For complex decisions, a decision matrix may involve multiple grouped sets of criteria. Within each group, criteria may be calculated using a simple or weighted formula, and the scores for each group can then be calculated to provide an overall score. You can then use the scores to evaluate the relative strengths of each potential option or alternative, and to sort, group, and filter the list.

By solving the Innovation Pipeline problem in detail, you solve a specific example of a decision matrix. You can apply the techniques and approach outlined in this chapter to similar problems in future.

TECHNICAL PATTERNS

While solving the Innovation Pipeline problem, you to implement the following technical patterns:

- **Pipe:** A pipe is used to support communication between two separate processes. The solution demonstrates how to use SharePoint lists to create a pipe between a master and child workflow.
- **Separation of concerns:** Each set of criterion and the weighting of measurement between each subject area should be distinct with no overlap, allowing subject matter experts to independently define and apply the specific criteria for their areas of specialization.

Beyond these patterns listed, you can also leverage some patterns discussed in earlier chapters.

BUSINESS PATTERNS

While solving the Innovation Pipeline problem, you implement the following business pattern:

- **Scorecard:** A pattern of converting observable performance into a specific set of measurements and related formulas that support the generation of a metric for evaluation and visualization.

The scorecard provides the foundation for the decision matrix, providing the raw measurements that can then be used to calculate a final ranking that identifies the best solutions with the set of choices.

BUSINESS PROBLEM DESCRIPTION

Before starting to solve the problem, spend some time getting a better understanding of the business problem. In this section you identify some high-level business requirements, and then gain a more detailed perspective by identifying use cases for key goals that need to be satisfied. The chapter ends by outlining some of the technical challenges that you need to address in your solution architecture.

Requirements Discussion

Bringing new innovations to market is never free. Because resources are required, and there is a cost to those resources, people in a position to provide those resources (or the capital to acquire them) need to be convinced of the value of an idea. The traditional model for documenting ideas for new products or services has been the venerable business plan.

You are probably familiar with the concept of a business plan. These traditionally have followed fairly well-defined formats that include an executive summary, a concept or a value proposition, a target market, competitive analyses, capital and operating cost projections, revenue and profit forecasts, and often spanned dozens to hundreds of pages that could take months to develop and present.

To assemble the resources required to develop these plans, innovation programs at companies were often delegated to special R&D (Research and Development) departments. These specialized groups were often located separately from other business locations and too often had limited interaction with a company's business operations or customers. Despite some well-documented successes, performance analysis of this approach to innovation indicated that overall the volume of ideas and cost per innovation were relatively poor.

As globalization, technology, and other factors increased business competition, the need to accelerate innovation demanded both an increase in volume, and more efficiency in preparing and evaluating ideas for innovation.

Today, many companies are recognizing that innovation is something that can be driven from anywhere and anyone. To accommodate for the increase in the volume of ideas, innovation processes are being stream-lined to augment existing R&D departments, or in some cases, replace them. Companies such as Toyota introduced the idea of a one-page business case that required innovation proposals to summarize the essentials of a business plan in a single-page document.

For your solution, the challenge is to create an efficient innovation pipeline satisfying the following high-level business requirements:

- **New proposal:** Enables any employee to complete an Innovation Proposal form and submit it for review
- **Evaluate proposal:** Enables subject matter experts (SMEs) distributed throughout the company to quickly assess each valid proposal against a set of subject-area specific criteria to produce a score
- **Review proposal:** Provides management with analysis and reporting tools to rank proposals based on a formula applied to the subject area scores

Of course, this is just the start. Whether you label them business requirements, goals or objectives, high-level requirements helps define the overall scope of the required solution.

Although SharePoint can provide the rapid application development tools and technologies you need to satisfy these requirements, you still need to employ proven analysis and design practices to ensure that you build an effective solution that meets the detailed user, functional and nonfunctional requirements as well.

Actors

Actors represent placeholders for individuals or groups that participate in your solution as providers or consumers of information and actions. The solution involves the following actors:

- **Users:** Submit a new proposal to the pipeline.
- **SMEs:** Score each proposal for their respective subject area.
- **SharePoint:** In the role of the system under discussion.

When implementing pipeline workflows that coordinate subprocesses, you often may not know the details of how each subprocess functions. In this case, you need to identify a surrogate actor: An actor that may be substituted for one or more roles at a more detailed level. In this example, the subject matter expert is a high-level actor or surrogate for the various specific subject matter experts that may be defined for each subprocess (that is, sales, marketing, legal, and so on).

Actions

The R&D Gateway pipeline responds to the actions on behalf of its supported actors. Now break these actions down by actor.

Users:

- Submit new proposal.

Subject Matter Experts:

- Evaluate and score proposals.

SharePoint:

- Send notifications to participants of assigned tasks and actions.
- Aggregate scores from each subject area survey.
- Review scored proposals against a pass/fail minimum score.
- Create a scorecard and apply a ranking formula for all accepted proposals.

Challenges

This chapter won't spell out in great detail how to address certain nice-to-have functions that a full-fledged solution might implement. Some of these functions include the following:

- **Checklist survey:** Instead of simply collecting a score for each subject area, each subject area workflow could present the SME with a checklist in the form of a survey and calculate the score based on numeric checklist responses.
- **Collect feedback task process:** Instead of requiring only a single SME from a group to evaluate a proposal, you can expand the evaluation workflow to assign checklist surveys to multiple members of a group and aggregate the responses.
- **Deferred/blocked:** There are cases in which an idea for innovation scores highly but includes a blocking factor that makes approving and executing on the idea impossible until the blocking factor is resolved. In this case, ideas that have been approved could be marked as deferred, or could have a post-workflow started to resolve the blocking factor.

You should meet some of these challenges on your own using techniques described in other chapters in this book. In other cases, you can look to online resources and other Wrox books for assistance, which are noted as they are warranted.

HIGH-LEVEL SOLUTION

This section describes the overall solution architecture and demonstrates analysis and design techniques that can help define workflow-driven business solutions. This section demonstrates two popular techniques: a cross-functional business flowchart and a wireframe used to demonstrate user-experience elements such as forms or notifications.

Solution Overview

To implement your R&D Gateway solution, you need to leverage out-of-box SharePoint components.

This solution includes more complexity than many of the workflows covered so far. The Pipeline pattern applies separation of concern by facilitating a master workflow and coordinating multiple child workflows through to the completion of an overall process. The Decision Matrix business pattern aggregates scores and a weighted formula to rank proposals on an executive dashboard.

You can divide the overall workflow process into four major steps:

1. **New proposal:** Enables users to submit new proposals for innovation. Users will be kept informed of progress through the decision process and will receive a final approval or rejection of the proposal.
2. **Subject area evaluation:** A SME for a subject area will be requested to score each new proposal.
3. **Proposal review:** Each survey score will be aggregated to produce an overall average score that will be compared to a minimum pass/fail requirement to be accepted or reject.
4. **Completion:** If a proposal is accepted, a scorecard will be created that includes a weighted formula to calculate a final ranking.

Swimlane Diagram

Figure 10-1 shows a cross-functional business workflow diagram with swimlanes showing the actors and key actions they take through the workflow similar to diagrams presented in previous chapters.

This chapter introduces two new elements: the subprocess shape representing the child workflows in your implementation for each subject area and horizontal swimlanes that break down the workflow into four major steps. Each step has a label that represents the overall workflow status displayed to the users during workflow execution.

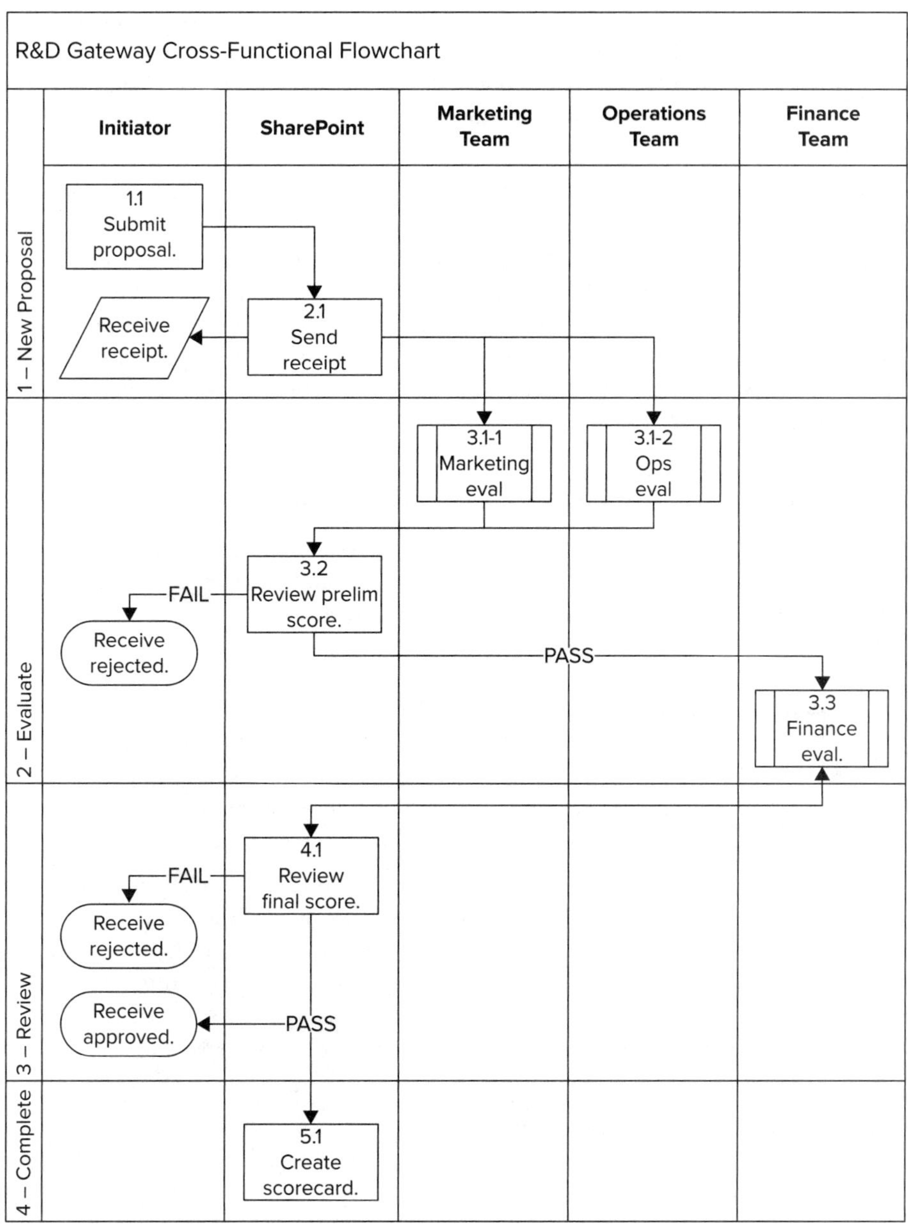

FIGURE 10-1

The process begins with a user submitting a new innovation proposal. How does the user submit a proposal? For the purposes of implementation, you could just as easily use an InfoPath Form, a Word or Excel document based on a document template, or a custom list with a supporting content type. (Remember, Chapter 8, "Enterprise: Authorization for Expenditure Capital," introduces InfoPath.) Regardless, a new item appears in a list or library, and the master workflow starts either automatically or manually by the user. The workflow sends the user a notification confirming receipt of the proposal. At this point, the Proposal Status defaults to 1 - New Proposal enabling users to easily see all the new proposals that have not yet been processed. The one-dash prefix on the status enables you to provide nicer sorted dashboards and views. Otherwise, SharePoint defaults to an alphabetical listing that's not going to be useful in the end.

In the second step, the master workflow is responsible for initializing and starting child workflows for each of the subject areas that evaluate the proposal, and then processing the response. For all intents and purposes, each child workflow is a "black box." The only requirement is that each child workflow returns a score for the proposal. In the sample workflow, finance is the most expensive subject area and may be influenced by scores generated by marketing or operations. To ensure efficient processing and also support this detailed requirement, the marketing and operations evaluations run in parallel, with a final sequential evaluation by finance after the previous evaluations have all been completed.

In the third step, an average score is compared against a minimum passing grade to automatically either accept or reject the proposal. Users are notified by email containing the result.

In the fourth and final step, if the proposal has been accepted, a scorecard item is created and linked to the original proposal to support an executive dashboard. A calculated weighted formula is applied to provide an overall ranking based on the subject area scores.

CROSS FUNCTIONAL FLOWCHARTS

Cross-functional flowcharts are an effective modeling tool for business workflow solutions. As workflows become more complex, involving more actors, steps, and subprocesses, it can help manage complexity to model business and technical flowcharts separately.

Cross-functional flowcharts can support both horizontal and vertical swimlanes. In the swimlane diagram in Figure 10-1, the vertical swimlanes represent the actors in the solutions, enabling you to visualize how processing is divided across roles. You have seen this demonstrated in previous chapters. This diagram also includes the use of horizontal swimlanes to divide the processing into a set of steps or phases.

This diagram introduced a new shape: the subprocess. For the purposes of the solution, this represents the parts of your process that are facilitated by a child workflow. It would be appropriate in a complete solution to also create separate flowchart models for each subworkflow.

Technical Implementation Overview

This section contains a summary of the technical elements of the overall solutions including site columns, content types, lists, workflows, and supplemental elements, such as forms or document templates, required to support implementation.

User Permissions and Groups

As you have seen in previous chapters, SharePoint Groups are a common way to both manage permissions on items participating in workflow processes but also to assign tasks to multiple users.

To support your solution, you need to create the following security groups:

- **Marketing reviewers:** A group containing members of the marketing team who complete the evaluation on proposals
- **Operations reviewers:** A group containing members of the operations team who complete the evaluation of proposals
- **Finance reviewers:** A group containing members of the finance team who complete the evaluation of proposals

To allow the workflow to perform steps using elevated privileges, you can also use impersonation that allows steps to execute under a Workflow Author account. You review how to create and apply permissions to a designated Workflow Author account that can be used for executing steps in a workflow with elevated permissions.

Proposals

Proposals are forms completed by employees to describe the server or product innovation. For a complex form, InfoPath and a Form Library could be a good choice.

For your workflow, use the same approach shown in previous chapters by creating a custom content type and associating with a custom list:

- **IP_Proposal** ***[Content Type]*****:** A content type containing fields describing the innovation proposal
- **Proposals** ***[Custom List]*****:** A custom list enabling users to create a new proposal

The list will also be configured with item-level security to enable only users to view and edit proposals they have submitted.

Master/Child Workflows

The complete solution requires four workflows: a master workflow with three child workflows designed to complete the evaluation and ranking of a proposal.

- **Innovation Pipeline** ***[Reusable Workflow]*****:** The master workflow that will be configured to start automatically when a new item is created. This workflow is responsible for coordinating the overall review and approval process.
- **Marketing Evaluation** ***[Reusable Workflow]*****:** A child workflow responsible for the evaluation and scoring of a new proposal by the marketing team
- **Operations Evaluation** ***[Reusable Workflow]*****:** A child workflow responsible for the evaluation and scoring of a new proposal by the operations team
- **Finance Evaluation** ***[Reusable Workflow]*****:** A child workflow responsible for the evaluation and scoring of a new proposal by the finance team

SharePoint Designer does not provide any specific workflow activities that support starting a separate workflow or monitoring a separate workflow for completion.

To support the ability to implement either a master/child workflow relationship, or implement a state machine model with transfer of control between peer workflows, you can implement a technical pattern that uses a control field and the Start on Change capability of SharePoint workflows, as shown in Figure 10-2.

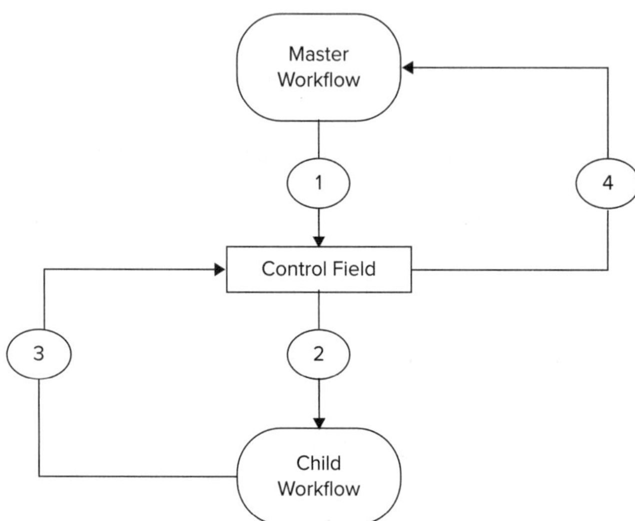

FIGURE 10-2

All workflows are associated with the same list or content type. This enables SharePoint Designer workflows to update and then listen for a change on the current item. Figure 10- 2 demonstrates the flow of control:

1. The master workflow updates the value of a control field on the current workflow item and then waits for the value of the control field to change.
2. The child workflow is configured to Start on Change. It evaluates the value in the control field to know whether it should execute. If the control field has not been set, it ends. If the control field has been set, it knows to execute.
3. The child workflow upon completing execution updates the control field indicating completion.
4. The master workflow, waiting for the update, continues execution.

When defining state machine-based or recursion-based workflow solutions, control fields can be any columns on a list or content type including fields updated by users. For a master/child workflow scenario in which the master workflow waits on a specific update from a child workflow, an exclusive control field is preferred. For your workflow solution, you define specific control fields for each child workflow.

Workflow Pipes

SharePoint Designer workflows do not provide a specific capability to enable workflows to communicate between each other. To allow parameters to be passed back and forth between the master and child workflows, you need to define a custom solution.

Pipes are a common term for a communication channel used for interprocess communication. To support the capability to pass input and output parameters between master and child workflows, you can use a custom list with a supporting content type.

Because the master and child workflows are all associated with the same list, and execute on the same item, you may be asking why you need a separate list to support the master/child communication. Although you can add technical columns to the original list or content type, there can be advantages to using a separate list including the following:

- **Secure communication:** Information passed between workflows may include sensitive data that should not be available to the workflow initiator. By using impersonation and a separate list, you can secure the communication pipe with separate permissions.
- **Custom parameters:** If you require communication between multiple workflows, each workflow may require a unique combination of columns to support input and output parameters between them. This could add a lot of additional columns to the original list or content type. By using a separate list and content types, unique sets of parameters can be defined between each set of workflows.

For your workflow solution, each child workflow is required to return the numeric score as an output parameter. To support this generic communication, you use a single list with a single supporting content type:

- **IP_WorkflowPipe** ***[Content Type]*****:** Content type with standard input and output parameters used for all child workflows.
- **Workflow Pipes** ***[Custom List]*****:** A custom list used exclusively to create a communication channel between each instance of a master and child workflow.

Because the communication between workflows is intended to be secure, impersonation and list permissions ensure that normal site users cannot view or edit list items. In addition, because this list is not intended to be viewed by any site users, and exclusively for the use of workflow processes, the list will also be hidden.

Scorecards

After a proposal has been evaluated and reviewed, if the proposal has been accepted, a new scorecard related to the original proposal will be created containing the aggregated scores and a calculated ranking based on a weighted formula.

Scorecards are only meant to be viewed by executive management and used for determining allocation of resources related to top-ranking proposals.

To support secure storage of scorecard values, you can use a custom list and supporting content type:

- **IP_Scorecard *[Content Type]*:** A content type containing fields for capturing scores and calculating a final overall ranking.
- **Scorecards *[Custom List]*:** A custom list used by the master workflow to record a scorecard for each approved proposal.

This list will be created using impersonation of the Workflow Author account. Scorecard items will only be visible to executive management.

DETAILED TECHNICAL IMPLEMENTATION

This section walks you through the process of building the solution.

Setup

Building solutions on SharePoint can encompass all three layers of a traditional N-Tier application: data, application and presentation. The data tier of SharePoint is represented by site columns, content types, and lists. The application or business tier is represented by your workflows. Finally, the presentation tier is composed of InfoPath Forms, list views, and pages containing web parts.

To set up your R&D Gateway solution, you build application in layers starting from the data tier and finishing with the application tier. In the following steps, you create lists, site columns, content types, workflows, and custom list views.

Create Lists

The solution is going to require three custom lists:

- **Proposals:** Custom list for innovation proposals and supporting workflows
- **Scorecards:** Custom list for scorecards associated with accepted proposals
- **Workflow pipes:** Custom list for pipeline items used to communicate parameters between the master and child workflows

Lists are created by selecting **View All Site Content** from the Quick Launch menu, and then selecting the **Create** command from the top-level toolbar, as shown in Table 10-1.

TABLE 10-1: List Specifications

LIST NAME	LIST TEMPLATE TYPE	ADDITIONAL SETTINGS
Proposals	Custom List	Quick Launch = Yes
Scorecards	Custom List	Quick Launch = Yes
Workflow Pipes	Custom List	Quick Launch = No

For now, you just want to create the basic list. You can customize these lists further as you continue your setup. When you finish, the three custom lists, and the default site Tasks list, should appear in the Lists area of the View All Site Content page (Figure 10-3).

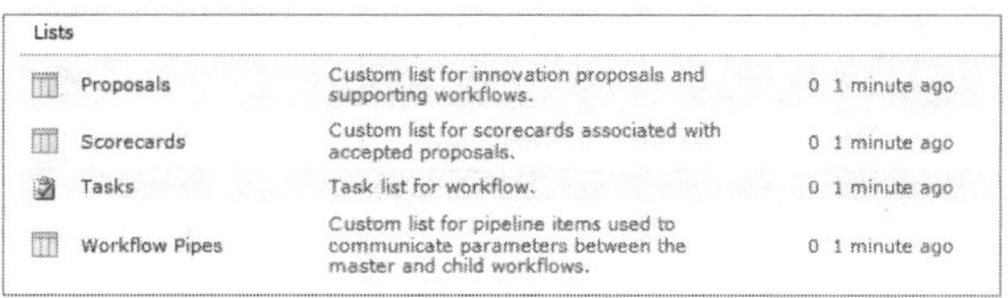

FIGURE 10-3

Create Content Types

Content Types are the foundation for content management and business process automation solutions, and are an essential building block for just about any customization.

As you've read over and over again in previous chapters, each supporting list in your solution is backed by a content type consisting of two categories of site columns: business and technical. End users enter data directly into business columns, and business columns appear on dashboards. Technical columns, on the other hand, do not generally appear to end users and instead support the technical needs of the solution.

Proposal

This content type captures details related to the employee proposal. Create a new content type named IP_Proposal using the details shown in Figure 10-4.

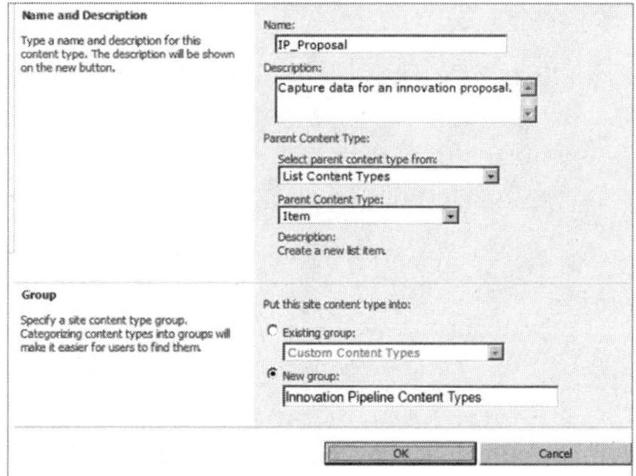

FIGURE 10-4

After you create the content type, add columns. For the proposal, you do not have any technical columns. The only columns added will be to allow a user to provide required data.

Business Columns:

- **Innovation:** A rich text description outlining the business case for the innovation
- **Innovation type:** Provides a type category for the proposal. This can be used on the dashboard to help group proposals by type
- **Benefit:** A description of the value that the proposal, if implemented, would provide
- **Benefit Type:** The type of improvement it generates

Add the site columns to the content type using the field specifications provided in Table 10-2. To help organize the columns, assign each new site column to an Innovation Proposal Columns group.

TABLE 10-2: Innovation Proposal Columns

COLUMN NAME	COLUMN TYPE	ADDITIONAL SETTINGS
IP_Innovation	Multiple Lines of Text	Required = True Type of Text = Rich
IP_InnovationType	Choice	Required = True Enter Choices: Service Process Product Display = DropDown
IP_Benefit	Multiple Lines of Text	Required = True Types of Text = Rich
IP_BenefitType	Choice	Required = True Enter Choices: Growth Profit Efficiency Sustainability Goodwill Display = DropDown

The completed content type is shown in Figure 10-5.

Scorecard

This content type records the scores from the subject areas captured during evaluation. Create a new content type named IP_Scorecard using the details shown in Figure 10-6.

Site Content Type Information

Name: IP_Proposal
Description: Capture data for an innovation proposal.
Parent: Item
Group: Innovation Pipeline Content Types

Settings

- Name, description, and group
- Advanced settings
- Workflow settings
- Delete this site content type

Columns

Name	Type	Status	Source
Title	Single line of text	Required	Item
IP_Innovation	Multiple lines of text	Required	
IP_InnovationType	Choice	Required	
IP_Benefit	Multiple lines of text	Required	
IP_BenefitType	Choice	Required	

- Add from existing site columns
- Add from new site column
- Column order

FIGURE 10-5

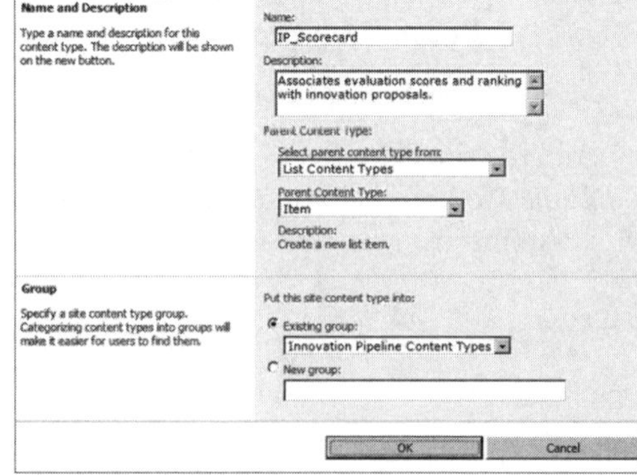

FIGURE 10-6

After you create the content type, add columns. For the scorecard, you do not have any technical columns. The only columns added will be used by management when viewing the dashboard. Security permissions that you configure later in this section will be responsible for ensuring that these fields are read-only for most users.

Business Columns:

- **Proposal:** Lookup column linking scorecard to the associated proposal
- **Marketing score:** Numeric value containing the score collected from the marketing evaluation
- **Operations score:** Numeric value containing the score collected from the operations evaluation
- **Finance score:** Numeric value containing the score collected from the finance evaluation
- **Proposal rank:** Numeric value calculated from the weighted formula used to determine overall proposal ranking

Add the site columns to the content type using the field specifications provided in Table 10-3. To help organize the columns, assign each new site column to an Innovation Scorecard Columns group.

TABLE 10-3: Innovation Scorecard Columns

COLUMN NAME	COLUMN TYPE	ADDITIONAL SETTINGS
Title	Single line of text	Hidden = True
IP_Proposal	Lookup	Required = True Source List = Proposals Source Column = Title
IP_MarketingScore	Number	Minimum = 0 Maximum = 100 Decimal Places = 0
IP_OperationsScore	Number	Minimum = 0 Maximum = 100 Decimal Places = 0
IP_FinanceScore	Number	Minimum = 0 Maximum = 100 Decimal Places = 0
IP_ProposalRank	Calculated	=([IP_FinanceScore]+[IP_MarketingScore] +[IP_OperationsScore])/3

The use of the IP_ProposalRank as a calculated column enables you to use the power of SharePoint calculated column formulas to determine the final rank for a proposal. For the solution you are just using a simple average, but some creative use of formulas supported by calculated columns. This rule could be more complex, applying a weighted average as an alternative.

Figure 10-7 shows the completed content type.

Workflow Pipe

This content type is used to facilitate passing parameters between the master and child workflows. Create a new content type named IP_WorkflowPipe using the details shown in Figure 10-8.

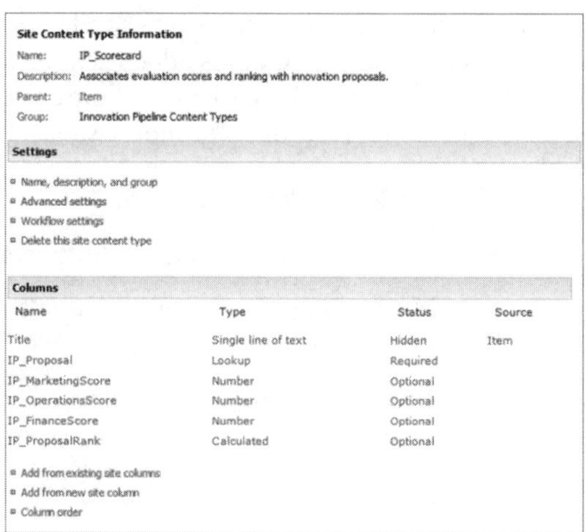

FIGURE 10-7

Name and Description
Type a name and description for this content type. The description will be shown on the new button.
Name:
IP_WorkflowPipe
Description:
Supports parameters between workflow processes.
Parent Content Type:
Select parent content type from:
List Content Types
Parent Content Type:
Item
Description:
Create a new list item.
Group
Specify a site content type group. Categorizing content types into groups will make it easier for users to find them.
Put this site content type into:
Existing group:
Innovation Pipeline Content Types
New group:
OK Cancel

FIGURE 10-8

After you create the content type, add columns. Workflow Pipe list items are used exclusively by workflows and are not intended to be viewed or edited directly by a user. All columns on this content type are technical.

Technical Columns:

- **Workflow instance:** Unique identifier of the instance of the master workflow that created the pipe.
- **Workflow item:** Unique identifier of the originating list item associated with the workflow process.

- **Workflow name:** The title or association name of the target subworkflow.
- **Workflow score:** An output parameter used by a child workflow to return a score to the master workflow.
- **Workflow key:** A calculated column creating a unique key that can be used by a child workflow to query the list.

USING SHAREPOINT SITE COLUMNS AND CONTENT TYPES

When designing any solution on SharePoint, you frequently are presented with a choice whether to use an out-of-the-box site column or content type versus creating your own custom item. In the case of this content type, there is already an out-of-box site column called Workflow Name that you can use instead of creating a custom site column.

Although there is no specific right or wrong answer, it is generally preferred that you create custom site columns and content types unless there is a specific technical requirement to use an out-of-the-box feature (for example, integration with a SharePoint service that requires use of a specific field such as Enterprise Keywords or Target Audiences). This can help protect your solution from any future changes introduced by Microsoft in service packs or the next major release and can also help ensure you can modify the item if necessary to address future requirements without being concerned how this may impact how the out-of-the-box item is used outside your specific purpose.

Add the site columns to the content type using the field specifications provided in Table 10-4. To help organize the columns, assign each new site column to an Innovation Workflow Pipe Columns group.

TABLE 10-4: INNOVATION WORKFLOW PIPE COLUMNS

COLUMN NAME	COLUMN TYPE	ADDITIONAL SETTINGS
IP_WorkflowInstance	Single Line of Text	Required = True
IP_WorkflowItem	Single Line of Text	Required = True
IP_WorkflowName	Single Line of Text	Required = True
IP_WorkflowScore	Number	Minimum = 0 Maximum = 100 Decimal Places = 0
IP_WorkflowKey	Calculated	Formula: =IP_WorkflowItem & "I" & IP_WorkflowName Data Returned = Single Line of Text
Title	Single Line of Text	Hidden = True

Figure 10-9 shows the completed content type.

Site Content Type Information

Name: IP_WorkflowPipe
Description: Supports parameters between workflow processes.
Parent: Item
Group: Innovation Pipeline Content Types

Settings

- Name, description, and group
- Advanced settings
- Workflow settings
- Delete this site content type

Columns

Name	Type	Status	Source
Title	Single line of text	Hidden	Item
IP_WorkflowInstance	Single line of text	Required	
IP_WorkflowItem	Single line of text	Required	
IP_WorkflowName	Single line of text	Required	
IP_WorkflowScore	Number	Optional	
IP_WorkflowKey	Calculated	Optional	

- Add from existing site columns
- Add from new site column
- Column order

FIGURE 10-9

Users Permissions and Groups

In this section, you set up security groups and assign permissions needed to implement your solution.

Subject Area Reviewers

Each subject area that is required to review a proposal needs to be assigned a task to collect feedback.

In earlier chapters, you examined the use of the Delegate pattern as a way to mitigate assigning tasks to a single user. In your solution, you make use of security groups. Using security groups for tasks instead of individual users can help make your solution more dynamic and easier to maintain. A task assigned to a group enables the task to be completed by any member of that group. An added benefit is that developers, testers, administrators, and other supporting users can be added to these groups to support implementation or support activities.

Create the security groups shown in Table 10-5.

TABLE 10: 5: Security Groups

GROUP NAME	PERMISSIONS	ADDITIONAL SETTINGS
Marketing Reviewers	Contribute	Edit Membership = Group Members
Operations Reviewers	Contribute	Edit Membership = Group Members
Finance Reviewers	Contribute	Edit Membership = Group Members

Task notifications will be sent to all members of the group when a new task is assigned. During implementation and testing, you probably want to assign only your own account to these groups.

SharePoint Workflow Author

Like many forms in common business processes, your innovation proposal template has an area to be filled out by the employee, and an area reserved for management. In your implementation, the various scores and other information assembled through the workflow process and eventually written out to the Scorecard list are confidential and are not intended to be shared with the proposal originator.

Additionally, your solution is using master/child workflows and has introduced the concept of using Workflow Pipes to facilitate passing input and output parameters between workflows. Passing workflow parameters may require exposing workflow state that would normally not be exposed outside a monolithic workflow, and is not intended to be viewed by the workflow originator.

To satisfy both of these requirements, your workflow needs to use an Impersonation Step to enable the workflow to run with elevated permissions, and create and update list items under the workflow author credentials instead of the workflow initiator.

SHAREPOINT DESIGNER WORKFLOW IMPERSONATION STEP

Workflows built and deployed using SharePoint Designer normally run under identity and with the associated permissions of the user who starts them. For example, if a workflow action creates a new list item, the Created By field on the new item reflects the user account who initiated the workflow.

Impersonation steps in SharePoint Designer enable child Steps, Conditions, and Activities to run under the account of the user that authors the workflow. In more concrete terms, it is based on the account that actually publishes the workflow from SharePoint Designer. This enables some or even all the logic in a workflow to run with an alternative (often elevated) set of permissions.

When building a workflow that uses impersonation, it is a good idea to use a special trusted account for the workflow author, rather than a normal user account. This ensures that the workflow does not inadvertently stop running if an employee leaves the company, or a contractor completes the project. The author uses a special account called SharePoint Workflow when publishing accounts. Regardless, when using impersonation, you need to identify the workflow author who publishes the workflow and grant the appropriate permissions to the site.

Grant the workflow author Designer permissions to the site, as shown in Figure 10-10.

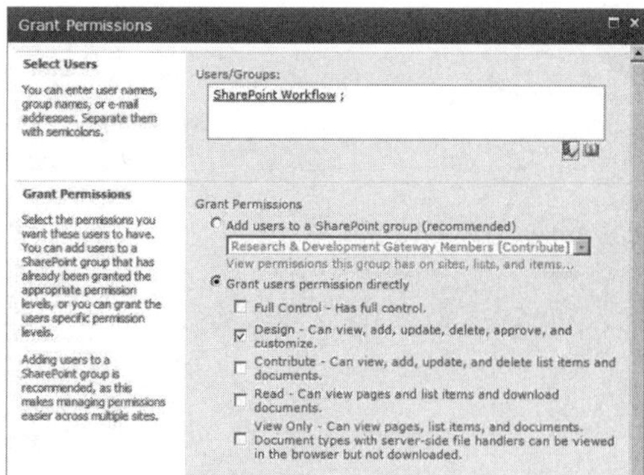

FIGURE 10-10

After you have completed applying security, site permissions should be similar to Figure 10-11.

Name	Type	Permission Levels
Finance Reviewers	SharePoint Group	Contribute
Marketing Reviewers	SharePoint Group	Contribute
Operations Reviewers	SharePoint Group	Contribute
Research & Development Gateway Members	SharePoint Group	Contribute
Research & Development Gateway Owners	SharePoint Group	Full Control
Research & Development Gateway Visitors	SharePoint Group	Read
SharePoint Workflow (LAB\sp_workflow)	User	Design
Viewers	SharePoint Group	View Only

FIGURE 10-11

Customize Lists

Now that you have completed your content types, customize the lists you created earlier in this section to use your content types, and make some other customizations.

Now walk through customizing the Proposals list. You need to customize the list to use a custom content type. Because users should have only the ability to edit the items they have submitted, you also need to set Item-Level Permissions.

From the Quick Launch menu, browse to the Proposals list, and from the Ribbon menu, open the List Settings page. Under General Settings, click the Advanced settings menu (Figure 10-12).

Click Yes to allow management of content types, and update the Item-Level Permissions settings, as shown in Figure 10-13. When complete, scroll to the bottom of the page, and click OK to apply the changes; then return to the List Settings page.

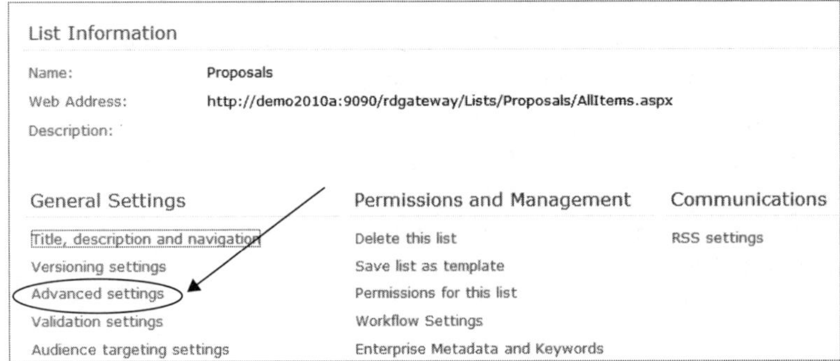

FIGURE 10-12

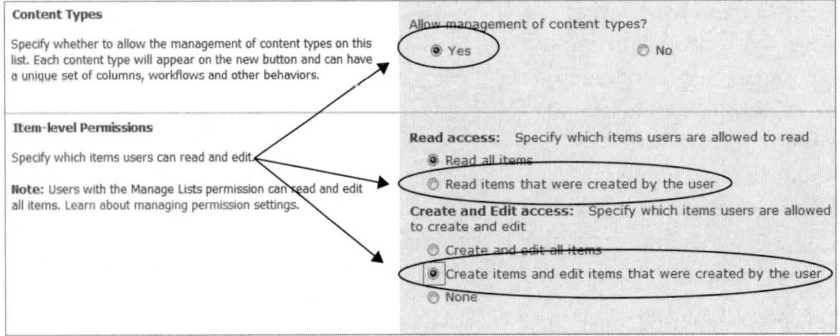

FIGURE 10-13

You can now add your custom content type to the list. Under the Content Types areas, click Add from Existing Site Content Types. Select the Innovation Pipeline Content Types group, and then add the IP_Proposal content type (see Figure 10-14). Click OK to complete.

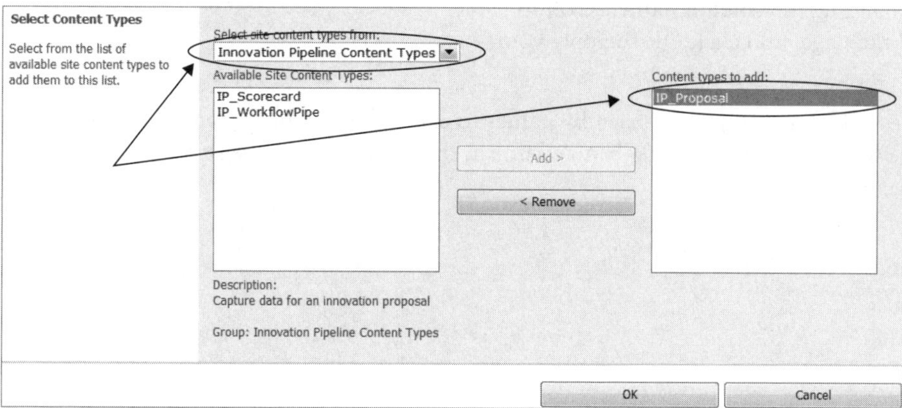

FIGURE 10-14

Next, set IP_Proposal to be the default content type, and remove the Item content type from the new menu. Under the Content Types areas, click the Change New Button Order and Default Content Type menu link. Uncheck the Visible column for the Item content type, and change the visibility order to ensure IP_Proposal is set to position 1, as shown in Figure 10-15.

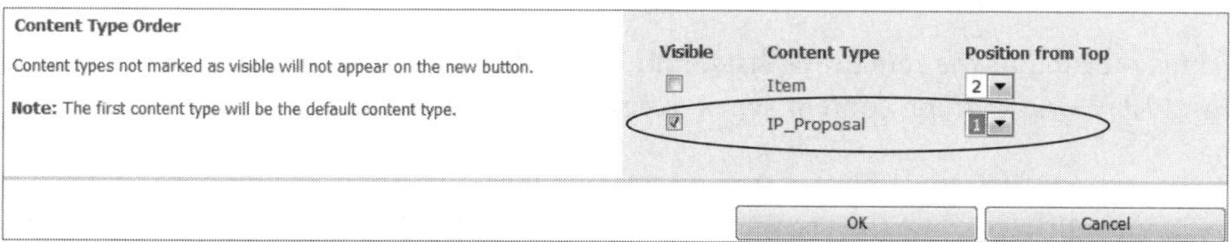

FIGURE 10-15

The completed changes are shown in Figure 10-16.

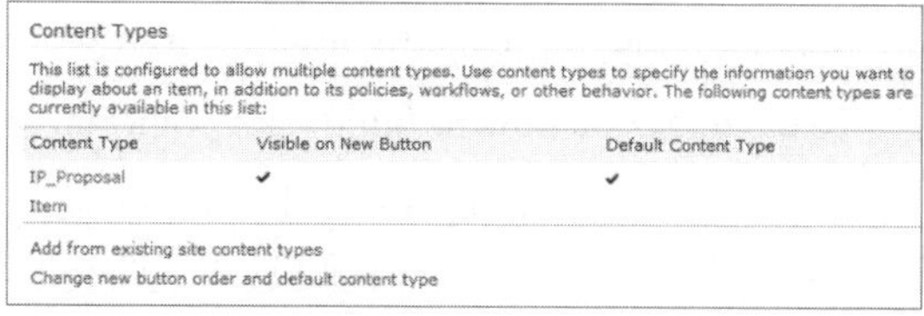

FIGURE 10-16

To complete your list customization, you can also now apply user-friendly naming to your list columns.

As discussed in previous chapters, when creating Site Columns and Content Types that are shared across your entire Site, you need to apply a good naming convention to ensure uniqueness and make your solution content types easily identifiable. When associating Site Columns and Content types with individual lists however, you can rename the columns on the local list to make them user-friendly. This change is largely cosmetic, and your workflow continues to use the original (also known as the Static Name) of the columns.

Under the Columns area, click any column to edit the display name of the column, as shown in Figure 10-17. After changing the column name, scroll to the bottom of the page, and click OK to apply your changes.

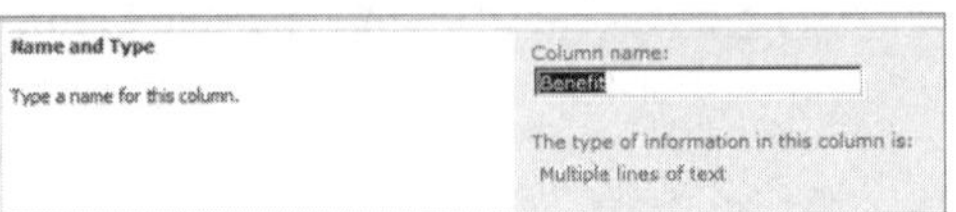

FIGURE 10-17

Repeat the previous step to give user-friendly names to each of the columns that were added to the list by the IP_Proposal content type. When you finish, the final list columns should be similar to Figure 10-18.

Columns

A column stores information about each item in the list. Because this list allows multiple content types, some column settings, such as whether information is required or optional for a column, are now specified by the content type of the item. The following columns are currently available in this list:

Column (click to edit)	Type	Used in
Benefit	Multiple lines of text	IP_Proposal
Benefit Type	Choice	IP_Proposal
Finance Status	Choice	IP_Proposal
Innovation	Multiple lines of text	IP_Proposal
Innovation Type	Choice	IP_Proposal
Marketing Status	Choice	IP_Proposal
Operations Status	Choice	IP_Proposal
Title	Single line of text	IP_Proposal, Item
Workflow Step	Choice	IP_Proposal
Created By	Person or Group	
Modified By	Person or Group	

Create column
Add from existing site columns
Indexed columns

FIGURE 10-18

The same steps need to be applied to the Scorecards and the Workflow Pipes custom lists used by your solution.

Open List Settings on each of the remaining lists, and perform the same steps using the IP_Scorecard and IP_WorkflowPipe content types, respectively, to complete the necessary list customizations.

Create Workflows

Your business solution uses Separation of Concern to abstract the details how each subject area determines the score for a proposal from a top-level workflow. To support this pattern, use a Master-Child approach to building your workflows.

To demonstrate how to build your solution, step through building two workflows:

- **Innovation pipeline:** The master workflow that manages the end-to-end process of evaluating and accepting or rejecting proposals.
- **Subject area evaluation:** A workflow to facilitate review of a proposal by a subject area.

Innovation Pipeline

The innovation pipeline facilitates the end-to-end business process and is responsible for delegating and aggregating the results of child workflows to accomplish the overall goals of the process.

Begin by starting SharePoint Designer. Make sure to run SharePoint Designer using a designated workflow authoring account because your workflows use Impersonation to run the workflows with elevated permissions. You can run SharePoint Designer using a specific account by using the Shift+Right-Click and selecting Run as Different User from the context menu.

Continue by opening the site where you have been building the solution, and select Workflows from the Quick Navigation menu.

Proceed with creating a new workflow by selecting Reusable Workflow from the Ribbon menu, as shown in Figure 10-19.

Enter the name and description, and select the content from the drop-down control, as shown in Figure 10-20.

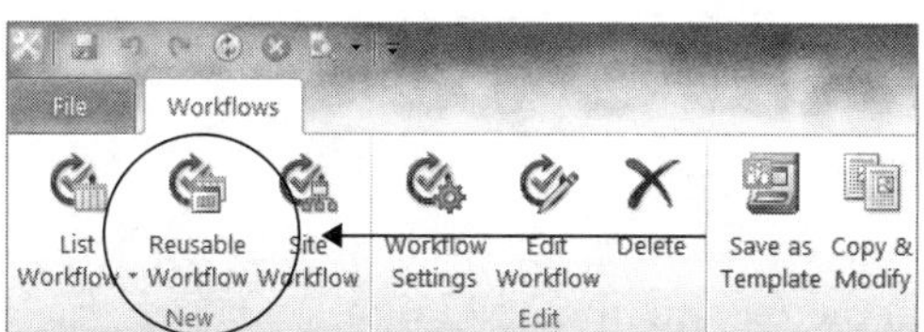

FIGURE 10-19

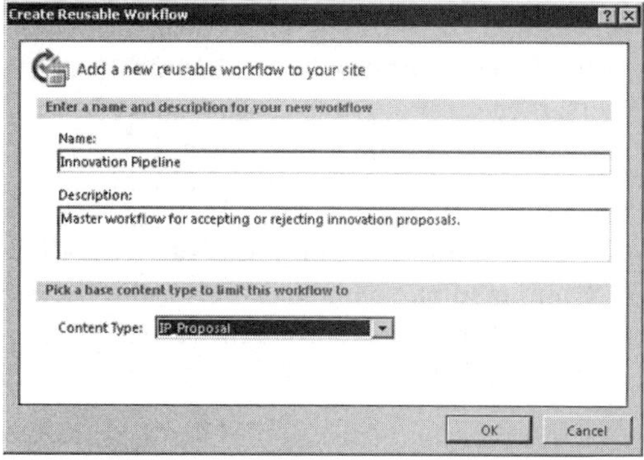

FIGURE 10-20

When the editor opens, create the skeleton for your workflow. This time, use the swim lane diagram (refer to Figure 10-1) to "stub out" the workflow first by adding all the steps at once. As you build the workflow, continue this practice by using nested steps to represent each process and subprocess.

Because the workflow runs with elevated privileges, start by adding an Impersonation Step to the designer. Within the Impersonation step, add an empty step for each major step in your workflow process, as shown in Figure 10-21.

FIGURE 10-21

To complete your workflow, complete the following steps:

1. Configure Initiation Form Parameters.
2. Configure Association Columns.
3. Build the New Proposal step.
4. Build the Evaluation step.
5. Build the Review step.
6. Build the Complete step.

Configure Initiation Form Parameters

Initiation Form Parameters enables you to create parameters entered by List Administrators when associating a workflow with a list, or by users when initiating a workflow manually.

Implement a business rule in your master workflow to auto-reject proposals that fail to achieve an average passing grade. Because you do not want to hard-code this value into the workflow, you allow it to be configured when the workflow is associated with a list.

To define an Initiation Form variable, click the Command button labled "Initiation Form Parameters" on the Ribbon, as shown in Figure 10-22; then complete the Add Field Wizard, as shown in Figure 10-23.

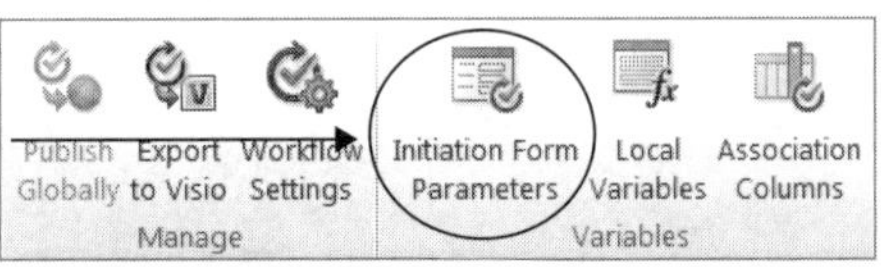

FIGURE 10-22

After you complete the Add Field, the field displays in the Association and Initiation Form Parameters dialog, as shown in Figure 10-24.

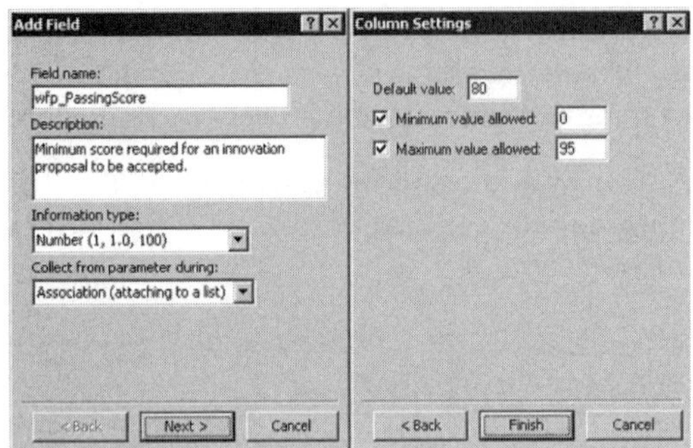

FIGURE 10-23

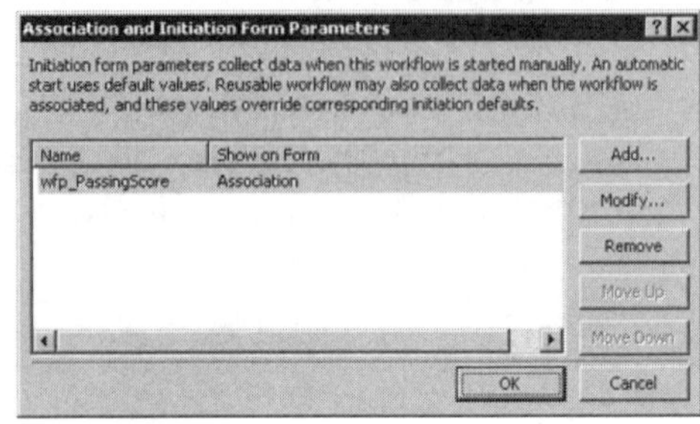

FIGURE 10-24

Configure Association Columns

Association Columns are columns that are automatically added to a target list or library when a workflow is associated with a list. They provide a good way to ensure that control fields and other technical columns that are specific to workflow processing exist on a target list.

Association Columns can be defined as new columns directly from the SharePoint Workflow editor; however, to reuse the columns, you can also add from existing Site Columns. Because your workflow will be using the same association columns as control fields between the master and child workflows, you need to pre-create them as site columns before configuring them in the workflow.

To support your workflow, create the following site columns:

Technical Columns:

- **Workflow Status:** Unique identifier of the instance of the master workflow that created the pipe.
- **Marketing State:** Unique identifier of the originating list item associated with the workflow process.
- **Operations State:** The title or association name of the target subworkflow.
- **Finance State:** An output parameter used by a child workflow to return a score to the master workflow.

To help organize your columns, assign each new site column to an Innovation Pipeline Columns group.

Innovation Pipeline Columns

COLUMN NAME	COLUMN TYPE	ADDITIONAL SETTINGS
IP_WorkflowStep	Choice	Choices: 1 - New 2 - Evaluate 3 - Review 4 - Complete Display Choices = Drop-Down
IP_MarketingState	Choice	Choices: Pending Not Applicable In-Progress Complete Display Choices = Drop-Down
IP_OperationsState	Choice	Choices: Pending Not Applicable In-Progress Complete Display Choices = Drop-Down
IP_FinanceState	Choice	Choices: Pending Not Applicable In-Progress Complete Display Choices = Drop-Down

The completed content type should appear as in Figure 10-25.

Innovation Pipeline Columns		
IP_FinanceState	Choice	Research & Development Gateway
IP_MarketingState	Choice	Research & Development Gateway
IP_OperationsState	Choice	Research & Development Gateway
IP_WorkflowStep	Choice	Research & Development Gateway

FIGURE 10-25

After you define the required Site Columns, return to the workflow editor in SharePoint Designer. To configure the Association Columns, click the Command button labeled "Association Columns" on the Ribbon, as shown in Figure 10-26.

Click the Select Site Column button to open a list of existing site columns (Figure 10-27), and add the four site columns you just created.

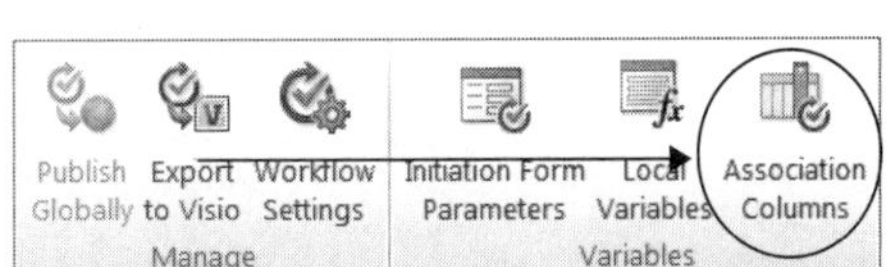

FIGURE 10-26

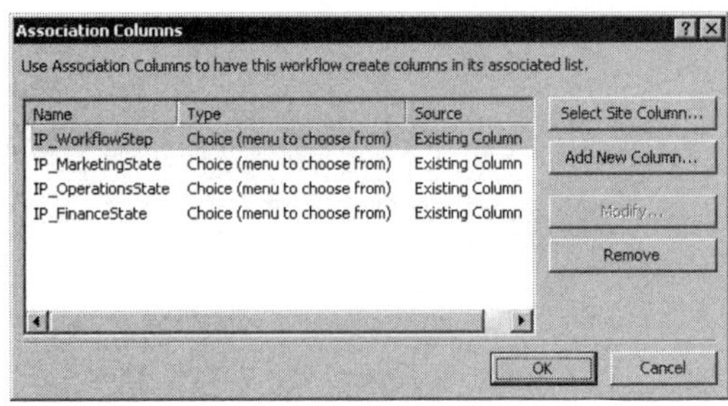

FIGURE 10-27

Build New Proposal Step

The New Proposal step is actually an initialization step. This step that is common to most workflows and initializes variables, validates parameters and sends acknowledgment receipts to the initiator to confirm the workflow process has started.

For your workflow, the initialization step is responsible for sending an acknowledgment to the workflow initiator.

From the Step menu on the Ribbon bar, add a new step inside the New step you previously created, and rename it Send Acknowledgement. From the Actions menu, add a Send an Email and a Log to Workflow History action, as shown in Figure 10-28.

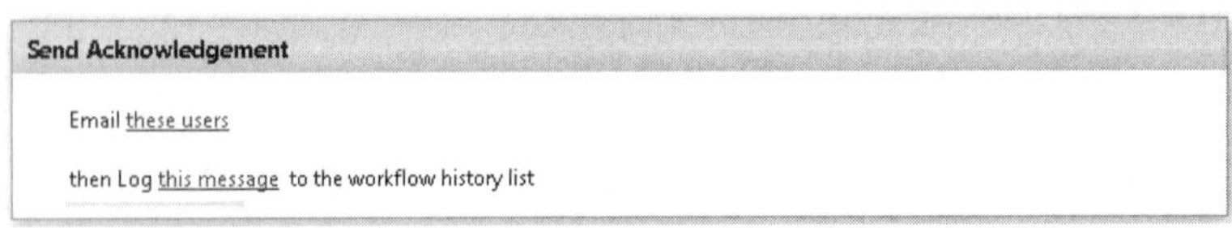

FIGURE 10-28

Click These Users and then configure the notification email as shown in Figure10-29. Give the email a clear subject line and body, and add lookup fields as appropriate to customize the content. It can also be a good practice to include hyperlinks in the email to the original workflow item, workflow status page, and workflow dashboard. This is a suggestion for you to explore on your own.

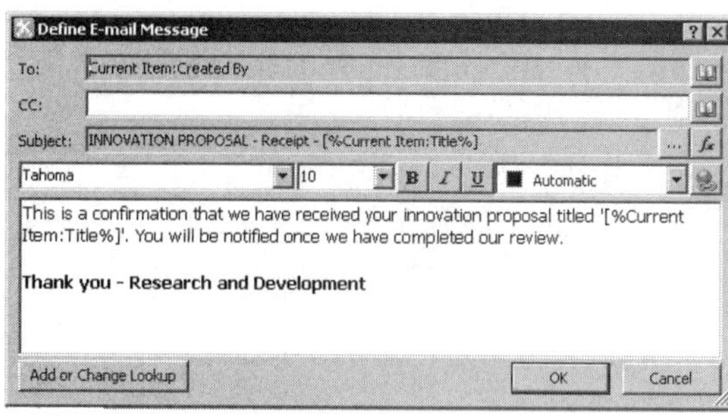

FIGURE 10-29

Finally, configure the Log to History list with a message confirming the acknowledgment email was sent. The final complete New Proposal step is shown in Figure 10-30.

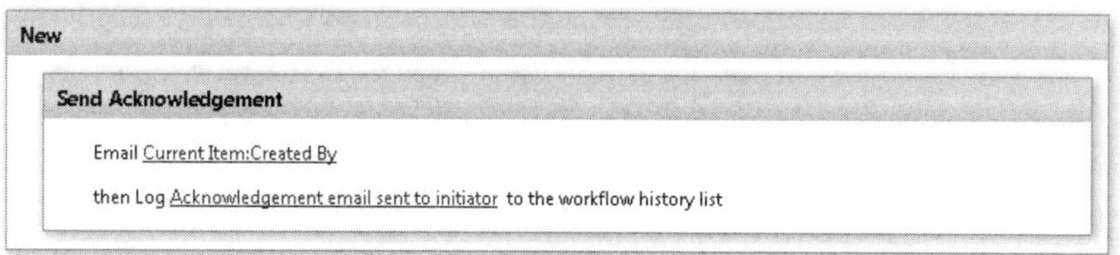

FIGURE 10-30

Build Evaluation Step

The Evaluation step is the most complex part of the master workflow and is where the master needs to facilitate the execution of the child workflows for each of the subject areas.

To keep track of the current major step of all running workflows, the first activity of each step is to update the workflow step column in the current list item. Use the Set Field in Current Item action, as shown in Figure 10-31.

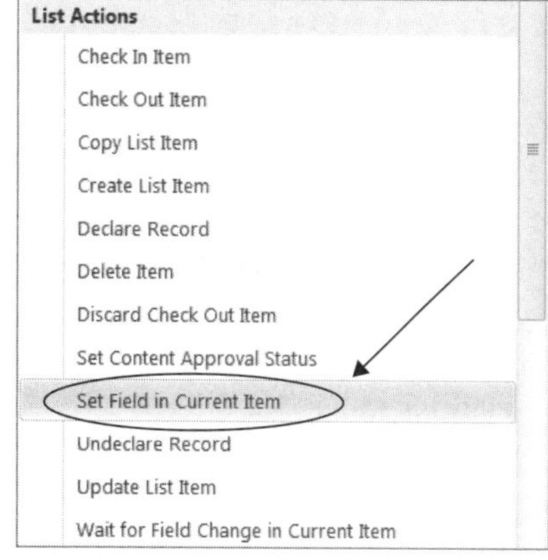

FIGURE 10-31

Update the workflow step to reflect the new status. (See Figure 10-32.) Repeat this action, at the beginning of each major step.

FIGURE 10-32

Next, add a Parallel Block to allow the Marketing Evaluation and Operations Evaluation steps to run at the same time (Figure 10-33).

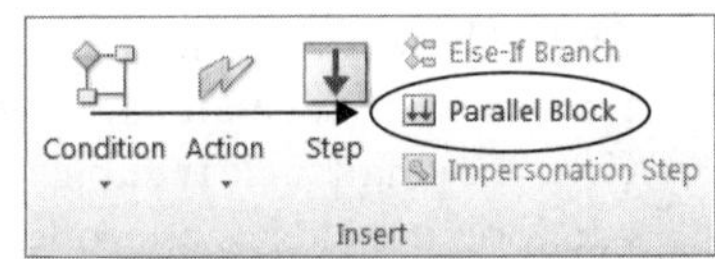

FIGURE 10-33

Inside the Parallel Block, add two steps and name them Marketing Evaluation and Operations Evaluation, respectively. The use of the parallel step allows the Marketing and Operations child workflows to run simultaneously; however, both must complete before the workflow proceeds with the Finance Evaluation step.

Lastly, below the Parallel Block, but still inside the outer Evaluate step, add a new step, and name it Finance Evaluation Rule. Add an If Any Value Equals Any Value condition as a placeholder for your rule, and inside the condition, add a new step named Finance Evaluation. When you finish, the skeleton Evaluate step should look like Figure 10-34.

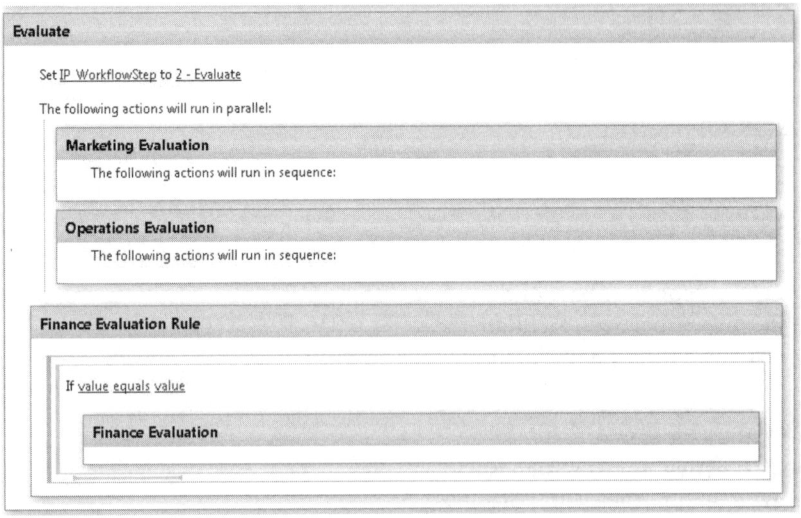

FIGURE 10-34

Now continue by completing the logic for the Marketing Evaluation step. Create a Workflow Pipe list item to communicate between the master and child workflow using the Create List Item workflow action (as shown in Figure 10-35).

Edit the This List variable on the action, and configure the field values for the new list item, as shown in Figure 10-36.

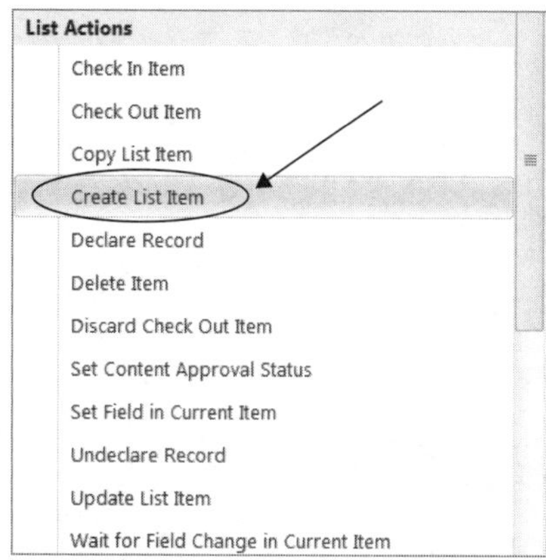

FIGURE 10-35

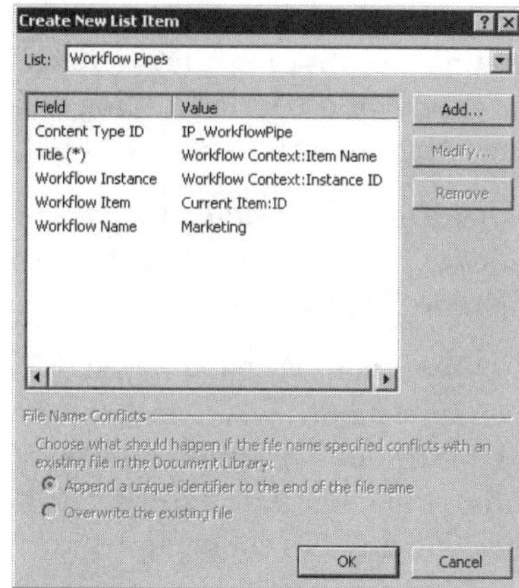

FIGURE 10-36

Configure the action to output to a new variable, as shown in Figure 10-37. You need this variable to later read, and then delete, the pipe when the child workflow has completed.

After you created the pipe, the next steps are to trigger the child workflow by updating the status of the child workflow control field, and then waiting for the status to be modified by the child workflow when it completes (Figure 10-38).

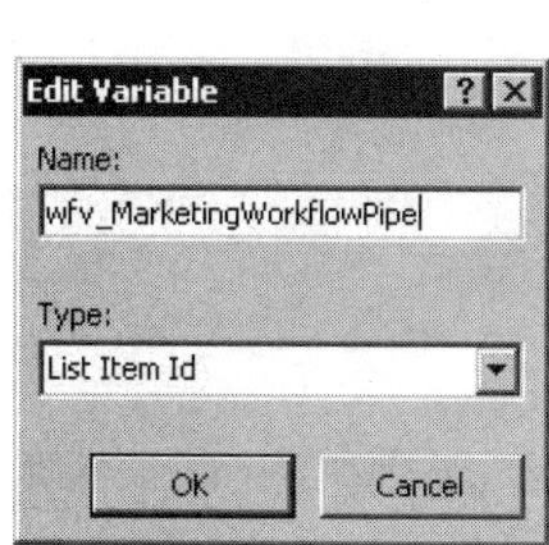

FIGURE 10-37

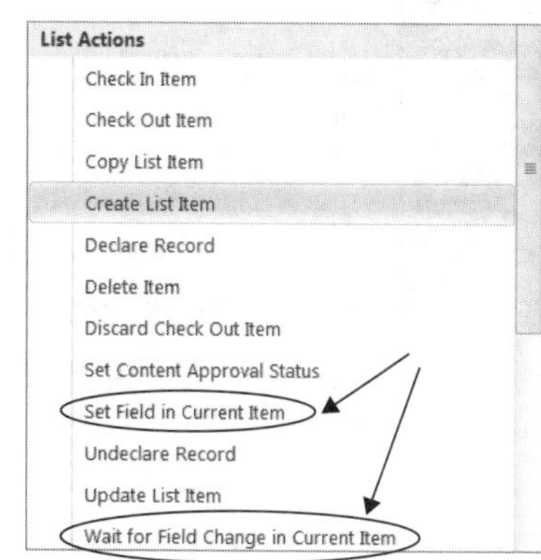

FIGURE 10-38

The updated step should now appear, as shown in Figure 10-39.

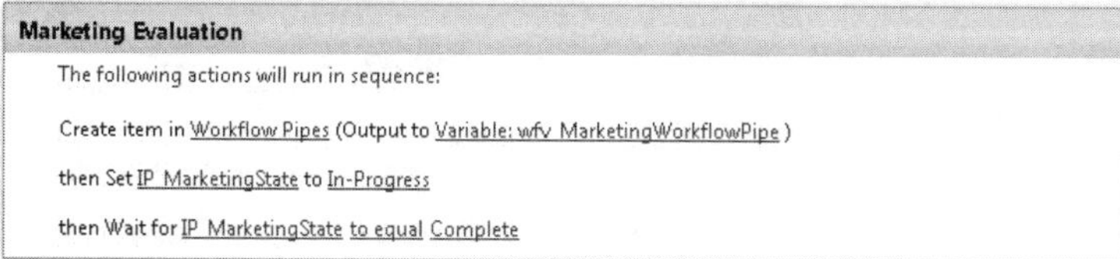

FIGURE 10-39

To complete the step, process the results of the child workflow by reading the workflow pipe to retrieve the score produced by the child workflow, and adding it to a variable for accumulating a total score.

Add two workflow (Do Calculation and Set Workflow Variable) activities to set a workflow variable, and then perform a calculation (Figure 10-40).

Configure the Set Workflow Variable action, by creating a new workflow variable named wfv_MarketingScore, and then set the variable to the Workflow Score field on the Workflow Pipe list item you create earlier. The Lookup dialog should be configured as shown in Figure 10-41.

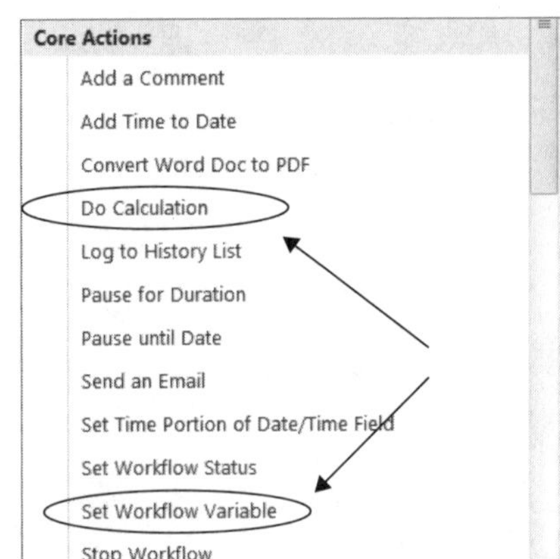

FIGURE 10-40

Configure the Do Calculation activity by creating a new local variable named wfv_TotalScore and adding the wfv_MarketingScore to the new variable (Figure 10-42).

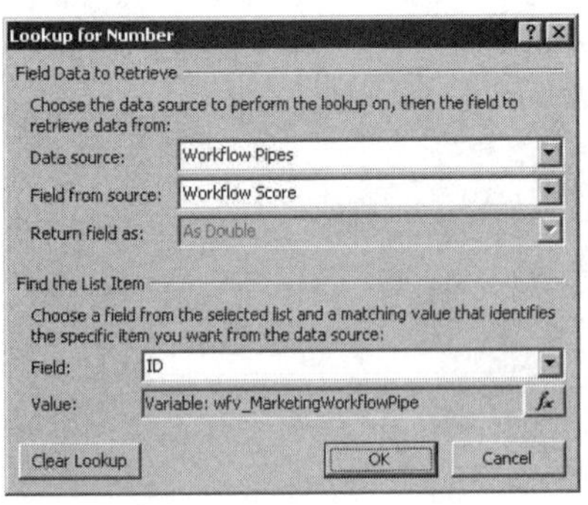

FIGURE 10-41

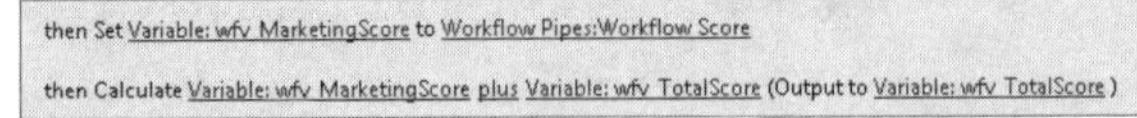

FIGURE 10-42

Lastly, delete the workflow pipe list item because you no longer need it. Add a Delete Item workflow action, and configure it to delete the item you created earlier using the List Item ID stored in the wfv_MarketingWorkflowPipe variable (Figure 10-43).

The completed Marketing Evaluation step should now look like Figure 10-44.

FIGURE 10-43

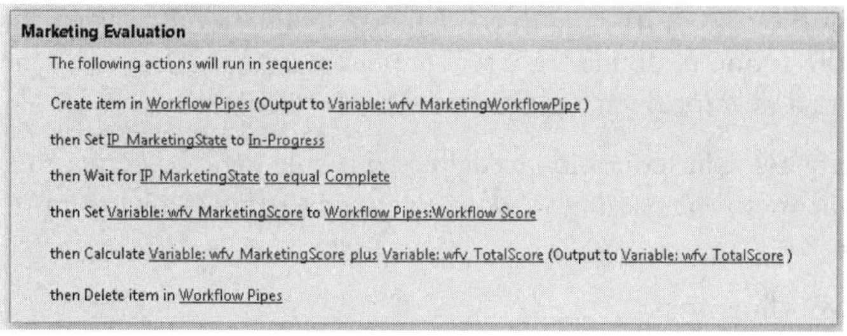

Marketing Evaluation

The following actions will run in sequence:

Create item in Workflow Pipes (Output to Variable: wfv MarketingWorkflowPipe)

then Set IP MarketingState to In-Progress

then Wait for IP MarketingState to equal Complete

then Set Variable: wfv MarketingScore to Workflow Pipes:Workflow Score

then Calculate Variable: wfv MarketingScore plus Variable: wfv TotalScore (Output to Variable: wfv TotalScore)

then Delete item in Workflow Pipes

FIGURE 10-44

The actions you configured to create the Marketing Evaluation are similar for both the Operations Evaluation and Finance Evaluation. Repeat these steps to complete the Operations Evaluation step. The completed step is demonstrated in Figure 10-45.

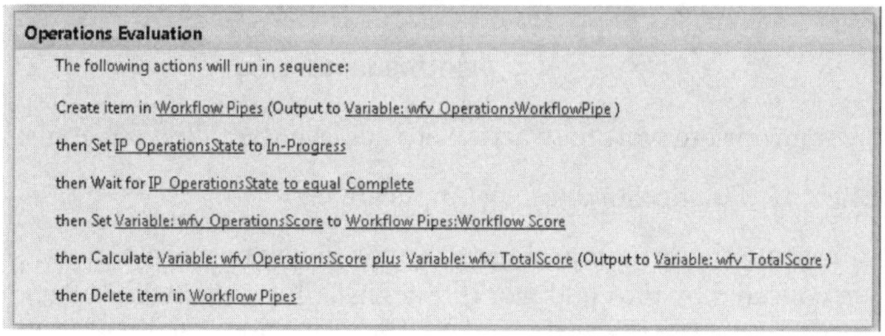

Operations Evaluation

The following actions will run in sequence:

Create item in Workflow Pipes (Output to Variable: wfv OperationsWorkflowPipe)

then Set IP OperationsState to In-Progress

then Wait for IP OperationsState to equal Complete

then Set Variable: wfv OperationsScore to Workflow Pipes:Workflow Score

then Calculate Variable: wfv OperationsScore plus Variable: wfv TotalScore (Output to Variable: wfv TotalScore)

then Delete item in Workflow Pipes

FIGURE 10-45

Now repeat the same steps to complete the Finance Evaluation. Again, create unique variables specific to the step. Figure 10-46 shows the completed step with the still incomplete outer Finance Evaluation Rule step.

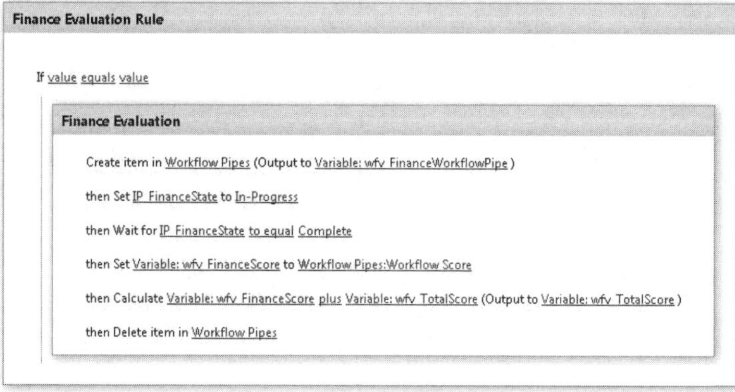
Finance Evaluation Rule
If value equals value
Finance Evaluation
Create item in Workflow Pipes (Output to Variable: wfv FinanceWorkflowPipe)
then Set IP FinanceState to In-Progress
then Wait for IP FinanceState to equal Complete
then Set Variable: wfv FinanceScore to Workflow Pipes:Workflow Score
then Calculate Variable: wfv FinanceScore plus Variable: wfv TotalScore (Output to Variable: wfv TotalScore)
then Delete item in Workflow Pipes

FIGURE 10-46

If you refer to your workflow model, you can avoid performing the Finance Evaluation if the previous evaluations have not produced a suitable intermediate average score.

Now add the final logic to implement the rule. At the top of the Finance Evaluation Rule step, add a Do Calculation activity. Configure the action to divide the wfv_TotalScore by 2 (for the two scores you currently collected) and output to a new local variable named wfv_AvgScore.

Next complete the existing If value equals value condition to define your rule logic by comparing the average score stored in wfv_AvgScore to the passing score you defined earlier as a workflow parameter named wfp_PassingScore.

Figure 10-47 shows the completed workflow step.

The final step is to add the alternative logic if you are going to skip the Finance Evaluation. Add an Else-If Branch from the Ribbon menu below the existing If Value Equals Value condition block (Figure 10-48).

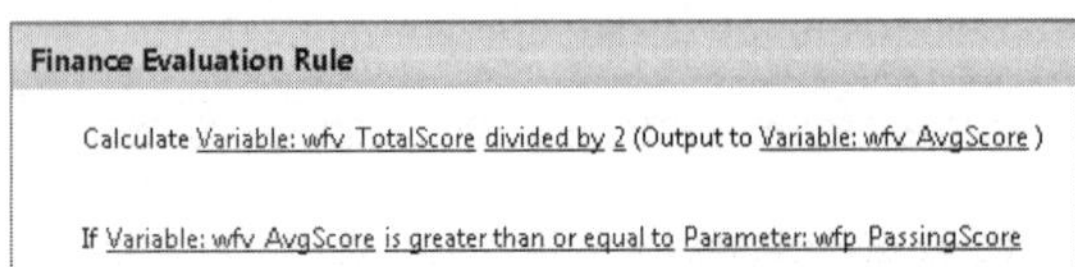
Finance Evaluation Rule
Calculate Variable: wfv TotalScore divided by 2 (Output to Variable: wfv AvgScore)
If Variable: wfv AvgScore is greater than or equal to Parameter: wfp PassingScore

FIGURE 10-47

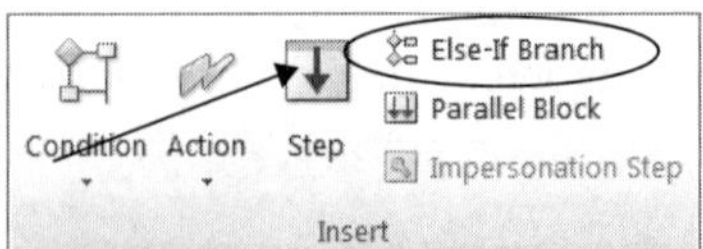
Condition
Action
Step
Else-If Branch
Parallel Block
Impersonation Step
Insert

FIGURE 10-48

To complete the else logic, pick the appropriate workflow actions to achieve the following goals:

1. Set the workflow control field IP_FinanceState to Not Applicable.
2. Perform a calculation to substitute the current average score for the finance evaluation score that would have been collected by the child workflow. This allows the Review step to recalculate the average score as if the finance evaluation had run without skewing the results.
3. Log a message to the workflow history indicating the finance review was skipped for informational purposes.

Figure 10-49 shows the final completed Finance Evaluation.

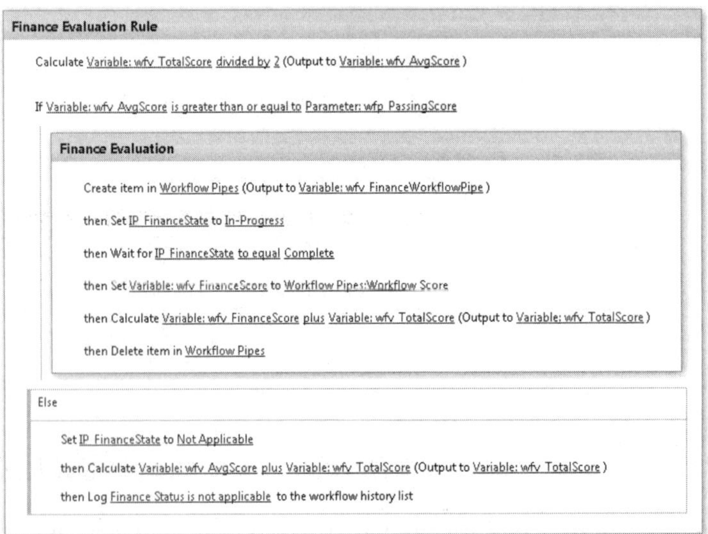
Finance Evaluation Rule
Calculate Variable: wfv TotalScore divided by 2 (Output to Variable: wfv AvgScore)
If Variable: wfv AvgScore is greater than or equal to Parameter: wfp PassingScore
Finance Evaluation
Create item in Workflow Pipes (Output to Variable: wfv FinanceWorkflowPipe)
then Set IP FinanceState to In-Progress
then Wait for IP FinanceState to equal Complete
then Set Variable: wfv FinanceScore to Workflow Pipes:Workflow Score
then Calculate Variable: wfv FinanceScore plus Variable: wfv TotalScore (Output to Variable: wfv TotalScore)
then Delete item in Workflow Pipes
Else
Set IP FinanceState to Not Applicable
then Calculate Variable: wfv AvgScore plus Variable: wfv TotalScore (Output to Variable: wfv TotalScore)
then Log Finance Status is not applicable to the workflow history list

FIGURE 10-49

This completes the overall Evaluation step. This was a fairly complex step in your overall workflow process due to the number of child workflows that needed to be managed, data aggregated for the various workflow pipes, and the conditional logic surrounding the Finance Evaluation subprocess.

Build Review Step

The Review step is where you can implement the business rule logic that ultimately determines whether the overall proposal is accepted or rejected based on whether an average of all the evaluation scores is greater than the minimum passing score you configured as the workflow association form parameter.

Begin filling out the Review step by repeating some earlier actions. Update the current workflow step to 3 - Review, and perform a calculation to determine the final average score by dividing the total scores by 3 for each of the evaluations performed (Figure 10-50).

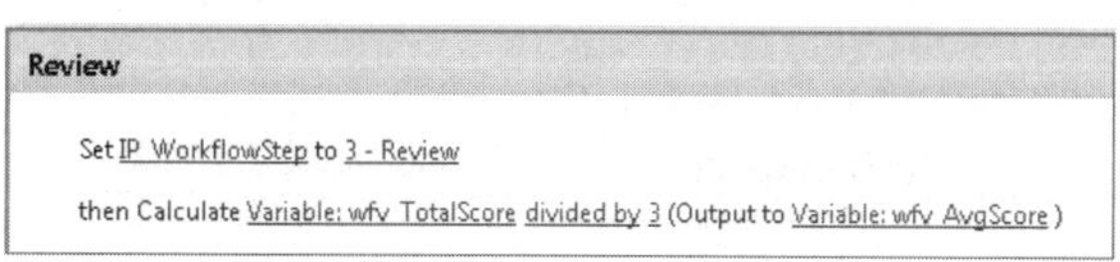

FIGURE 10-50

Next, implement a conditional If/Else Block to notify the initiator that the proposal was accepted or rejected, and update the workflow state appropriately.

Add an If Any Value Equals Value from the Condition Ribbon menu, and configure it to evaluate if wfv_AvgScore is greater than or equal to wfv_PassingScore. Next, add an Else-If Branch, as shown in Figure 10-51.

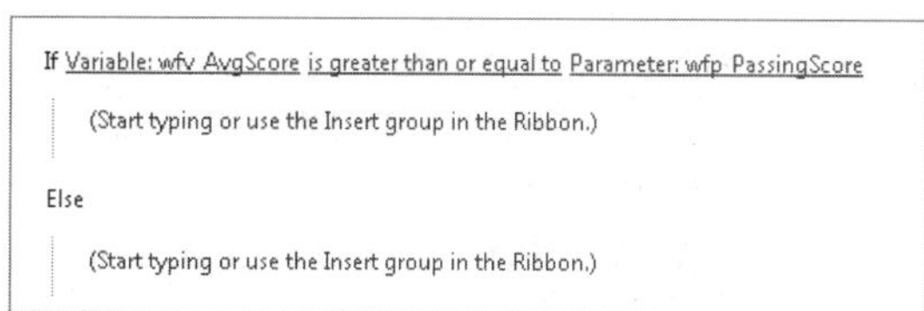

FIGURE 10-51

For each path, you need to accomplish the same steps:

1. Update a workflow variable indicating whether to create a Scorecard. Name the variable wfw_CreateScorecard, and make it a Boolean.
2. Email the workflow initiator, and advise them that the proposal was accepted or rejected.
3. Log a message indicating the result to the Workflow History.
4. Set the workflow status to Approved or Rejected.
5. From the Actions menu, select the appropriate actions, and add them to the If and Else paths.
6. Edit the Send an Email actions for If and Else paths, and enter an appropriate message for the initiator (Figure 10-52).

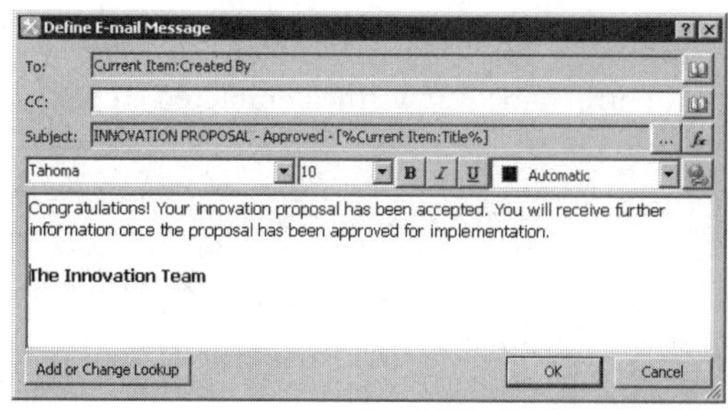

FIGURE 10-52

Figure 10-53 shows the complete review.

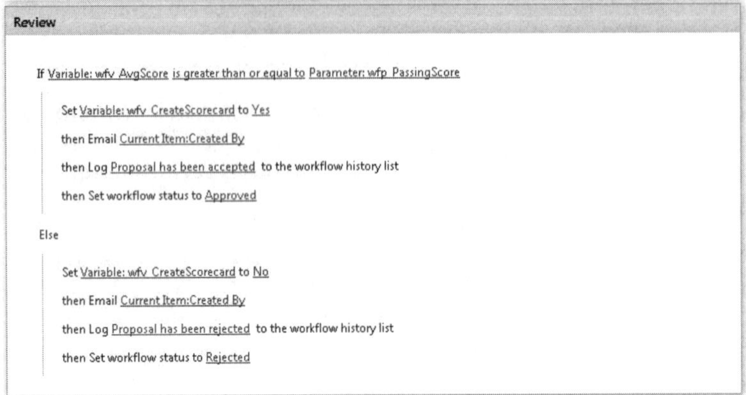

FIGURE 10-53

Build Complete Step

The Complete step is where you perform any final actions that need to be performed, perform any cleanup, and update any final status or state fields.

The key actions that need to be completed in this step are to create a Scorecard item if the proposal has been accepted, and to update the final workflow state:

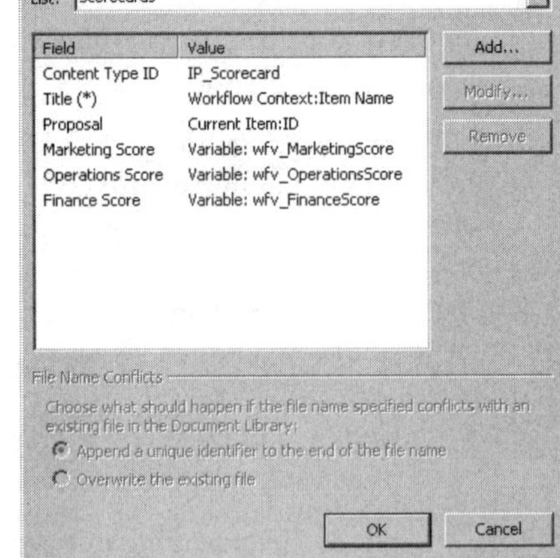

FIGURE 10-54

1. Add an If Any Value Equals Value action, and update to set wfv_CreateScore to Yes.
2. Inside the If block, add a Create List Item action, so you can create a new Scorecard item.
3. Configure the action to save the scorecard values you collected to the list item, as shown in Figure 10-54.
4. Lastly, add the Set Field in Current Item action, and configure it to update the IP_WorkflowStep field to 4 - Complete.

Figure 10-55 shows the completed step.

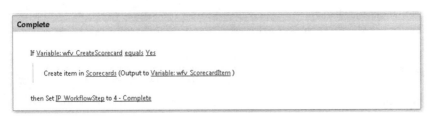

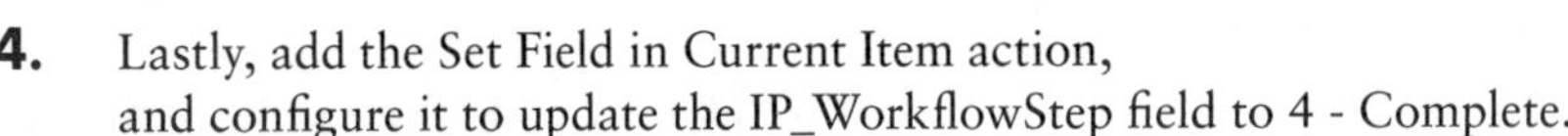

FIGURE 10-55

This complete the end-to-end workflow process for the master workflow satisfying the requirements to keep the proposal originator informed of the overall workflow status, coordinating the execution of subject area reviews, and creating a scorecard for accepted proposals.

Subject Area Evaluation

The subject area review workflow includes a child workflow demonstrating a single example of how a SME or team might implement a scoring process for a proposal.

Although it is possible, and even probable, that each team could implement a custom process, each child workflow can accept parameters and return the same output values to the master workflow. For this perspective, the implementation of each child workflow utilizes the same foundation, which is demonstrated here. For your example, you create and build the evaluation workflow for marketing.

If you continue from creating the previous workflow, SharePoint Designer should already be open and ready to begin. If not, run SharePoint Designer using a designated workflow authoring account because your workflows will be using Impersonation to run the workflows with elevated permissions. You can run SharePoint Designer using a specific account by using the Shift+Right-Click, and selecting Run as Different User from the context menu. Continue by opening the site where you have been building the solution, and select Workflows from the Quick Navigation menu.

Proceed with creating a new workflow by selecting Reusable Workflow from the Ribbon menu. Enter a name and description, and select the content type IP_Proposal, as shown in Figure 10-56.

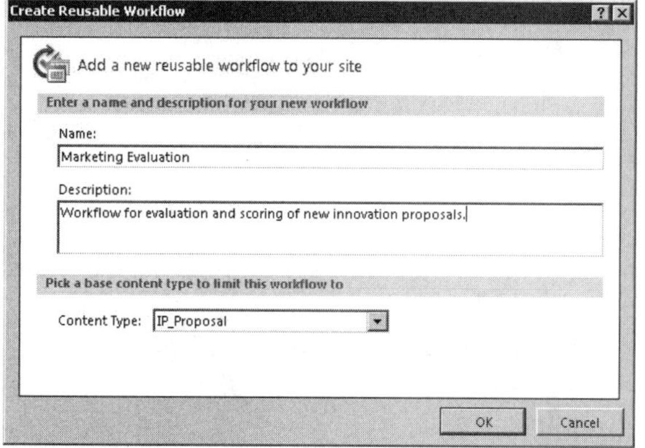

FIGURE 10-56

When the editor opens, create the skeleton for your workflow. Because your workflow will be running with elevated privileges, start by adding an Impersonation Step to the designer.

Within the Impersonation, add an If Any Value Equals Value condition. Within the If block, add two sequential steps, and name them Score Proposal, and Update Pipeline, respectively. Figure 10-57 shows the completed workflow skeleton.

Impersonation Step

The contents of this step will run as the workflow author:

If value equals value

Score Proposal

Update Pipeline

FIGURE 10-57

To finish the workflow, complete the following steps:

1. Configure Association Columns.
2. Configure Execution Rule.
3. Build the Score Proposal step.
4. Build the Update Pipeline step.

Configure Association Columns

When configuring the master workflow, you defined a number of Site Columns to use as control fields between the master and child workflows. You added these site columns as workflow Association Columns to communicate and monitor the execution of child workflows.

To configure your required Association Columns, click the command from the Ribbon menu, as shown in Figure 10-58:

Click the Select Site Column command button to open a list of existing site columns, and add the IP_MarketingState column (Figure 10-59).

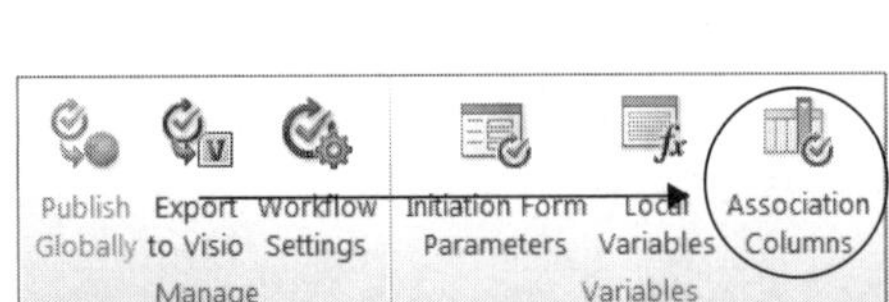

FIGURE 10-58

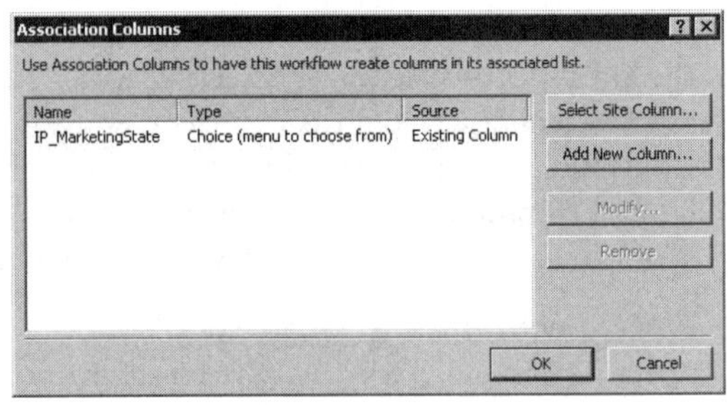

FIGURE 10-59

Your workflow can use this control field to evaluate whether it needs to execute, and can update this field to communicate to the master workflow when it finishes.

Configure Execution Rule

The child workflow is associated with the Proposals list and configured to start when the Proposal item is changed. It is entirely likely that an item may be changed in any number of ways that do not necessarily indicate you should execute your Evaluation step.

As part of cooperating with the master workflow, the child workflow needs to monitor the value of a designated control field to know when to execute. When configuring the skeleton outline of the evaluation workflow, you added an If block as a placeholder for this rule.

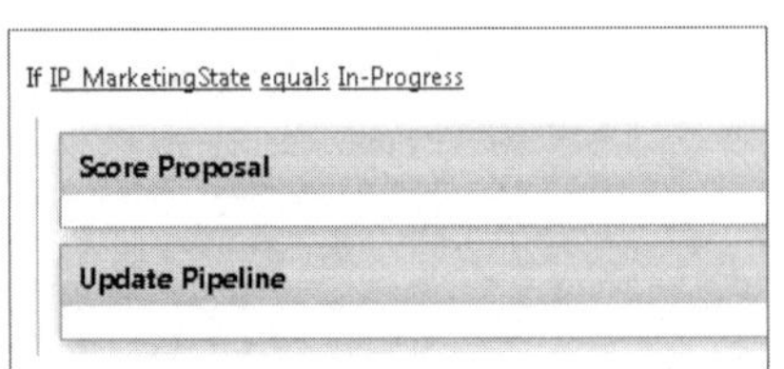

FIGURE 10-60

Configure the If Any Value Equals Value action to determine if the IP_MarketingState field equals In-Progress. Figure 10-60 shows the configured action.

Later in the workflow, you update this field again to communicate to the master workflow that you have finished.

Build Score Proposal Step

The Score Proposal step is responsible for implementing the subprocess logic of collecting feedback from SMEs and returning a score to the master workflow.

The benefit to use separation of concern principles is that you can accomplish this goal any way you choose without impacting the master workflow. One example might be an InfoPath form with a survey or questionnaire that generated a score based on an average or calculated value based on the results of the questionnaire. This could be accomplished in parallel by assigning the same survey to an entire group, or could be accomplished through a set of sequential steps in which different specialists completed a part of the survey.

For the purpose of demonstration, you can accomplish your goal in a fairly simple fashion using a Collect Data from a User action. You can assign this action to a single user or group, and request them to provide one or more fields of data associated with a Workflow Task. When the task is complete, you can access the fields on the task that were completed by the user.

Within the Score Proposal step, select the task action from the Ribbon menu (Figure 10-61).

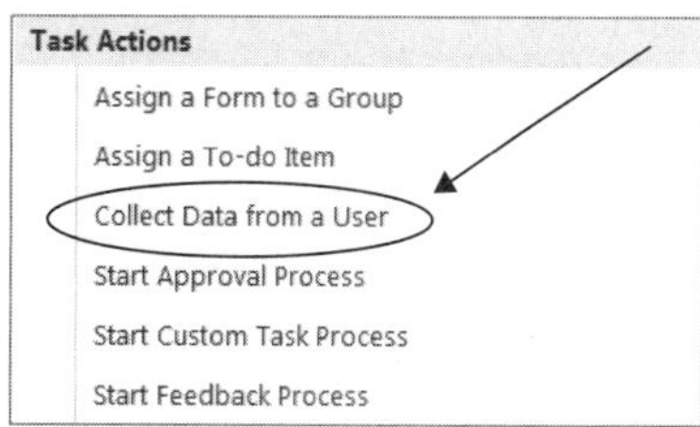

FIGURE 10-61

To configure this action, you need to configure what data needs to be collected from the user by completed a wizard with a series of dialogs. Click the data parameter, and click Next to proceed past the welcome page of the Custom Task Wizard dialog.

Enter a title and description for the workflow task that will be assigned to the user to complete, as shown in Figure 10-62. When complete, click the Next command button.

On the final dialog page, click the Add command button to add a new form field. Enter Score for the field name, enter a description, and select Number from the Information Type drop-down. Click Next > to configure the columns settings, as shown in Figure 10-63.

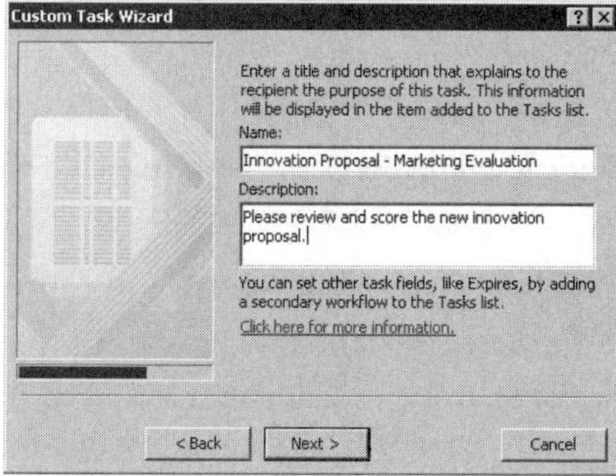

FIGURE 10-62

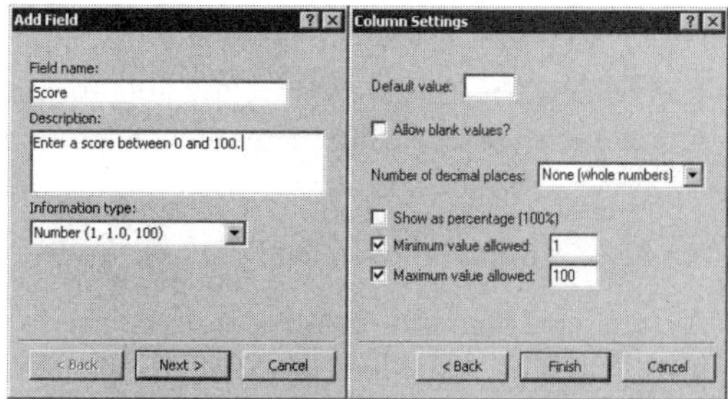

FIGURE 10-63

When finished, click Finish to complete configuration of the data form. For a simple demonstration, you simply collect only a score value.

Next click the This User parameter to configure who will be completing the form. Previously, you created a number of SharePoint Groups containing members available to evaluate and score proposals. By assigning the task to a SharePoint group, all members of the group will be notified of the pending task, and any member can complete the evaluation.

From the Select Users dialog, select People/Groups from SharePoint Site, and click Add (Figure 64). From the Select People and Groups search dialog, enter Marketing, and select Marketing Reviewers (Figure 10-65).

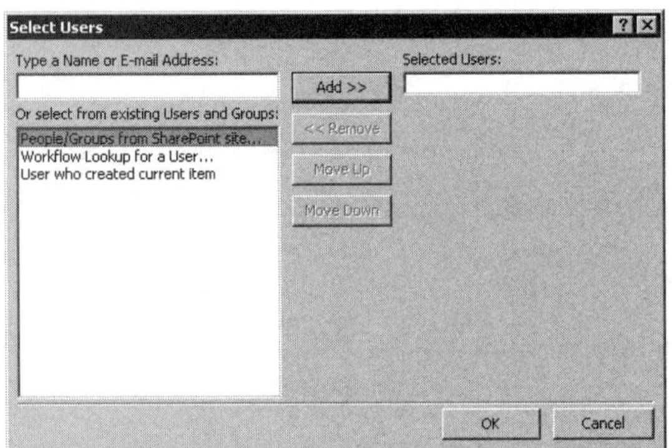

FIGURE 10-64

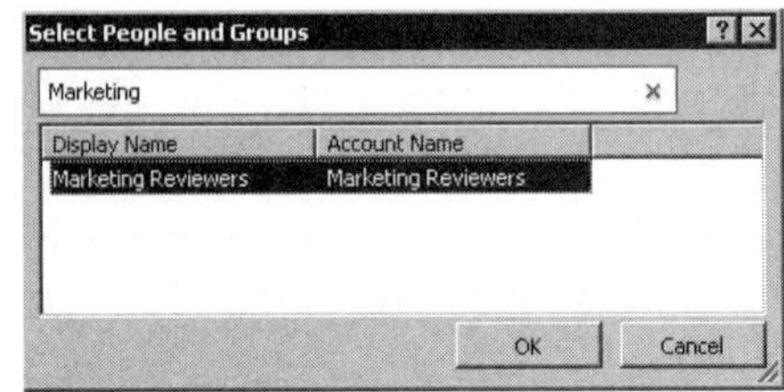

FIGURE 10-65

Lastly, create a new variable to hold the List Item Id of the task item and name it wfv_FeedbackTaskItem. Figure 10-66 shows the completed step.

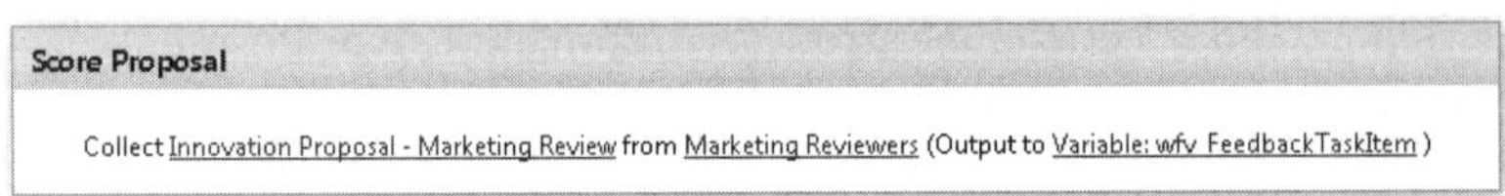

FIGURE 10-66

Build Update Pipeline Step

The Update Pipeline step is responsible for updating the Workflow Pipe item with the collected score, and then updating the workflow control field to show that the process has been completed.

The first activity you need to accomplish is to locate the Workflow Pipe list item created by the master workflow to exchange data with your child workflow.

As you have seen in previous chapters, the lookup capability of SharePoint Designer can query only a list based on a single field value. To locate the Workflow Pipe, a unique key has been created by combining the unique ID of the proposal with the association name of the child workflow. The format of the key field is <Id>|<Workflow Name>.

Within the Update Pipeline step, add a Set Workflow Variable action. For the workflow variable parameter, create a new variable named wfv_PipelineKey. Select the value parameter, and using the String Builder dialog you learned to use in previous chapters, format a string value, as shown in Figure 10-67.

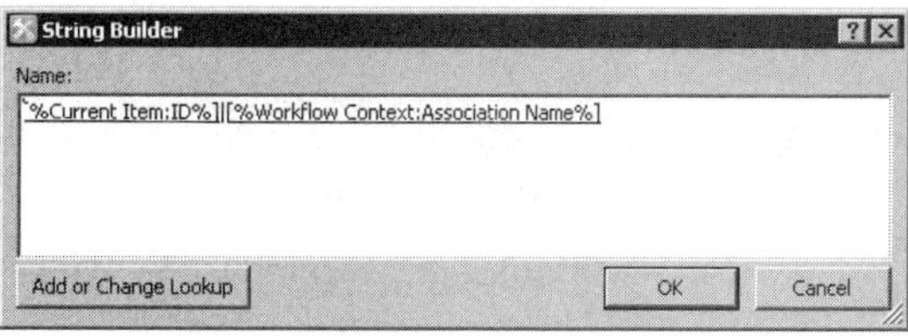

FIGURE 10-67

Now that you have your unique key, you can update the Workflow Pipe item with the collected score. Add an Update List Item action, and configure the action to update the Workflow Score field, as shown in Figure 10-68.

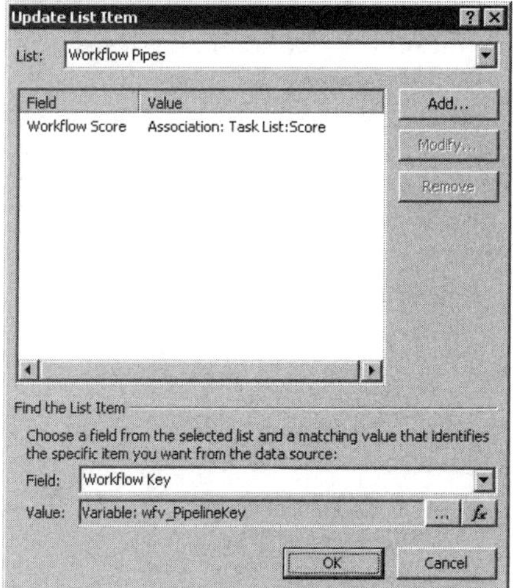

FIGURE 10-68

To complete your step, you need to communicate to the master workflow that we have finished processing by updating the control field. Add a Set Field in Current Item action to the step, and configure to set the IP_MarketingState field to Complete.

Figure 10-69 shows the completed workflow step.

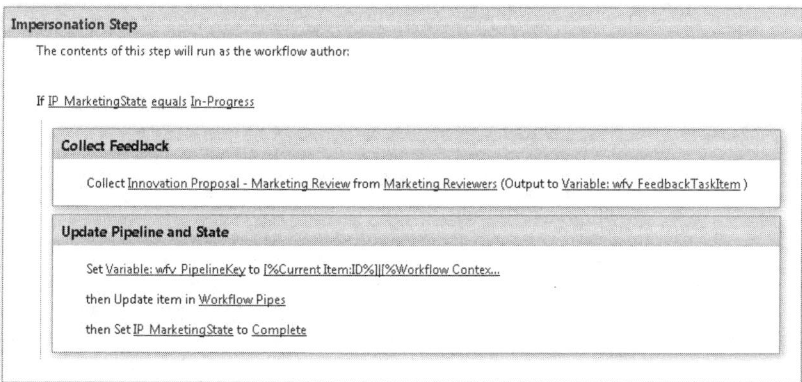

FIGURE 10-69

SUMMARY

This chapter introduced some advanced topics when designing and building workflow solutions that can address the complexity of advanced business processes.

Knowledge work and measurement of creative processes are notoriously hard to measure, making objective and fair management an ongoing challenge for many organizations. Through the implementation of the Scorecard pattern, you learned how to collect measurements from knowledge workers through workflow, which can assist management is making better decisions.

Through the implementation of the Pipeline pattern, you learned how to coordinate multiple workflows as a way to create abstraction layers within the overall process. This can help manage complexity and improve maintainability of advanced workflow solutions. As long as the defined inputs and outputs of each subprocess do not change, the overall process can remain consistent even when the details of how each subprocess performed can evolve and change over time.

11

Enhancing the User Interface

WHAT'S IN THIS CHAPTER?

- Using InfoPath to Create Advanced Data Entry Forms
- Improving SharePoint User Interfaces with jQuery
- Leveraging the Data View Web Part
- Selecting the Best Option for Your Needs

So far, this book has spent a lot of time describing business solutions and emphasizing the importance of workflow patterns. Of course, the *workflow* component of a business process is important. However, it's sort of invisible to end users and is only one part of the three key components of business solutions. Recall that business solutions follow an arc. They begin with some kind of data entry process to kick things off. Then, a business process ensures the process operates correctly, step by step. Finally, you implement a dashboard to manage the process, preferably managing exceptional conditions only (such as missed due dates and the like). It's fair to say that two of these three components (data entry and dashboards) have been given short shrift. It's time to remedy that situation.

It's not that data entry and dashboards have been ignored. It's clear, however, that the kind of user interfaces you'd present to your end users if you followed the book verbatim so far would be poor at best. You need to provide better user interfaces to your end users. This chapter offers you three different techniques that power end users ("activist users") can leverage to accomplish that.

HOW TO BUILD GREAT USER INTERFACES

SharePoint provides two direct and one indirect method for creating great data entry screens and dashboards. The use of "direct" and "indirect" is literally true, but don't think that a "direct" method is necessarily better than an "indirect" method or vice versa. As you'll see, each technique has its time and place. Following are the techniques:

- InfoPath
- Data View Web Part (DVWP)
- JavaScript and, in particular, jQuery

The following sections describe each of these in detail, how they work, and when you should (and should not) use them and ends with detailed walk-throughs using them for good effects. Begin with InfoPath.

ENHANCEMENT TECHNIQUES IN DETAIL

The next three major sections describe each of these techniques. You learn what they are at a high level, when you should use them, and when you should not. Each section concludes with one or two detailed walk-throughs that illustrate how to use the technique to meet a real-world business need that you're likely to encounter while building solutions in SharePoint.

UI ENHANCEMENT AND WORKFLOW

Although this book is obviously primarily about SharePoint workflow, these enhancement techniques transcend workflow. Everyone wants better data entry screens and list views. Despite the emphasis here to use these UI builder tools to address gaps in the solution "arc" (data entry and dashboards), don't limit your imagination. Use these tools anywhere you think they are appropriate — as a component of a workflow solution or something else entirely.

InfoPath

Previous chapters in the book mentioned InfoPath. InfoPath is a Microsoft product that is actually one of the more specialized Microsoft office products. Microsoft Office is like that: You likely use a handful of bread-and-butter apps such as Microsoft Word, Excel, and Outlook all the time. InfoPath, like Microsoft Publisher, Communicator, OneNote, and others represent a second tier in the Office family. That's not to say that they are second class, but they are specialized apps for specific purposes and a more narrow scope.

What Is InfoPath?

InfoPath is a dual-purpose Microsoft product. First, use it to create data entry forms for your end users. Second, use InfoPath to fill out those data entry forms at runtime. This book calls the kind of user that creates forms a *developer*. Don't get caught up in the "D" word. By the time you finish with this section and its walk-through, you can lay claim to the title if you so choose, whether you know coding or not. In other words, you don't need to know anything about code or bring any special experiences to the tool to succeed with it.

How is that? InfoPath, as a member of the Microsoft office family, provides a friendly interface for the activist users this book targets (that is, you) to learn and use effectively. Like Microsoft Word, Excel, or most other office applications, you fire it up and use its friendly WYSIWYG interface to do your work. Unlike Microsoft Word or Excel, you use InfoPath to create data entry screens. At run-time, end users fill out those forms using a web browser.

INFOPATH WITH AND WITHOUT SHAREPOINT

When working with InfoPath in a SharePoint environment, at run-time your end users most often (99%+ of the time) fill out InfoPath forms directly in their web browser. Because the form is entirely browser-based, these end users don't need InfoPath installed on their work station. You should know, however, that InfoPath forms can also be filled out by the client application and, indeed, don't need SharePoint at all. In this scenario you (as the developer) would provide the form by email or a number of other distribution methods to your end users. They would also have InfoPath installed on their work station. As with Word and Excel, when they click the attached form, the InfoPath client opens up and enables them to fill out the form. This book won't cover that scenario but it's good to know.

How Does InfoPath Work?

Just like it takes two to tango, it takes two to effectively use InfoPath. First, someone needs to create a form. Second, someone needs to fill out that form.

You use the InfoPath client to create forms. This means that you need the InfoPath client installed on your work station. Your IT department can obtain and install it for you. Failing that, you can obtain a trial version from Microsoft's website. Figure 11-1 shows the opening InfoPath screen.

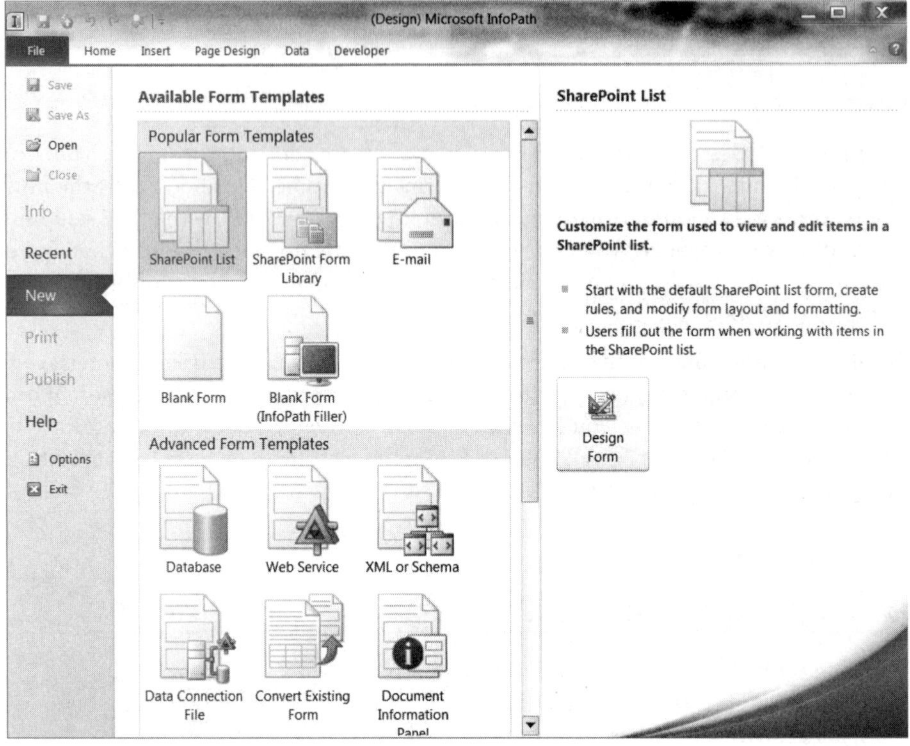

FIGURE 11-1

When you create an InfoPath form, you're actually creating a template. The template is a collection of individual files that operate together at run-time to provide the user who fills out the form with the best experience you can provide, limited by your skills and InfoPath's core capabilities. (Following are some guidance on this.) After you create the perfect template, you *publish* it to SharePoint. The publishing process saves the template in a library in SharePoint. The template is actually no different from any other document that you might want to upload to SharePoint. It's just a file with a specific extension (XSN) but is otherwise not special as far as SharePoint is concerned.

It becomes special when your end users fill out the form at run-time. SharePoint uses the template to provide the form-filling experience. This includes the actual data entry fields, any custom validations that you added, dynamic enabling or disabling of fields, and other UI niceties. At some point, the end user will want to save the form, which is normally accomplished with a button or other "save me" control. When end users save their forms, SharePoint and InfoPath work together to create a straightforward XML document. This XML document refers to its original InfoPath template but is otherwise no different from any generic XML document that you've seen before. InfoPath saves these documents to a library in SharePoint, and like their template masters, SharePoint doesn't consider them special. They are just ordinary documents in a library. All the usual SharePoint functionality applies (that is, versions, check-in/check-out, recycle bin, and so on).

How Do You Use InfoPath?

To use InfoPath, you need two things at a minimum:

- Microsoft InfoPath installed on your work station
- An appropriately licensed SharePoint environment

The second bullet point is a little tricky. You cannot use InfoPath in a SharePoint Foundation environment. At a minimum you need SharePoint 2010 Standard Edition to effectively use InfoPath with SharePoint, and even then, it's limited. It gets more complicated with Microsoft's cloud offerings. The only unrestricted environment is SharePoint 2010 Enterprise edition, and you may as well assume that you need Enterprise. Talk with your IT department for help on this topic if you're not sure you have the correct edition.

When you have these prerequisites in place, you create an InfoPath form. You can create these forms completely standalone. (You begin with nothing and create a new form starting with a blank page.) Alternatively, you can use InfoPath to customize SharePoint's default data entry screens: the CRUD screens that SharePoint automatically creates for you for any custom list. This approach is more appropriate for beginners and is effective for beginners and advanced users. That's the approach you learn about in the walk-through.

InfoPath, What's It Good For?

InfoPath is good at solving a number of problems that the previous business solutions chapters ignore (or waved their hands at). They include the following:

- **Radical user interface enhancements:** Not only can you completely change the layout of the page, you can change the colors, add images and hyperlinks, and change fonts, field widths, and much more. As a result, you can create an exciting data entry function that provides a professional and pleasing look to your end users.
- **Change field labels:** In the previous chapters, you created CRUD data entry forms based on content types. Those content types follow a name convention and as a result, the default SharePoint CRUD screen looks odd and stilted to end users. Use InfoPath to change the labels, but also retain the important naming convention of the underlying content type.
- **Data entry validations:** Use InfoPath to enhance the data entry experience through validations. Consider the time off request example from Chapter 5, "Time Off Management." One of the core rules of that solution was that everyone must request time off in 4-hour increments. You implemented this rule directly in the workflow via the modulo function. Although this got the job done, it's still a little confusing to end users. If the end users entered an invalid number of hours, they could still submit the form. They wouldn't find out until after the workflow had fired. Use InfoPath to both provide instant feedback to users and disallow submitting the form if it's destined to fail in any case.

The three categories described cover some of the primary uses of InfoPath. After you start using it, more ideas will occur to you.

InfoPath — When Not to Use It

InfoPath is good for enhancing SharePoint's standard data entry forms. However, it's not appropriate for dashboards. (Although some advanced scenarios make sense.) Use it for data entry, and leave it at that.

Obviously, if you can't meet the prerequisites, it's not appropriate. You must have at least one license of the InfoPath client and then SharePoint must be appropriately licensed to use InfoPath. Don't fall into the trap of thinking that because you have InfoPath on your work station that you can use it with SharePoint. Check with your IT department first.

InfoPath Walk-Through

Now walk through two scenarios using InfoPath. First, you change the labels on one of SharePoint's default CRUD forms and learn how that works. Next, you attach some validation to a date field. (You can't request something in the past.) Begin with changing form labels. Both walk-throughs assume that you have met the minimum requirements for using InfoPath in your environment.

Example: Change the Labels on a Form

To execute this walk-through, you'll need the following:

- Content type
- Custom list

You create a content type with columns deliberately named in a "funny" way so that you have a clear and obvious reason to change them. Then, you add the content type to a custom list. Lastly, you use InfoPath to change those labels.

First, create a content type with three site columns named and described as follows:

- Funny Date Requested: Data and Time
- Funny Hours Requested: Number
- Funny User ID: Person or Group

Look to Figure 11-2 for help.

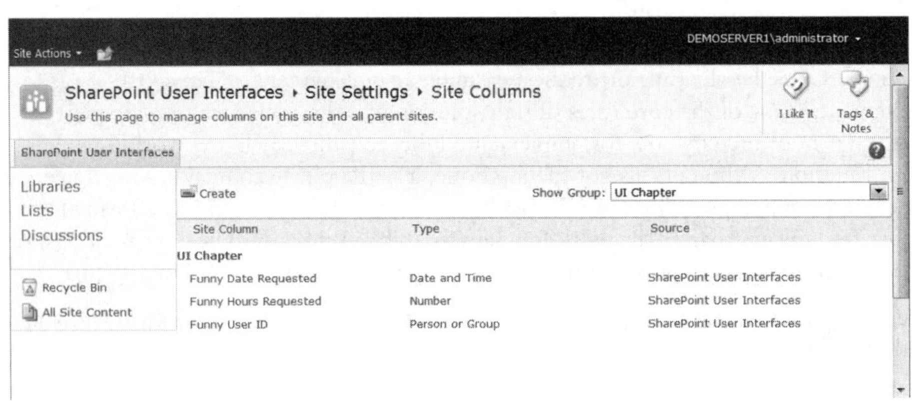

FIGURE 11-2

Add those columns to a content type named Funny Time Off Request.

Next, create a list called Abbreviated Time Off Request, and add this content type to it. When finished, it should look like Figure 11-3.

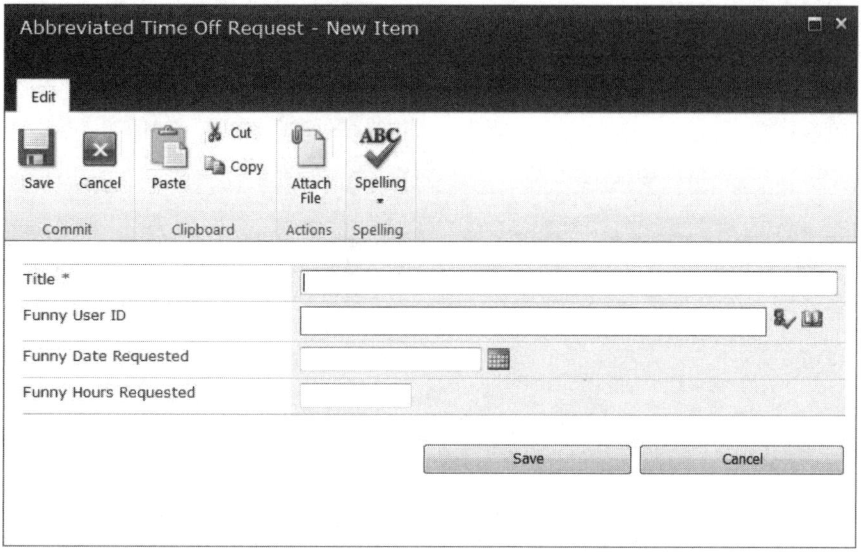

FIGURE 11-3

To edit this form's CRUD screen, navigate to the list, and then click List in the ribbon. If you've met the prerequisites, SharePoint lights up a button labeled Custom Form on the Ribbon (see Figure 11-4). Click it to launch InfoPath.

FIGURE 11-4

SharePoint responds by opening up the page, similar to Figure 11-5.

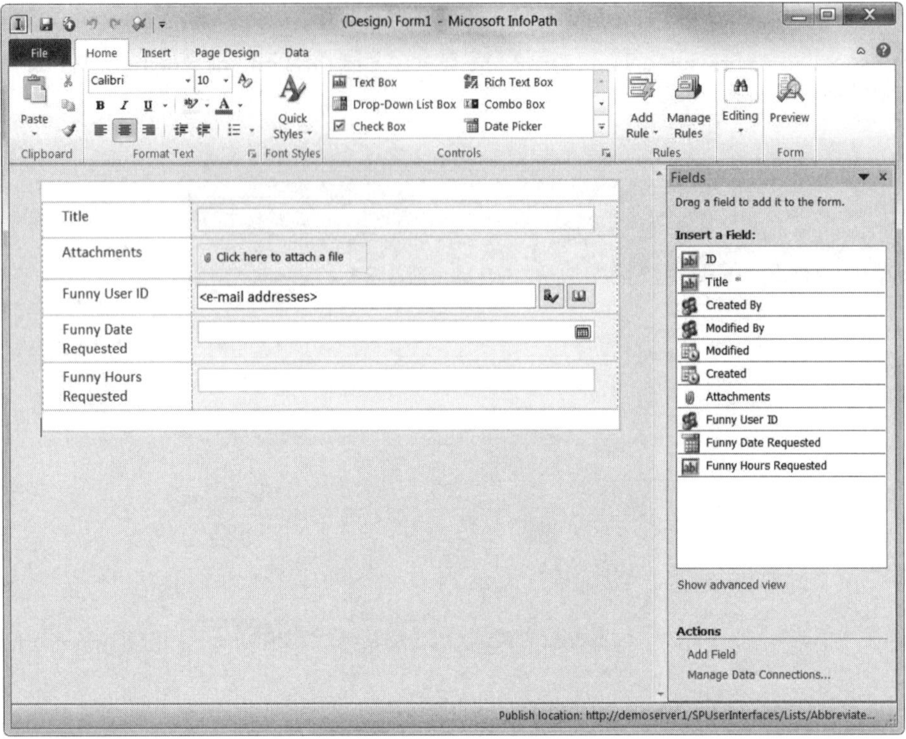

FIGURE 11-5

To change the labels, simply click with your mouse and make the change on the screen. See Figure 11-6 for a view of that activity.

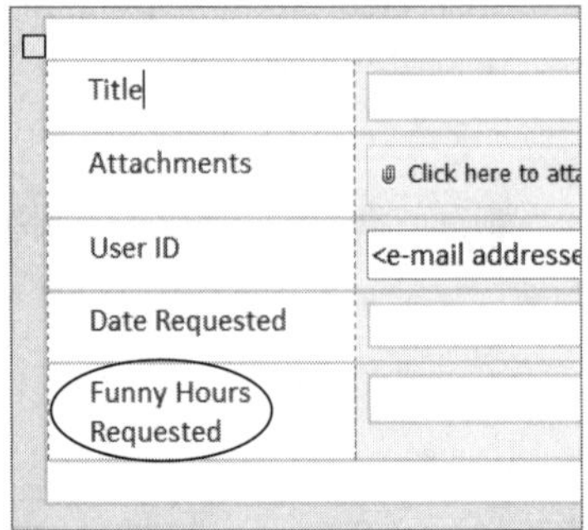

FIGURE 11-6

After you complete making the changes, it's time to publish the form. Publish it by clicking File and then Publish. InfoPath responds with two big-button options: SharePoint list and Export Source Files. For this exercise, just click SharePoint List. However, at some point, go ahead and click Export Source Files to get an insider view of the template and its many components. There is a great deal of educational value in doing so.

When you click SharePoint list, InfoPath publishes the form to SharePoint. When it finishes, it displays a dialog box confirming that the form was published and offers you the option to open the SharePoint list in the browser. Feel free to do that or simply click OK, and then test the form by navigating your browser to the list and clicking Add Item. Your new form will look similar to Figure 11-7.

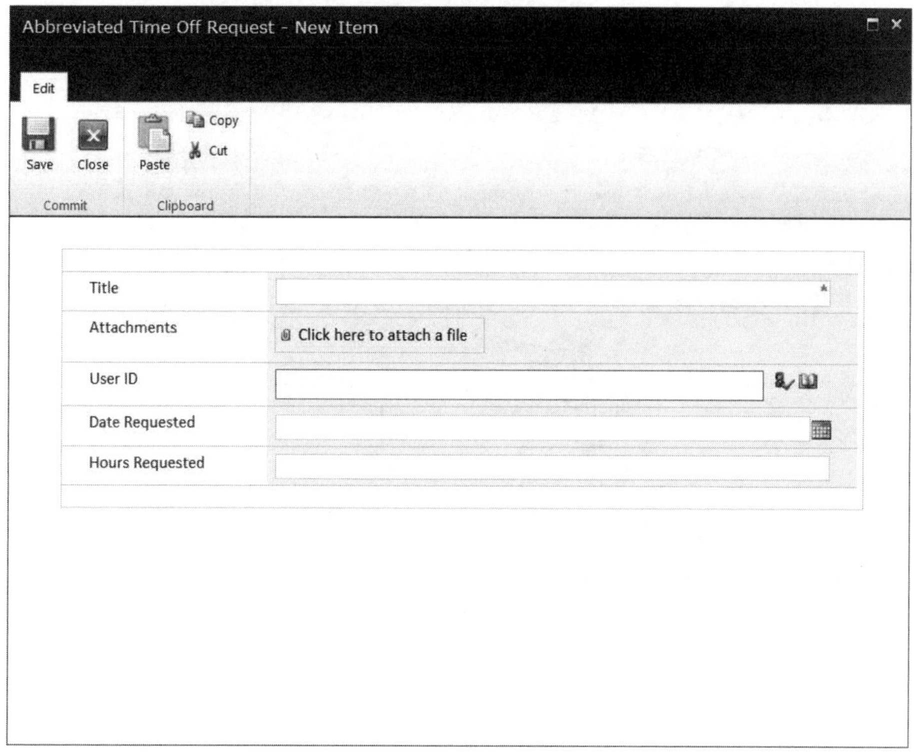

FIGURE 11-7

Repeat the edit/publish cycle a few times until you're familiar with the process. Consider performing the following steps:

1. Reduce the width of the form fields to more realistic sizes.
2. Right-justify the field labels, and append a colon.
3. Remove the Attachments column altogether. (Hint: Right-click and select Delete Row.)

Keep at it until you think you have the hang of it.

The data entry form is quite a bit different from SharePoint's default, even while it shares some commonality. It still has a Ribbon, but now it's showing Attachments as if it were a first class data entry field. This is par for the course and expected behavior.

Example: Add a Date Validation

In this walk-through, you add some validation to the form. This validation prevents the user from submitting the form if the request date isn't in the future. (You can't make a request in the past.)

Step 1: Create a Rule

You can create rules in InfoPath. These rules fire in response to the user's actions. Create a rule on the Date Requested Field.

Select the Date Requested field by clicking it. On the Ribbon, click Managed Rules. This is the top-right corner of the Ribbon. Use Figure 11-8 as a guide to create a new rule.

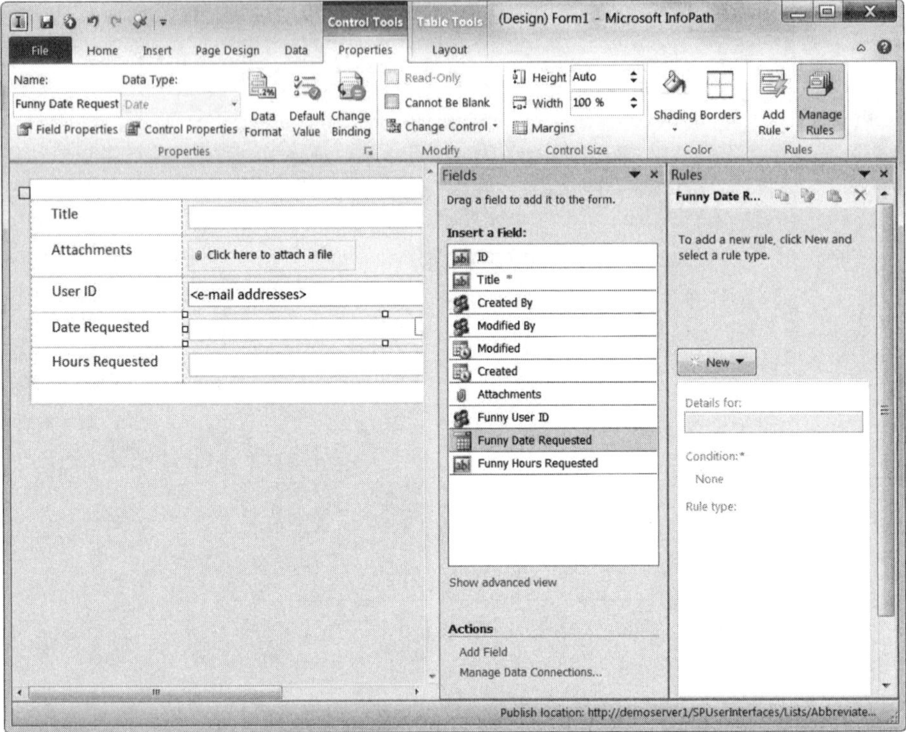

FIGURE 11-8

Click the New button in the rules tool pane, and select Validation from the drop-down list. Name the rule `Must Be Greater Than Today`, as shown in Figure 11-9.

Change the rule by clicking the hyperlink None under Condition. InfoPath responds with the rules maker dialog. Use that dialog to specify that the Funny Date Requested is greater than the current date. InfoPath, which is (sadly) a click-happy Office product, forces you through a couple of dialog boxes to get this done. First, look at Figure 11-10. This shows that you can pick Funny Date Requested. Even though you changed the label on the screen to simply Date Requested, InfoPath remembers the name of the actual field, so don't be confused. Next, select Is Greater Than and then Use a Formula to get to yet another dialog box.

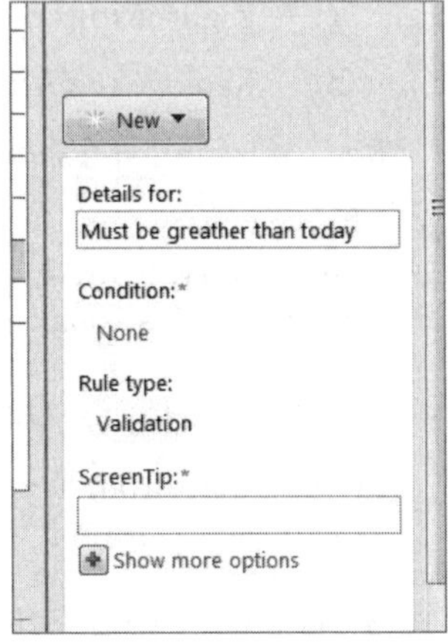

FIGURE 11-9

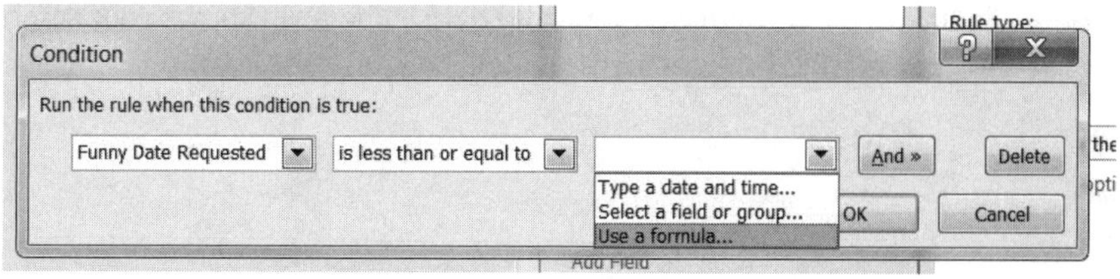

FIGURE 11-10

When you click Use a Formula, InfoPath responds with the Insert Formula dialog box. Click Insert Function. This enables you to pick the Today function from the Date category. Look at Figure 11-11 to see how this works.

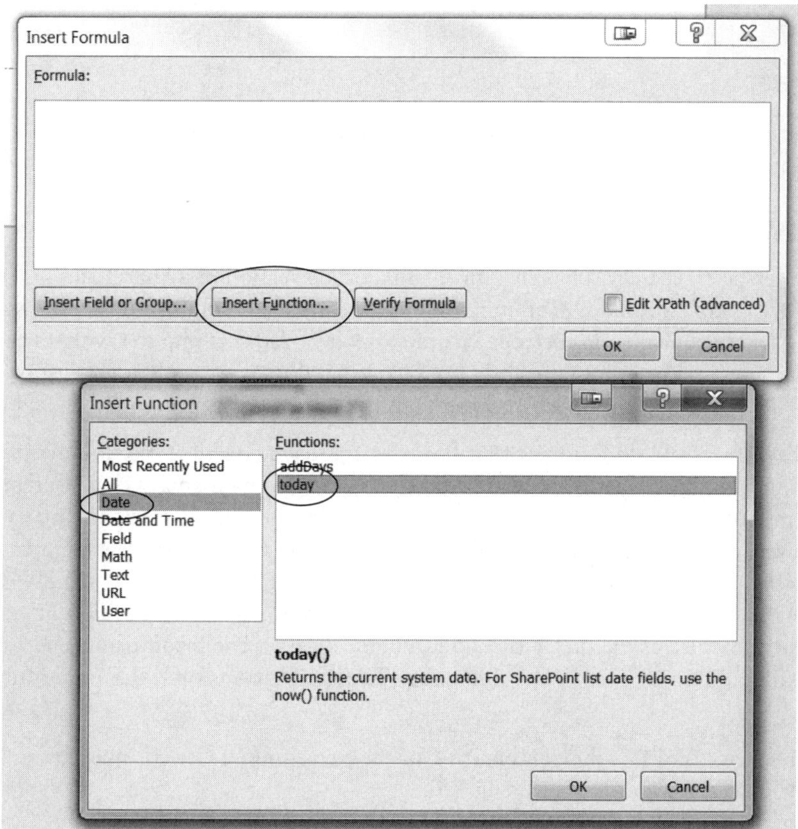

FIGURE 11-11

Click OK buttons until you return to your main screen.

In the screentip on the rule definition (refer to Figure 11-9), enter `Date Must Be in the Future`.

Publish the form the same way you did in the previous exercise.

Fill out the form and enter an invalid date. (Blank is an invalid date.) The form shows your screentip message as a tooltip. See Figure 11-12.

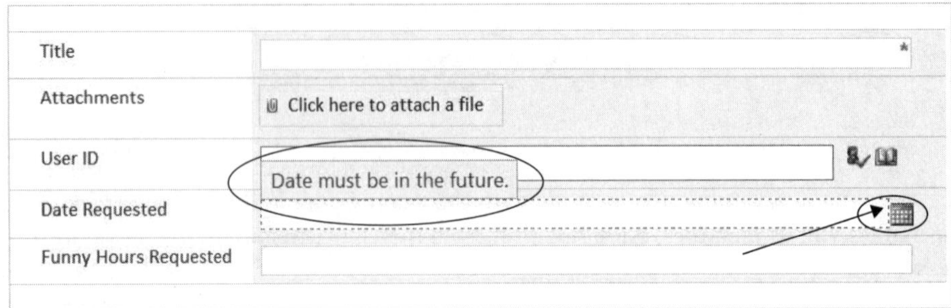

FIGURE 11-12

Data View Web Part

Second in the customization lineup, Data View Web Parts (DVWPs) can play greater in your dashboards than they do on data entry screens. Now see how.

What Is a Data View Web Part?

From an IT professional perspective, a DVWP is the "raw," unadorned version of a SharePoint list or document library in its "web part" form. So, in an important sense, any SharePoint list or library is a data view web part. This isn't technically 100 percent accurate, but it is also accurate to say that nearly all SharePoint lists and libraries can be represented as a DVWP. What does it mean that it's a list or library in a "raw" form? The explanation is fairly technical but not difficult to conceptually understand.

At its simplest, a SharePoint list (and don't forget that libraries are just a specific type of list) is a query plus a view. The query runs against content in a database, and a view displays that content. SharePoint provides abstractions for both the query and the view. SharePoint abstracts the query up several "layers." The lower layer (and one that SharePoint people rarely interact with) is a bunch of SQL calls. After all, SharePoint is backed by a Microsoft SQL database. The layer at which DVWP works with data is a CAML Query. CAML is pronounced "camel" and stands for Collaborative Application Markup Language. After the query runs, SharePoint displays the result using a mouthful of a process called Extensible Stylesheet Language Transformations or XSLT (and often shortened to just XSL).

For our purpose, a SharePoint DVWP is the combination of the preceding: a CAML query that returns and renders data onto the web browser using XSL.

It may sound technical, but it's actually easy to work with it, as you see next.

How Do You Use DVWPs?

DVWPs are easy to use. Follow two steps. First, add an existing list to a web part page. Second, edit that using SharePoint Designer.

It's as easy as that, and you see how when you go through the detailed walk-through.

DVWP, What's It Good For?

DVWP is an excellent choice for building informative list-based dashboards. DVWP enables you to do things such as the following:

- Highlight a row in a list view when a task has passed its due date
- Reformat a column
- Highlight an individual column in a view when it exceeds normal safe boundaries
- Replace a column with an icon, or possibly append an icon to a row, to build a traditional KPI view

These kinds of conditional formatting and display tweaks are simple and straightforward.

DVWP is actually a deep set of SharePoint functionality. You won't learn about it in this book, but a DVWP can use custom data sources and can even use more than one data source at the same time. For instance, you could define a data source that pulls weather data from a web service (for instance, at http://www.weather.gov/xml). You could then merge the content from that secondary data source with your primary data source to provide a dashboard that shows a list of company locations and current weather at the same time. This is powerful stuff.

These advanced scenarios are actually not hard to implement, but they are outside the scope of this book.

DVWP — When Not to Use It

DVWP has wide applicability, and it's hard to say when you shouldn't use it. At some point, DVWP dashboards can become unwieldy. This happens when you have overly complex formatting or too many secondary data sources. This can lead to nearly impossible-to-debug problems. At this point, it's best to use dedicated tools, such as SQL Server Reporting Services, PerformancePoint, or just plain custom coding.

Walk-Through: Color Code a List's Row

Now see the DVWP in action. In this detailed walk-through, you change a row's background color. The business driver for this walk-through is based on a time-sensitive task. The task has both a due date and a warning date. If the task has passed its warning date, you want to change the row's background to indicate that fact. This can prove to be a more effective dashboard element because the business process manager's eye will be drawn to these exceptional conditions.

In this walk-through, you'll learn the following:

- How to create a DVWP
- How to conditionally set the background color of an entire row

Step 1: Create a Custom List

Create a new list and add just two columns: Warning Date and Due Date. You create just these two columns so that you can focus on the mechanics of learning the DVWP. Use Figure 11-13 as a guide.

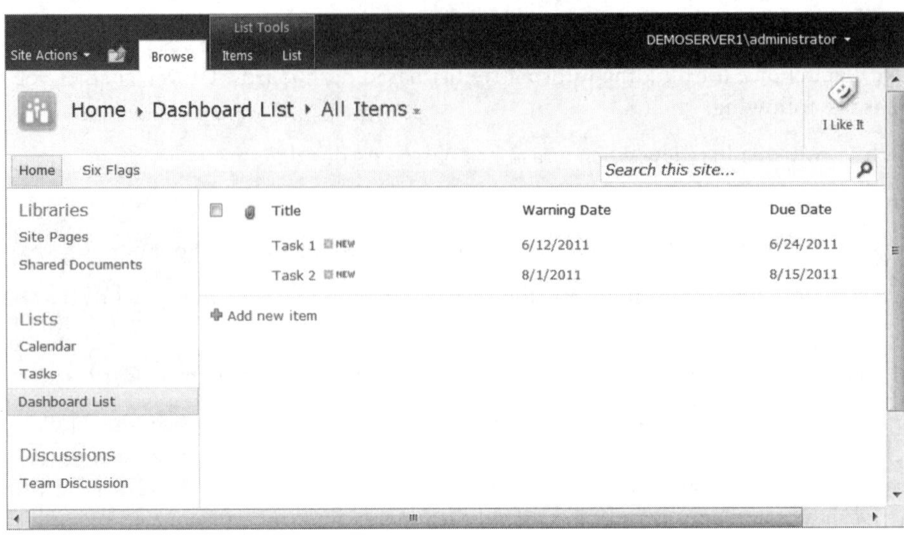

FIGURE 11-13

Be sure to add a couple of rows of data. For testing purposes, make sure you add a row whose warning date is earlier than today's date and a warning date that is not.

Step 2: Create a Dashboard Web Part Page

As you've done many times by now, create a web part page to serve as your dashboard. Add the Dashboard List to this web part page (see Figure 11-14). Your completed dashboard should look similar to Figure 11-15.

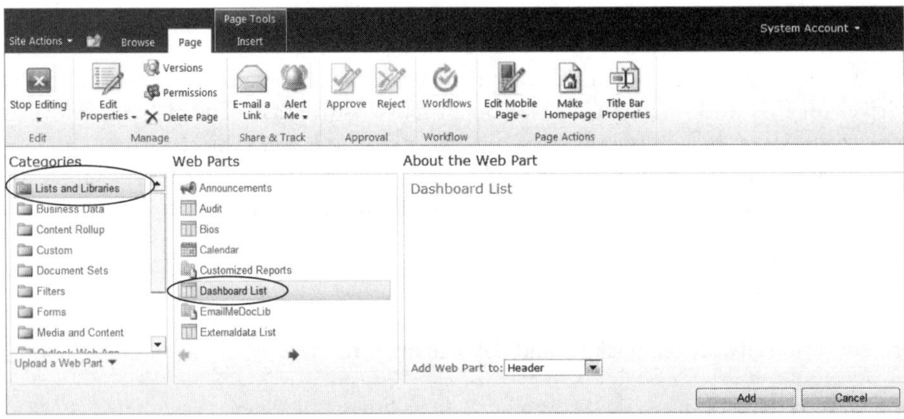

FIGURE 11-14

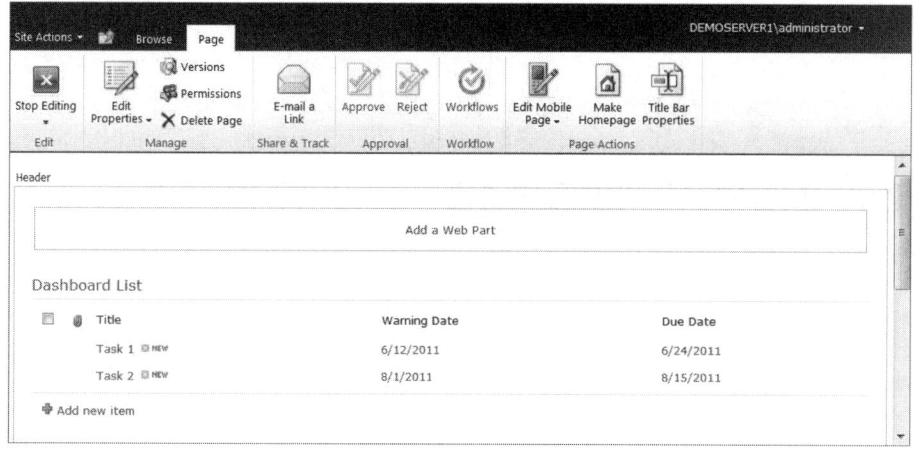

FIGURE 11-15

Step 3: Edit the Web Part Using SharePoint Designer

Use SharePoint Designer to edit the DVWP. Connect to your site, and navigate to the web part page that represents your dashboard. Use Figure 11-16 as a guide.

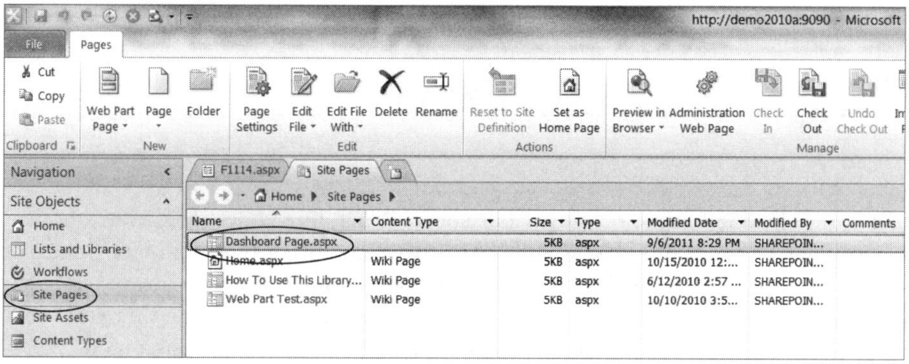

FIGURE 11-16

When you click the Dashboard Page.aspx link (Figure 11-16), SharePoint Designer pulls up your dashboard page's properties. Click Edit File. This link is located in the lower-left quadrant of the properties screen. SharePoint Designer then pulls up your dashboard page. It should roughly look like Figure 11-17. If it does not, make sure you're in Design mode. You can check by looking at the bottom of SharePoint Designer. The word Design should be highlighted, as shown in Figure 11-18. If you're not in design mode, click Design to bring you there.

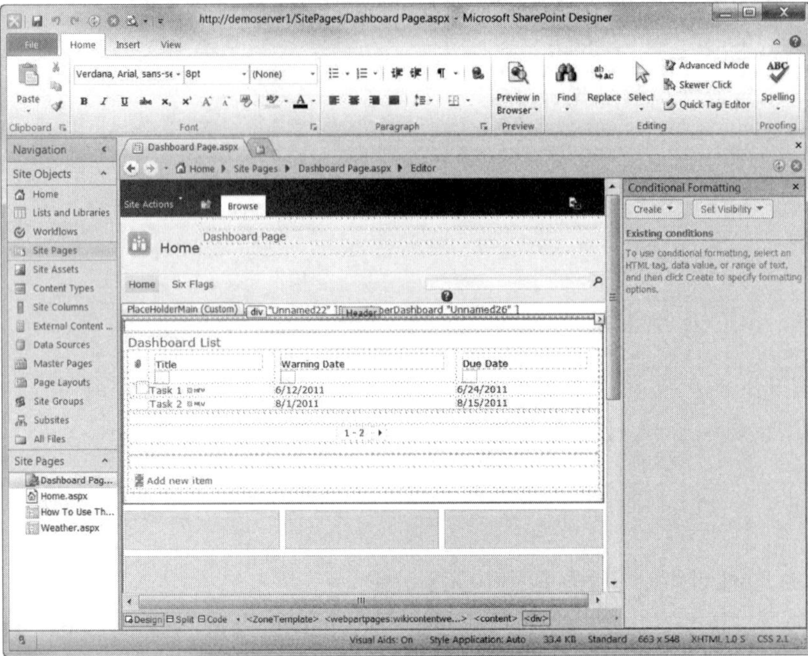

FIGURE 11-17

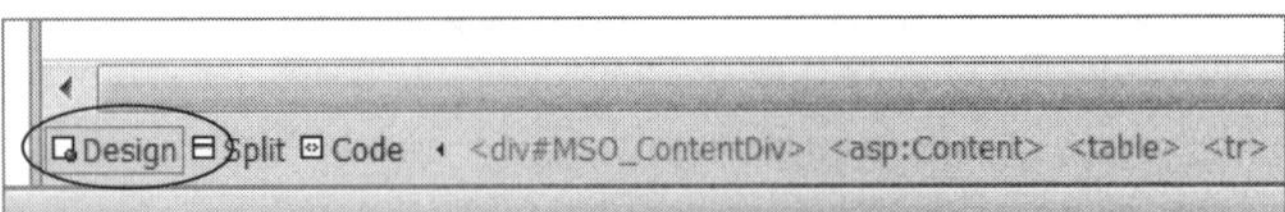

FIGURE 11-18

While you're there, try clicking Split and Code. Code shows you a pure code-based view of the web part page consisting of a mix of HTML, XSL, JavaScript, and other technical bits. Split mode shows both the design view and the code view with an adjustable slider. As you click in one area, the other area follows your typing. This can be useful to find a specific bit of code that you want to manipulate. After you finish exploring these modes, make sure you're back in design mode.

Unlike SharePoint Designer's workflow editor, SharePoint Designer is at times (most times, unfortunately), quite slow. After it "warms up" it gets reasonably performant, but be patient at the beginning. As bad as it may seem now, it was far, far worse in the 2007 world, so be thankful for that!

Recall that the DVWP is a SharePoint query and a lot of XSL to render results. The design mode in SharePoint Designer enables you to edit the presentation via menus and drop-downs without making any code changes. (You can also change the query and how it works without code, but that's an advanced topic and not covered in this book.) The objective of this walk-through is to color code an entire row. To do so, click your mouse on one of the rows of data, as shown in Figure 11-19.

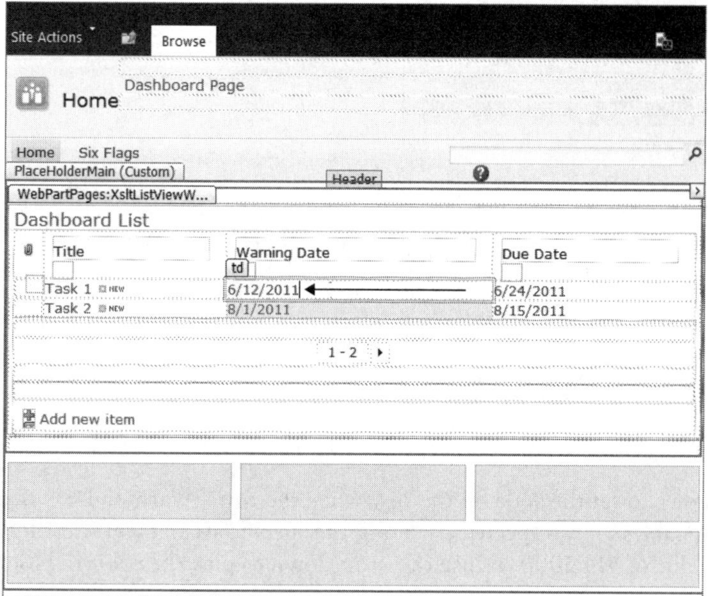

FIGURE 11-19

It's better to click a row with data rather than a column label; although both work. If you click on a data row, instead of a column header, SharePoint Designer makes things a little harder on you. This walk-through assumes that you click a data row.

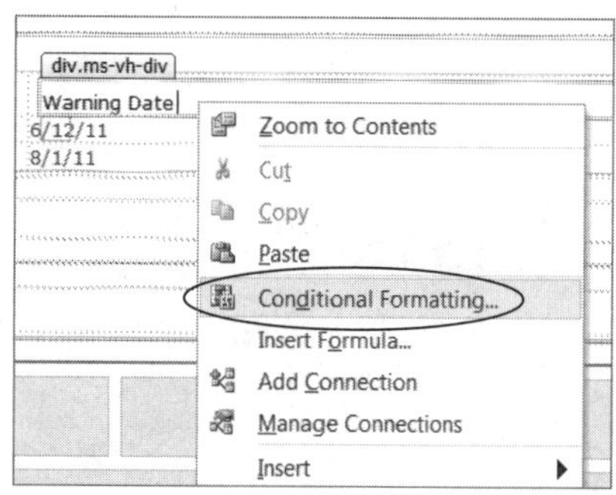

FIGURE 11-20

Right-click and select Conditional formatting from the drop-down menu. You can also select Conditional formatting from the Ribbon. See Figure 11-20 for a guide.

When you do this, SharePoint Designer opens up a new pane on the right side of the screen labeled Conditional Formatting. Click the Create button and select Apply Formatting, as shown in Figure 11-21.

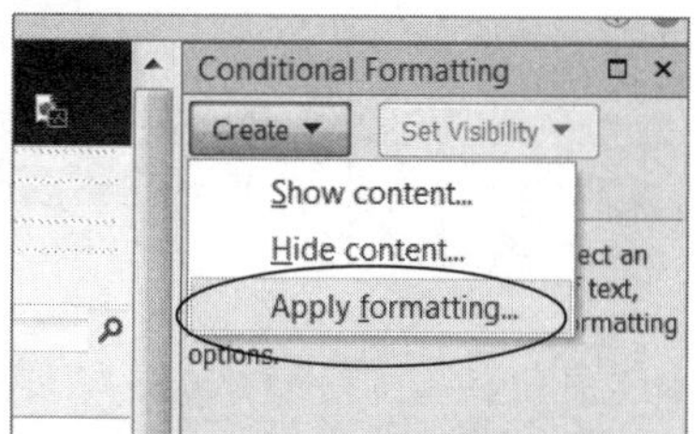

FIGURE 11-21

SharePoint Designer responds with a rules maker dialog. Use this dialog to specify what must be true to apply a specific format to the row. In this case, you want the formatting rule to execute when the warning date is less than or equal to today's date. (That is, it happened in the past.) SharePoint Designer's rule maker dialog enables you to specify "today" by putting in the [Current Date]. Try it out, using Figure 11-22 as a guide. When you have the rule just right, click Set Style.

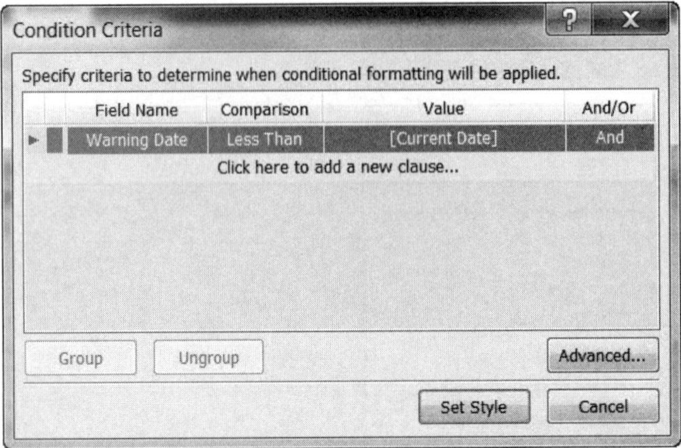

FIGURE 11-22

You've just told SharePoint Designer to set the style on the row when the row's Warning Date occurs in the past. The Set Style dialog enables you to specify, in detail, the specific styling you want for the row. Enter a background color value of #FF0000, or use the drop-down to pick the color red (or any color you want) (see Figure 11-23).

Click the Save button and then return to the web browser. Pull up you dashboard page. If you've done everything correctly, you see a result similar to Figure 11-24.

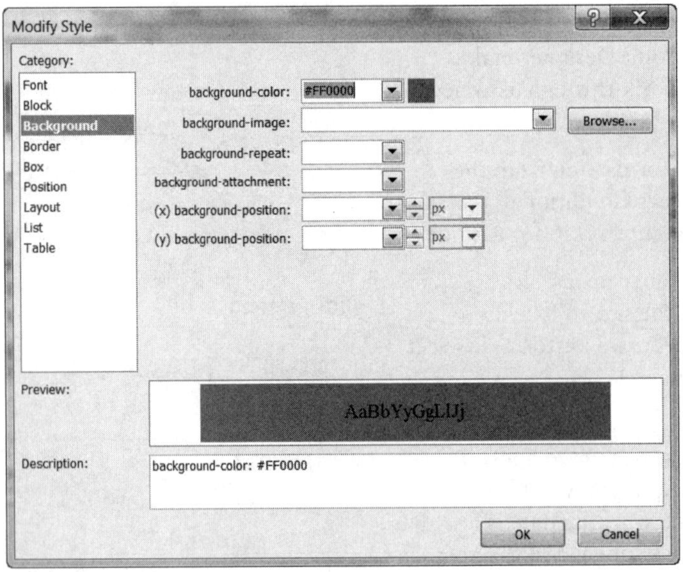

FIGURE 11-23

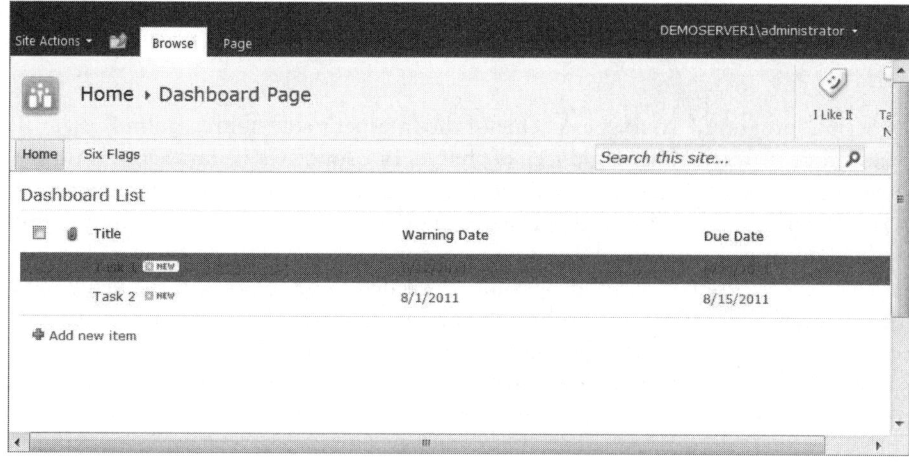

FIGURE 11-24

In the real world, you'd find the row-coloring rule too simplistic. You want to highlight this row only if the task is past its due date *and* it's not finished. Refer to Figure 11-22. You can see that SharePoint Designer enables you to add multiple conditions (where clauses). This is how you can craft a rule that meets your needs. Go ahead and try it out before leaving this section.

Walk-Through: Summary

You've just walked through the process to enhance a dashboard to highlight potential problem areas that could and hopefully will facilitate timely intervention on tasks in the "danger zone." It's a fairly straightforward process:

1. Create a dashboard page (a web part page).
2. Add your list (or lists) to the page.
3. Use SharePoint Designer to modify the underlying DVWP using SharePoint Designer's design mode capabilities.

This no-code approach is quick and easy when you get the hang of it.

jQuery

The third and final option is relatively new to SharePoint: jQuery. This section introduces you to jQuery (and its parent, JavaScript). Like the other chapters, it explains when you should and shouldn't use it. It then ends with a couple of walk-throughs designed to help you learn this interesting and useful technique.

What Is jQuery?

To understand jQuery you need to begin with JavaScript, which is a programming language that all modern browsers (including all the browsers supported by SharePoint) understand. JavaScript programs are run by the browser. They don't run on the server, in the cloud, or anywhere else. For this reason, JavaScript is often called client-side script. The code runs on or in the client, which is the web browser.

JQuery is a JavaScript "program," so to speak. One of the Internet's star figures, John Resig, created jQuery and gave it away to the world free of charge. In a lot of ways, JavaScript is "just" JavaScript. However, Microsoft, Apple, Mozilla foundation, and many others released web browsers with JavaScript "engines" that varied from each other. As a result, a JavaScript program developed and tested on Apple's Safari web browser wouldn't work perfectly on Internet Explorer. Until jQuery came on the scene, JavaScript programmers needed to be aware of these many minor (and major) differences. jQuery solves this problem by providing a portable set of functions that enable you to create a single set of JavaScript code that you can confidently share with the rest of the world and know it works regardless of their web browser. (This is a bit of an oversimplification because if there's one rule in computer programming it is that things are never as simple as they seem.)

One of the most important take-aways from this discussion is that jQuery *is* JavaScript. Going forward, the chapter uses jQuery interchangeably with JavaScript to cut down on clutter.

How Does jQuery Work?

Because jQuery is a JavaScript library, using it is natural (provided you know JavaScript in the first place). JQuery works by providing a set of functions that enable you to do things like the following:

- Find field elements on a page by their name, style, or location on the page
- Change field element attributes; for instance, disable a text field
- Add events and execute JavaScript code; for instance, add an event when the user's mouse moves over a tab to color its background color and give the tab appearance on a web page
- Invoke a web service, passing parameters and consuming the result

It does all of this in the page, typically after the page finishes loading (more on this later).

Why Use jQuery?

You may be asking yourself, "Why is the book talking about jQuery at this point? It sounds complicated and a lot like coding." You're right, it is complicated and does involve coding. However, it's extremely powerful and as hundreds of blogs and online articles on the subject attest, IT professionals and activist users have embraced this technology.

They've embraced jQuery because it enables SharePoint shops to affect SharePoint's behavior in ways that SharePoint itself just doesn't allow. You normally code jQuery programs to kick in after SharePoint has fully rendered a page. This means that if you don't like SharePoint's default label, you can change it with jQuery. If you want to enable or disable fields on a SharePoint custom list's CRUD form, you can do that with jQuery. If you want to implement a cascading drop-down list, you can do that with jQuery. In a certain sense, it's a bit of sneaky "rewrite."

SharePoint has already served up its page, and then you take over and do whatever you want with it. As you will see in the second walk-through, it can be both powerful and quite simple (as far as coding solutions are concerned).

How Do You Use jQuery in SharePoint?

To use jQuery, you need just two components: A reference to the jQuery library and some jQuery on a SharePoint page.

You can get to the jQuery library in several ways. The easiest way is to use a Content Delivery Network (CDN). Microsoft, Google, and some other major players provide publicly accessible CDNs. They provide a single-known location for jQuery and a number of other public tools. For example, Google's jQuery CDN is located here at `http://ajax.googleapis.com/ajax/libs/jquery/1.6.1/jquery.min.js`.

You can also download jQuery directly from `www.jquery.com`. If you go this route, you would then add the jQuery to a document library or somewhere else in your SharePoint environment. There are good reasons to avoid CDNs, but they are unusual and won't be covered by this chapter. This chapter makes use of Google's CDN to emphasize jQuery's independence from Microsoft.

After you figure out how to get the jQuery library in your SharePoint site, you need to figure out how and where to reference it. A "reference" in JavaScript terms looks like this:

```
<script
  src="http://ajax.googleapis.com/ajax/libs/jquery/1.6.1/jquery.min.js"
  type="text/javascript">
</script>
```

The preceding code snippet makes the jQuery library available to JavaScript running anywhere in its scope. Scope basically means that as long as your custom JavaScript runs near the jQuery reference, you can use jQuery in your JavaScript. You have three options for referencing the jQuery code:

1. Master page
2. Page layout
3. Individual SharePoint page

Because end users and IT pros don't normally have the ability to edit the master page or page layout, the default choice is normally option #3, an individual SharePoint page. Use the master page to make jQuery available to every page in SharePoint. Use the page layout to make jQuery available to a class of pages in SharePoint. Use individual SharePoint pages when you can't edit the master page or page layout.

Finally, with the jQuery reference worked out, you write JavaScript code that leverages the library. You soon see how this works in the walk-through.

JQuery Library Extensions

Just as jQuery is one big giant extension of sorts to the JavaScript programming language, jQuery can be extended. Programmers can created a plug-in. Plug-ins are JavaScript and jQuery code that follows certain conventions. People write jQuery plug-ins for a variety of reasons and topics. Learn more about general-purpose plug-ins via a bing search or at `www.jquery.com`. Of course, this book is about SharePoint, and it's time to call attention to a free jQuery plug-in for SharePoint.

SPServices, located at `http://spservices.codeplex.com`, extends jQuery's already rich set of functionality by providing simple jQuery statements that "know" about SharePoint. SPServices was created by Microsoft SharePoint MVP Marc Ambinder who (at least at the time of writing this chapter), actively maintains and extends this free plug-in. You see this library in action in the walk-through.

JQuery — When Not to Use It

When you fully embrace jQuery, you may find yourself falling into the old "When you use a hammer all day long, everything starts to look like a nail." Remember that you have a number of other tools at your disposal and use them when appropriate.

Of course, many talented IT pros and activist users simply don't have the background or interest in learning how to create coding of any kind. If you're one of those people, shrug it off and use the other good tools available to you. When a client coded solution is needed, work with your colleagues to create it (possibly by gifting them a copy of this book!).

jQuery Walk-Throughs

With the background and theory out of the way, it's time to get your hands dirty. You create two jQuery programs. First, you create one that simply displays an alert on the screen. This simplistic program doesn't achieve much but serves to teach you how to pull all the various pieces together so that you can do the second example, rearranging radio sets horizontally rather than vertically (SharePoint's inconvenient default).

Walk-Through: Introductory jQuery Program

Step 1: Create a Custom List

First, create a new custom list with the following columns:

- Book Name Sounds Like (text)
- Book Type: Radio set with values: Sci-fi, Fantasy, Historical, Politics, and Other
- Other Description (text)

When finished, it should look like Figure 11-25.

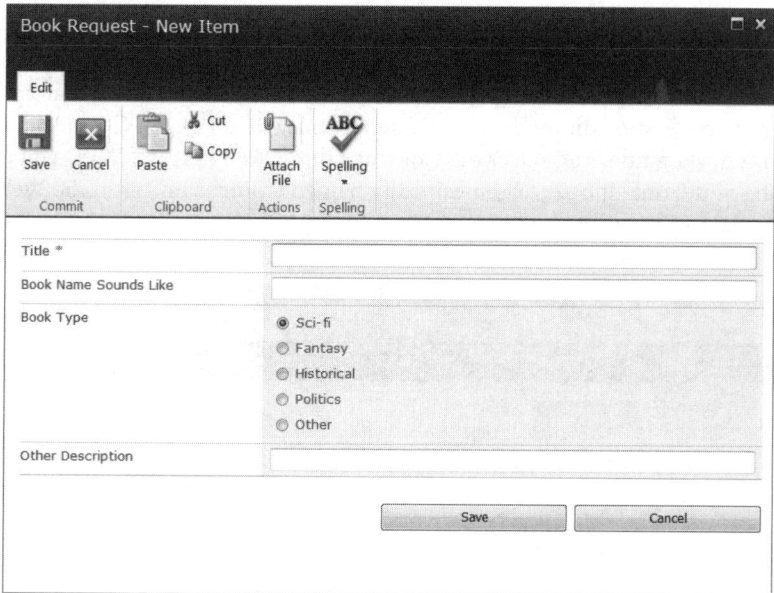

FIGURE 11-25

Step 2: Create the jQuery Code:

To create the code, open up your favorite text editor, such as notepad. Enter the code as shown in Figure 11-26. This code does two things. First, it makes the jQuery library available via the reference to Google's CDN. Second, it displays an alert (Ping!) after the page finishes loading.

"After the page finishes loading" is important. This bit of code is responsible for ensuring that happens:

```
$(document).ready(function() { … });
```

That's your first bit of jQuery and it says in English, "Once the document (the page) is ready (finished loading), execute the code inside the function." You almost always want your code to wait for the page to finish loading. Why? Because JavaScript begins to execute as soon as the browser finds it. If your browser starts to execute code before the entire page is downloaded, strange things can and will happen.

jQuery1.txt - Notepad

File Edit Format View Help

```
<!-- Obtain jQuery from Google's content delivery network (CDN) -->
<script
  src="http://ajax.googleapis.com/ajax/libs/jquery/1.6.1/jquery.min.js"
  type="text/javascript">
</script>

<!-- When the page finishes loading, ping the user. -->
<script type="text/javascript">
  $(document).ready(function() { alert("Ping!"); });
</script>
```

FIGURE 11-26

Step 3: Add the jQuery to the Page

Now it's time to get the code out of notepad, where it's not doing anyone much good, and get it into SharePoint. You can do this via a content editor web part. Navigate to the Book Request custom list you just created, and bring the page into edit mode. (Click Site Actions ➪ Edit Page). Click Add a Web a Part using Figure 11-27 as a guide, and select the Content Editor Web Part (CEWP). You can find the CEWP in the Media and Content category, specifically named Content Editor in the Web Parts pane in the web part selector dialog.

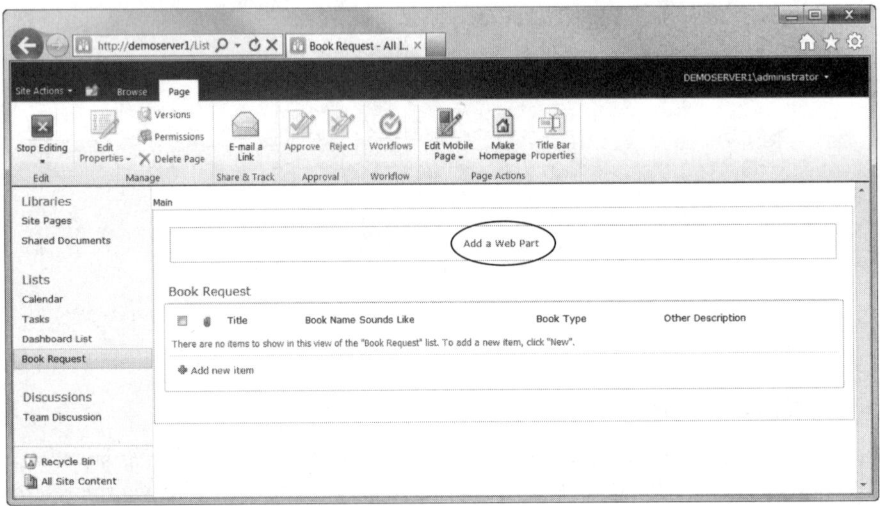

FIGURE 11-27

After adding the CEWP, follow it's helpful advice and Click Here to Add New Content. Normally, you use the CEWP to add richly formatted text to the page. In this case, you use it to add JavaScript to your page. To do that, you need to work with the CEWP in HTML mode. Get into this mode by clicking the HTML button on the Ribbon, using Figure 11-28 as a guide.

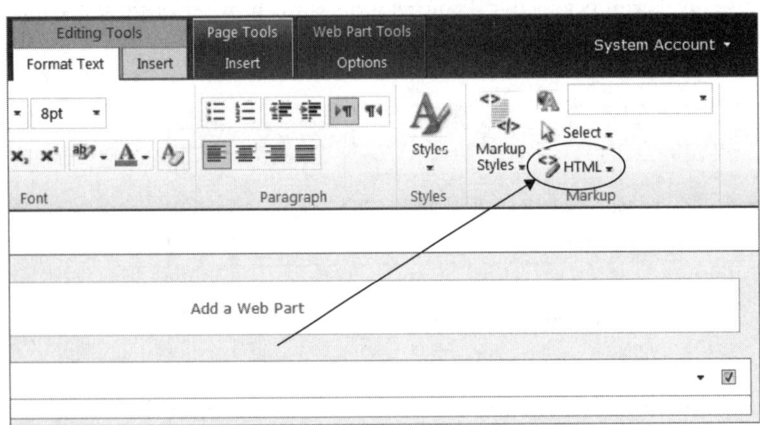

FIGURE 11-28

Copy the code from notepad into this resulting SharePoint dialog box. Click Save to save that change to the CEWP.

Finally, click Stop Editing on the Ribbon to finish this change to the page. If you did it all correctly, you get the Ping! alert box, as shown in Figure 11-29.

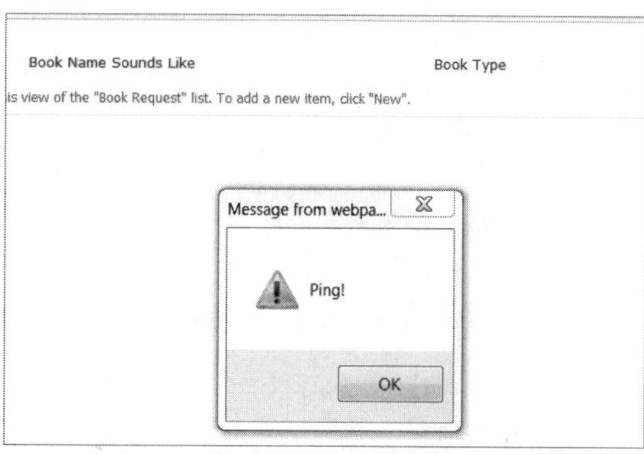

FIGURE 11-29

Before wrapping this chapter up, consider why you use notepad. In practice, you won't actually use notepad, but you will use some editor other than the CEWP. This is because SharePoint's CEWP mangles JavaScript code. It's not clear why, but it's a fact and we all have to live with it.

Congratulations! You just created your first jQuery program.

Walk-Through: Use SPServices to Change Radio Set Layouts

In this walk-through, you download and install SPServices. You use SPServices to change SharePoint's default layout of a radio set on a CRUD screen.

Step 1: Make SPServices Available in Your Environment

Unlike jQuery, SPServices doesn't benefit from a big name player such as Google or Microsoft hosting it on a CDN. Therefore, you need to download and install it into your SharePoint environment.

Start by creating a vanilla document library named, easily enough, jQuery.

Next, access the jQuery library from codeplex. Open up your web browser and go to `http://spservices.codeplex.com`. Click the big Download button and save the resulting .zip file to your favorite download location. Unzip the file.

SPServices, like most plug-ins, comes in two flavors. There is a simple .js file, and a minified version of the same. The minified version has been processed to remove all unnecessary white space and to compact it as small as possible to reduce page load times. You can use either. The walk-through uses the expanded version. For production solutions, you would normally want to use the minified version, if it's available. As a follow-up to this walk-through, swap it out for learning purposes.

After unzipping the file, upload the .js file to your jQuery library. At the time of this writing, it was named jquery.SPServices-0.6.1.js.

Step 2: Write the jQuery Code

Using notepad again, write the following jQuery code:

```
<!-- Obtain jQuery from Google's content delivery network (CDN) -->
<script
  src="http://ajax.googleapis.com/ajax/libs/jquery/1.4.2/jquery.min.js"
```

```
    type="text/javascript">
  </script>

  <!-- Obtain the SPServices Plug-in -->
  <script
    language="javascript"
    type="text/javascript"
    src="/jQuery/jquery.SPServices-0.6.1.js"></script>

  <script type="text/javascript">

  $(document).ready(function() {

    $().SPServices.SPArrangeChoices({
      columnName: "Book Type",
      perRow: 9
    });

  });

  </script>
```

This code does several things. First, it references a minified version of jQuery from Google's CDN. It references jQuery version 1.4.2, which differs from the previous walk-through. Keep this in mind as there can be breaking differences between jQuery libraries. The next things the code does is reference the SPServices jQuery plug-in. As you can see, it's pulling it directly from /jQuery. If your jquery document library is located somewhere else, be sure to correctly reference it. Finally, it uses the SPServices `SPArrangeChoices` plug-in command to rearrange Book Type to show nine choices per row instead of SharePoint's default of one per row.

After you've tested this solution in step 3 (coming up next), play around with the "perRow" parameter. Change it to values from 1 to 3 to see how the plug-in handles it all.

Step 3: Add the Code to the Page

Next, it's time to add the code to the page. Use a CEWP this time, just like you did in the previous walk-through. However, which page? It's actually not as obvious as it seems. Unlike the last walk-through, you need to add the code to a different page than what SharePoint shows you by default. You can get to this page in several ways. Follow these short steps to do this the easiest way.

First, go to the list's settings, and click Advanced. Scroll to the bottom of the page and answer No to the question, Launch Forms in a Dialog? (as shown in Figure 11-30).

Next, navigate back to the list, and add a new item. You'll see that SharePoint shows the old style MOSS/WSS data entry screen instead of the new pop and sizzle shadowed dialog box that

SharePoint 2010 gives you. From here, edit the page, add the CEWP, and do the copy/paste trick to get the code from notepad onto the page.

If you add an item now, you can see that the radio buttons have rearranged themselves. Because the dialog box is nicer, go back to the list's advanced settings, and answer Yes to the Launch Forms in a Dialog? question.

If all is well, your final result should look similar to Figure 11-31.

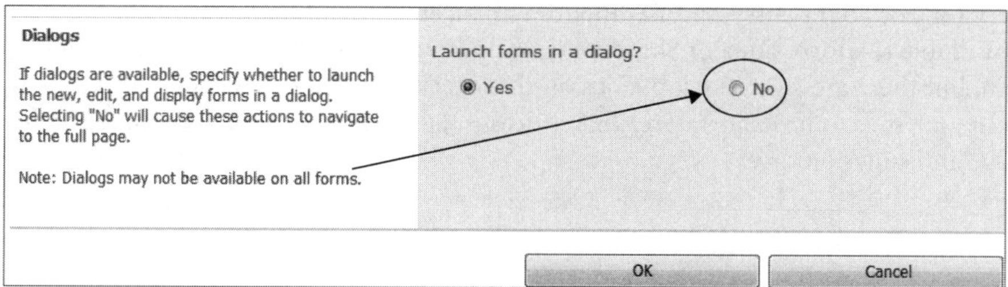

FIGURE 11-30

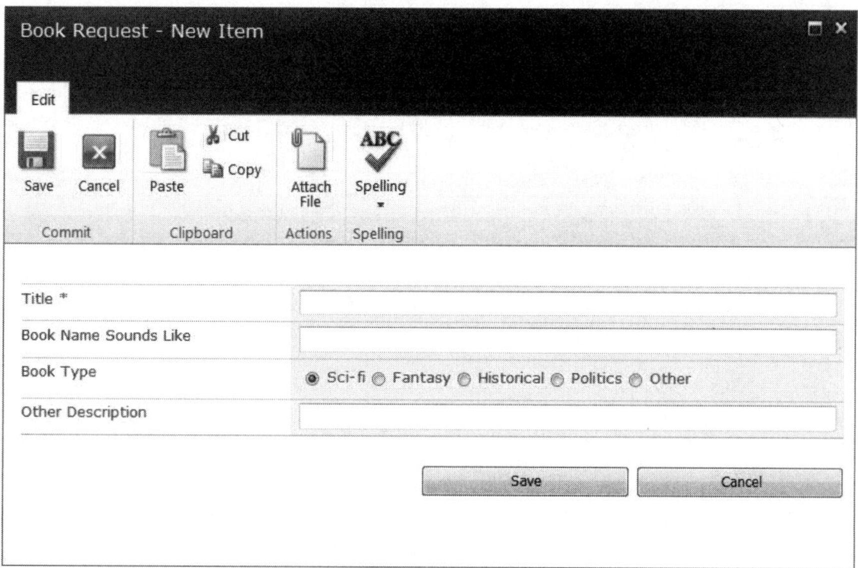

FIGURE 11-31

SUMMARY

As stated in the introduction to this chapter and referenced in many places throughout the book, you can create minimal but effective dashboards using SharePoint's default look and feel. However, you can create even more effective dashboards and data entry screens using advanced techniques.

Use InfoPath to create extensive and complex data entry forms. InfoPath enables you to validate individual fields, change the look and field via its drag-and-drop interface, create repeating sections, and do many other useful things. InfoPath is only available in SharePoint enterprise.

The Data View Web Part should be your first choice for interactive, colorful dashboards. Use SharePoint Designer to edit DVWPs to create snappy dashboards that call the dashboard manager's attention to extraordinary conditions that require human intervention. Use DVWP in advanced scenarios to pull data from more than one SharePoint list at the same time or even from data sources outside of SharePoint.

Lastly, use jQuery for both data entry and dashboard enhancements. JQuery runs in the web browser and is available to all versions of SharePoint, including hosted SharePoint. It is a code intensive solution, but there are so many job aides on the Internet, it's not as difficult as it may seem. If you go that route, be sure to look at the free SPServices jQuery plug-in for SharePoint-specific jQuery knowledge and functionality.

12 Custom Activities

WHAT'S IN THIS CHAPTER?

- Creating custom activities
- Deploying custom activities
- Making custom activities available in SharePoint Designer
- Troubleshooting custom activities

By now, you've learned you can go quite far in building out a full and complete business solution with SharePoint Designer when you're confronted by a wide array of business problems. You've also learned that SharePoint Designer falls short, infuriatingly short, at times. This chapter explains how you can close the gaps.

Be warned: This is an advanced chapter, and the material it covers is far beyond the skills of your typical activist user. This chapter is the most technically deep in the book. Why break the pattern of the other chapters in the book and cover this? The rationale behind this chapter is that if you're not a coder, you know some coders in your organization. Describe the gaps you need to close and ask them to read this chapter. Soon enough, you'll have with the technical solution you need to close some of these frustrating gaps.

As with every chapter in this book, you learn about custom activities in the context of a business problem. Specifically, how to calculate weekend and holiday-aware due dates that take place [x] business days in advance. This chapter keeps the business aspect deliberately simple and narrow so that you can focus on technical challenges and not get bogged down in the business details. Don't worry, however; the chapter relates this deep technical discussion to a wide array of business problems so that you'll have a good idea when it makes sense to invest the time and effort to create a custom activity.

THE WHAT, WHY, AND HOW OF CUSTOM ACTIVITIES

Custom activities are an advanced topic and nontrivial to implement and deploy. There are compelling reasons to do so, however, as you learn in this chapter (and likely realized in earlier chapters). Before diving deeply into the "how," examine what custom activities are, why you create them, and how you can start creating one.

What Is a Custom Activity?

At a high level, custom activities are simply new activities (and conditions) that you can use to create SharePoint Designer workflow solutions. You've been using activities throughout this book. SharePoint Designer provides more than 40 actions and about eight conditions out-of-the-box. (See Figure 12-1 for a quick reminder.)

Microsoft provides a useful number of activities with the product when it ships, but as you've seen in this book, even more are needed. Fortunately, Microsoft provides an open framework upon which you can create entirely new custom activities and conditions. The framework defines a process. When you correctly follow the process, you can install your custom activity into the SharePoint environment, and it looks, feels, and operates just like any of the out-of-the-box activities that Figure 12-1 depicts. Figure 12-2 shows an example of this. This capability, although on the hard side to implement, is powerful stuff.

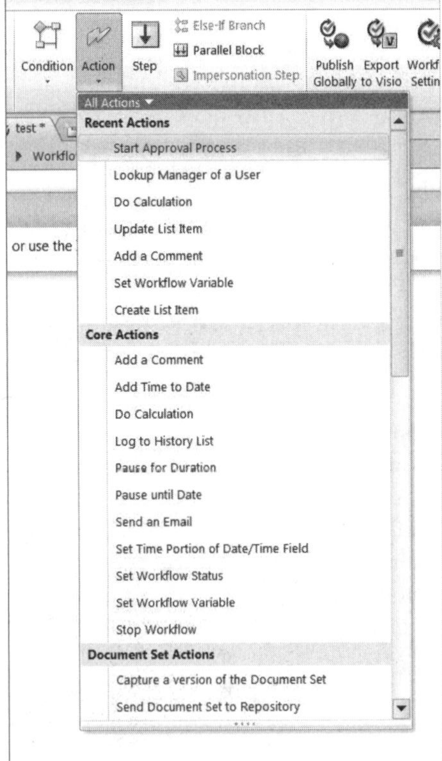

FIGURE 12-1

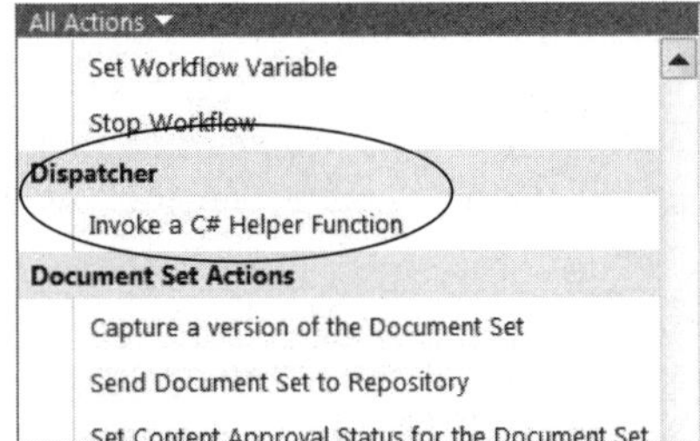

FIGURE 12-2

You can create a new custom activity, and SharePoint Designer shows it in its own group (Dispatcher) with its own label (Invoke a C# Helper Function).

Why Create a Custom Activity?

The short answer to that question is that you create custom activities when you need to do something that you can't do using an out-of-the-box activity. Consider one of the early business problems first raised in Chapter 3, "HR On-Boarding." Recall that your on-boarding workflow assigns tasks to a number of different business units (IT, AP, and Security). These tasks have a due date. Your workflow assigned that task to be completed three days before the new hire showed up for work the first time.

The problem is easy to spot: If the new hire is due to start on Monday, the due date for all those tasks will be Friday (three days before Monday). If something goes wrong and the task isn't completed on time for some reason, it's too late to do anything about it.

It would be better to assign a due date that is three *business* days prior, not three calendar days. That way, the HR management team has some time to react to slow departmental responses. You may be thinking that's relatively easy — just figure out the weekend days and then use that fact to calculate week days and translate that to business days. It's actually a little more complicated than that; you also want to account for company holidays.

It just isn't possible to meet this business requirement using SharePoint Designer out-of-the-box. To meet it, you need to use a custom activity.

There's another strong answer to this question, too — although an answer only a developer would love. Developers want to create custom actions so that they can *get end users off their backs*. Of course, no good developer actually views end users as burdens, but you get the idea. Custom activities empower end users. Empowered end users can take on development tasks and projects that are, frankly, too simple for developers to actually care about. When end users can take over some of these relatively simple (albeit extremely valuable!) projects, developers are freed up to do far more complicated and heavy-duty work. Developers should view this as a wonderful opportunity to clear their plate of mundane work so that they have more time for the really hard and interesting work.

What Tools Do You Need to Create a Custom Activity?

Custom activities fall firmly within the realm of developers, and developers use Microsoft Visual Studio to create them.

Visual Studio is Microsoft's development tool and is the starting point for all custom SharePoint development. You can download an evaluation license from Microsoft's development network (MSDN) site at `http://msdn.microsoft.com` (see Figure 12-3). Figure 12-3 shows Visual Studio 2010 Premium edition, but you can use Visual Studio 2010 Professional.

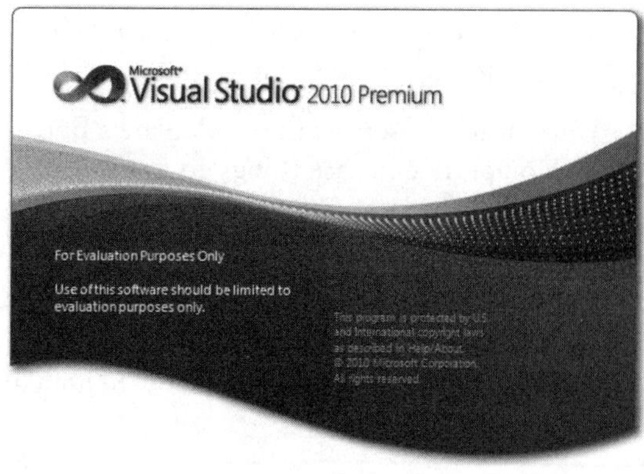

FIGURE 12-3

Visual Studio is a complex product and far beyond the scope of this book to cover in any great level of detail. Therefore, to create a custom activity, you must either be a developer, or you must have a developer friend, colleague, or contractor available to do the work for you. Fortunately, SharePoint is a wildly popular platform, so if you don't have anyone at arm's length today, you can easily find a good contractor on the open market.

Of course, you can't hand this kind of work to any old developer. This is, after all, SharePoint. Although SharePoint is a platform in and of itself, it's also built on top of a number of other platforms, starting with a Windows server and on through to ASP.NET. Your developers don't need to be experts in all the layers between the hardware and SharePoint, but it helps to be familiar with ASP.NET. Furthermore, this chapter's walk-through shows how to create a custom activity by way of the C# programming language. Although VB.NET is mostly interchangeable with C#, this chapter does not provide an equivalent example in VB.NET.

Lastly, custom SharePoint development like this must take place on a server. As you've executed the walk-through's in the book, you may have been doing the work directly on a server, but SharePoint Designer enables you to connect to a server remotely. You have no such luck with Visual Studio and SharePoint. (See the note for more on this.)

SHAREPOINT DEVELOPMENT AND SERVERS

Back in the early days of MOSS development, if you listened carefully from your backyard patio, you could hear the frustrated cries of ASP and ASP.NET developers across the world as they came to realize that they couldn't follow their old and familiar development practices because SharePoint development required a server. Microsoft ameliorated this requirement with SharePoint 2010, and you can now do some limited development directly on a Windows 7 desktop/laptop.

THE BUSINESS SCENARIO

Before hitting the walk-through, here's a business scenario to give some context. As previously mentioned, Chapter 3 introduced the HR On-boarding business process, and you know there is a serious flaw/weakness in the solution as provided. Namely, it's not weekend or holiday-aware. As a result, due dates can and often are set dangerously close to "zero hour," leaving little or no time to account for mistakes and missed dates.

Your business users want to calculate a due date for on-boarding tasks that provide a nice cushion of time in case things go awry. Security people might be on vacation, vendors deliver laptops a little late, and so on. You work with your end users and decide that 3 business days is enough notice.

But, wait! It's even a little more complicated. You're in a multinational company. (And these days, even small companies may be multinational.) You want the flexibility to use a different set of country-specific holidays, not just U.S. holidays.

All this leads to a simple set of requirements that underlie the business scenario and dictate what the technical solution must accomplish:

- Weekends are universal. Regardless of the country, never count Saturday or Sunday as a business day.
- Use an out-of-the-box SharePoint calendar to specify company holidays. This enables the company to update the company calendar independently of the workflow solution. This kind of decoupling is always a good thing.
- Create a separate calendar for each country. End users can go to the United States calendar to specify U.S. holidays. End users can go the Spain calendar to specify Spanish holidays.

The technical walk-through can help you create a SharePoint solution that meets these requirements.

TECHNICAL OVERVIEW

SharePoint Designer custom workflow activities have a number of specific components:

- Visual Studio solution
- Visual Studio project that defines the business logic
- Visual Studio project that you use to install and deploy the activity to the SharePoint farm
- Actions file — an XML file that contains declarative information about the custom activity
- One or more source files that contain the actual logic

Figure 12-4 shows a straightforward example of what this looks like in the Visual Studio Solution Explorer.

Many of these components depend upon each other, including an almost bewildering number of dependencies that do so in obvious and not-so-obvious ways. These dependencies are the worst kind possible — you find out if you made a mistake only at run-time. It's even worse because runtime failures are frustratingly vague with things partly working or partly failing in breathtaking variety. Later in the chapter, you'll see some common errors and how to fix them. Before that, consider each of these components and how they interplay.

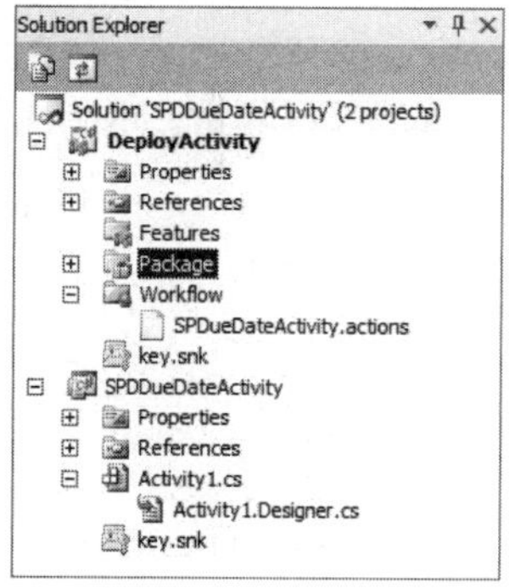

FIGURE 12-4

SharePoint Designer

SharePoint Designer is an end-user tool that organizes actions and conditions into a workflow process. When you connect to a SharePoint site and create a workflow solution, SharePoint Designer actually communicates with the SharePoint environment to find out all the available actions. SharePoint Designer does this only when you first click a button to create or edit an existing workflow in any given session. A *session* means that you opened SharePoint Designer and did any work. A session ends when you close SharePoint Designer. The key takeaway here is that when you develop and debug a SharePoint Designer workflow using your custom activity, you need to close and reopen SharePoint Designer when you make changes on the server. (Detailed-oriented and picky readers: See the note on opening/closing SharePoint Designer.)

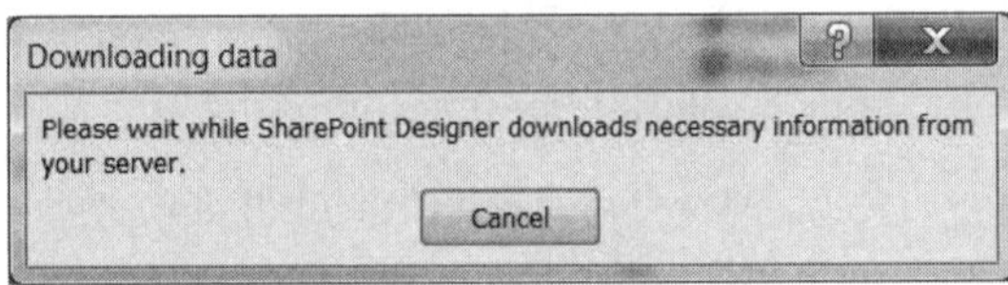

FIGURE 12-5

Depending on the speed of your desktop/laptop and your SharePoint server, you may see this happening when you first create a workflow, as shown in Figure 12-5.

> **OPENING AND CLOSING SHAREPOINT DESIGNER**
>
> It's not literally true that you need to close and reopen SharePoint Designer every time you make a change on the server; however, it's a good habit. Even though some server-side changes don't require recycling SharePoint Designer, it's quite easy to do and can save you a lot of grief — especially when you first learn how to create custom activities.

Actions File

An xml file, called the `actions` file, describes how SharePoint Designer should show the custom activity to the workflow developer, what parameters are available for the custom action and whether those parameters are provided to the action (an input parameter) and which parameters are returned from the custom activity (an output parameter).

In addition, the `actions` file maps the parameters and the action to a .NET assembly. You create the assembly using Visual Studio, and the assembly is stored in the Global Assembly Cache (GAC).

Following is an example actions file:

```
<WorkflowInfo>
  <Actions Sequential="then" Parallel="and">
    <Action Name="Demo Action"
        ClassName="ActivityLibrary1.Activity1"
        Assembly="ActivityLibrary1, Version=1.0.0.0, Culture=neutral,
PublicKeyToken=3381109f55920d8e"
        AppliesTo="all"
        Category="Chapter 12">
      <RuleDesigner Sentence="Demo activity, try out DueDays: [%1]">
        <FieldBind Field="DueDays" Text="Due Days" DesignerType="TextArea" Id="1"/>
      </RuleDesigner>
      <Parameters>
        <Parameter Name="DueDays" Type="System.String, mscorlib" Directions="In"/>
      </Parameters>
    </Action>
  </Actions>
</WorkflowInfo>
```

That `actions` file defines an action named `"Demo Action"`. That action defines a "sentence" that displays in SharePoint Designer. The sentence uses a simple substitution mechanism: the percent sign and a number, called a token. SharePoint Designer replaces a given token with `parameter` whose ID equals the token's number. In the preceding example, the token `%1` is replaced with `"DueDays"` at runtime.

Web.config

The activities are implemented as .net assemblies. SharePoint Designer and SharePoint won't let any assembly be used as a custom activity, even if it's an assembly that is otherwise coded correctly. SharePoint needs to both trust that assembly, and it must be recognized as "authorized." You authorize an assembly by creating an entry in the web.config file for the web application in which you want to use the custom activity.

Web.config files are saved on the SharePoint servers in their respective web application's web root folder. Typically, this would be c:\inetpub\wwwroot\wss\VirtualDirectories\[port] where [port] is the port number of the application. Each custom activity's DLL must have an entry in the `<authorizedTypes>` section of web.config. Following is an example:

```
<System.Workflow.ComponentModel.WorkflowCompiler>
  <authorizedTypes>
    <authorizedType
Assembly="ActivityLibrary1, Version=1.0.0.0, Culture=neutral,
PublicKeyToken=3381109f55920d8e"
Namespace="ActivityLibrary1"
TypeName="*"
Authorized="True" />
…
…
</authorizedTypes>
</System.Workflow.ComponentModel.WorkflowCompiler>
```

The .NET Assembly

Last, but certainly not least, you need the compiled C# code that implements the logic of your custom activity. This is typically implemented with two separate Visual Studio projects bundled into one Visual Studio solution: one for the activity's custom code and another to package the solution for deployment purposes.

This assembly is saved into the GAC. Its code follows a pattern that includes defining properties decorated with workflow-specific attributes. These properties map back to the `actions` file. It also implements the actual logic, which as you'll see, can sometimes be less involving than setting up the plumbing itself.

DETAILED WALK-THROUGH: CREATE A CUSTOM ACTIVITY

The next sections walk you through the process to create a custom activity in great detail. You'll do the following:

- Create a new Visual Studio solution and project based on the workflow activities library template and write your business logic.
- Add an empty SharePoint project.
- Create an `actions` file and assembly reference to GAC.

- Deploy the solution to SharePoint.
- Modify web.config by hand.

You need to carefully follow these steps because many small and common errors can creep into your solution without your knowledge. The section, "Error Scenarios and Fixes" can help you when you get stuck.

Creating the Custom Activity Project

Fire up Visual Studio 2010 and create a new project named SPDCustomActivity. Use Figure 12-6 for guidance. In Installed Templates, select Workflow, and in the main section, select Workflow Activity Library. Visual studio responds with a graphical view of the workflow. You won't use that view, so even though it's interesting, it's not relevant to the work you complete in this chapter. Instead, right-click Activity1.cs, and select View Code, as shown in Figure 12-7.

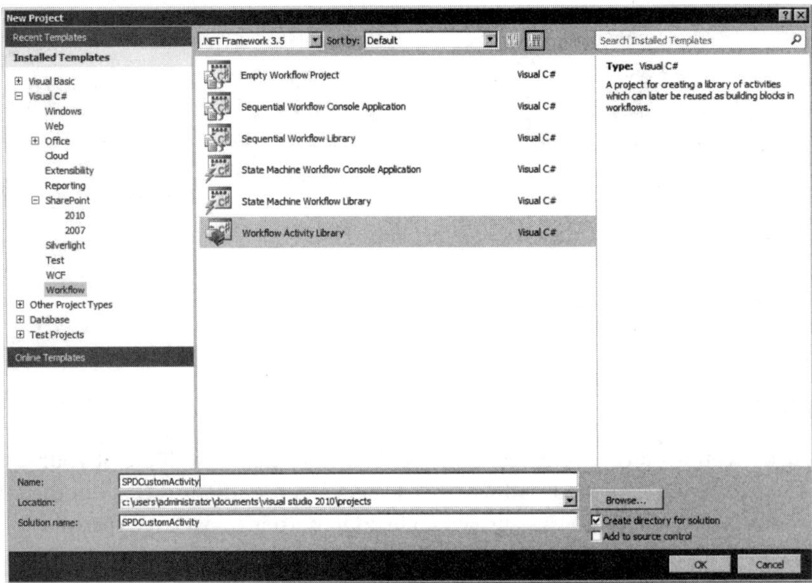

FIGURE 12-6

At this point, you have a skeleton C# code file that has all the references and other plumbing it needs to be a SharePoint Designer custom activity. Next, you need to define the activity's parameters and its logic.

As per the business requirements previously discussed, you need an activity flexible enough to handle the diverse needs of your international company, meaning that you need multiple holiday calendars (one per country). If you need multiple calendars, you need one parameter that enables the user to specify the correct calendar (in this example, as a custom list).

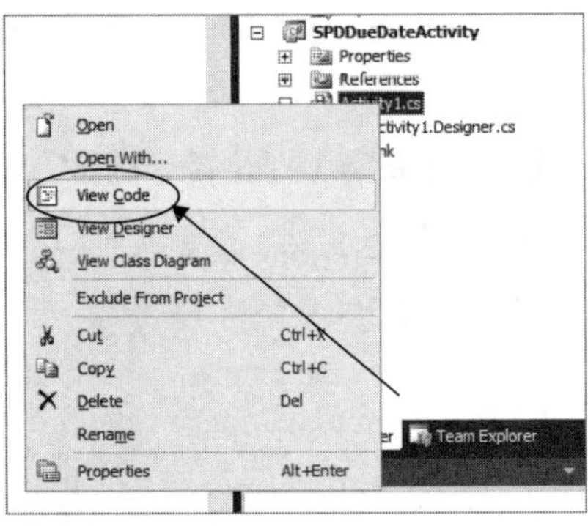

FIGURE 12-7

Next, the activity needs to calculate business days in relation to a particular due date. Therefore, you need a parameter for the due date. Because you plan to reuse this activity, you want to keep it generic, so call it a reference date. This activity can return a date that is a certain number of business days earlier than that reference date. In the HR case, the reference date is the date that the employee plans to show up for his first day on the job.

Lastly, your activity needs the number of business days. You have a hard requirement for HR that tasks should be completed three business days in advance of the employee's start date, but other business scenarios may call for two days before, one week before, and so on. Some scenarios may even call for a future date. So, rather than hard coding three days, use a parameter to gain greater flexibility.

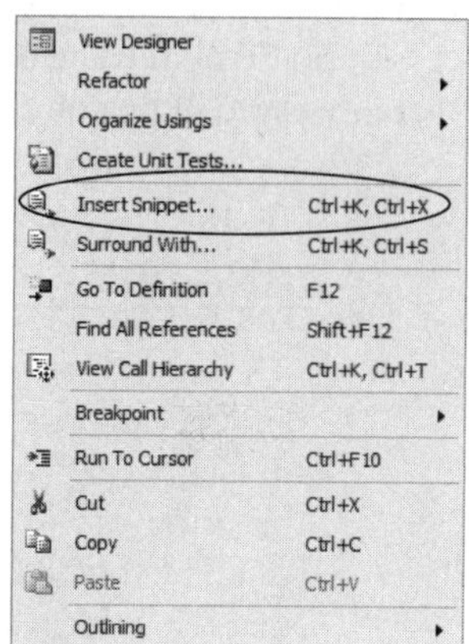

FIGURE 12-8

Coding Parameters

The following code snippet shows how to create a parameter for the Business Days parameter. The easiest way to create the property definition is to use the Insert Snippet feature in Visual Studio 2010. Right-click and select Insert Snippet, as shown in Figure 12-8, and choose an appropriate category, as shown in Figure 12-9, to insert the property definition to the class, and then just change the name and type of the property as per requirement.

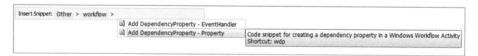

FIGURE 12-9

```
        public static DependencyProperty BusinessDaysProperty = DependencyProperty.
Register("BusinessDays",
                typeof(string),
                typeof(Activity1));

        [Description("BusinessDays")]
        [Category("BusinessDays Category")]
        [Browsable(true)]

        [DesignerSerializationVisibility(DesignerSerializationVisibility.Visible)]
        public string BusinessDays
        {
            get
            {
                return ((string)(base.GetValue(Activity1.BusinessDaysProperty)));
            }
            set
            {
                base.SetValue(Activity1.BusinessDaysProperty, value);
            }
        }
```

The first line of code defines the parameter and sets up the plumbing so that the .NET workflow engine can read from and set the values of workflow parameters. The rest of it is a more or less standard getter/setter for a property in the Activity1 class. It's married to the `DependencyProperty` by way of the getter and setter's code.

At this point, you've taken the first steps needed to enable bidirectional communication between your SharePoint Designer workflows and your custom activity's code via this parameter-based interface. Even though there are a few more parameters to create, move on to other parts of the solution. You'll come back to parameters when you've proven that one works. (See the note for more cheerleading on this topic.)

ITERATION IN CUSTOM ACTIVITY DEVELOPMENT

It's generally good practice to make small changes in code: compile, test, rinse, and repeat. It's even more important to follow a pattern like this for custom activity development. This is because there are a lot of opportunities to introduce a small bug into your work (either in code or somewhere in the actions file XML) and you can find yourself totally lost at sea when you hit one of the many mysterious errors that this effort can present you with. Make small focused changes and test them so that you know the scope of your debugging effort every step of the way.

Create a Deployment Project

There actually isn't any such thing as a deployment project. You won't find a deployment project template in Visual Studio. Instead, you create an empty SharePoint project whose only purpose is to deploy your custom activity to SharePoint.

Go to File, click Add, and select New Project in Visual Studio's File menu. From the Installed Templates panel, select SharePoint 2010 and then Empty SharePoint Project, as shown in Figure 12-10.

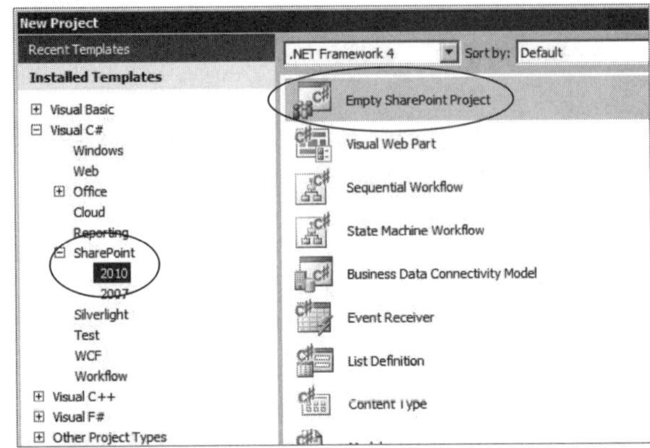

FIGURE 12-10

Name the project `DeployActivity`. Visual Studio asks you what site to use for debugging. Enter any valid site. (It doesn't matter because you won't debug it this way.) Lastly, be sure to click the Deploy as a Farm Solution check box. SharePoint Designer activities cannot be deployed as sandbox solutions because the activity must be in the GAC. This deployment project doesn't know that, so it offers up this choice, and unfortunately, it's the default option. Figure 12-11 shows what it looks like. Click Finish to create the project.

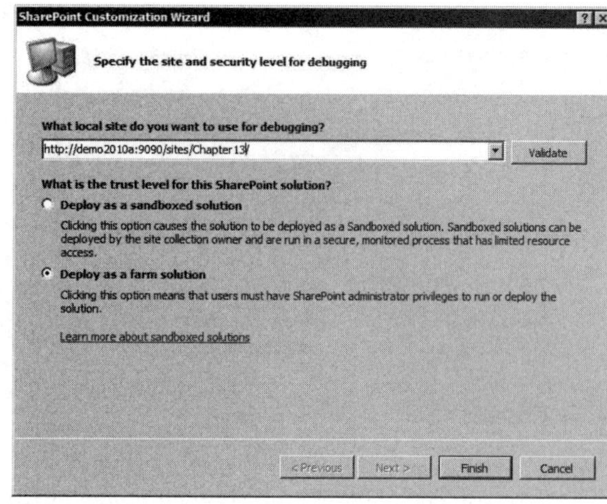

FIGURE 12-11

This new project is a convenience project. It's convenient because when you build this project, Visual Studio creates a .wsp (solution file) and automatically deploys it to your development environment. As you see, you still need to do some manual work, but the manual work you need to do is far, far less than it would be without this project.

This project is going to do two things for you: deploy the actions file to the 14 hive and deploy the assembly into the GAC. Read on to learn about both.

Deploying the Actions File

You haven't created an `actions` file as yet, but you will shortly. The `actions` file has to be deployed to at least each web frontend in the environment. When it goes to these web frontends, it has to be stored in a specific place: the workflow folder in the 14 hive. The 14 hive is the root location on the hard drive underneath which most the SharePoint data resides (excepting SQL itself). You could copy the actions file to each of these servers manually, but that's error prone and painful, and it breaks best practices to boot. You can and should use this deployment project for that purpose instead.

Given that the activity file belongs in the 14 hive, you need to configure the deployment project to place it there. You need two things to make this happen: a mapped folder and an activity file. Start with the mapped folder.

When Visual Studio deploys the solution to the farm, it needs to save the actions file to the [14hive]\template\[language code]\workflow directory where [language code] is a number representing the language to which your actions file belongs. U.S. English is language code 1033. Typically, this would be C:\Program Files\Common Files\Microsoft Shared\Web Server Extensions\14\TEMPLATE\1033\Workflow. For a list of language codes go to `http://msdn.microsoft.com/en-us/library/0h88fahh(VS.85).aspx`.

You can get SharePoint to do this for you automatically by mapping a SharePoint folder in the project. To do this, right-click the `DeployActivity` project, click Add, and click SharePoint Mapped Folder, as shown in Figure 12-12.

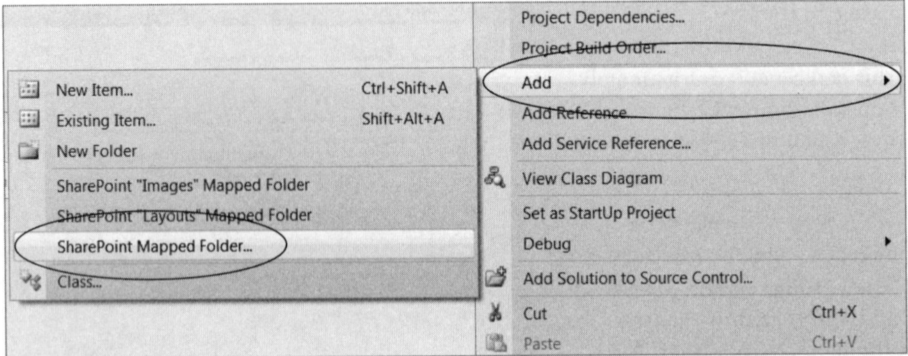

FIGURE 12-12

When you click SharePoint Mapped Folder, Visual Studio calls out to SharePoint and obtains a list of folders in the 14 hive, as show in Figure 12-13.

Navigate to the correct workflow directory, and click OK.

Now that you have the mapped folder, it's time to create the `actions` file.

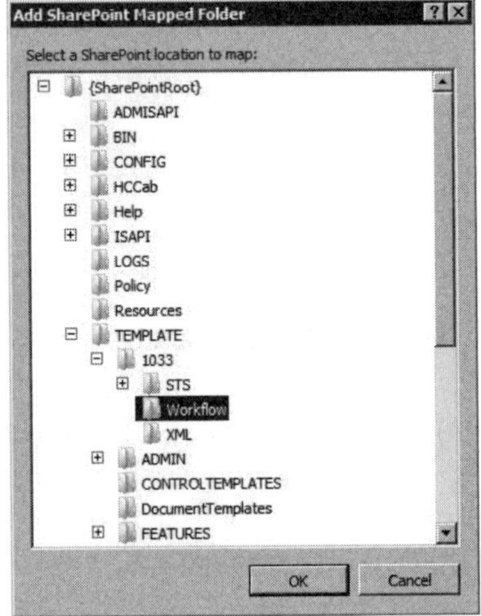

FIGURE 12-13

Crafting an Actions File

`Action` files are XML files with a somewhat counterintuitive extension, "actions." Create an `actions` file by right-clicking the Workflow folder in Solution Explorer under the `DeployActivity` project. Click Add and then click New Item. In the Installed Templates panel, click Data, and select XML File. Give it a name, `SPDueDateActivity.actions` and save it. When finished, your `DeployActivity` Visual Studio Solution Explorer windows should look like Figure 12-14.

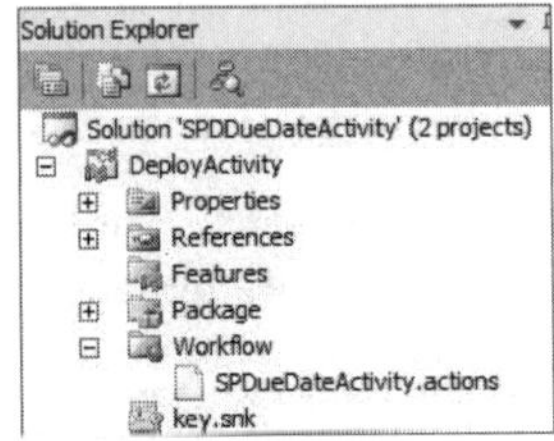

FIGURE 12-14

ACTIONS FILE AS XML

You can add the `actions` file as a text file or any other file that you want. However, if you tell Visual Studio it's an XML file, intellisense kicks in and gives you clues and other assistance. These `action` files are so picky, you need all the help you can get.

The actions file isn't too complicated, but once again, small errors here can cause headache-inducing errors, so be careful. Consider the following XML:

```
<WorkflowInfo>
  <Actions Sequential="then" Parallel="and">
    <Action Name="Calculate Due Date"
        ClassName="SPDDueDateActivity.Activity1"
        Assembly="SPDDueDateActivity, Version=1.0.0.0, Culture=neutral,
        PublicKeyToken=0606bf2a15d08c6d"
        AppliesTo="all"
        Category="My Custom Activities">
      <RuleDesigner
        Sentence="Calculate a date that is [%1] business days before or after
        a reference date.">
        <FieldBind Field="BusinessDays"
          Text="Business Days" DesignerType="TextArea" Id="1"/>
      </RuleDesigner>
      <Parameters>
        <Parameter
           Name="BusinessDays" Type="System.String, mscorlib"
           Directions="In"/>
      </Parameters>
    </Action>
  </Actions>
</WorkflowInfo>
```

The opening and closing of the action file's XML is boilerplate stuff. The interesting part begins with the <Action> node, which specifies the following key pieces of information:

- **Name of the activity:** SharePoint Designer displays this as the action's name, so pick something clear and obvious that your end users will understand.
- **Class name behind this activity:** The previous example shows this starting with the Namespace, therefore SPDDueDateActivity.Activity1.
- **Strong name of the assembly:** Assembly strong names are strangely difficult to obtain. One of the easiest ways to get the strong name is via a populate tool, .NET Reflector. This tool used to be free, but the owner started to charge for it in early 2011. You can obtain the strong name in a number of ways. You need to compile the project at least once to generate a DLL with the strong name.

The <Action> node basically maps the activity to its assembly in the GAC in a secure manner.

The next node of interest is the <RuleDesigner> node:

```
<RuleDesigner
  Sentence="Calculate a date that is [%1] business days before or after
  a reference date.">
```

This node defines the actual sentence that appears in SharePoint Designer when you select this activity in a step. It also closes the loop on the communication plumbing between SharePoint Designer workflow, windows workflow foundation, and the custom code you write to implement the activity. Now take them one at a time.

The sentence attribute is straightforward. It's the actual sentence that SharePoint Designer displays for the activity. It uses a token replacement scheme in the form of a percent sign (%) concatenated with a number. This number refers to a `<FieldBind>` node:

```
<FieldBind
  Field="BusinessDays"
  Text="Business Days"
  DesignerType="TextArea"
  Id="1"/>
```

The `<FieldBind>` node maps a `%n` token to a label (`Text="Business Days"`) and a data entry behavior (`DesignerType="TextArea"`). It instructs SharePoint Designer to treat the Business Days parameter as a text string. The `%n` token is matched up with a particular `<FieldBind>` node by the `<FieldBind>` node's ID attribute.

```
<Parameter
  Name="BusinessDays"
  Type="System.String, mscorlib"
  Directions="In"/>
```

Finally, the `<Parameters>` node matches up this SharePoint Designer field with your workflow parameter in your custom activity's code. Type defines the data type of the parameter, and the direction sets the `action` type of the parameter as `In` (Value can be set from Designer) or `Out`. (Value can be set from workflow activity code through property.)

In summary, the `actions` file defines what the user sees in SharePoint Designer, it maps tokens (`%n`) to fields, and it maps fields to parameters in your workflow. There are a lot of dependencies in there, and you must pay close attention to detail to keep it working.

Deploying the Activity's Assembly to the GAC

With the `actions` file out of the way, it's time to learn how you can use Logic's assembly to SharePoint. Start by looking at the deployment package. Do this by double-clicking the Package node in the `DeployActivity` project in Solution Explorer. See Figure 12-14 for help. This opens up the Package GUI, as shown in Figure 12-15. Click Advanced and you're provided with an opportunity to add an assembly to the package. Click the Add button, and select Add Existing Assembly. Visual Studio responds with the Add Assembly from Project Output dialog, as shown in Figure 12-16. Click OK and Visual Studio responds with Figure 12-17.

At this point, you almost have a deployment project that can install your action's assembly and actions file to the GAC for each server in the farm. The final missing ingredient is a strong name. This solution must be deployed to the GAC and therefore it must have a strong name. Nearly every .NET developer knows about strong names, but if you need to brush up on this topic, check out this MSDN article: `http://msdn.microsoft.com/en-us/library/ms247123(v=VS.100).aspx`.

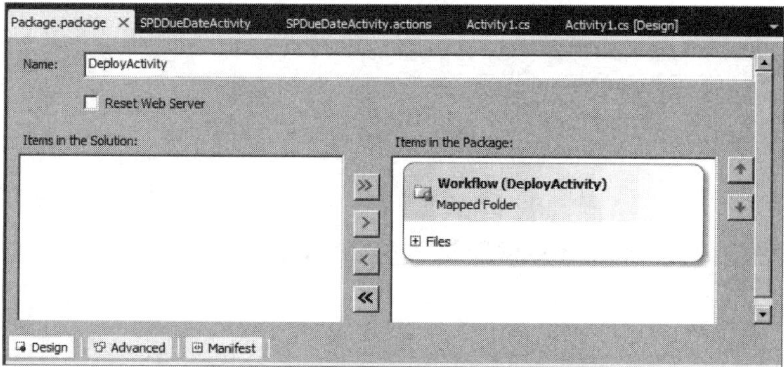

FIGURE 12-15

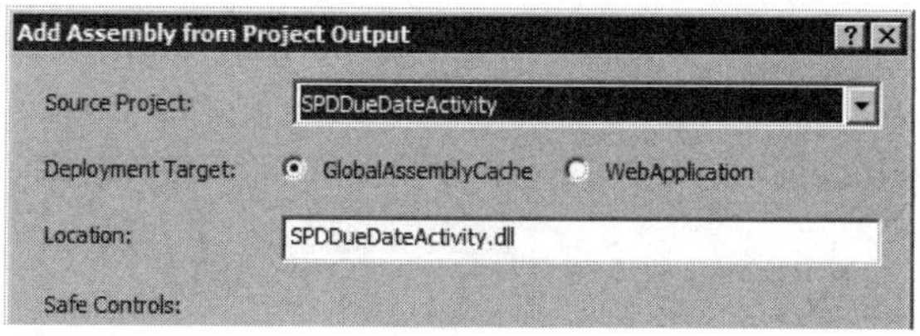

FIGURE 12-16

Click OK and it looks like Figure 12.17.

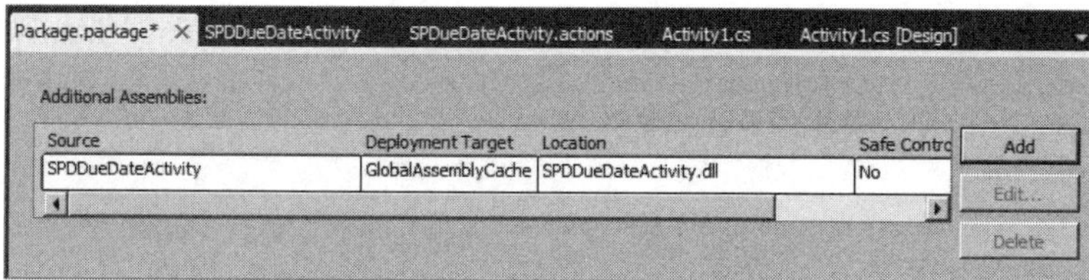

FIGURE 12-17

Deploy, Test, and Debug — Part 1

SharePoint 2010 and Visual Studio 2010 make the deploy, test, and debugging process far easier than its MOSS 2007 counterpart. Simply right-click the Solution node in Solution Explorer, and select Deploy Solution. SharePoint Designer creates a WSP file, installs it in the farm, and deploys it for you, all in that one click.

At this point, you are almost ready to test, but there is one last configuration change you need to make. You must manually edit the web.config file. There is a web.config file for every web application in the farm. The web.config file is typically located in c:\inetpub\wwwroot\wss\VirtualDirectories\[port]\web.config. See Figure 12-18. The ".config" part might be truncated depending on your Windows Explorer settings. You can edit web.config with Notepad; although, if you double-click it, Visual Studio may open it for you.

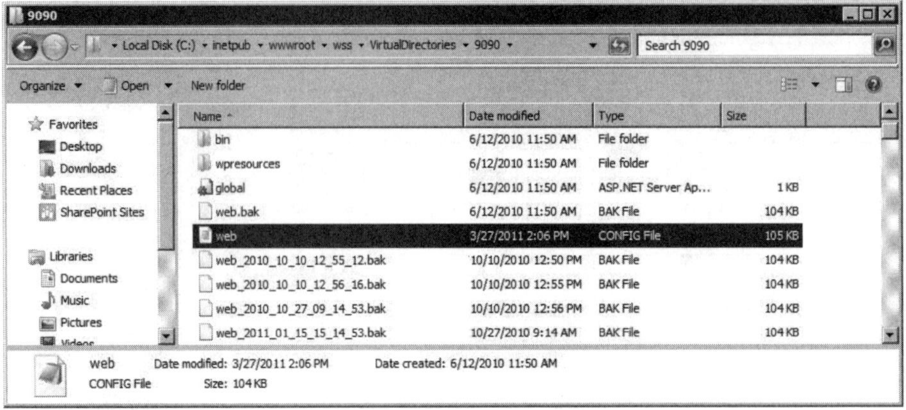

FIGURE 12-18

AUTOMATING WEB.CONFIG UPDATES

Is it necessary to manually edit the web.config file? The answer is no. The correct course of action is to add a feature receiver to your deployment project. The feature receiver would add the necessary authorized types and other web.config updates for you. Learn more about feature receivers at `http://msdn.microsoft.com/en-us/library/ee231604.aspx`.

You need to add an entry to the `<authorizedTypes>` element in the web.config file. This element's immediate parent is `<System.Workflow.ComponentModel.WorkflowCompiler>` and is located near the last third of a typical web.config file. See Figure 12-19.

```
</location>
<location path="_layouts/mobile/mblmultilogin.aspx">
  <system.web>
    <authorization>
      <allow users="*" />
    </authorization>
  </system.web>
</location>
<System.Workflow.ComponentModel.WorkflowCompiler>
  <authorizedTypes>
    <authorizedType Assembly="SPDDueDateActivity, version=1.0.0.0, Cuture=neutral, Public
    <authorizedType Assembly="System.Workflow.Activities, Version=3.0.0.0, Culture=neutra
    <authorizedType Assembly="System.Workflow.Activities, Version=3.0.0.0, Culture=neutra
    <authorizedType Assembly="System.Workflow.Activities, Version=3.0.0.0, Culture=neutra
```

FIGURE 12-19

You insert a new element there as shown:

```
<authorizedType
   Assembly="SPDDueDateActivity, Version=1.0.0.0, Culture=neutral,
   PublicKeyToken=0606bf2a15d08c6d" Namespace="SPDDueDateActivity"
   TypeName="*" Authorized="True" />
```

This is another one of those tricky things that must be absolutely perfect, or you'll have with confusing, hard to debug errors. It breaks down as follows:

- **Assembly:** The fully qualified strong name of the assembly.
- **Namespace:** The namespace that encompasses the activity.
- **TypeName:** The name of the type (object) that implements your logic. Leave it as `"*"` to include all the types in your assembly.
- **Authorized:** Obviously, set this to `"true"`.

Save the web.config file, and you're finally ready to start.

One last note before firing up your first test; you need to make this web.config change only once. The deployment project doesn't make this entry for you when it deploys to SharePoint, but it also doesn't remove it when you retract the solution, so at least you don't need to worry about it after you get it right the first time.

It's finally time to test things out. Fire up SharePoint Designer, connect to a SharePoint site, and create a workflow on a list. For this initial test, you won't bother saving it, so you don't need to be careful about which list or the name you give the workflow. After you get to the entry screen, click Actions and scroll down, searching for My Custom Activities. You should see something like Figure 12-20.

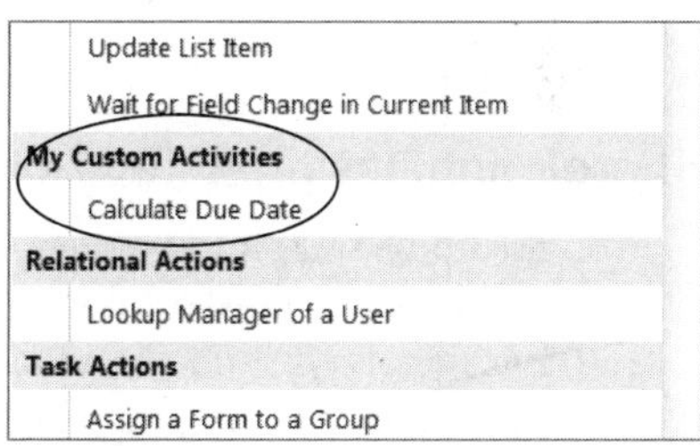

FIGURE 12-20

Error Scenarios and Fixes

There's an excellent chance at this point that something went wrong. The following sections cover the most common errors that you're likely to see and provide advice on how to solve them.

The "Nothing Happens" Click

Sometimes, you deploy the solution and your custom activity shows up in a list (refer to Figure 12-20) but when you click on it, nothing happens. This happens when you made a mistake in the web.config file. If you don't get it *just so,* you can expect this behavior. Consider these two XML snippets:

Snippet #1:

```
<authorizedType Assembly="SPDDueDateActivity, Version=1.0.0.0,
Culture=neutral, PublicKeyToken=0606bf2a15d08c6d"
Namespace="SPDDueDateActivity" TypeName="*" Authorized="True" />
```

Snippet #2:

```
<authorizedType Assembly="SPDueDateActivity, Version=1.0.0.0,
Culture=neutral, PublicKeyToken=0606bf2a15d08c6d"
Namespace="SPDDueDateActivity" TypeName="*" Authorized="True" />
```

Can you tell the difference? Snippet #1 has the correct strong name in the Assembly attribute, whereas snippet #2 misspells SPDDueDateActivity.

The Assembly Does Not Exist Error

You fire up SharePoint Designer and try to create a new workflow. Everything is looking good when SharePoint Designer stops and throws up a dialog box similar to Figure 12-21.

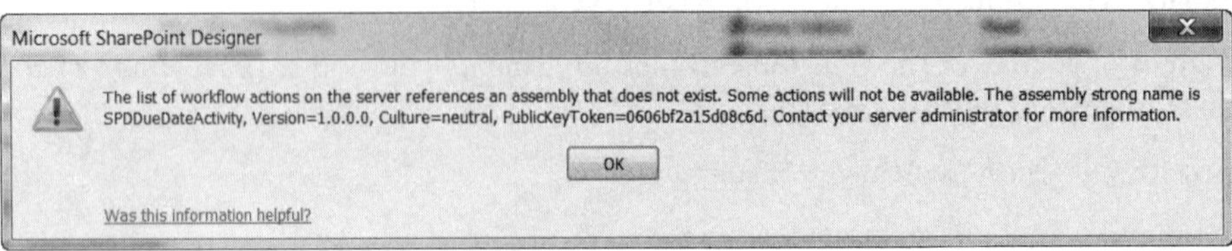

FIGURE 12-21

This error occurs when the `actions` file was successfully deployed, but the activity's assembly was not. One way this could happen is that the deployment project's package didn't deploy the assembly at all. Recall that you need to go to the package's Advanced tab to tell it to include the output of the activity project.

SharePoint Designer Tells You: Cannot Find Property Named

You fire up SharePoint Designer, create a workflow, and see your activity right where you expect it. You add it to your workflow and so far, so good, as shown in Figure 12-22. You enter a value into Business Days, and SharePoint Designer responds with something like Cannot Find Property Named, as shown in Figure 12-23. This can happen when your activity's source code has a mismatch between the `DependencyProperty` and the property itself, as shown in Figure 12-24. The `DependencyProperty`'s `Register` method is passing "BusinessDays" (with two letter s's) while the corresponding property in the object itself is named "BusinesDays" (just one letter s).

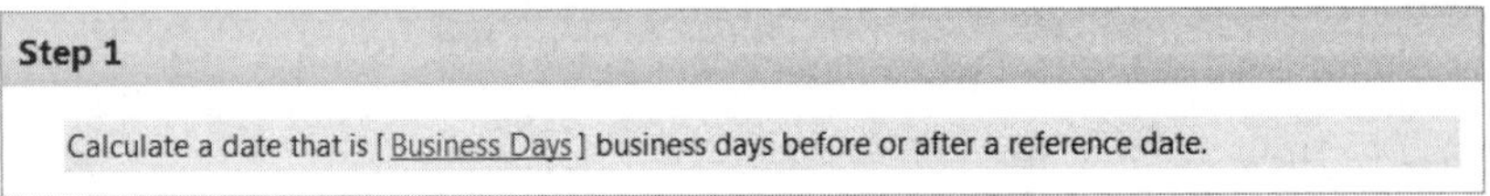

FIGURE 12-22

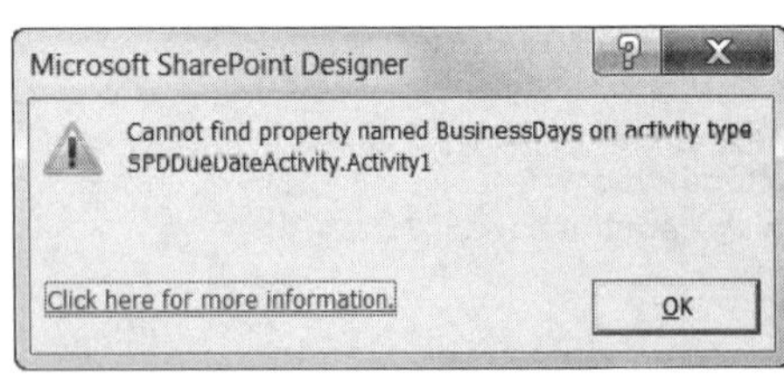

FIGURE 12-23

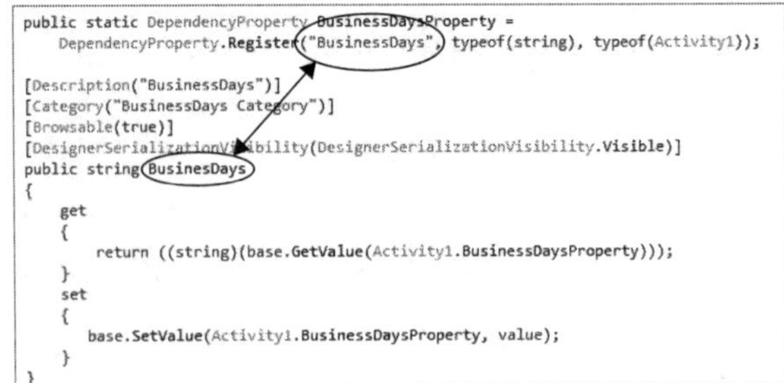

FIGURE 12-24

The %1 Token Appears, Not Its Label

The SharePoint Designer action appears in the actions list, but when you select it, the token itself shows in the sentence, and you can't edit it. This can happen when there's a mismatch in the actions file between ID attributes on the <Fieldbind> node and the <Sentence> token. See Figure 12-25. It shows that the sentence is referencing a <Fieldbind> node whose ID is "1" based on the %1 token. However, the only <FieldBind> node in the actions file has Id = "11".

```
<RuleDesigner Sentence="Calculate a date that is [%1] business days before or after a reference date.">
    <FieldBind Field="BusinessDays" Text="Business Days" DesignerType="TextArea" Id="11"/>
</RuleDesigner>
```

FIGURE 12-25

Everything Seems to Work but Then Check for Errors Fails

You can add your action, and you can edit the Business Days parameter with no problem. Everything looks good, but when you click Check for Errors or attempt to publish the workflow, SharePoint Designer tells you This Action Has Required Parameters That Are Missing (see Figure 12-26).

Step 1

Calculate a date that is [3] business days before or after a reference date.

This action has required parameters that are missing.

FIGURE 12-26

This can happen when there's a mismatch between the Name attribute of the Parameter and the corresponding Field attribute in the <FieldBind> node. See Figure 12-27.

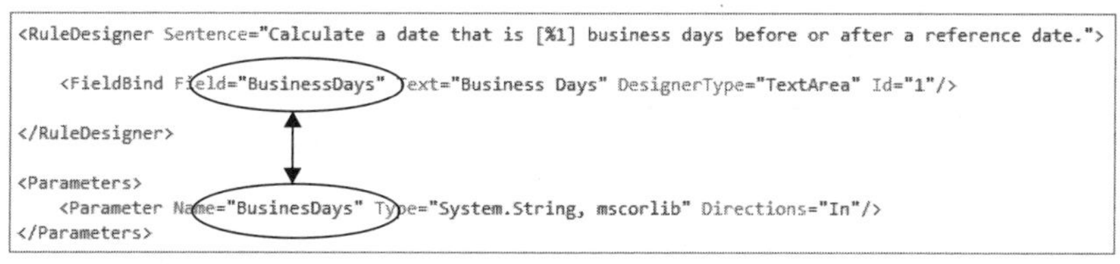

```
<RuleDesigner Sentence="Calculate a date that is [%1] business days before or after a reference date.">
    <FieldBind Field="BusinessDays" Text="Business Days" DesignerType="TextArea" Id="1"/>
</RuleDesigner>
<Parameters>
    <Parameter Name="BusinesDays" Type="System.String, mscorlib" Directions="In"/>
</Parameters>
```

FIGURE 12-27

Finishing the Logic

After you get this basic activity working, it's time to make it actually do something. To this point, all you've accomplished is to allows SharePoint Designer to show an activity that enables you to enter a value into the Business Days field. It doesn't actually do anything at this point. To do that, you need to add some additional parameters and extend the logic in your activity code file to calculate business days.

Add References

This solution uses core components from your SharePoint 2010 environment. They are encapsulated in two different DLLs that must be added as references to the project. They are:

- Microsoft.SharePoint.dll
- Microsoft.sharepoint.WorkflowActions.dll from ISAPI folder in 14 hive path (C:\Program Files\Common Files\Microsoft Shared\Web Server Extensions\14\ISAPI\microsoft.sharepoint.WorkflowActions.dll)

Update the Actions File

The first step is to update the `actions` file. Replace your `actions` file with the following XML:

```
<WorkflowInfo>
  <Actions Sequential="then" Parallel="and">
    <Action Name="Calculate Due Date"
        ClassName="SPDDueDateActivity.Activity1"
        Assembly="SPDDueDateActivity, Version=1.0.0.0, Culture=neutral,
        PublicKeyToken=0606bf2a15d08c6d"
        AppliesTo="all"
        Category="My Custom Activities">
      <RuleDesigner Sentence="Calculate a date that is [%1] business days before
      or after a reference date [%2] using a holiday list named [%3] from a site
      link: [%4], and store the return date into [%5].">
        <FieldBind Field="BusinessDays"
                   Text="Business Days"
                   DesignerType="TextArea" Id="1"/>
        <FieldBind Field="ReferenceDate"
                   Text="Reference Date"
                   DesignerType="TextArea" Id="2"/>
        <FieldBind Field="ListName"
                   Text="List Name"
                   DesignerType="TextArea" Id="3"/>
        <FieldBind Field="SiteURL"
                   Text="Site URL"
                   DesignerType="TextArea" Id="4"/>
      <FieldBind
                   Field="DueDateVal"
                   Text="Due Date"
                   DesignerType="ParameterNames" Id="5"/>

      </RuleDesigner>
      <Parameters>
        <Parameter Name="BusinesDays"
                   Type="System.String, mscorlib"
                   Directions="In"/>
        <Parameter Name="ReferenceDate"
                   Type="System.String, mscorlib"
                   Directions="In"/>
        <Parameter Name="ListName"
                   Type="System.String, mscorlib"
                   Directions="In"/>
```

```
            <Parameter Name="SiteURL"
                       Type="System.String, mscorlib"
                       Directions="In"/>
           <Parameter Name="DueDateVal"
                       Type="System.String, mscorlib"
                       Directions="Out"/>
          </Parameters>
        </Action>
      </Actions>
    </WorkflowInfo>
```

The new XML defines five parameters for your action:

- `ReferenceDate`: To use for the basis of the date calculations
- `BusinessDays`: This is number of days before or after the reference date you want to calculate.
- `ListName`: The name of a list that has the company holidays. The logic assumes this is also a calendar list. This does not include the URL of the list.
- `SiteURL`: The URL of the list itself
- `DueDateVal`: Calculated due date based on the business logic will be returned through this parameter and bind to the variable in SharePoint Designer.

Update the Activity Code File

Now it's almost time to get into the meat of the matter and write some code that does more than plumbing. But there is still a little more plumbing to take care of.

Add Remaining DependencyProperty Pairs

For each of the five properties in the `actions` file, you need a corresponding set of `DependencyProperty` pairs.

```
        #region BusinessDaysProperty
        public static DependencyProperty BusinessDaysProperty =
            DependencyProperty.Register("BusinessDays",
            typeof(string),
            typeof(Activity1));

        [Description("BusinessDays")]
        [Category("BusinessDays Category")]
        [Browsable(true)]

        [DesignerSerializationVisibility(DesignerSerializationVisibility.Visible)]
        public string BusinessDays
        {
            get
            {
                return ((string)(base.GetValue(Activity1.BusinessDaysProperty)));
            }
            set
            {
```

```
            base.SetValue(Activity1.BusinessDaysProperty, value);
        }
    }
    #endregion
```

Override the Execute Method

When the SharePoint workflow engine pulls up the XOML file that defines your workflow process, it interprets the XML, finds activities, and invokes a method, `Execute`, for each one it finds. Your code file overrides the `Execute` method, as shown here:

```
protected override ActivityExecutionStatus
  Execute(ActivityExecutionContext executionContext)
{
    CalculateBusinessDaysOffset();
    return ActivityExecutionStatus.Closed;
}
```

This code does two things:

- It invokes a method: `CalculateBusinessDaysOffset`.
- Upon completion, it lets the workflow engine know that it has finished this activity.

Calculate the New Offset Date

Finally, it's time to write the actual logic that calculates the new date. This logic needs to look up the calendar that contains all the holidays and use that, plus the hard-coded assumption that weekend days are never business days, to calculate the date. Add one more helper method that identifies holidays:

```
private bool CheckHolidayList(DateTime dtHol)
{
    using (SPSite oSite = new SPSite(SiteURL))
    {
        using (SPWeb oWeb = oSite.OpenWeb())
        {
            SPList oList = oWeb.Lists[ListName];
            SPQuery oQuery = new SPQuery();
            oQuery.Query =
"<Where><Eq><FieldRef Name='HolidayDate'/>" +
"<Value IncludeTimeValue='FALSE' Type='DateTime'>" +
dtHol.ToString("yyyy-MM dd") + "</Value></Eq></Where>";

            SPListItemCollection oColl = oList.GetItems(oQuery);

            if (oColl.Count > 0)
                return true;
            else
                return false;
        }
    }
}
```

This method uses the supplied SiteURL (that the workflow designer entered into SharePoint Designer) to look up a list using its name (`ListName`). It then executes a query to find an entry in that list that matches the test date passed as the method's one and only parameter. If the search returns a result, it's a holiday date. Otherwise, it isn't.

The helper method is invoked from `CalculateBusinessDaysOffset` itself:

```
        private void CalculateBusinessDaysOffset()
         {
                         using (SPSite _site = new SPSite(SiteURL))
            {
                using (SPWeb _web = _site.OpenWeb())
                {
                    SPList _list = _web.Lists[ListName];

                    DataContext data = new DataContext(_site.RootWeb.Url);

                    int NoOfDays = Convert.ToInt32(BusinessDays);
                    int ProposedNoOfDays = NoOfDays;

                    for (int i=1; i<=NoOfDays; i++)
                    {
                        if ((DateTime.Today.AddDays(i).DayOfWeek ==
                          DayOfWeek.Saturday) ||
                          (DateTime.Today.AddDays(i).DayOfWeek ==
                          DayOfWeek.Sunday)
                            || (CheckHolidayList(DateTime.Today.AddDays(i))))
                        {
                            ProposedNoOfDays++;
                        }
                    }

                    if (string.IsNullOrEmpty(RefDate))
                    {
                        DueDateVal =
    System.DateTime.Today.AddDays(ProposedNoOfDays).ToString();
                    }
                    else
                    {
                        DueDateVal =
    Convert.ToDateTime(RefDate).AddDays(ProposedNoOfDays).ToString();
                    }
                }
            }
        }
```

`CalculateBusinessDaysOffset()` simply starts off with the reference date and increments (or decrements) by one day, checks if it's a weekend or holiday date and iterates until it finishes the calculation. The method ends when it finishes iterating and assigns the new offset date, which is passed back to SharePoint Designer.

At this point, you're done and ready for the deploy/test/change cycle until it all works. After deploying the solution package, open the site in SharePoint Designer, create or edit the existing workflow, and look for the `CalculateDue` action in the custom `actions` list. When you select the action, it should display, as shown in Figure 12-28.

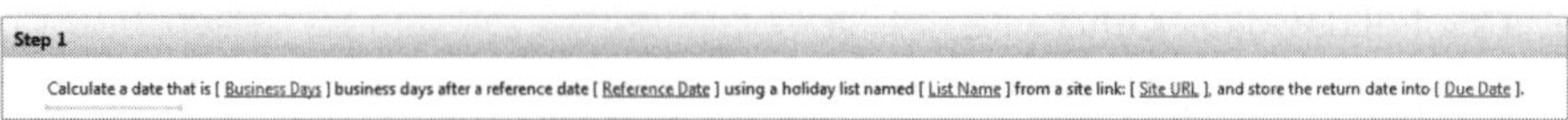

FIGURE 12-28

Code Summary

A lot is going on with this project, but when you boil it all down it comes down to a lot of plumbing and a little bit of actual implementing of business logic in code. You have your `actions` file that helps SharePoint Designer provide a user interface. The `actions` file maps to a bunch of properties in your code. Those properties need to follow a pattern and naming convention that pairs up exactly with the parameters defined in the `actions` file. Lastly, your activity code file overrides the `Execute` method, and you finally have full control over what's happening.

The code presented in this chapter has some holes. It doesn't do any validation of any kind. As a result, there are many, many opportunities for uncontrolled errors. The user might specify a nonexistent list. The user might specify a calendar list to which other users won't have security access. The user might enter an alphanumeric value for the business days offset or the reference date itself. All this can be managed by checking the values in the code, and you should always do that.

ADVANCED TOPICS

To some extent, this chapter is an advanced chapter by itself, but there are additional avenues to explore and opportunities to significantly advance the solution from where it ended in the walk-through.

Troll for Ideas

Just as you created your own `actions` file for your custom activity, so has Microsoft created an `actions` file for all of its activities. Believe it or not, it's just sitting there in the 14 hive in the same workflow directory where you deployed your `actions` file. If you browse to that directory, you can see several `actions` files, including `WSS.ACTIONS`, `moss.actions`, and `moderationworkflow.actions`. If you like the behavior and flair of a given OOB SharePoint Designer activity, look it up here, and model your custom activity after it.

Debugging Workflows

Debugging workflows at runtime is a bit of a nuisance. There's a fair amount of setup work required. The first step is to set your breakpoints as normal and deploy the process.

The real key is to use Visual Studio's Attach to Process function under the Debug menu, as shown in Figure 12-29. Visual Studio shows a list of all running processes. You want to scroll through the list, looking for Processes named w3w.exe (the Internet Information Services worker process). There will likely be more than one, and there's no convenient way to know which one will be running your workflow, so attach it to all of them. (You can multiselect from this list.) You may need to click Show Processes from All Users and/or Show Processes in All Session to see the w3wp.exe processes. See Figure 12-30 for an example.

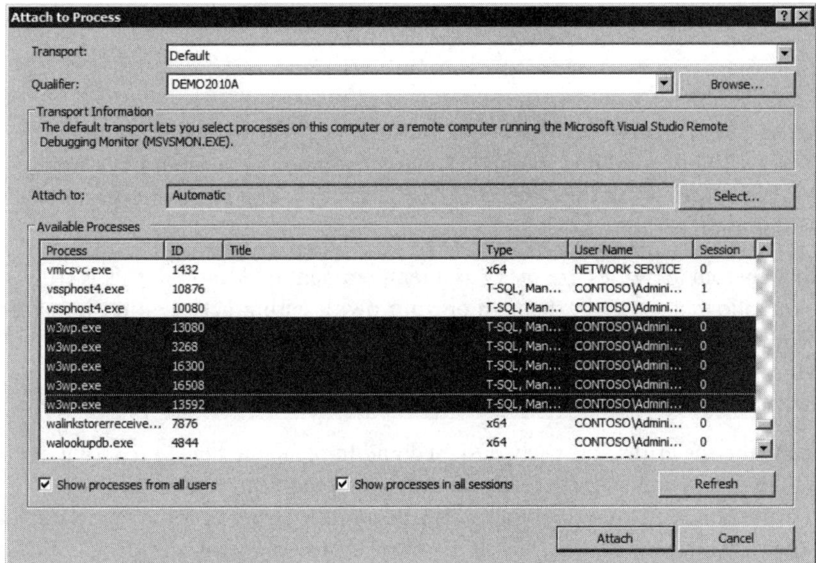

FIGURE 12-29

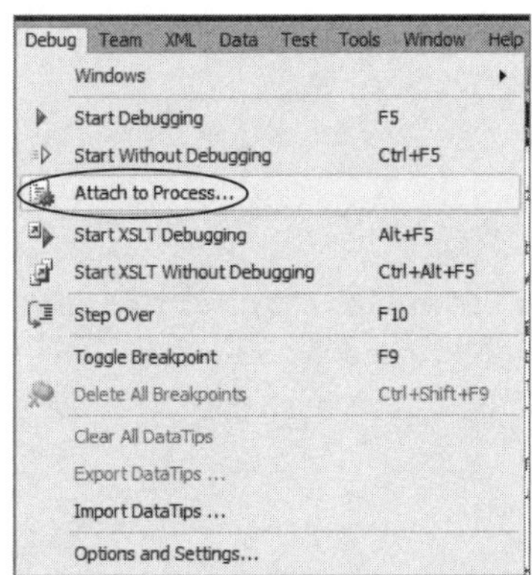

FIGURE 12-30

Lastly, launch a web browser and start a workflow. When the SharePoint workflow engine executes your custom activity and hits a breakpoint, you can debug as you would with any other server-side application.

Automatically Update web.config

As you'll recall, the walk-through made you edit the web.config file and add an entry to the `<AuthorizedTypes>` element. You can automate this with a feature receiver that updates web.config via a support API. Read about that API set on Microsoft's site at `http://msdn.microsoft.com/en-us/library/ms481167.aspx`.

SUMMARY

In this chapter, you learned about custom activities — what they are, why they are useful and important, and how to create them from nuts to bolts. You learned about a number of common problems that developers encounter when they create custom activities, and more important, you learned how to fix these common errors.

This chapter stressed that custom activities are picky and temperamental. Although this is true (as you no doubt know if you followed the walk-through on your own), with practice (and the expert advice from this book!) you'll be writing, deploying, and quickly debugging custom activities like there's no tomorrow. Most of the common errors are easy to identify and fix after you've been through the process a few times.

There's a good reason to make the effort. Properly designed and implemented custom activities cannot only close gaps (like the business days offset scenario presented here) but actually change the rules of the game. For instance, custom activities can access information everywhere in the farm, not just in the current site — a limitation of all the OOB SharePoint Designer workflow activities. They can update multiple rows in a list or lists conditionally. They can do advanced calculations and manipulations that greatly expand the scope of work that SharePoint Designer and end users can accomplish and are well worth the effort to learn.

13

Site Governance

WHAT'S IN THIS CHAPTER?

- More SharePoint Designer Custom Activities
- Creating and Installing Timer Jobs

This chapter describes how to implement a site governance solution (sometimes called a site life cycle management solution). It begins by defining governance (an important subject in SharePoint) and then explains the "site" part of "site governance." In short, it describes how to create an automated process that enables end users to request and automatically create sites with a defined purpose and lifetime. As you'll see in the chapter, this goes far beyond SharePoint's "self service" features.

This highly technical chapter builds upon the previous chapter's introduction to custom activities. You build a new, more complex custom activity to support site governance.

Site governance provides value to end users and IT management alike. End users request new sites by way of an online form. SharePoint Designer workflow can use the custom activity to create a new site. First, however, it uses an interesting security trick to decide whether the user should be granted the site automatically or if an IT administrator must first approve the request.

Lastly, the solution introduces a new platform feature: the timer job. The timer job ensures that sites are properly disposed of over time and takes responsibility for implementing reminders.

The problem is now defined in greater detail.

WHAT IS SITE GOVERNANCE?

Before discussing the "site" in site governance, consider governance, which in the SharePoint world, describes the rules, policies, and procedures that your organization puts in place to ensure that employees use SharePoint correctly and according to plan. As you probably know, SharePoint is a Swiss-Army-Knife kind of platform. Governance plans guide users and the organization at large to ensure that the right tool is used at the right time for the right job. SharePoint governance covers a lot of territory, ranging from branding to security and site ownership to backup and restore policies. Sites are just one of those items. It's easy to mistake governance as a bunch of rules with the unintentional (or intentional) purpose to stand in your way to getting your work done. A poor governance plan does just that. A good governance plan, on the other hand, is an indispensable tool.

Governance plans tend to be rules-oriented, and humans are prone to finding reasons to avoid following them even when they agree with the rules. Sometimes, people view governance policies as a hindrance to getting "actual" work done. Sometimes, they don't know much about the governance plan at all. Sometimes, they derive only indirect benefit; a particular governance rule or policy exists to benefit the "greater good," and it's hard to follow that kind of rule when faced with the reality of hard deadlines and the like. As a result, a gap normally exists between the on-paper version of the governance plan and the real living, breathing SharePoint environment it supposedly supports. The site governance solution tries to narrow this gap by simultaneously forcing the user to follow the rules while paradoxically making it easier to do so through automation.

Many aspects of a governance plan can and should be automated. One such aspect is when and how temporary ad hoc sites should be created, archived, and eventually deleted. This need arises in the common scenario around project sites. A company's many employees are always starting, executing, finishing, and occasionally abandoning projects. SharePoint provides excellent support for many, many different kinds of projects. As a result, educated project managers and other interested parties clamber IT for project sites. By automating the process, your company can both ensure that the governance plan is followed and that employees can quickly and reliably create their project sites with a predictable, easily understood process.

The site governance solution automates the process by which end users request new sites while enforcing the governance plan.

PROBLEM CLASS

The site governance solution solves a problem in the "governance enforcement" problem class. As you see in the chapter's closing sections, governance automation solutions cover a wide array of ordinary and routine scenarios. When you begin automating one part of your SharePoint governance plan, you'll want to automate more.

The site governance solution also finds uses further afield. As you see in the requirements section, this solution serves as a kind of night club bouncer. Anyone is allowed to walk up and ask to enter, but the bouncer may decide you're not ready yet. SharePoint can provide this gatekeeper role to other valuable resources, not just SharePoint sites. For instance, if you replace "sites" with "motorcycle," you can imagine that SharePoint would support rules that ensure that no untrained wannabe cyclist gains access to a motorcycle until properly trained. We call this the privileged-user scenario. Some people have earned the privilege while others have not. You need to control access.

This solution lends itself to a number of business scenarios and after you have this one in your back pocket, you'll be ready to tackle additional governance problems for the betterment of your SharePoint environment.

TECHNICAL PATTERNS

While solving the interview scheduling problem, you're going to implement the following technical patterns:

- **Simple approval:** One-level approval process that ensures that only properly trained and vetted end users are allowed to create and designate themselves as site owners.
- **Run-time security check:** This pattern establishes best practices for defining who is allowed to automatically create a site versus those that require IT's specific approval.
- **Custom activities:** You create a new custom activity for this solution, following the same development pattern you learned about in the previous chapter.
- **Timer jobs:** You learn how to create a SharePoint timer job, install it, and configure it.

As always, you will use more than a handful of technical patterns described here.

BUSINESS PATTERNS

While solving the time off management problem, you need to implement the following business patterns:

- **Reminders:** As you'll read shortly, one of the key rules in site governance is that "nothing is forever." The kinds of sites that fall under the auspices of site governance are, by definition, time-limited and should be archived and removed when they hit their expiration date. Of course, you don't want to cause any calamity by accidentally deleting an active site, so the reminders pattern ensures that this doesn't happen by accident or through laziness.
- **Resource Request and Approval:** Just like a mobile projector or conference room, a SharePoint site is a resource that comes with responsibility and a cost. Admittedly, the "cost" of a SharePoint site may be miniscule in day-to-day operations (a little disk space and processing power in a SharePoint farm). However, a long-term cost (consider upgrade-time) and unconstrained environments can be messy. Follow this pattern to ensure that the right people create sites quickly and easily while the "wrong" people can't or must provide additional justification.

BUSINESS PROBLEM DESCRIPTION

The following sections describe the business requirements, lists the actors and actions they take, and explain some of the special challenges that this problem and the requirements present to you as a SharePoint workflow developer.

Requirements Discussion

Unlike most of the problems in this book, and indeed, in the real world, this is a more technical kind of requirements discussion than, say, Human Resource on-boarding. This isn't to say that you should book a conference room deep in the bowels of the IT department and exclude everyone else. Just keep in mind that end users may come to view automated governance solutions as a hindrance. You need to walk a fine line with enforcement on the one side and mayhem on the other. End users tend to push for fewer rules, whereas some folks in the IT department push in the opposite direction, putting together a rules list that would be the envy of Hammurabi himself (if he were around, that is). Walk the middle way, and you can craft a solution that may not perfectly satisfy all your constituents but can help your company's success with SharePoint.

IS "MAYHEM" TOO STRONG A WORD?

Is it possible for mayhem to break out in a SharePoint environment? Absolutely! The author has worked with clients who had "hundreds" of site collections — "most" of which were no longer needed or useful, or ever used. "Hundreds" and "most" are in quotes because no one really knew how many were used, but IT was sure that few were actively used. Imagine this confused and incoherent environment. How do you implement an effective backup/restore strategy? Disaster recovery? What about upgrading to SharePoint 2010 and the next big version of SharePoint? So no, "mayhem" is not too strong a word.

Now that the social scene is set, you can consider the details.

The vision that drives site governance requirements is stated simply: "Allow the right users to create easily managed SharePoint sites quickly and easily." Now unpack that statement.

What is the "right" user? These are users who have been trained and know enough about SharePoint that IT can trust them do things correctly. These "right" users have normally been trained (by IT or externally). They understand those basic SharePoint features (such as basic page editing, managing lists and libraries, and how to add and remove user access to their site) needed to use their site properly.

What is "easily manage?" In this case, you want to create a system whereby the IT department can manage all these ad hoc sites. You don't want to fall into the "mayhem" trap. How to avoid it? These sites need to be tagged with metadata much like you tag lists and libraries with content types. With metadata in hand, your IT department can use dashboards to keep track of site activity, backup, and restore; figure out when sites are abandoned; and finally, decide when it's safe to archive and eventually delete them. (As you probably know, SharePoint sites don't provide a mechanism for collecting metadata at the site level; you'll learn about a site metadata solution shortly.)

What is "quickly and easily?" Although this is fairly self-evident; explore it a bit. Some people consider that out-of-the-box SharePoint user interface for creating sites is "quick and easy." See Figure 13-1 for an example. Most people, however, view that as quick and easy for IT, but confusing for end users. Besides that, you have relatively little ability to customize SharePoint's default behavior in this area. Therefore, "quickly and easily" in this case means that you need to make a more suitable site creation method available to your end users.

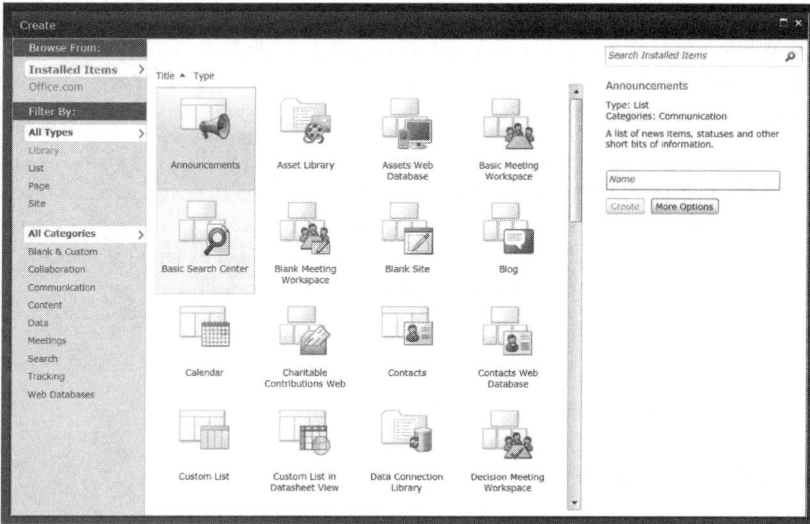

FIGURE 13-1

Quickly and easily doesn't just mean that it's fast. A quick-and-easy site creation solution just means that lots and lots of sites get created. That's no good to anyone if those sites aren't well suited to the business need at hand. To reduce the risk that end users select inappropriate sites, you want to offer them a menu of templates, much like those that SharePoint provides out-of-the-box. However, you create those templates yourself. Beyond that, you need to capture important information from the end user so that the dashboard feeder pattern can populate IT's dashboard and meet its requirements.

You can summarize this discussion as follows:

- There must be a way to identify a properly trained end user separately from others.
- Validated end users create a site using a simple, clean interface that helps ensure end users create appropriate sites.
- IT must generate reports that show all sites — abandoned sites, sites ready for archive, and other metrics.

With these requirements in hand, now formally identify actors and actions.

Actors

The following actors play a role in the site governance solution:

- **End users:** Use the solution to create new sites, obviously enough. End users also receive and respond to email notifications that their site is due for deletion. End users request a new site by means of a simple data entry screen.
- **IT:** Although to a certain extent, the whole point of this solution is to enable IT some much deserved down time so that it can play Hearts in the back office, it does play an important

role. IT must maintain a list of authorized end users who are allowed to automatically create new sites. When other end users request sites, IT reviews and approves (or denies) these requests. In addition, IT must monitor sites and make decisions about early archival (in the case of abandoned sites).

- **SharePoint:** Plays a bigger role than most in this solution. It provides the core workflow solution for approvals but is also responsible for email notifications over the long term. These kind of sites may be useful for a short-term project (4 to 6 weeks) but also much longer, pushing a year or maybe even longer. Of course, if the site needs to be around a lot longer than that, it may make sense to add it to the official taxonomy.

Actions

The actions that these actors take are now described in greater detail.

Information Technology Department

The IT department needs to take the following actions in this solution:

- Set and enforce standards for site ownership.
- Intervene when necessary, but try to keep hands off and let the system work as designed.
- Archive and purge abandoned sites.

The information technology department shepherds the entire process, and "shepherd" is probably an apt term. End users are not sheep. However, they do need help, starting with appropriate training. Training, and possibly other criteria, enters into whether IT allows them to create a site in the first place. This means that IT must maintain a list of authorized users who have met those criteria.

Occasionally, IT may need to intervene. For instance, end users may create a site and configure it to their needs but then leave the company. In this case, IT should assign new site owners so that it doesn't take over maintenance responsibilities. In such cases, the system should aid the IT department by capturing metadata about the site when it's first created. That way, when IT becomes involved, it knows such things as its intended purpose and deletion date and other potentially valuable information.

Finally, IT owns the environment and that includes when to shut down sites. End users may abandon a site, but more likely (or so you hope) the reason for the site naturally concludes. For instance, a 6-month project actually wraps up in 6 months. Before the final expiration date, end users should save any data they need, and the system should delete the site. Note: There's an important discussion at the conclusion to the chapter on what to do at end-of-life scenarios for the site.

End Users

End users execute two actions: Request a new site and then use it for its intended purpose.

When requesting a new site, end users should provide some basic information about the site's purpose, such as "ERP Enhancements" and provide an expected closure date. Keeping in mind that dozens, hundreds or in some real-world cases, thousands of SharePoint sites may be created, it's important to provide accurate information here. Later, when someone has to do some analysis of this site, a proper set of site metadata will go a long way toward making maintenance easier and more productive.

End users obviously use the site to conduct the business of the project or otherwise support their effort. Of course, to use it effectively, they must be trained. This kind of site management training feeds into the overall solution. IT won't create a site for untrained end users (or allow the system to do it automatically) if they haven't been trained first. At least, IT *shouldn't* allow them to create a site.

There's another reason why end users need to use the site. If they don't, it will be marked as an abandoned site. IT doesn't want abandoned sites sitting around, taking up space and resources or interfering with future migrations and upgrades. Using a site ensures that it stays on IT's radar, safe from abandonment actions.

Lastly, end users need to update their site's metadata. When they create a site, they provide that basic metadata (purpose and anticipated expiration date). If this information changes over the course or the project, they need to update the site to reflect it.

SharePoint

SharePoint does a lot of heavy lifting in this solution, and you'll do some interesting solutioning in this chapter. More on that soon. In the meantime, focus on the actions that SharePoint takes at one point or another in this solution.

First, SharePoint's SharePoint Designer workflow can create the sites. It may do this automatically in some cases. In other cases, it waits for IT to approve or deny the request. In both instances, SharePoint audits the requests and results.

When sites are in place, SharePoint provides a dashboard style interface so that IT can track what's going on.

SharePoint takes proactive steps, more so than most other solutions. It looks for abandoned sites and reports these to IT by means of the dashboard.

Lastly, SharePoint notifies end users of incipient site deletion events. The manner in which end users respond to these messages dictate whether SharePoint deletes a site, holds off, or merely informs IT.

Challenges

Although site governance seems like a straight-forward request/approve/process kind of solution, it's actually technically challenging. This chapter walks you through how to handle some of the challenges such as deleting a site at the end of its life. In other case, it would simply take too long and require too much detail to cover here. The concluding sections in the book give you some points, however.

One such challenging area is the answer to the question, "How do I know if a site is abandoned?" This question may not be easy to answer in every case. A dashboard or notification process that tries to answer it may come up with false positives (claim a site is abandoned even though it isn't) or the opposite — fail to identify an abandoned site.

Requirements Summary

In summary, the requirements for this business solution follow:

- Via self-service functionality, end users create sites when they need them.
- IT implements policies that enforce the site governance rules of your company.
- SharePoint resources are put to best use and your company derives maximum benefit from them.

HIGH LEVEL SOLUTION

To implement this solution, use all the bread-and-butter techniques described throughout the book (content types, custom lists, and dashboards implemented as custom list views rendered on web part pages). You can expand upon the previous chapter's write-up on custom activities. Finally, you create a SharePoint timer job to execute this solution's requirements.

Solution Overview

To build out this solution, you need to start with the obvious first step: Create a data entry function so that end users can request their site. Of course, as soon as you think about this data entry screen, you realize a few things. First, you don't want to approve every person's request for a site. At the same time, you don't want people at IT to sit around all day approving new site requests — they have much better things to do with their time. Instead, you want to automatically approve the request. You can manage this by way of a custom list. It can hold a list of approved site owners. The approval workflow can consult this list. If the requestor has access to the list, the request is approved automatically.

When end users fill out the online form, they need to specify a purpose for the site. You may want them to request a specific site template, or you may provide a menu of choices. Either way, you need to create some site templates in the first place.

With data entry out of the way, it's time to consider the workflow itself. For this solution, it's fairly light. It reviews the information provided by the end user, consults the auto-approve list, and eventually creates a new site. Of course, there isn't any "create site" SharePoint Designer activity. Therefore, you need to create one. You use the same approach as explained in great detail in the previous chapter. This custom activity will go ahead and create the SharePoint site for you. In addition, it populates that new site with metadata. Unlike lists and libraries, SharePoint sites don't actually have any obvious mechanism for storing metadata. (See the Note for some of these options.) You have several good options, and in this case, you can use the site request list as a master catalog of sites. This can help you feed content to the all-important dashboards for which IT will be ever so grateful.

METADATA FOR SITES

Unlike documents and custom lists, SharePoint sites don't provide any out-of-the-box method for end users to enter site metadata. You can't assign a content type to a site and then use a nice edit function to perform CRUD activities against it. You do have at least two good options above and beyond the master catalog approach described by this chapter. First, at a programming/object model level, sites have a Property Bag property. This is just a collection of name/value pairs. You can access a site's PropertyBag via code and the object model. Read more about it at `http://msdn.microsoft.com/en-us/library/ff649798.aspx`. A good second option is to create a custom list at the site level designed to contain just one row of information. Associate this list with a content type and then populate as needed. The advantage to this approach is that you don't need to write any custom code, and the custom list is visible to SharePoint search, making it easy to search for a site in a complex environment via keywords.

Finally remember that these sites have a shelf life. You don't want them sitting around taking up resources. That goes for abandoned sites as well. The best way to determine these facts is to inspect both the site's metadata and analyze site-specific activity. As sites approach their expiration date, or as you can safely identify an abandoned site, the system should email the site owner of record. Three results are possible: The site owner responds, asking to extend the site's life; the site owner responds and agrees that the site can be deleted; or the site owner fails to respond altogether. The best way to do this kind of automated site auditing is via a SharePoint timer job. SharePoint timer jobs run on a schedule (ever few minutes, hours, days, weeks, and so on) and perform their logic. In this case, a timer job searches for all the sites that fall within its search parameters and takes the appropriate action.

In summary, you can create the following components for this solution:

- Data entry function
- Straight-forward SharePoint Designer workflow with a custom activity
- Timer job to inspect sites for scheduled expiration and abandonment

It's a lot to chew on; you won't take big bytes at once with this solution, but rather just start nybbling.

Swim Lane Diagrams

The actors and actions underlying this solution work together as per the swim lane diagram shown in Figure 13-2.

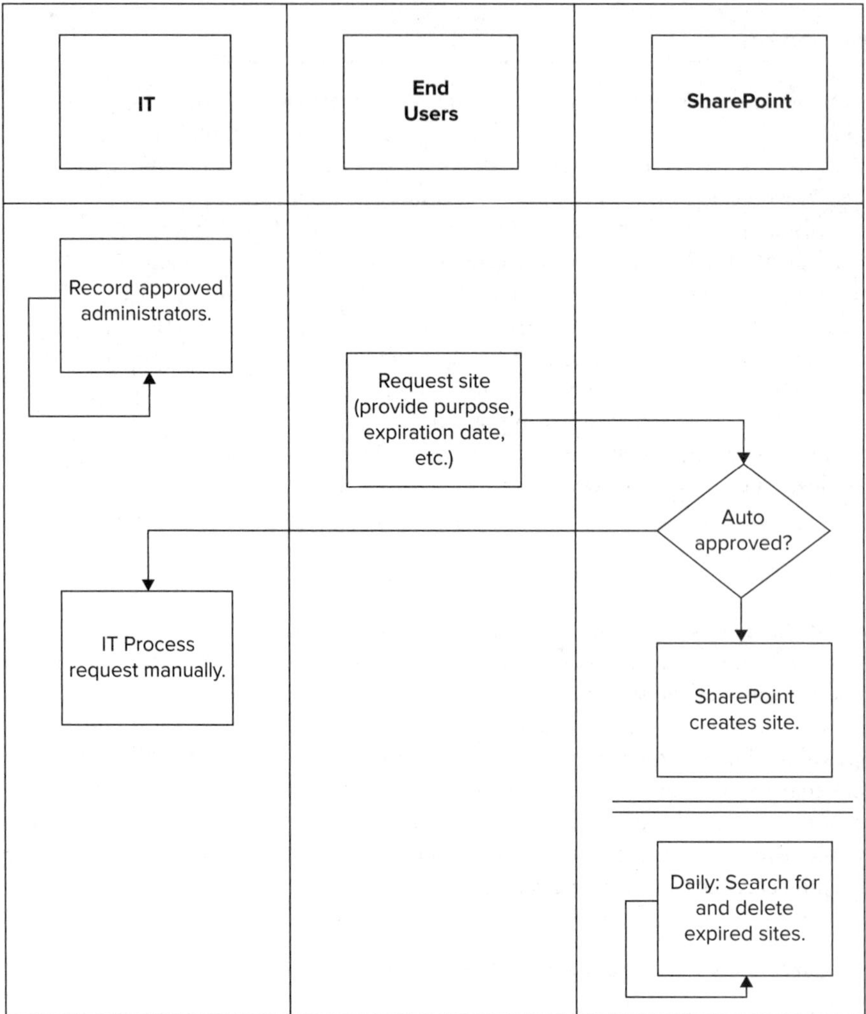

FIGURE 13-2

Periodically, the IT department runs classes or provides one-on-one training that teaches end users how to properly administer a SharePoint site in accordance with the rules of the organization. IT then records these approved users in a SharePoint list.

Separately, end users request sites. They document the purpose, the expiration date, and other important data about the site they want.

SharePoint determines whether the user is allowed to do this (i.e., whether IT recorded the user as being approved). If the user is allowed, SharePoint creates the site. Otherwise, SharePoint routes the request to IT for manual processing.

Finally, SharePoint periodically checks these sites to determine whether they have passed their expiration date. At that time, SharePoint deletes the site.

TECHNICAL IMPLEMENTATION OVERVIEW

The technical solution that meets this chapter's requirements relies upon a new SharePoint designer activity. You already learned about custom activities in Chapter 12, "Custom Activities." This more complex activity takes as input the ID of a list item and then uses that list item to create a new SharePoint site.

To send email reminders and to actually purge sites, you create a timer job. SharePoint runs timer jobs as per their individual schedule. This timer job inspects all the sites created and managed by this process to determine whether they have met their expiration date. If they have, it deletes them.

As per the requirements, the solution should create sites for end users automatically when they request them. However, it should not create the site if the user hasn't been properly trained on the responsibilities for site management. You can meet this requirement by creating and securing a SharePoint custom list. If the requestor has access to the list, the system can automatically create the site. Otherwise, the request is added to a queue (a SharePoint task list) for IT to manage manually.

Like everywhere else, this solution follows the same overall pattern as all the rest of the solutions in the book. Define and create the content types necessary to capture and track information from a data entry perspective and to meet process and dashboarding needs.

Now begin.

Content Types

As described in the previous section, you need a content type that represents the actual end user request. The goal is to create a data entry screen similar to Figure 13-3.

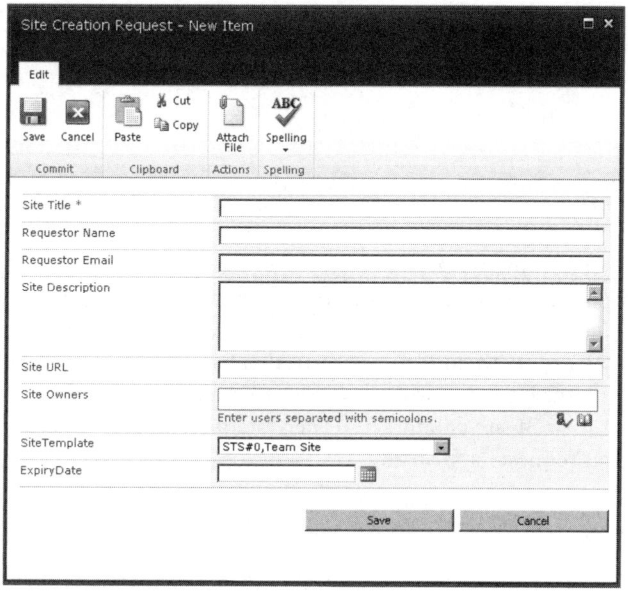

Site Creation Request - New Item

Edit

Save Cancel Paste Cut Copy Attach File Spelling

Commit Clipboard Actions Spelling

Site Title *

Requestor Name

Requestor Email

Site Description

Site URL

Site Owners

Enter users separated with semicolons.

SiteTemplate STS#0,Team Site

ExpiryDate

Save Cancel

FIGURE 13-3

Figure 13-3 shows the following columns of information:

- **Site Title:** A text field that becomes the actual title of the newly created SharePoint site. This title appears in the web browser title bar, as shown in Figure 13-4.
- **Requestor Name:** The full name of the person requesting the site
- **Requestor Email:** The email address of the end user requesting the site
- **Site Description:** The description of the site in plain English (or your language of choice). When you train end users on how to use this form, you should emphasize how important it is for them to provide a full and complete description. This helps IT down the road for maintenance purposes.
- **Site URL:** This would be the URL of the requested site. It may not be available, and you can use jQuery to provide immediate feedback on site URL availability. See Chapter 11, "Enhancing the User Interface," for more information on jQuery.
- **Site Owners:** One or more end users who take ownership of the site
- **Site Template:** Every SharePoint site is based off a *template*. A template is a predefined set of lists, libraries, features, and other SharePoint artifacts that serve as the initial set of data and functionality for your site. You can constrain your users here by way of a drop-down list so that they don't accidentally create a new records center, for example.
- **Expiry Date:** This key date determines when and whether the site will be archived. Your custom timer job uses this expiry date to determine whether it should delete the site.

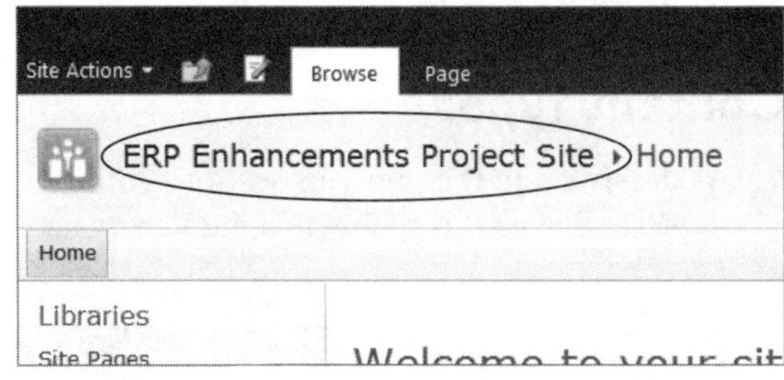

FIGURE 13-4

Custom Lists

Users make requests by adding an entry to a custom list. You can wire the request/approval workflow to this list.

A second, less obvious list enables you to determine whether a user's new site request is automatically approved or whether IT needs to review it first. You populate this list with just one row of information. You break inheritance on that one row and secure it individually. If users are allowed to automatically create sites, IT grants them read access to this list. Otherwise, they won't have read access. At runtime, SharePoint Designer workflow tries to read from that row. If it succeeds, the users are considered authorized site creators and the system creates the sites automatically. Otherwise, it notifies IT and requests approval.

> **ON CREATING A MASTER SECURITY LIST**
>
> You may find that you want to provide a more finely tuned auto-approve function. For instance, the system should automatically approve all of Aidan's requests. On the other hand, the system should auto-approve only Paul's requests for basic sites because he has not completed necessary training for the advanced features of other sites. You can do this, but it's a bit of work. To do so, follow the same technical pattern you learned about in Chapter 3, "HR On-Boarding," and specifically, delegation. To meet this kind of requirement, you need a dual key lookup, but SharePoint doesn't enable that kind of lookup. The delegation pattern from Chapter 3 enables you to meet this need, should it arise.

Workflow

Just one SharePoint Designer workflow lies at the heart of this solution.

When users add a new list item to the Site Creation Request list (see Figure 13-4 for a reminder), SharePoint Designer workflow starts automatically. By way of the security list, workflow determines whether the site should be created automatically or whether manual intervention is required by IT. Assuming the request is approved, SharePoint Designer workflow needs to create the actual site and update some status information for dashboarding purposes. As you no doubt know, SharePoint Designer doesn't provide a Site Provisioning custom activity. To accomplish this, you need a custom activity.

Custom Activity

SharePoint Designer can't create a site directly. As you learned in Chapter 12, however, you can create a custom activity to do this for you. This chapter's custom activity operates a little differently from the previous custom due date activity.

Aside from the obvious (it creates a site instead of calculating a business-days-aware due date), it also works with parameters a little differently. Instead of passing in individual parameters, such as site name and template and all the other eight or so key parameters, it passes in the list item itself. When the custom activity executes at runtime, it has access to the entire list item and all its site columns. Happily, SharePoint Designer workflow provides a nice interface to which your end users will already be accustomed, as you can see in Figure 13-5.

FIGURE 13-5

The action will be added to the step, as shown in Figure 13-5, and you can click the List Item link to specify the current item.

SharePoint Timer Job

SharePoint ships with a number of built-in timer jobs (dozens, actually). These timer jobs run in the background on a scheduled basis. SharePoint administrators manage timer jobs via SharePoint Central Administration. Figure 13-6 and Figure 13-7 show the Central Administration and a few timer job listings.

FIGURE 13-6

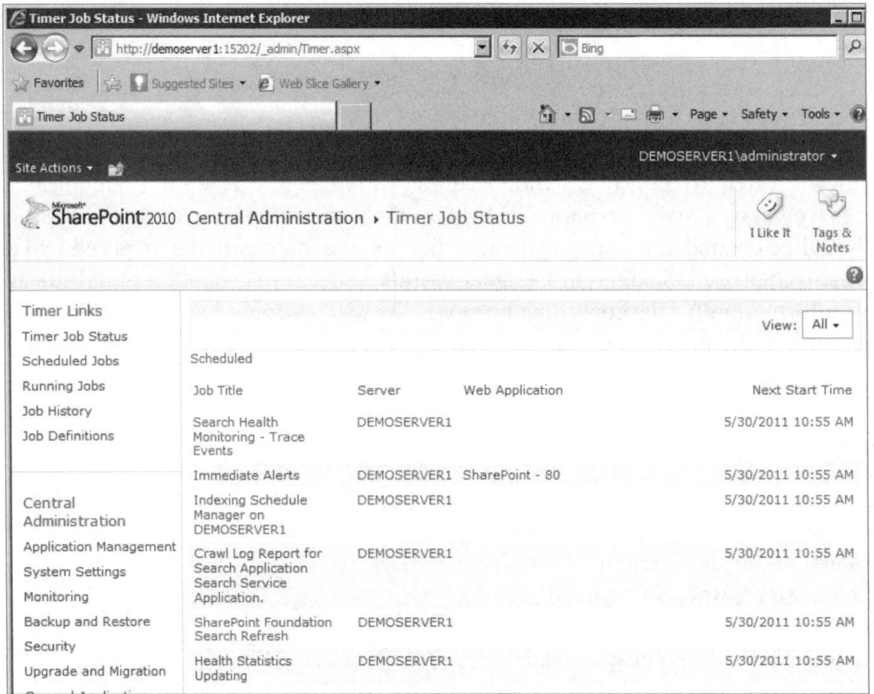

FIGURE 13-7

Microsoft provides a mechanism that enables you to create your own timer jobs. The overall pattern is similar to what you already know for custom activities; although, it's a little easier because you don't need to make manual changes to web.config files. By writing some C# code (or other supported .NET languages, such as VB.NET) and making sure you follow some rules, you can create a custom DLL that deploys to SharePoint and is managed administratively through the same interface as SharePoint's default timer jobs, as shown in Figure 13-8.

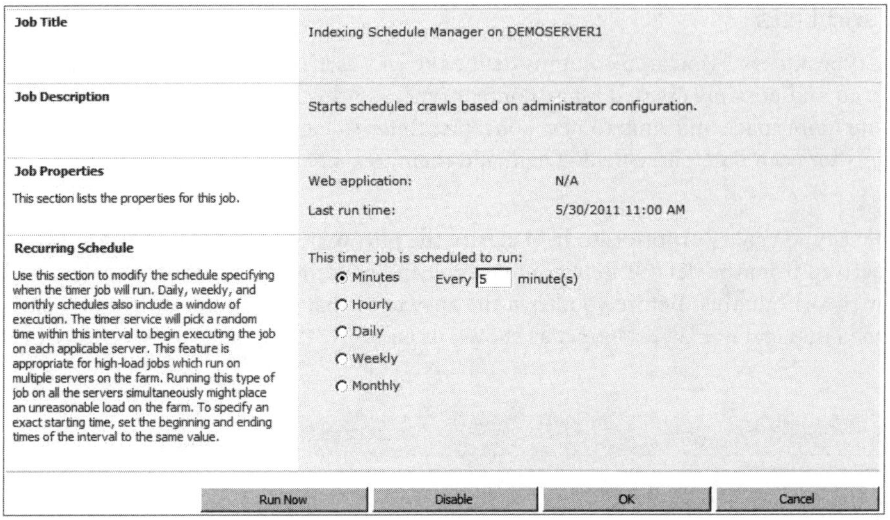

Job Title	Indexing Schedule Manager on DEMOSERVER1
Job Description	Starts scheduled crawls based on administrator configuration.
Job Properties This section lists the properties for this job.	Web application: N/A Last run time: 5/30/2011 11:00 AM
Recurring Schedule Use this section to modify the schedule specifying when the timer job will run. Daily, weekly, and monthly schedules also include a window of execution. The timer service will pick a random time within this interval to begin executing the job on each applicable server. This feature is appropriate for high-load jobs which run on multiple servers on the farm. Running this type of job on all the servers simultaneously might place an unreasonable load on the farm. To specify an exact starting time, set the beginning and ending times of the interval to the same value.	This timer job is scheduled to run: Minutes Every 5 minute(s) Hourly Daily Weekly Monthly

Run Now | Disable | OK | Cancel

FIGURE 13-8

Dashboard

As with every solution, you need to provide a dashboard. The objective of this dashboard is two-fold:

- **Show those requests that require manual approval and intervention by IT:** This represents new site requests by users who are not allowed to automatically create sites.
- **Show up-coming scheduled site deletions:** This dashboard view is visible to IT, but just as important, end users need to see what the system intends to do with their site. If they don't want SharePoint to delete their site, they need to take action to prevent it.

The approach taken to designing this solution makes for a relatively easy dashboard process. Because all site requests and related site metadata reside in one custom list, it's just a matter of creating appropriate views.

DETAILED TECHNICAL IMPLEMENTATION

This solution's technical implementation is fairly complex. It begins with a setup step. Create content types and custom lists. Then, you create a custom activity that then enables you to create the SharePoint Designer workflow. Then, you create the timer job that automates email reminders and site deletion. Lastly, you close it out with a dashboard.

Setup

This solution requires two content types and two custom lists.

Content Types and Lists

The first content type and its associated columns define the end user's request to create a new site. By now, you've read and possibly created many content types, so this section skimps a bit so that the chapter can devote more space and time to new concepts. Refer to Figure 13-3 as a guide, and go create site columns for each data entry field. Then, add them to a site content type named `Site Request`.

The second content type's sole purpose is to help clarify the purpose of a SharePoint list to IT. This content type is derived from the default Item content type and contains no site custom columns. You may wonder why this is valuable. Before you learn the answer to that question, create a new site content type named `SLM Authorized Users`, as shown in Figure 13-9.

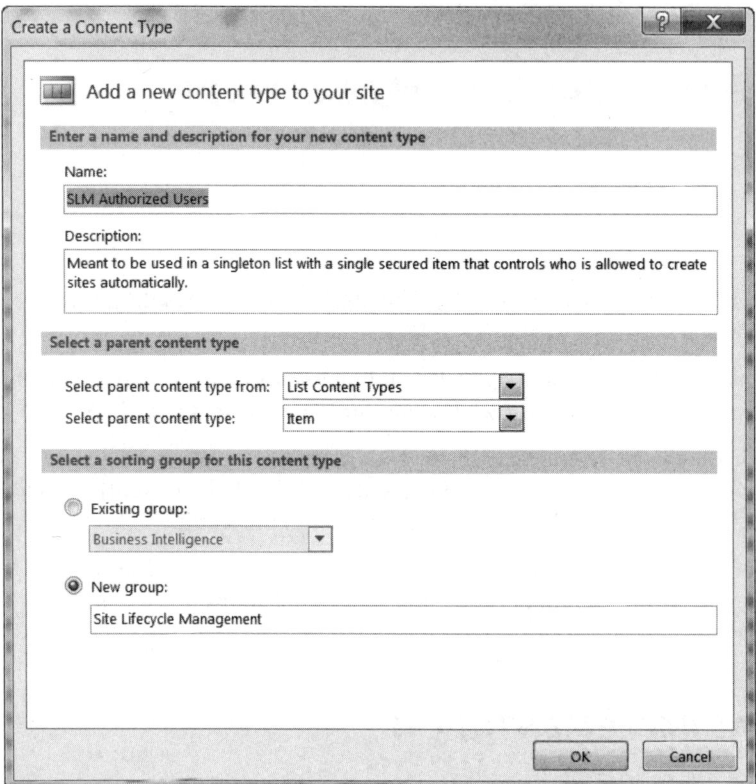

FIGURE 13-9

Next, create a custom list backed by this content type. Add the content type to the list's set of managed content types and remove the default Item. This list now contains just that content type. When IT goes to manage this list, it's more clear what it's used for.

Lastly, this list contains just one item (it's a singleton list) and that one item will be secured. Recall that SharePoint security leverages an inheritance mechanism. Securable objects, such as list items, typically inherit security from their parent container. List *items* are contained by lists. *Lists* are contained by sites. *Sites* are contained by site collections. *Site collections* are contained within web applications. Finally, *web applications* are contained within farms, which are the highest level container.

Follow these steps to configure item level security. First, create one item in the list with a title `Site Lifecycle Management`. Then, select the row, which causes the Ribbon to change context. This lights up the Item Permissions button, as shown in Figure 13-10.

SharePoint shows you a list of the SharePoint groups, AD groups, and individual users who have been granted access to the item. It also shows the type of access they've been granted (such as contribute, View Only, and such). Configure security on this specific item by clicking the Stop Inheriting Permissions button in the Ribbon. Accept SharePoint's warning. At this point, you would typically remove all the permissions for the default users and then add in the individual users, SharePoint groups, and Active Directory groups that are allowed to create sites automatically.

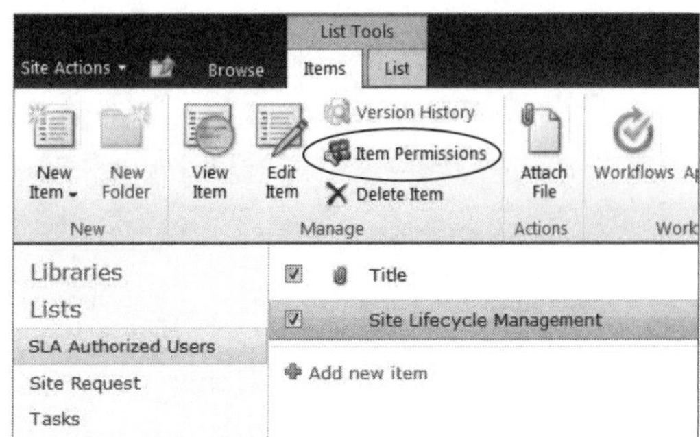

FIGURE 13-10

> **ITEM LEVEL SECURITY FEELS SO RIGHT**
>
> It's almost never a good idea to enable item level security in SharePoint. There are just a few good times to do it (like now) and a lot of very bad places to do it that "feel so right" but which are terribly wrong. Item level security may seem like a panacea, but it can cause an administrative nightmare and cause difficult-to-track performance problems because SharePoint needs to take individual permissions into account everywhere and every which way they are used. Avoid it most of the time.

At this point, you have finished the setup steps required to build this solution.

Custom Activity

Follow the steps outlined in Chapter 12, "Custom Activities," to create a new custom activity. Like the due date calculation activity from Chapter 12, this activity is composed of two major components: An `actions` file and some C# code that follows SharePoint's rules for SharePoint Designer custom activities.

Actions File

Consider the following `actions` file:

```
<WorkflowInfo>
  <Actions Sequential="then" Parallel="and">
    <Action Name="Site Provisioning"
     ClassName="SiteCreationActivity.Activity1"
```

```
        Assembly="SiteCreationActivity, Version=1.0.0.0, Culture=neutral,
        PublicKeyToken=e320b08afc1741ae"
        AppliesTo="all"
        Category="Extras">
         <RuleDesigner Sentence="Provision Site Based on Values Given in %1">
         <FieldBind Field="ListId,ListItem" Text="List Item"
         DesignerType="ChooseListItem" Id="1"/>
         </RuleDesigner>
         <Parameters>
           <Parameter Name="__Context" Type=
           "Microsoft.SharePoint.WorkflowActions.WorkflowContext" Direction="In"/>
           <Parameter Name="ListId" Type="System.String, mscorlib" Directions="In"/>
           <Parameter Name="ListItem" Type="System.Int32, mscorlib" Directions="In"/>
         </Parameters>
      </Action>
    </Actions>
  </WorkflowInfo>
```

As compared to Chapter 11, there are a couple of new elements to review.

The `<FieldBind>` element lists a new type of `<Field>` node with the value `"ListId, ListItem"`. It's paired with a `<DesignerType>` node whose value is `"ChooseListItem"`. These operate together so that when the SharePoint Designer workflow user uses this custom activity, SharePoint Designer provides the user with its standard List choose dialog box. Refer to Figure 13-5 for a reminder.

You should understand one more important difference. In this `.actions` file, the `<Parameters>` don't match `<FieldBind>` elements one for one. As you can see, there is just one `<FieldBind>` element, whereas there are three `<Parameter>` elements. This is for two reasons: 1) The one `<FieldBind>` element actually returns two different values to your custom activity at runtime: the Guid of the SharePoint list and the Guid of the individual list item. Second, a parameter is named `"__Context"` (that's two underscore characters in front of the word `Context`). Pass the `__Context` parameter to your custom activity so that you can inspect the overall set of data related to the workflow at runtime. This includes a pointer to the SharePoint site (the SPWeb in object model terms). The SharePoint site, combined with the ID of the list and the ID of the list item, gives your custom activity everything it needs to do its job.

Activity Code File

The site provisioning activity's code file follows the same pattern as Chapter 11's due date activity. It includes `DependencyProperties` that map to the parameters in your `.actions` file and contains an `Execute()` method.

Your `DependencyProperty` code must define a property for each of the three parameters:

- `__Context` (`WorkflowContext` variable to get current execution context)
- `ListId` (`List GUID`)
- `ListItem` (`ListItem Id`)

Here's the code:

```
[Category("__Context Category")]
[DesignerSerializationVisibility(DesignerSerializationVisibility.Visible)]
{
    {
    }
    {
    }


[Category("ListItem Category")]

[DesignerSerializationVisibility(DesignerSerializationVisibility.Visible)]
{
            return ((int)(base.GetValue(Activity1.ListItemProperty)));
    set
        base.SetValue(Activity1.ListItemProperty, value);
}
public static DependencyProperty ListIdProperty =
DependencyProperty.Register("ListId", typeof(string), typeof(Activity1));
[Description("ListId")]
[Browsable(true)]
public string ListId
    get
        return ((string)(base.GetValue(Activity1.ListIdProperty)));
    set
        base.SetValue(Activity1.ListIdProperty, value);
}
```

Execute Method

The execute method creates the actual SharePoint site in response to the user's approved request. It uses the `__Context` to get the SPWeb of the list item. It then uses the Guid of the list item and the list item's ID (these representing the Site Request custom list and individual site request within that list, respectively) to find the correct list item. It pulls the new site title, description, URL, and site template from the request and adds a new site to the site collection. Here is the code:

```
{
    SPList _list = _ctxWeb.Lists[new Guid(ListId)];

    {
        {
            string SiteDesc = _item["Site_x0020_Description"].ToString();
            string SiteTemplate = _item["SiteTemplate"].ToString()

            .Substring(0,_item["SiteTemplate"].ToString().IndexOf(','));
            SPWeb newWeb = _site.RootWeb.Site.AllWebs.Add(SiteURL,
            SiteTitle, SiteDesc, 0, SiteTemplate, true, false);
        }

}
```

If this weren't a custom activity, it would just look like code that you or your colleagues have probably written many times before.

Timer Job

Timer jobs are straightforward to create. Fire up Visual Studio and create a new empty SharePoint 2010 project. Add a class file and name it "SiteCleanUp.cs." As with a custom activity, you need to follow a few rules in your code.

First, your timer job's object inherits from the SharePoint object model class, `SPJobDefinition`. SPJobDefinition is part of the SharePoint.DLL and should already be included as a reference in your project.From here, you override the `Execute` method. SharePoint runs the `Execute()` method of every timer job as per the job's schedule (more on that in a minute).

As part of governance process, the sites that users created in the past need to be deleted/archived after the expiry date. The timer job runs once a day to verify the expiry date. If the expiry date occurs in the next 3 days, the timer job triggers the reminder email about site deletion. The end user (site owner) receives this email. If the end user doesn't want the site to be deleted, he simply updates the date to reflect the new expiration date. If the timer job finds a date and its expiry date is today's date, the timer job deletes the specific site.

BUSINESS DAYS INSTEAD OF CALENDAR DAYS

We've kept the code simple, so when you look at the `Execute()` method's code, you can see that it's checking and sending emails three calendar days in advance. This should be business days, not calendar days. You should use the same business day logic you implemented in the previous chapter here.

Here is the code:

```
using System;
using System.Collections.Generic;
using System.Linq;
using System.Text;

using Microsoft.SharePoint;
using Microsoft.SharePoint.Administration;
using Microsoft.SharePoint.Utilities;
using System.Web.Configuration;
using System.Web;

namespace SiteCleanUp
{
    class SiteCleanUp : SPJobDefinition
    {
        const string LIST_NAME = "Site Creation Request";

        public SiteCleanUp() : base()
```

```
        {

        }

        public SiteCleanUp(string jobName, SPWebApplication web) : base(jobName,
        web,null,SPJobLockType.ContentDatabase)
        {
            this.Title = "Site ClenUp";
        }

        public override void Execute(Guid targetInstanceId)
        {
            CleanSites(LIST_NAME);
        }

        private void CleanSites(string listName)
        {
            SPSecurity.RunWithElevatedPrivileges(delegate()
            {
                SPWebApplication webapp = this.Parent as SPWebApplication;

                SPSite _site = new SPSite(webapp.Sites[0].Url.ToString());
                SPWeb _web = _site.OpenWeb();

                SPList _list = _web.Lists[LIST_NAME];

                SPQuery _query = new SPQuery();
                _query.Query = "<Where><Eq><FieldRef Name='ExpiryDate'/><Value
                IncludeTimeValue='FALSE' Type='DateTime'>" + DateTime.Today
                .ToString("yyyy-MM-dd") + "</Value></Eq></Where>";

                SPListItemCollection _listItems = _list.GetItems(_query);

                if (_listItems.Count > 0)
                {
                    for (int i = 0; i < _listItems.Count; i++)
                    {
                        DeleteSite(_listItems[i]["Site URL"].ToString(), _site);
                    }
                }
            });
        }

        private void DeleteSite(string WebName,SPSite DelSite)
        {
            SPSecurity.RunWithElevatedPrivileges(delegate()
            {
                SPWeb DelWeb = DelSite.AllWebs[WebName];

                DelWeb.Delete();
                DelWeb.Update();
            });
        }
    }
}
```

Again, the code is just regular C# code, and there is nothing special about it, aside from the various rules you must follow to make it a timer job that SharePoint can manage.

Installing Timer Jobs

Unlike SharePoint 2010 web parts, you need to write some code that specifically install and activates your timer job. To do so, add a new C# code file to your project named `TimerJobInstaller.cs`. The code here inherits from `SPFeatureReceiver` as shown:

```
using System;
using System.Collections.Generic;
using System.Linq;
using System.Text;

using Microsoft.SharePoint;
using Microsoft.SharePoint.Administration;

namespace SiteCleanUp
{
    class TimerJobInstaller : SPFeatureReceiver
    {
        const string JOB_NAME = "Governance - Site Cleanup";

        public override void FeatureActivated(SPFeatureReceiverProperties
        properties)
        {
            SPSecurity.RunWithElevatedPrivileges(delegate(){
                SPSite site = properties.Feature.Parent as SPSite;

            foreach (SPJobDefinition jDef in site.WebApplication.JobDefinitions)
            {
                if (jDef.Name == JOB_NAME)
                    jDef.Delete();
            }

            SiteCleanUp CleanUpJob = new SiteCleanUp(JOB_NAME,site.WebApplication);

            SPDailySchedule schedule = new SPDailySchedule();
            schedule.BeginHour = 0;
            schedule.BeginMinute = 0;
            schedule.BeginSecond = 0;

            schedule.EndHour = 23;
            schedule.EndMinute = 59;
            schedule.EndSecond = 59;

            CleanUpJob.Schedule = schedule;
            CleanUpJob.Update();
            });
```

```
            }

            public override void FeatureDeactivating(SPFeatureReceiverProperties
            properties)
            {
                SPSite site = (SPSite)properties.Feature.Parent;

                foreach (SPJobDefinition jobdef in site.WebApplication.JobDefinitions)
                {
                    if (jobdef.Name == JOB_NAME)
                        jobdef.Delete();
                }
            }

            public override void FeatureUninstalling(SPFeatureReceiverProperties
            properties)
            {
                //throw new NotImplementedException();
            }

            public override void FeatureInstalled(SPFeatureReceiverProperties
            properties)
            {
                //throw new NotImplementedException();
            }
        }
    }
```

When the SharePoint project is deployed and its feature is activated, SharePoint executes the overridden `FeatureActivated()` method. The logic then instantiates a new instance of the timer job and then sets a schedule to run once a day at 11:59PM.

Workflows

With all of that out of the way, it's time to create the workflow. This chapter doesn't introduce anything new from a workflow perspective that you haven't seen before. Your workflow runs automatically when the user creates a new site request. Workflow uses the same technique described in Chapter 6, "HR Interview Scheduling," to determine whether the user is on the auto-approve list. It does this by trying to assign a workflow variable to the value of the ID of the SLM Authorized Users list. If the current user has security access to the list, the result is nonzero. Otherwise, the result is zero.

Based on that, it either assigns an approval task to IT or goes ahead and automatically creates the site. Use the task approval activity as described in Chapter 4, "Helpdesk Ticketing," to assign the approval task and inspect the result.

Use the new Site Provisioning activity (Figure 13-11) to create the actual SharePoint site. Select the current list item as input to the activity (Figure 13-12).

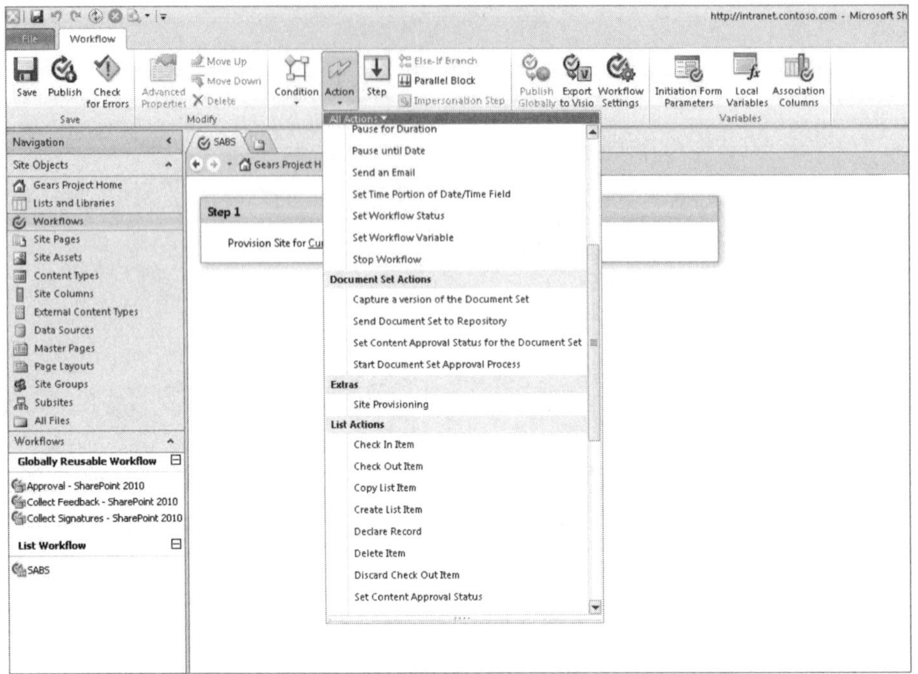

FIGURE 13-11

The action is added to the step, as shown in Figure 13-11. Click the List Item link to specify the current item.

Save and publish the workflow to the list, and test it out.

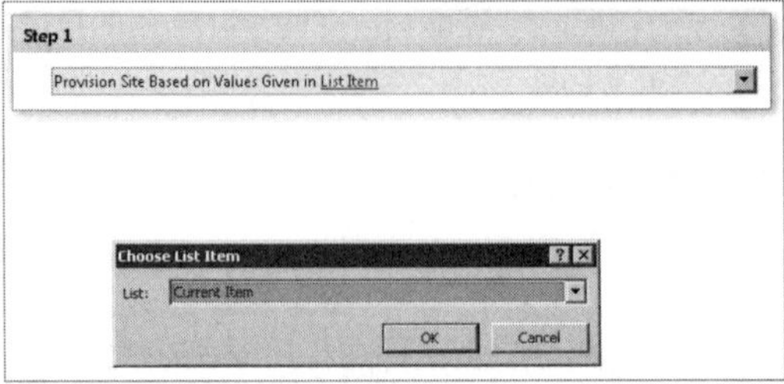

FIGURE 13-12

Create the Dashboard

As with the workflow, there isn't anything new to describe to create an appropriate dashboard. Follow the same pattern described in most of the book's prior chapters:

- Create several views on the site request list. At a minimum, create one view that shows any site scheduled to be deleted in the next 7 days. Create another view showing sites that have already expired. Create a third view that shows all sites grouped by requestor.
- Create several web part pages, one for each view.
- Create one additional web part page that has a content editor web part. Use this CEWP to provide a menu that links to the three different web part pages.

With these web part pages and their respective list views, you can provide your end user community and the IT department with the information they need to properly manage these sites.

Extending the Solution

As you can probably tell, the solution meets the bare minimum requirements but leaves open a lot of interesting possibilities that you should plan to exploit when you build this solution for the real world. They include the following:

- Auditing
- Identifying abandoned sites
- Archiving instead of deleting
- Improving security
- Creating parameter-driven timer jobs

Now dive into them one by one.

Auditing

Despite that end users are reminded and provided tools, such as dashboards, to ensure that their site isn't deleted without their knowledge and consent, it may happen anyway. In such cases, you need to provide them with a detailed explanation showing when SharePoint reminded them that their site was marked for cleanup. The timer job should create an entry in an audit custom list for this purpose, making a note each time it sends an email to the site owner.

Identifying Abandoned Sites

Because the timer job is waking up and inspecting sites for possible deletion, it may as well check to see if a site has also been abandoned. This can be a tricky because there's no easy "last used" kind of flag on a SharePoint site. You need to write some code that inspects the timestamps of documents in the site's libraries and lists. It can be done, and it's highly recommended. It is potentially a fair amount of work, however.

After you identify an abandoned site, you can seek verification from the site owner. If he responds one way or the other, you at least have a positive response to use as a basis for your next decision: Delete the site or keep it around. If the site owner fails to respond, you can probably treat the site as abandoned and delete it.

Archiving Versus Deleting

This chapter's timer job code deletes sites when they expire. In most cases, you need to perform some kind of backup. You have a couple of good options here. First, you could simply mark the site as "ready" for deletion. Then, leave it up to IT to manually delete the site. Of course, with this approach, you could end up with a big backlog of "ready to delete" sites that are never deleted because IT is too busy with other things. However, it does prevent the potentially nightmare scenario of SharePoint automatically deleting an active site.

The next and truly the best method is to archive the site first and then delete it. Archiving in this context means to take some kind of backup snapshot and save that to disk. If it turns out that the site were deleted in error, you can just restore it from disk with a minimum of fuss. This introduces a new set of issues and questions such as "How long does this archive file exist? Where is it stored? Do I provide a user interface so that end users can restore their own archived sites?"

The detailed walk-through glossed over a couple of important points (mainly to give space for a more full treatment of dashboards). The following sections list them and offer some guidance on how to solve them.

Security Considerations

This chapter uses SharePoint security to determine whether a site request is approved automatically. It doesn't address the security of the newly created site nor does it address the site request list. Both require treatment.

First, the newly created site should probably be secured by way of the usual visitors, contributors, and owners paradigm. To some extent, you could just leave that up to the new site owner, but why not prompt him when he first requests the site? That way, the initial security configuration will be set up, and it provides a more friendly interface.

Second, there's a potential flaw in the site request list. Suppose that HR wants to run a project named Director of A/P Replacement Search. Well, if the *current* Director of A/P sees that project site, it could be the cause of a major concern. You can solve this in a couple of ways. First, create an entirely new site for "secured HR project site requests." Then, secure that site so that only HR is allowed to see it. A more thorough solution, however, would be to create a new custom activity that secures the site request list item itself. This way, you get the best of both worlds — a single master list that is the authoritative location for all ad hoc sites but which is properly secured.

Parameter-Driven Timer Job

The solution as described in this chapter defines a timer job matched to a specific site and specific custom list. As such, it's inflexible in where it locates the information that drives its execution. If you want the timer job to work with site requests in another site collection or with a different list name, you're out of luck.

Unfortunately, SharePoint doesn't provide a great mechanism for timer jobs to get parameters at run time. Use web.config for this purpose.

SUMMARY

The Site Governance solution does it all. It follows the same pattern described for every other business solution: custom lists backed by content types, workflow to obtain approval, and a dashboard to manage the process. It extends your solution-building ability by means of custom activities and the new notion of a timer job. Timer jobs run independently of your workflow. This timer job inspects the site request list to determine whether the site is ready for deletion.

Beyond the new techniques you learned here (timer jobs and using SharePoint item level security to identify qualified/trained end users for auto-approval), you should take away one core fact: SharePoint is a platform upon which you can build a wide variety of business solutions. This solution uses many of those platform features, and you should too as you work in the future.

INDEX

Symbols

A

H

I

N

O

P

S

T

U

X

Y